FAIRY TALES *and* SOCIETY

FAIRY TALES *and* SOCIETY:

ILLUSION, ALLUSION, *and* PARADIGM

Edited by

RUTH B. BOTTIGHEIMER

University of Pennsylvania Press · Philadelphia · 1986

upp

Library of Congress Cataloging-in-Publication Data

Main entry under title:

Fairy tales and society.

Bibliography: p.
Includes index.
1. Fairy tales — History and criticism — Addresses,
essays, lectures. 2. Fairy tales — Social aspects — Addresses, essays, lectures. I. Bottigheimer, Ruth B.
GR550.F25   1986   398.2'09   85-29629
ISBN 0-8122-8021-0 (alk. paper)

Printed in the United States of America

Designed by Adrianne Onderdonk Dudden

Nicht die Kinder bloß speist man mit Märchen ab.

Gotthold Ephraim Lessing, *Nathan der Weise*

La qualité d'ambassadeur
Peut-elle s'abaisser à des contes vulgaires?
Vous puis-je offrir mes vers et leurs grâces légères?
. . . .

Quoi? de contes d'enfants son peuple s'embarrasse!
. . . .

Si Peau d'âne *m'étoit conté,*
J'y prendrois un plaisir extrême.

Jean de la Fontaine, *Fables*

Contents

 *Preface*

This book explores the many and various functions of fairy tales in society and the way they are used by or appear to their tellers, their listeners or readers, or society at large. As a Germanist concentrating in early nineteenth-century literature, I have a special interest in the *Märchen* as a genre and in Grimms' *Fairy Tales* in particular. Recognizing how this little volume of more than two hundred tales was utilized in German society in the nineteenth and twentieth centuries as a prop and proof for widely divergent child-rearing, political, and psycho-social aims led me to wonder how fairy tales functioned within other societies and how they were regarded and analyzed in other disciplines. Although other possibilities exist, three principal functions emerged: the fairy tale as an illusion, as an allusion, and as a paradigm.

As illusion, fairy tales regularly suggest that events may develop according to a pattern that diverges sharply from that which daily experience would lead the fairy tale narrator or listener (or reader) to expect. Walt Disney's American versions of some of the best-known fairy tales provide an illusion of good and evil which in no way corresponds to the far more subtle surfacing of malevolence in society. He and his animators sketched an equally illusory set of feminine qualities which corresponded to widely held post–World War II notions about femininity.

Allusive use of fairy tales frequently involves social institutions, personal relationships, and individual development. By alluding to a widely known body of material, a writer may, for example, utilize fairy tale elements as a contrapuntal ground for plot and character development, safely assuming that readers share the knowledge referred to. Fairy tale figures often appear in advertisements for household products in Western Europe, Japan, and the United States. At the opposite extreme, Jungian fairy tale analysts accept fairy tale characters and events as allusions to a deep psychological reality generally hidden from view.

And, finally, in many societies fairy tales function as a paradigm both for understanding the community and for determining and developing individual behavior and personality within that community. Within a given corpus, these paradigms are generally consistent both with each other and with society's requirements. Bruno Bettelheim's influential study, *The Uses of Enchantment,* best represents this approach. However, when these paradigms no longer overlap with individual, group, or societal expectations, as is true with many fairy tales whose current form was fixed during the nineteenth century, radical reinterpretations or rewritings occur, as in Germany in the 1970s.

These three theoretical functions provided points in a framework for thinking about fairy tales and their relationship to society. As a group we took advantage of the looseness of the term "fairy tale" in English and thus we were also able to include tales which shade off into other genres, such as the folktale, the wonder tale, and the literary fairy tale, as well as the fairy tale as it is rendered in illustrations. This flexibility opened the door to considering fairy tales and their social functioning from numerous points of view: anthropological, folkloristic, literary, historical, juridical, artistic, psychoanalytical, semiotic, and architectural.

This volume of essays unites several separate but related aims. The first is to explore the interpenetration of fairy tales and society, a subject so boundless that thousands of pages would be required to encompass it adequately. Nonetheless, the varied and sometimes opposing perspectives express the disparate concerns of different disciplines and attempt at least to begin that fascinating study, with the fairy tales which emerge from a long-published past considered along with those from oral tradition.

The second aim is to describe and assess current research on fairy tales. A regrettable lacuna exists where I had hoped to address the subject of fairy tales in Africa, Asia, and the Pacific Basin. Numerous efforts to secure contributions representing these areas produced promises but no papers. A historical perspective is also sadly missing, an area in which much productive work has been done in recent years.

A third aim is to acquaint both the scholarly and the lay fairy tale–reading public with contemporary German research in addition to research originally presented at the conference entitled "Fairy Tales and Society: Illusion, Allusion, and Paradigm." The essays by Heinz Rölleke and Rudolf Schenda further this aim. Also, Hans-Jörg Uther's account of the *Enzyklopädie des Märchens* taps into work that is relatively unfamiliar among the non–German-reading public, while Rainer Wehse's contribution sums up the results of international narrator research.

Finally, the brief annotated bibliographies pinpoint those studies which each contributor has identified as important for the development of his or her essay.

It is my hope that this collection will broaden the purview of serious readers and investigators of fairy tales. The articles offered here suggest the range of interpretive possibilities by introducing the broad variety of contemporary approaches to fairy tale research in the United States and Europe.

The conference from which the majority of these papers derive was remarkable both for its liveliness and for the public interest it aroused. Held at Princeton University in 1984 and supported by the Departments of Anthropology, Architecture, Comparative Literature, English, and Germanic Languages and Literatures, the Graphic Arts Collection, the Program in European Cultural Studies, and the Program in Near Eastern Studies, it brought together an unusually broad assortment of scholars and professionals, students and lay participants. Social workers, jurists, and psychiatrists joined professional storytellers and folklorists in vigorous discussions.

I would like, in particular, to acknowledge several individuals who chaired sessions at the conference and who contributed greatly to its success: James R. Beniger, James W. Fernandez, John W. Fleming, Walter H. Hinderer, Ulrich G. Knoepflmacher, Robert M. Maxwell, and Anthony Vidler. Others presented papers which for one reason or another could not be included here: Gillett G. Griffin, Hermann G. Rebel, Dale R. Roylance, and Anthony Vidler. The Council of the Humanities, in the person of its chair, W. Robert Connor, generously supported first the idea and then the implementation of the conference, a collegial act for which I am particularly grateful. The conference owed its existence to the unstinting support and assistance of the New Jersey Committee for the Humanities, whose executive director, Miriam Murphy, provided continuing encouragement. I am very grateful for additional grant support from the New Jersey Committee for the Humanities to defray the expenses incurred in preparing this book.

In closing I would like to make two personal acknowledgments. The first is to the Department of Comparative Literature at the State University of New York at Stony Brook, which has exemplified academic hospitality during the year in which this book was in preparation. The second is to my companion of many years, my husband, Karl S. Bottigheimer, with whom a thirty-year conversation has provided continuing delight.

Ruth B. Bottigheimer
Stony Brook, NY

December 1985

Introduction

LUTZ RÖHRICH

The fairy tale is the first poetic form with which people come into contact in their lives. For most of us it is one of the deepest and most enduring childhood impressions. Even those of us who as adults no longer read or listen to fairy tales still recognize "the hundred years' sleep." We also speak of a "Cinderella existence" or "the forbidden door," phrases we understand whether we are highly educated or not and which indicate how much more deeply fairy tales have penetrated our general consciousness than any other book-based memories.

Public interest in fairy tales has been rekindled in a quite astonishing manner in recent years, exceeding all expectations. Fairy tales have won new adherents among both the young and the old. This phenomenon has nothing to do with nostalgia, nor does it simply signal a flight from a technically rational world into neo-irrationalism. Instead, I believe, more and more people are recognizing that fairy tales are essential and substantial stories which offer paradigmatic examples of conflicts in decisive life situations.

Associations and societies for the preservation and investigation of fairy tales annually gather a large international public which is

Translated by Ruth B. Bottigheimer.

both learned and broadly interested in the subject. An immense fairy tale literature in translation has made accessible the fairy tales of exotic countries and distant peoples. Publications series and encyclopedias attempt to collect and present national fairy tale treasures.

At the same time, emphasis in fairy tale research has shifted noticeably in the past decade. More and more frequently, contemporary folkloristic, sociological, psychological, pedagogic, functional, and structural research has joined traditional cultural-historical, philologically literary, or comparative studies.

The collection of essays in this book is due to the indefatigable energy and the active involvement of Ruth B. Bottigheimer. These essays approach questions inherent in *Märchen und Gesellschaft* ("fairy tales and society") from diverse points of view and with a variety of methods. The tales taken as the basis encompass vast geographical areas and great spans of time: from the Grimms to the *Thousand and One Nights*, from the Greece of antiquity to the present. Nearly all the important questions that have recently been directed at fairy tales, their narrators, and their audience converge here. These include

- the question of the reality and of the cultural-historical background of fairy tales;
- the question of what social prototypes fairy tales should convey to contemporary readers and in particular to children;
- the question of who the narrators were and whether, consciously or unconsciously, they wove autobiographical reminiscences into their narratives;
- the question of the narrative event itself as a social communicative act.

Yet other research perspectives in this book allow us to see the world of the fairy tale with fresh eyes. One literary critic poses questions about how ancient mythology was received and accepted literarily in the medieval period and now. Other critics examine the problems of genre definition, such as the difference between literary fairy tales or legends and folk and fairy tales. Modern folk narrative research makes allowance for traditional genres themselves having changed, with the orally recounted tale frequently becoming a "book tale." But other related stories, such as the memoir, the gossip tale, and the joke, have come within the purview of folklorists. Even within the limited circle of folklorists and textual scholars, more scholarly points of view differ widely in these essays.

Scholarship never comes to a halt. A hundred answers here will spawn a thousand new questions somewhere else: monographs and case studies on individual fairy tales that seemed to have long belonged to the past are enjoying great popularity, especially when they pass beyond their own ethnic borders instead of simply adding to existing studies or searching for an archetype; Eurocentrism in folk narrative research has begun to fade; the investigation of black African folk narrative has struck out in completely new directions.

A question that has perhaps not been treated at sufficient length in this volume and in which I have been interested for a long time is the question of fairy tales and folk narrative as a source for cultural and socio-historical information about cultural change and evolution. The tales themselves certainly declare nothing about their own date of composition, saying only: "Once upon a time . . . ," "In days of old, when wishing still worked . . . ," "Many, many years ago. . . ." Naturally, certain indicators of both era and culture remain; they speak of kings, for example, and thus establish a monarchical era. Professions, however, are almost totally absent. Any number of poor people exist in fairy tales — woodcutters, woodsmen, charcoal burners, hunters, and shepherds. This group is expanded by soldiers and a few artisans like millers or tailors. Merchants, however, seldom appear. Why are there no teachers, no postmen, no railwaymen, no electricians, gas station attendants, or mechanics? Fairy tales clearly belong to a preindustrial period, but nonetheless they continue to survive, accommodating themselves with very few basic changes.

Dragons, giants, and dwarfs make us think of magic days of yore; witch burnings, torture, and horrible punishments remind us of late medieval and early modern systems of punitive justice. If we accepted "Lucky Hans" at face value, we would have to conclude that we are still in an age of barter and agrarian economy, not yet in a money economy. But in other tales different circumstances obtain.

The history of fairy tales or folk narratives can be inferred from preserved texts and from historical sources or the indications of age offered by motifs. Even contemporary fairy tales mirror an earlier world view with their beliefs about life and death, the here and now, and the hereafter; the appearance of demonic figures like giants, dwarfs, fairies, sorcerers, dragons, and trolls; the use of supernatural intervention in the form of blood, hair, and spittle as power-bearing entities; and the presence of sympathetic animals and plants and of archaic beliefs such as taboos and the power of names. Fairy tales retain what appear to be traces of an ancient hunter culture beliefs, such as the help of a grateful animal whom the hunter has spared; death and subsequent revival by means of bones; totemistic characteristics like comprehending animal speech; and shamanistic traits recognizable in the elaborated motif of the world tree and the journey to the nether world.

In the area of law and custom the fairy tale has also preserved ancient material — like matriarchal inheritance and horrifying penalties — as remnants of judicial procedures. Fairy tales depict human sacrifice, the exposure of infants and children, and even cannibalism. They portray practices paralleling initiation customs and ancient customs connected with wooing a bride, with marriage, and with birth, such as assigning an unborn child to a supernatural being. But the characteristic quality of fairy tales only appears when magical and supernatural forces are somehow sublimated, made harmless, and rendered formulaic.

Fairy tales continually modernize themselves and replace older cultural features with more recent ones. From the earliest stages of storytelling, there has presumably also existed a rather more fantastic yarn-spinning tendency along with apparently archaic fairy tale content. Other kinds of tales which surface in ludic forms and fictions of wish-fulfillment, such as the tales about lazy and industrious people or the shrewd and the simple folks, probably never had anything to do with folk belief. In the ancient world stories already existed which one may regard rather as novellas alongside tales of magic, one prototype for which is the tale of Rhampsinitus's treasury told by Herodotus in the fifth century B.C., which corresponds to the Grimm tale about the master thief.

Philological questions join cultural-historical ones in fairy tale research. For instance, which texts are authentic and which are only compilations, reworkings, or counterfeits? Are the Grimm texts only "fakelore"? There is also the rediscovery of fairy tales by the hermeneutical disciplines, expressed in the theme of the 1984 International Folk Narrative Research Congress, "The Quest for Meaning." But philological answers are needed to determine which texts should be the basis for exegeses and interpretations. Is it, one must ask, even admissible to base an interpretation on a single version? And then one wonders for whom these interpretations have any value: for the narrators, for the collector and publisher, for the "people," or only for the interpreter?

The social role of fairy tales can be analyzed — as this volume proves — on many different levels. "Fairy Tales and Society" is indeed a broad field which extends into each of the directions considered above.

In the past decade the women's movement in particular has sharpened our view of the role of the feminine in fairy tales. Completely new perspectives have resulted. This volume repeatedly addresses this theme, not only because women are the authors of these articles, but also because their interest seems justified by the material itself, for it is principally female figures who occupy central positions in fairy tales. They are as important in the frame tale of the *Thousand*

and One Nights as in the spinning-chamber tales of European peoples. Concepts like the "Cinderella complex" or the "Sleeping Beauty syndrome" have entered general parlance, and women's roles in Grimms' *Fairy Tales* stretch from "The Virgin's Child" to "The Clever Peasant Girl."

As feminist commentators contend, there are, indeed, astonishing relics and role constraints in connection with gender from the patriarchal realm. While the man carries out heroic deeds, the woman generally plays a menial role. She is abased as goosegirl, or else she leads a cindermaid existence at the domestic hearth. As Frau Holle's serving maid she is rewarded for diligent and devoted housework. Or else she keeps house for the seven dwarfs, while they — as men — leave home for work in the morning. Negative female stereotypes reveal themselves particularly in the female antagonist roles of wicked stepmother or witch. Can tales which pass on such material continue to lay claim to a legitimate place in the modern world? Or have these tales perverted children's sense of reality, leading parents to rear their children with unrealistic dreams? And will such reading cause children to see a witch in every old woman?

The scholarly contributions to this volume accord with the urgency of these questions. There are titles such as "Silenced Women in Grimms' Tales," which balance the fact that women themselves have begun to publish collections of women's fairy tales which accentuate previously hidden active female qualities, for example, *The Woman Who Left Home to Save Her Husband* (*Die Frau die auszog, ihren Mann zu erlösen*, Frankfurt, 1983). Analyzing gender-specific female roles naturally casts doubt on male heroic roles, which must now be rethought. (See Katalin Horn, *Der aktive und der passive Märchenheld*, Basel, 1983.)

Fairy tales always reflect the society in which they are told. This statement is valid for contemporary texts as well as for historical ones like the salon tales of the ancien régime in France or the predominantly bourgeois tales of the Grimms. It is valid also for the lower social levels at the turn of the century, from which highly interesting authentic texts have emerged. That leads to the question of where fieldwork is still possible or where it should and can be undertaken. Efforts to revive and to organize storytelling have gained attention in America as well as in Europe. In part these renewers of the taletelling tradition are "neotraditional," that is, they are concerned with conveying traditional tale material, and in part they have a completely new repertoire. Especially in conjunction with fairy tale "renewals" and reformulations of well-known traditional material, one has to ask whether there is not a lot of ballast in the form of motifs that should be tossed overboard. Social criticism has been kindled by fairy tales over and over again. People have charged the fairy tale with being untrue, fanciful, and anachronistic. In fairy tales, antiquated social relationships are thought to emerge, which are reproached with being rooted in the feudal period and with offering role models from the patriarchal world. It is claimed that fairy tales were used to discipline children and that they expressed out-of-date, repressive, and authoritarian child-rearing methods.

In response to such criticism one must agree that fairy and folk tales have served the church for centuries as an integral part of sermons and as a secular means of instruction. The Grimm tales teach preponderantly nineteenth-century bourgeois "productive" social virtues—diligence, moderation, cleanliness, obedience to parents and to constituted authority, contentment with existing conditions, and gratitude. Scholars, especially in socialist countries, have elaborated sociocultural inclinations in folk tales which had previously been neglected or suppressed. Other scholars have seized upon erotic motivations omitted by nineteenth-century prudery. Fairy tales, it is clear, have generally been told neither naively nor without specific intentions. Why should they fare differently now? Thus there are many storytellers who modernize, humanize, democratize, purify, politicize, and emancipate old fairy tales.

Two subjects that interest me particularly are contemporary fairy tale rewriting and the way fairy tale "meaning" explains the survival of this genre.

Contemporary fairy tale rewriting creates its own problems. Whether one assists female emancipation and the women's liberation movement by turning the brave little tailor into a courageous seamstress is one question. Whether one benefits people in general and the juvenile fairy tale audience in particular with a false sense of animal protection by taking the big bad wolf to the zoo or chasing him off instead of having his belly filled with rocks is quite another question. To finish off the Grimm abominations with their patriarchal structures of yesteryear, some newspapers in Germany publish modernized fairy tales week by week, though certain people who do not want to relinquish the Grimm book write protesting letters to the editor. Authors themselves have come to grips with the question of updating fairy tales and have rewritten them in modern language.

I would like to illustrate this train of thought in connection with one traditional fairy tale character, the figure of the king, which no longer seems to fit into a modern democratic society at all when it is scrutinized closely. In the first place it must be said that the folk who told these tales could not begin to comprehend either an actual monarch or anything much about court life. Thus in many fairy tales the king is only a variation on the figure of the wealthy peasant: flax to be spun lies outside the queen's chamber; the king "likes nothing so much as spinning," and at his departure for a trip he leaves his daughters a great chest of flax which must be spun before he returns; or when the king and queen go out, the castle is unpeopled. The fellow who asks for work in the castle has to deal with the maid. Or, at her father's wish, the princess takes a sprinkling can to the meadow to bleach the wash. Or there are not enough plates at the baptismal banquet in the palace, and the king is put into a highly awkward position when a thirteenth guest arrives.

The depictions of the fairy tale castles we read about clearly do not proceed from the inhabitants of real castles. Instead, they are recast from the narrator's day-to-day world, and this perspective is connected with the fact that fairy and folk tales were recorded in the nineteenth and twentieth centuries from the lowest social levels among day laborers, woodsmen, navvies, old people in the chimney corner, invalids, poorhouse inmates, basket weavers, berry pickers, the blind, and the crippled. A good example is that of the completely illiterate Ödenburg street sweeper, Tobias Kern, who was the sole source for all 122 tales of the famous Bünker collection from Burgenland. Thus the description of the social milieu in these tales corresponds to this environment.

Longing for good fortune is one central theme in fairy tales that seems to follow from the outward social circumstances of the tale tellers, who may well have sought an escape from their mundane existence in the utopian world of fairy tales. It is not accidental that most fairy tales deal with poor people and their paths to good fortune. For these simple and frequently illiterate narrators, fairy tales perform a compensatory function. Whether as an ideal or as an exemplary warning tale about deviations from the norm, fairy tales always offer a likeness of the narrators' social and economic environment, a snapshot of the cultural process. A simple storyteller who in reality can never rise to kingship must somehow compensate for his situation psychologically, and so he depicts the king's existence as less than enviable. Thus, the king may be rich, but he isn't happy. He can't laugh. He's sick and has to locate someone who can undertake a journey to the water of life for him. He is a widower. He needs a hero to defend him against enemies threatening his country. He has to ensure that his daughter finds a qualified husband who, as his son-in-law, can succeed him. The lie that money solves all problems is revealed in the figure of the king. Paramount, however, is the fact that the king himself is removable. Anybody, no matter what his background, can aspire to his throne. Even the poor man, the beggar, or the swineherd can become king.

* Fairy tales rest on the opposition between high and low, but they are more likely to emphasize the disruption of social structure than they are to confirm sovereign power. Social relationships are turned topsy-turvy. The poor man becomes king; the king is toppled — by the powerless. The proud princess has to marry the swineherd. The poor cinderboy becomes the heir apparent. Poverty turns to wealth and the high fall low. There is an aspiration toward freedom which shatters every social barrier.

One should not overlook the fact that social oppositions in fairy tale plots are less an image of actual feudal attitudes than they are an artistic and narrative prerequisite. Folk and fairy tales love oppositions, and it is a law of effective storytelling that the hero who ultimately becomes king should previously have been poor. The hero's ancestral social lowliness is indispensable for the polar tension of fairy tales.

Of greatest importance in fairy tales is the fact that the king is neither a feudal lord nor a subconscious father figure. In the symbolic language of fairy tales he represents a high estate in the sense of a higher psychical development, a human being's maturation. Kings are able to become and to remain the symbolic figure for the goal most worth striving for precisely because we no longer have real kings. Precisely because outward appearances stand for inner conditions in fairy tales, the king is not simply an actual ruler, a representative of political power. In fairy tales, self-control is a path to sovereign authority, a test for him who intends to exercise power beyond himself. Many fairy tales have described this path to inner sovereign rule. Visible kingship is only an image and symbol of a higher and therefore true goal for human life: the perfectly mature human being in control of his or her own life. The fairy tale ending in wealth, glory, and a life of abundance conceals more than the simple satisfaction of material desires and social advancement. Such an ending means to convey an inner contentment far beyond physical gratification. That a wealth quite different from the merely material is in question here is something that fairy tales are well aware of, and they hint at it. Fairy tales express profound wisdom in asserting that true wealth is only to be attained through poverty.

In the example of the king we have, so to speak, a materialistic conception of the fairy tale ranged in opposition to an idealistic one; both are clearly valid. But here, finally, the weighty question in contemporary analysis of fairy tales is posed, Do the content, motifs, and dramatis personae in fairy tales only express what is said in so many words or do they express a deeper meaning? The narratives themselves and not the interpretations are naturally of central importance in fairy tales. But the appearance of folk narratives in a similar or identical form among so many peoples indicates that they also share a common meaning beyond linguistic boundaries. And if fairy tales did not offer models for the solution of problems, they would not have demonstrated such staying power for centuries if not for millenia. Only what is important and what touches people immediately is passed along in story form. Only what "means" something is handed on.

Investigations of how folk and fairy tales are received lead inevitably to the psychological question, Why? Interpretations try to answer the question of why folk and fairy tales are passed on at all. The Why-question is passé in terms of psychological inquiry, and it is undeniable that most contemporary studies of fairy tales have been written by authors schooled in psychoanalysis or depth psychology, but often with no folkloristic dimension. Literary critics, philologists, and folklorists must ask why and with what justifications "their" field is now so successfully cultivated by those who harvest there without having sown.

The simplicity, linearity, and one-dimensionality of fairy tales have led to a belief in their allegorical nature, a conviction that fairy tales mean something quite different from what stands in the text. Folktales with supernatural contents, the "fantastic genres," have always been destined for and susceptible to psychoanalytic exegesis, for the same reason that dreams or the utterances of psychotics or neurotics lend themselves to interpretation. Folktales can be understood on various levels: on the first level accessible to everyone; on a higher level only understood by the initiated; and, finally, on a third level which can only be disclosed with the assistance of psychoanalytic interpretation. Stories are necessarily ambiguous, and interpretations which are frequently only subjective can lay no claim to certainty; they are opinions about likelihood. On the other hand, striving for valid interpretations is the goal of all the humanities. It can be said with certainty that fairy tales exhibit "archetypal" contents and that with reference to their contents they correspond to elementary anthropological models. Fairy tales concern everyone, because they reproduce an Everyman-Reality and an Everyman-Ideal.

Part One

FAIRY TALES AS ORAL PHENOMENA

1. Oral Narration in Contemporary North America

KAY F. STONE

Fairy tales, for both scholars and general readers alike, most often mean printed texts in books. Folklorists are aware that behind each printed text are hundreds of unrecorded tales by hundreds of traditional artists, with no single telling capturing the full potential of any story. Nonfolklorists, however, place far too much weight on a single text or at best a handful of variants, without giving much attention to the dynamics of oral context. Traditional tales were meant to be heard, not read, and exist in specific geographical, historical, and cultural settings. No traditional tale can be fully comprehended without some understanding of its vitality in these settings.

For the past few decades folklorists have examined traditional tales and tellers within specific tale-telling societies and have contributed greatly to our understanding of narrative traditions.[1] However, scholarly attention has focused totally on traditional tales, tellers, and listeners. It is my intent here to expand this perspective to include what has been described popularly as "the storytelling revival," a

This article has had many retellings since its oral delivery in March 1984. I have particularly welcomed the comments of Ruth B. Bottigheimer, John Harrell, Margaret Mills, and Ruth Stotter, among others. Material on storytellers was gathered on the East Coast in 1982–83 when I had a leave of absence.

phenomenon of the past two decades. To provide a context for this "revival" I will briefly examine traditional narration in English only as it continues to exist in some rural areas of North America, as well as the nontraditional urban storytelling that preceded and continues to exist along with revivalist storytelling. This is unexplored territory, a new continent whose coastline can only begin to be described here. My hope is that other scholars, folklorists and nonfolklorists, will see the value in including contemporary tale-telling in their various examinations of the *Märchen*.

I will concentrate here on the process of narration rather than on the *Märchen* as a unique genre, but I emphasize that *Märchen* continue to exist alongside other narrative forms favored by traditional and nontraditional tellers. I am constantly surprised at the resistance I receive from students, listeners, and other scholars when I insist that *Märchen* are still very much alive (along with the other oral forms) beyond the printed page. I insist that anyone who studies *Märchen* with serious intent should be aware of their continuing oral vitality within known geographical and historical settings. I intend this essay, then, to provide a useful framework for anyone attempting an examination of *Märchen* or of oral tale-telling.

To clarify the literary and verbal artistry of traditional tales and tellers, I will briefly examine four key folkloric studies offering complementary approaches. The earliest of these is Max Lüthi's literary and philosophic work, *The European Folktale: Form and Nature*, which explores the traditional *Märchen* as a unique form of human expression. Lüthi challenges folklorists by insisting that the full power of the *Märchen* lies in the text itself, without reference to either individual narrators or specific storytelling communities:

> Although in many ways, like everything human, the folktale is to be interpreted historically, I have preferred to search for its lasting truths. Today more than ever I am convinced that, despite increased interest in the functions of tales and in what has been called folktale biology, the tales themselves merit the greatest attention, just as always. Even though much is clarified by their context, the texts themselves take on an ever new life with the passage of time. They speak to all kinds of people and to widely separated generations; they speak in terms that sometimes differ and yet in many ways remain the same. Only a small part of the secret and the fascination of folktales can be grasped by research into the present-day context of their performance in days past. The secret of the folktale resides essentially in its message, structure and style.[2]

Lüthi's careful examination of oral tales in print explains the continuing vitality of old tales in today's world of written literature.

Linda Dégh's study of Hungarian peasant narrators presents traditional tales in their oral and social contexts.[3] In another article on this contextual approach, termed "the biology of storytelling" by folklorists, Dégh insists on the necessity of looking at tales as they actually live for the people who tell and listen.

"Biology" indicates a significant switch of focus in scholarship, from text to context. The term signals a change in concentration from the static view of artificially constructed and isolated oral narrative sequences, to the dynamics of telling and transmitting stories from person to person and from people to people, through means of direct contact, interaction, and resulting processes responsible for the formation and continual recreation of narratives.[4]

Another classic study of oral material in context, Albert Lord's *The Singer of Tales*, examines the ways in which traditional narratives are learned, practiced, performed, and received.[5] Based on the Yugoslav heroic epic, his observations are nonetheless relevant to other narrative forms, particularly the complex *Märchen*. Like Dégh, Lord concentrates on the actual existence of oral narratives in specific communities, and like Lüthi he is interested in the artistic and historic merits of specific texts. He is also aware of the misunderstandings literate societies impose on oral creativity.

A culture based upon the printed book, which has prevailed from the Renaissance until lately, has bequeathed to us — along with its immeasurable riches — snobberies which ought to be cast aside. We ought to take a fresh look at tradition, considered not as the inert acceptance of a fossilized corpus of themes and conventions, but as an organic habit of re-creating what has been received and is handed on. It may be that we ought to re-examine the concept of originality, which is relatively modern as a shibboleth of criticism; there may be other and better ways of being original than that concern for the writer's own individuality which characterizes so much of our self-conscious fiction.[6]

Taken together, these three works are indispensable to a full understanding of traditional narratives as forms of artistic, social, and personal expression. A fourth and more recent work, Richard Bauman's *Verbal Art as Performance*, is even more immediately relevant to the subject of oral narration.[7] Bauman emphasizes the necessity of viewing verbal arts in actual performance as well as in broad social contexts. He defines performance flexibly enough to cover the various aspects of verbal creativity addressed here, and I will refer to it throughout this essay.

Fundamentally, performance as a mode of spoken verbal communication consists in the assumption of responsibility to an audience for a display of communicative competence. This competence rests on the knowledge and ability to speak in socially appropriate ways.[8]

While in a broad sense his definition could also be applied to nontraditional arts such as drama or opera, he expands on the essential quality of verbal material as ever-changing rather than static, as in dramatic scripts or literary texts.

The emergent quality of performance resides in the interplay between communicative resources, individual competence, and the goals of the participants, within the contexts of particular situations. We consider as resources all those aspects of the communication system available to the members of a community for the conduct of performance.[9]

Bauman includes with his theoretical statements texts and textual analysis by folklorists and anthropologists working in many world cultures. Thus he combines the considerations expressed by Lüthi, Dégh, and Lord. These works and others are familiar to traditional narrative scholars but are generally not so familiar either to those studying texts alone (as in literary and psychological studies) or to those writing about nontraditional storytelling.[10] Folklorists, in devoting their attention to traditional narration alone, have not considered other forms of nontraditional storytelling found today in schools and libraries and at concerts and festivals.[11]

Oral narration of both traditional and nontraditional stories is carried on in three broad public contexts in North America today:[12] among traditional storytellers in predominantly rural communities such as the maritime provinces of Canada and the mountains of the southern United States, among nontraditional storytellers in predominantly urban school classrooms and libraries, and among "neo-traditional" storytellers in concerts and festivals in both urban and rural areas. Traditional storytellers (excluding native Americans) were active from the beginnings of European settlement here, nontraditional urban storytellers since about the 1870s, and neo-traditional storytellers since the late 1960s. The term *neo-traditional* is deliberately paradoxical since these storytellers, despite their recent emergence, blend old and new in challenging ways.

Within each of these contexts storytellers learn and perform their tales differently, and the listeners receive them differently. I am more interested in the connections than the differences and will illustrate how storytellers, tales, and performances interweave in North America today.

Traditional Oral Narration

Folklore scholarship reveals that oral tales are the products of chains of individual, though usually anonymous, narrators. In the sense that each verbal artist contributes to any single tale, this literature can be regarded as a communally created product. We should remember that this communal creativity is not superorganic, not some mystical concept suspended above human culture, but can only come into being when actual people retell actual tales. The first people to retell tales on this continent were native Americans, for whom tale-telling continues to provide a body of oral literature. Other ethnic and racial groups, notably black Americans, also continue the active recreation of their traditional literature. Much of this literature — native American, ethnic, black American — has been gathered in published collections available for use by storytellers from any background.[13] In fact, these traditions are extensive enough to deserve complete attention, and the scope of this essay is too narrow to do them justice here. Hence most of my remarks are relevant to tales and tale-telling adapted to this continent from the traditions of the British Isles.[14]

Much popular and scholarly attention centers on storytelling in the southern mountains. In two compilations of reworked tales from North Carolina by Richard Chase, for example, we meet storytellers whose tales can be traced to ancestors alive in the 1700s.[15] The descendents of one such family, Ray Hicks, Stanley Hicks, and Hattie Presnell, are still performing today. Another contribution, Marie Campbell's descriptions of tellers, tales, and community, was inspired by her years as a school teacher in the Kentucky mountains.[16]

Within tale-telling communities such as these, tellers learn tales in the same way that they learn language, as part of a holistic complex of cultural expression. Tale texts are not isolated, consciously memorized, and formally performed. Instead they are gradually learned and absorbed through watching, listening, and imitating. Traditional tellers with the opportunity of hearing a variety of tellers and tales over long periods develop a flexible concept of verbal creativity quite different from our perceptions of a story as a fixed text. They also learn, by observing many different narrative styles and techniques, to balance between the traditional limitations of old tales and their own

The public at large no longer regards storytelling as a significant literary expression. The *Märchen* in particular is seen at best as child's play, and at worst as inappropriate even for young ears.[25] Thus urban storytellers cannot rely on a knowledgeable audience of peers to judge their "communicative competency." Often tales are not *told* at all but are read or recited from memory, with none of what Bauman calls "emergent quality." Nontraditional urban storytelling often resembles cooking from a recipe rather than recreating dishes learned from watching other cooks.

Few urban tellers have been aware of the dynamics of oral telling beyond nostalgically sentimental notions of quaint old peasants sitting beside glowing fires enchanting rapt listeners with their tales of wonder.

Yet despite their great distance from traditional storytelling, these urban nontraditionalists have kept the remnants of storytelling alive and thus have provided the basis for neo-traditional tale-tellers.

In summary, urban nontraditional storytelling has not been regarded as a significant literary expression for the public at large. It has been consciously learned and performed in a restricted milieu such as a classroom or library and primarily for children. Women, who have predominated as teachers and librarians, have most often been the narrators. The dissemination of tales has been mainly from books and has been neither horizontal nor vertical, but individual. Listeners have not been expected to pass tales on to others.

Neo-Traditional Tale-Telling

The spontaneous appearance of a more dynamic style of storytelling in the early 1970s is directly traceable to the earlier urban pattern. Many of the first performers were teachers and librarians who had given up their stable jobs for the risky life of the performer. Tale-telling began to move closer to traditional models as more tellers became full-time professionals who traveled the folk-festival circuit, learning tales and techniques from other performers rather than from printed sources. They began to create and perform in their own words rather than reciting fixed texts and to adapt old tales to the new urban milieu. Gradually such tellers began to attract audiences of adults who reevaluated the potential of old tales, and of new tales formed on old models.

Since this phenomenon has not been formally studied, its precise origins can only be guessed at. Certainly the rich soil of the countercultural movement of the 1960s nourished many revived craft and art forms. However nostalgic such revivals were initially, many have now become firmly established as artistic expressions. The concerts and festivals of folksong revival of earlier decades also provided models for professional performances. One teller describes his beginning as a storyteller in Berkeley in the 1960s.

> I was too old to be mistaken for a "Hippie," but as a "Beat" poet who identified with the new movement I was accepted by that generation ["Hippies"] and moved easily within it. Pete Seeger and Joan Baez were (and still are) very important to me, and folk music festivals were deeply moving. The performance *skills* and *personal warmth* of Pete and Joan (among others), won me over. That's when I began storytelling. I'm not a singer, so I started telling stories, and that filled a vacuum I so keenly felt in what I was doing at the time.[26]

As storytelling grew, tellers began to experiment with a variety of creative oral styles, using many narrative models. Some, following the well-established model of the stand-up comedian, favored brief humorous anecdotes strung together as personal-experience stories. Increasingly, performers turned to the wonder tale as a more challenging medium for their messages. Such tellers viewed their performances as a deeper form of communication beyond entertainment. One well-known teller, a former priest and social activist, saw his storytelling as a balance between entertainment and enlightenment: "I think stories should always be entertaining. It's the basic responsibility of the storyteller. But I think the kinds of stories I like are stories that disturb too — that raise questions."[27]

Other tellers spoke of involving, provoking, and challenging listeners, of engaging them more fully in the creative process. To this end some favored traditional *Märchen* and sacred tales of all sorts, while others created their own tales of serious fantasy. Even the most individualistic of these performers, however, emphasized originality far less than did literary writers. The teller quoted above, for example, comments:

> I call myself a storymaker as well as a storyteller. So almost all the stories I tell never existed before, until I created them inside of me. That's true in one sense but there's also a sense that they probably pre-existed in some form I wasn't aware of — I just happened to be a vessel for that form and it became me.[28]

Such tellers bridged the gap between oral and written composition, using both written and oral sources for their tales, first writing them, then performing them orally, not reciting them as fixed texts.[29]

The connection between teller and tale remained philosophical and psychological rather than socio-cultural, and the emphasis was on a dramatic performance separating teller and audience more clearly than in traditional oral narration. Thus the teller as an individualistic performer often became more important than the tale. Concerts and festivals aimed at adult audiences encouraged the further development of storytelling on a theatrical model more appropriate to a public familiar with mass entertainment rather than traditional storytelling.

Storytelling settings for festival and concert performances today are even more circumscribed than those of school and library contexts. Not only are stories told in specific places at specific, pre-announced times, but they are most often told from a raised stage with a microphone, special lighting, and occasionally other stage props. Audiences, mainly adult, range in size from fifty to two hundred or more. In a concert setting two or more performers entertain listeners in turn, one following the other with a full performance of several tales. In a festival setting, several performers share the stage and take turns telling one or two stories each. In both settings tellers have to contend with increased distances between themselves and their audiences. The continuing popularity of seminars and workshops devoted to the development of individual style and technique has further encouraged storytelling as a theatrical performance.

In a narrow sense, a storytelling community of tellers and listeners has emerged in many urban areas. The establishment of a non-commercial national storytelling center, NAPPS, has encouraged the development of such "communities" throughout the continent.[30] This national center is situated in a tiny town in Tennessee rather than in a major urban center, and its annual storytelling festival has always featured traditional narrators along with urban tellers. Among traditional tellers regularly featured at the festival are members of the Hicks family, one of whom, Ray, inspired the first storytelling festival.[31] NAPPS now sponsors year-round workshops in addition to its major festival in the fall, publishes a newsletter and a journal, and serves as a central resource and a model for hundreds of regional organizations.[32]

It is impossible to say how long-lived these artificial storytelling "communities" might be, since they are less stable than traditional communities. Also, tale-dissemination tends to be horizontal rather than vertical: certain tales and styles are periodically in fashion before they are replaced by other tales and styles. Neo-traditional storytelling has continued to grow steadily since the early 1970s, attracting performers with widely varied backgrounds, interests, and narrative styles. *Märchen*, both traditional and newly created, are central in the neo-traditional movement.

With the reevaluation of *Märchen* as adult entertainment, men have reentered the scene as important performers. This does not mean that women have stepped back. They continue to retain their centuries-old position as storytellers and are experimenting with new tales and techniques. In North America today both women and men perform at large public gatherings such as the tenth-anniversary NAPPS-sponsored festival in 1983 in Tennessee, at which 22 women and 26 men performed.[33] Of the ten performers from traditional backgrounds, only three were women, a clear reflection of the pattern in traditional tale-telling communities. This festival continues to offer a variety of traditional narration. In 1985, for example, performers from Bengal, Ethiopia, and Acoma Pueblo were featured.

Neo-traditional storytelling blends the old with the new: the flexibility of true oral composition with the rigidity of self-consciously created individual performances; the gradual absorption of tales learned orally from other performers with the memorization of printed texts; the individualistic position of the isolated modern professional performer with the old ties with a quasi-communal storytelling "society." If verbal creativity is at the heart of folklore scholarship, this new form of verbal expression deserves attention not only from folklorists but also from other observers of contemporary society and culture.

In summary, neo-traditional tale-telling has regained some significance as a literary expression for adults as well as for children. Both women and men are recognized public performers in concerts, festivals, and workshops. Stories are learned both from books and from other tellers. Tales are spread both horizontally, with peers as listeners and fellow narrators, and vertically, within family groups. The interaction between neo-traditional, nontraditional, and traditional artists continues to blur the boundaries between all contemporary tale-tellers.

Contemporary tale-telling in North America is a complex phenomenon. I will describe three storytellers whose verbal artistry illustrates both the differences and the connections in the three broad categories discussed here: Donald Davis, Laura Simms, and Jay O'Callahan.[34] They all appear regularly at concerts, festivals, and workshops, and they all have written about their storytelling.[35]

Donald Davis is the only one of the three with a background of traditional tale-telling. His family has lived in Haywood County, North Carolina, since the late 1700s and has kept alive a rich body of old tales. Davis's primary narrative models were his grandmother, who told wonder tales, and his uncle, who preferred humorous tales. Davis did not set them apart as "storytellers," however, nor did he think of storytelling as a special activity:

On days like that, storytelling was going on, but we didn't know it. There was no formal time set aside as "storytime" or any real separation of story from the total fabric of conversation. Story was the language of normal communication and the natural result of talking, much as going somewhere is the result of walking.[36]

His casual view of tales and tale-telling almost caused their demise in his own life, since he at first rejected them when he began university studies. When he read the stories of Chaucer and Shakespeare, however, he began to reexamine his narrative heritage and to retell some of the stories he remembered. "I recognized some of my stories there, and I also recognized that mine were better."[37] He had never thought of tale-telling as a special activity for children.

In the storytelling of my childhood, there was no distinction between stories for children and stories for adults. A story was told because it was to be told, not to entertain or hold an audience. As we grew up we absorbed stories so often that the deeper and deeper levels of meaning emerged as we heard the same stories at a different age.[38]

Now a minister in Charlotte, North Carolina, Davis still performs and teaches traditional tales though he does not regard himself as a full-time professional.

People are always asking me when I am going to become a "full time" storyteller. I guess I've been a full time storyteller all my life, but I just can't see myself making storytelling the end of what I do rather than the means by which I am who I am. Storytelling is not what I do for a living, but instead it is how I do all I do while I am living.[39]

For Davis, stories are no more separate from his life than is language itself.

In contrast, Laura Simms began as a library storyteller in the nontraditional urban milieu, learning exotic tales from books and consciously performing them for children. Without oral models on which to draw for tales and techniques, she has had to develop her own way of finding, learning, and performing stories. For her, research and rehearsal are critical in preparing a story for performance, and she has become a major performer in less than a decade. She now performs for adults as often as for children, has founded a storytelling center in Oneonta, New York (an urban "storytelling community"), and has developed an effective workshop program for formally teaching her techniques.

Because her learning experiences, unlike those of Donald Davis, were of necessity formal and conscious, Simms's connections with her tales are philosophical and personal rather than cultural and familial, and thus she often expresses herself more abstractly.

> Storytelling is the direct and shared communication of something true about being alive. It is not only the story, but a combination of a living storyteller, situation, sound and rhythm of voice, silence, gesture, facial expressions, and response of listeners that makes it potent.[40]

Her own performance experiences have taught her what Davis learned by observing others as he grew up. But unlike him, Simms views storytelling as a separate, specialized form of literature. She considers herself a full-time professional carrying on an ancient art.

> We have lost touch with the time when an entire village hung on story; when every aspect of life was presented, questioned and given meaning by story, music, dance, art, architecture and metaphor. But we still possess that common bond of existence whose continuous story we share with everyone. This is the source and the power of the revival in storytelling today.[41]

In her own way Simms has come to understand that story and society are intimately connected, yesterday and today.

Yet another perspective is offered by Jay O'Callahan, a writer who performs his own stories and traditional wonder tales. O'Callahan was a writer by profession but a storyteller at heart and has found a new voice in combining the two.

> In four years as a writer I earned $40, but I developed a hobby of entertaining children at a library by telling stories. One day a group offered me several hundred dollars to do the same thing, and soon after the school system of Brookline [Massachusetts] paid me $2,500 to tell stories to the upper grades and in the high school. It had never occurred to me that I could be a professional storyteller, but suddenly I had become one.[42]

Like Simms, O'Callahan lacks Davis's traditional background and came to his understanding about stories and storytelling — as opposed to story writing — through his own experiences as a live performer. He describes storytelling today as "the liveliest, most probing art in America — touching drama, dance, healing, history, mime, music, poetry, politics — and all with a powerful intimacy."[43] While he usually performs his own compositions, he also uses traditional materials.

O'Callahan has performed nationally and internationally for large audiences of adults but has not lost sight of the storyteller's advantage of immediacy and intimacy. He expresses this not only in the stories he tells but in the classes and workshops on storytelling he offers. Perhaps more important in understanding the intricacies of tales and society, he functions within a small but vibrant community of urban tale-tellers in the Boston area and rehearses his stories orally with them. The potential impersonality of urban existence has made him acutely aware of the importance of storytelling as an art form capable of touching modern audiences in the same way that listeners have always been touched by a well-told tale: "Nothing has a chance to touch us very deeply these days. We need an opportunity to get away from other people's images and finally learn what is inside us."[44]

Although he performs his own written compositions rather than traditional tales, O'Callahan senses the creative possibilities offered by interaction with a participating audience. Thus his stories remain flexible and "emergent," in Bauman's terms.

The fundamental difference between traditional tellers and neo- and nontraditional tellers is the relationship between teller and community. To return to Bauman's definition of performance, all tellers discussed here assume "responsibility to an audience for a display of communicative competence" each time they perform. However, the "ability to speak in socially appropriate ways" — that is, to understand and react immediately to one's live audience — is perceived differently by both tellers and audiences in all three oral contexts. In a traditional setting where stories may more easily arise spontaneously, the teller determines social appropriateness by judging the responses of the listeners. In the more restrictive and less spontaneous setting of classroom, library, and concert hall, tellers more often present a predetermined program with less immediate responses to listeners. The fact that the listeners do not form a true storytelling community, since they represent only a very small and age-specific part of the community at large, also encourages tellers to dominate rather than to exchange.

In general, traditional and nontraditional tellers are at opposite ends of a continuum in the relationship between teller and community. Between them are the neo-traditionalists, who attempt to respond to their audiences in socially appropriate ways, to create an interplay between themselves and their listeners that provides their narrative performances with "emergent quality." Those who reject dramatic models of mass entertainment in favor of developing this emergent quality manage to overcome the lack of a stable storytelling community and emerge as full oral performers.[45]

In a recent article Donald Davis suggests an alternative for the theatrical stage as a model for storytellers — the courtroom.

As a storyteller I do not work with a behaving audience but with an unpredictable jury. If it is clear the jury is not following my argument, I must respond to their challenge with a new approach. The evidence, the facts (the real story) don't change; by my approach, my presentation, my clothing of the facts (the words) must be retailored to suit this jury.[46]

Davis's words illustrate the dynamic tensions between traditional stability ("the real story") and individual innovation (his presentation of it) that is at the heart of storytelling.

The only connection most revivalist tellers have with the traditional "oral medium" is the printed page on which they find a story. However, with the increased contacts between traditional and revivalist tellers at contemporary festivals, concerts, and workshops, storytelling as a full expression in the oral medium is coming into bloom. As I noted earlier, the relationship between written and oral literature has always been synchronic rather than diachronic, and this increasing synchronicity is well illustrated by the three tellers Davis, Simms, and O'Callahan. Revivalist tellers have begun to free themselves from the printed page and the scripted dramatic performance while continuing to use traditional tales as an important source for their performing events. Still, some see themselves as inheritors of the ancient tradition of storytelling, failing to understand the absence of diachronic relations between traditional and revivalist narration. One writer warns against such a nostalgic view of modern telling: "As literate persons, raised in a literate society, there is no way we can carry on oral tradition. We never belonged to it in the first place, and we cannot reenter it like an astronaut coming back into earth's gravitational field."[47]

I am intrigued by the willingness of many contemporary performers to understand and to review their position as inheritors of an ancient form of human expression. Neo-traditional performers in particular maintain a tenuous position between the full oral creativity of traditional narration and the literate traditions to which they belong, and in which they attempt to practice their art. Many insist that their art is, despite their literate backgrounds, a truly oral accomplishment. As storyteller Ruth Stotter observes, for example:

The tradition has changed. Folklore is, by definition, dynamic. I feel I am a teller in the oral *tradition*. I feel comfortable calling myself a storyteller in the oral tradition because part of that tradition is people sitting down and listening to new and old tales. It is not the material alone that makes the tradition, it is the experience.[48]

Many folklorists might insist that such narrators are not "in the oral tradition" no matter how they might view themselves, since they are not historically or culturally connected with long-standing narrative communities. I find it more useful to admit that while revivalist tellers might not be the legitimate heirs of a full oral tradition, they are its stepchildren who demand recognition in their own right. Every *Märchen* reader will recognize the powerful claims of the stepchild.

I have no intention of claiming that revivalist narrators fully parallel or succeed or even replace traditional narrators. They learn, present, and view their stories and listeners differently than do traditional narrators. They do, however, function as verbal artists in a rich variety of ways. In contemporary settings we can view artists from all backgrounds and see how they diverge and converge: some, like Donald Davis, draw their tales from a vibrant oral tradition; others, like Laura Simms, bring new oral life to traditional tales in print; still others, like Jay O'Callahan, create new tales on old models. All offer us new perspective on *Märchen* as verbal art, as an expression of the people. They provide us with the timeless literary artistry of the wonder tale as examined by Max Lüthi, as well as with more immediate social and artistic connections as suggested by Albert Lord, Linda Dégh, and Richard Bauman. The *Märchen* continues its emergent quality in contemporary performances.

Notes

1. As it is impossible to list all of even the most significant contributions here in this limited space, I can only suggest a beginning. See Dan Ben-Amos, *Sweet Words: Storytelling Events in Benin* (Philadelphia: Institute for the Study of Human Issues, 1975); Daniel J. Crowley, *I Could Talk Old Story Good: Creativity in Bahamian Folklore,* Publications in Folklore Studies, no. 17 (Berkeley: University of California Press, 1966); Diane Wolkstein, *The Golden Orange Tree and Other Haitian Folktales* (New York: Alfred A. Knopf, 1978).

2. Max Lüthi, *The European Folktale: Form and Nature* (Philadelphia: Institute for the Study of Human Issues, 1982), p. xv.

3. Linda Dégh, *Folktales and Society: Story-Telling in a Hungarian Peasant Community* (Bloomington: Indiana University Press, 1969).

4. Dégh, "Biology of Storytelling," *Folklore Preprint Series* 7 (March 1979): 1.

5. Albert Lord, *The Singer of Tales* (New York: Atheneum, 1970); see also Milman Parry and Albert Lord, *Serbocroatian Heroic Songs,* vol. I (Cambridge, MA: Harvard University Press, 1954).

6. Lord, *The Singer of Tales,* p. i.

7. Richard Bauman, *Verbal Art as Performance* (Prospect Heights, IL: Waveland Press, 1984).

8. Ibid., p. 11.

9. Ibid., p. 38.

10. In the oft-quoted *Uses of Enchantment* (New York: Alfred A. Knopf, 1976), for example, Bruno Bettelheim offers lip-service to tale variants and to the importance of hearing the stories, but he shows little comprehension of the nature of oral creativity.

11. European scholars have been more attentive. See, for example: Johannes Merkel and Michael Nagel, eds., *Erzählen* (Reinbek bei Hamburg: Rowohlt, 1982) and Klaus Doderer, ed., *Über Märchen für Kinder von heute* (Weinheim: Beltz, 1983).

12. In determining these contexts I have employed the concept of "organized story-telling" developed by Richard Alvey in his study of the history of storytelling on this continent. See n.22, below. Obviously a great deal of oral creativity takes place outside organized contexts — joke-telling at parties, for example — but I could not possibly examine all forms of verbal art for all groups in North America. Thus I am confining myself to organized storytelling in English.

13. For black American material, begin with various studies by Roger Abrahams, *Deep Down in the Jungle*, rev. ed. (Chicago: Aldine Press, 1974); for native material, begin with Dennis Tedlock, *Finding the Center: Narrative Poetry of the Zuni Indians* (New York: Dial, 1972). (Tedlock includes an excellent bibliography for further reading.) Particularly relevant for contemporary storytelling is a master's thesis by Ruth Stotter, "Interpretive Performance of Traditional Native American Narratives," Sonoma State University, 1984.

14. Marie Campbell, *Tales from the Cloud-Walking Country* (Bloomington, Ind.: Indiana University Press, 1958, repr. Westport, CT: Greenwood Press, 1976); Richard Chase, *The Jack Tales* (Cambridge: Houghton Mifflin, 1943) and *Grandfather Tales* (Boston: Houghton Mifflin, 1948); Arthur Huff Fauset, *Folklore from Nova Scotia* (New York: American Folklore Society Memoire 24, 1931); Emelyn Gardner, *Folklore from the Schoharie Hills, New York* (Ann Arbor: University of Michigan, 1937); Vance Randolph, *The Devil's Pretty Daughter* (New York: Columbia University Press, 1955), *Sticks in the Knapsack* (New York: Columbia University Press, 1958), *The Talking Turtle* (New York: Columbia University Press, 1957), and *Who Blowed Up the Church House?* (New York: Columbia University Press, 1952); Leonard Roberts, *South from Hell-fer-sartin* (Lexington, Ky.: University of Kentucky, 1964), *Old Greasybeard* (Detroit: Folklore Associates, 1969), *Sang Branch Settlers* (Austin, Tex.: University of Texas, 1974); Carol Spray, *Will o'the Wisp: Folktales and Legends of New Brunswick* (Fredericton, New Brunswick: Brunswick Press, 1979). These collections include only Anglo-American materials. The wealth of tales from other groups can hardly be covered here.

15. These tales appear in Richard Chase's two books listed above. For a recent scholarly study see: W. F. Nicolaisen, "At 1535 in Beech Mountain, North Carolina," *Scandinavian Yearbook of Folklore* 36 (1980): 99–106.

16. Campbell's description of the Kentucky community in which she taught is found in *Cloud-Walking*. All narrators mentioned in her tale collections are described in *Cloud-Walking*. (Bloomington: Indiana University Press, 1960).

17. A fine example of original composition based on traditional models is found in Lord, *The Singer of Tales*, pp. 272–75. Here epic singer Milovan Vojičić composes an epic poem dedicated to Milman Parry.

18. In many tale-telling communities this is not true: Certain kinds of narratives can only be told at certain times by certain individuals. For example, Ojibwa sacred versions of the culture-hero Nanabush are properly told by religious specialists during initiation rites for the Midewiwin, or Great Medicine Society.

19. See, for example, Dégh, *Folktales and Society*, esp. pp. 92–93 and 99–102. The dominance of male narrators can also be seen in the Anglo-American collections mentioned in n.14, above. Folklorist Margaret Mills, who has conducted field research in Afghanistan, commented to me in a personal communication: "Women (in traditional societies) are left in the cultural-educational backwaters, holding the bag of traditional culture. Dialectologists treat it as a truism that if you want to study archaism in dialects, women often predominante as subjects, because their opportunity to travel and to learn to talk to outsiders are limited compared to men's. So their lore tends to be more local or regional — in modern times and, perhaps, always. Men tend to have the floor, but women have the lore!"

20. Ray Hicks and Stanley Hicks have appeared at several of the national festivals in Jonesborough, Tennessee. This information was gathered from NAPPS festival programs for the past ten years. See n. 30, below.

21. Dégh, *Folktales and Society;* also Nicolaisen, "At 1535 in Beech Mountain."

22. Richard Alvey, "The Historical Development of Organized Story-Telling to Children in the United States" Ph.D. dissertation, University of Pennsylvania, 1974.

23. Ibid., p. 36.

24. See, for example: Sara Cone Bryant, *How to Tell Stories to Children* (New York: Houghton Mifflin, 1924); Ruth Sawyer, *The Way of the Storyteller* (New York: Viking Press, 1942; repr. 1962). Both of these early classics warn against forcing tales into narrow pedagogic channels.

25. The *Märchen* has excited controversy since its first appearances in print. See Kay Stone, *"Märchen to Fairytale: An Unmagical Transformation," Western Folklore* 40, no. 3 (July 1981): 232–44; and Michael C. Kotzin, *Dickens and The Fairy Tale* (Bowling Green, Ohio: Bowling Green University Popular Press, 1972).

26. John Harrell, letter to the author, 5 November 1984.

27. David Holt, "An Interview with Ken Feit," *The Yarnspinner* 6 (March 1982): 3.

28. Ibid., p. 2.

29. Canadian children's writer Robert Munch, for example, composes his stories orally in school performances before writing them down. "It may take me as long as three years of telling to get a story ready for print" (CBC radio interview, 16 November 1984). American writer Jane Yolen, on the other hand, writes her stories and then performs them orally — not reciting or reading them (conversation with the author, 20 March 1984).

30. The National Association for the Preservation and Perpetuation of Storytelling offered its first annual festival in October 1973, in Jonesborough, Tennessee.

31. From a conversaton with Doc McConnell, a founding member of NAPPS, in Jonesborough, July 1983.

32. *The Yarnspinner,* formerly a monthly newsletter, is now a bimonthly supplement alternating with the bimonthly *National Storytelling Journal*, the first issue of which was published in January 1984.

33. As described in the 1982 National Storytelling Festival program.

34. Comments are based on conversations with these performers in 1982–83 and on material by and about them in NAPPS publications.

35. Many pieces have appeared over the past several years in *The Yarnspinner* and *The National Storytelling Journal.*

36. Kay Stone and Donald D. Davis, "To Ease the Heart: Traditional Storytelling," *The National Storytelling Journal* 1, no. 1 (Winter 1984): 3.

37. Conversation at the John C. Campbell Folk School in Brasstown, North Carolina, December 1982.

38. Stone and Davis, "To Ease the Heart," p. 5.

39. Ibid., pp. 4–5.

40. Laura Simms, "Storytelling, Children and Imagination," *The Yarnspinner* 6 (June 1982): 2.

41. Laura Simms, "The Lamplighter: Storytelling in the Modern World," *The National Storytelling Journal* 1 (1984): 8.

42. "Profile: Jay O'Callahan," *The Yarnspinner* 6 (January 1982): 3.

43. Ibid., p. 2.

44. Ibid.

45. Storyteller Ruth Stotter, for example, writes: "Another thought triggered by your paper was a reappraisal of what happened at my Bookseller Cafe evenings. The same people (basically) attended twice a month for 3½ years . . . mostly singles, a few couples, a few families. They would stay and talk afterwards, almost as if sharing the stories (time?) created a bond. There was a sense of community. Whenever I do regular storytelling programs like this it is an entirely different experience than a one-time performance for entertainment." (Letter to the author, 20 November 1984).

46. Donald D. Davis, "Inside the Oral Medium," *National Storytelling Journal* 1, no. 3 (Summer 1984): 7.

47. John Harrell, *Origins and Early Traditions of Storytelling* (Kensington, Calif.: York House, 1983), p. 63.

48. Ruth Stotter, letter to the author, 20 November 1984.

Bibliography

Alvey, Richard. *The Historical Development of Organized Storytelling to Children in the United States.* Ph.D. dissertation, University of Pennsylvania, 1974. A very detailed description of storytelling in schools, libraries, churches, and playgrounds.

Bauman, Richard. *Verbal Art as Performance.* Prospect Heights, IL: Waveland Press, 1984. Bauman's theoretical statements on the nature of oral performance, supported by articles by other anthropologists and folklorists.

Ben-Amos, Dan. *Sweet Words: Storytelling Events in Benin.* Philadelphia: Institute for the Study of Human Issues, 1975. A study of tellers and performances in Nigeria.

Crowley, Daniel J. *I Could Talk Old Story Good: Creativity in Bahamian Folklore.* Publications in Folklore Studies, no. 17. Berkeley: University of California Press, 1966. A description of several tellers and their stories, including full texts of the tales.

Dégh, Linda. *Folktales and Society: Storytelling in a Hungarian Peasant Community.* Bloomington: Indiana University Press, 1969. A careful examination of traditional narrators, the society in which they function, and occasions for tale-telling. Some story texts are included.

Lord, Albert. *The Singer of Tales.* New York: Atheneum, 1970. This study of how Yugoslav epic singers learn and practice their art employs the Parry-Lord formulaic theory, a model for verbal creativity relevant to the *Märchen* as a complex verbal expression.

Lüthi, Max. *The European Folktale: Form and Nature.* Philadelphia: Institue for the Study of Human Issues, 1982. Originally published in 1947 as *Das Europäische Volksmärchen: Form Und Wesen.* A careful study of the folktale as a literary form, heavily reliant on the Grimm collections and other important gatherings of German tales.

Stone, Kay. "I Won't Tell These Stories to My Kids." *Canadian Ethnic Studies* 7, no. 2 (1975): 33–41. A brief description of a young Polish Canadian and the texts of two folktales.

———. "*Märchen* to Fairy Tale: An Unmagical Transformation." *Western Folklore* 40, no. 3 (July 1981): 232–44.

———. "Der Goldene Schlüssel." *Erzählen,* ed. J. Merkel and Michael Nagel. Hamburg: Rowohlt Taschenbuch Verlag, 1983.

Stone, Kay, and Donald D. Davis. "To Ease the Heart: Traditional Storytelling." *The National Storytelling Journal* 1, no. 1 (Winter 1984): 3–7.

Part Two

FAIRY TALES IN SOCIETY

2. *Madness and Cure in the* Thousand and One Nights

JEROME W. CLINTON

The stories of the *Thousand and One Nights* appear on first encounter to appeal principally through their exotic, fantastic, and sensational features. And, indeed, they are filled with kings and caliphs and all the panoply of court life, with enormous and terrifying jinns, with magicians both good and evil, and of both sexes, and with adventures that are by turns horrible, wonderful, bloody, and sublime. Yet the collection opens with the instruction that we are to read these tales, not to be amused or distracted, but to be admonished and restrained.

> The lives of former generations are a lesson to posterity. A man may review the remarkable events that have befallen others, and so be admonished. He may consider the history of people of preceding ages, and so be restrained. Praised be He who has ordained that the history of former generations be a lesson to those which follow. Thus are the tales of the Thousand and One Nights.[1]

We are invited to see events and characters in them that are so like us that reading about them will illumine our understanding of ourselves and of others like us.

I presented an earlier version of this paper at the MESA meetings in Philadelphia in November 1982. At various stages in the revision of it into its present form I have benefited from the comments of a number of colleagues and friends. I would like to thank Andras Hamori, Nahoma Clinton, Peter D. Molan, and Betsy Halpern, in particular, and to absolve them of responsibility for any deficiencies that remain.

The very first tale in the collection, and the one that both introduces the others and sets their narration in motion, seems to deny
that promise. The elements of the fantastic, exotic, and sensational
are so strong within it that it is difficult to see beyond them. Yet, at
bottom, the tale of Shahriyar and Shahrizad is about male wounding
and how it can destroy the bond between men and women.[2] The
theme is one that is both general and ordinary. It is also a story about
justice, and about madness and its cure. If on first encounter it excites
our interest by its strangeness, it is its profound familiarity that en-
grosses us at last.

The Madness of Shahriyar

The world to which the tale of Shahriyar and Shahrizad first introduces us is one of apparent tranquility and order. Shahriyar has ruled
in justice for twenty years. His brother, Shahzaman, is so secure
upon his throne that he feels free to leave his kingdom in his vizir's
charge while he goes off on a prolonged visit to his brother. The infidelity of Shahzaman's wife makes an ugly ripple in this serene surface, but that of Shahriyar's wife shatters it with destructive force.
After Shahriyar witnesses her debauch, he first abandons his throne
altogether, then, after his encounter with the jinn and the kidnapped
bride, he returns to his throne, but transformed into a monster of
injustice.

Shahriyar, in a word, has gone mad. That is, for a monarch who is
loved and admired throughout his kingdom first to abandon his throne
without a moment's warning or reflection, and then to make war on
his subjects in this calculated but violent way are acts of madness.
The task which the clever and heroic Shahrizad sets herself is to cure
him of this madness, both "to rescue the daughters of Muslims from
death," and to restore that peace and order which initially reigned in
the state. The means by which she attempts this cure is the series of
tales that fills up their nights for the next three years or so. Since the
cure works, she has arguably understood the king's affliction correctly. But as she does not present her diagnosis anywhere in explicit
terms, we are obliged to infer it from the symptoms, just as she did. A
formidable task, but not an impossible one, particularly since we
have, as she did not, the considerable advantage of being able to witness the event that traumatizes Shahriyar as he is experiencing it.

That infidelity, and particularly the manner of it, tells us a good
deal. Shahriyar's wife has chosen not only to cuckold him, an act of

tremendous hostility by itself, but also to do so with a man who is as opposite and inferior to him as Islamic court society can provide, a black slave. She has made her act of infidelity a kind of rite of the harem by involving forty of her male and female slaves. Moreover, it is a rite that she apparently celebrates every time the king leaves the palace. And although it is carried out in the apparent seclusion of the harem, with so many privy to the secret, it can hardly have been a secret at all, except from Shahriyar. When Shahriyar confronts both the fact and the manner of his wife's betrayal of him, he has to confront as well the realization that what has only now become known to him has long been common knowledge in the court.

The physical context of this traumatic event gives added symbolic weight to it. As Shahriyar looks down on his wife and her attendants, he is observing her in what was for him both the most secret and secure point in his kingdom. The garden is at the heart of the castle and protected by its walls, and the walls of the castle are protected both by his own twenty years of just rule and by those of his father as well. The garden is not simply a quiet and beautiful place within the palace, it is a symbol and metaphor both for Shahriyar's psyche and self, and for the quality of his performance as ruler of his kingdom.[3] Shahriyar's wife has invaded, violated, and betrayed him in the very center of his personal and public being. The blow is too much for him to endure, and as the author says, "his wits flew off." He physically flees as well, abandoning throne and state, and deferring vengeance, to find if anyone in all the world has suffered as he and Shahzaman have.

Let us leave him there and return for a moment to the traumatic scene that put him to flight. The adultery of Shahzaman's wife foreshadows that of Shahriyar's. Since events rarely come singly in such tales, when we learn that Shahzaman's wife has betrayed him, we know, or can reasonably assume, that we will shortly encounter the infidelity of his elder brother's wife. Yet, psychologically, the first betrayal cannot altogether prepare us for the second. The adultery of Shahzaman's wife, however surprising and unpleasant, is private and has the air of a more routine act of infidelity. The only hint of symbolic defiance is in her choice of a black slave as her lover. What Shahriyar must confront is on a much vaster scale and is much more heavily freighted than what his brother has endured.

Our first introduction to Shahriyar has also not prepared us to see him humiliated in quite this way. On the contrary, Shahriyar has been described to us as a just ruler, and the presumption is that a ruler who is just and equitable with his subjects will be so with his family and friends as well. Nor should we interpret his justice as rigid and authoritarian. The Perso-Islamic ideal of justice is one that rests

as much on the exercise of wisdom and mercy as on the strict enforce-
ment of the law. That Shahriyar conformed to this ideal may be inferred from the statement that his subjects loved him. The adultery of
Shahriyar's wife is a puzzling response to such justice, or, rather, its
ferocious and defiant character is. It obliges us to look at the question
of justice, his justice, again. For unless we can find something in the
story to show that Shahriyar at least mistreated his wife, her actions
will appear as inexplicable or as arising from some inborn predisposi-
tion to malice.

This latter assumption is, in fact, the one that informs most interpretations of the tale.[4] The argument runs that the wives of Shahriyar,
Shahzaman, and the captive of the jinn are innately wicked women
who treat their respective mates with unjustified and excessive cruelty.
Based on this sample of womankind, Shahriyar's policy of bride murder is certainly extreme, but not altogether wrong-headed. The problem is only that his sample is skewed. What Shahrizad does through
her tales and her own example is to expand his sample to include a
number of virtuous women.

This reading is supported in the text principally by the expectations set up by the infidelity of Shahzaman's wife. Since she is arguably "in the wrong," by implication Shahriyar's wife is as well. The
norms of the society in which the story takes place, and of which the
audience that heard it was also a part, reinforce this view. That society takes for granted that women are morally inferior to men and
are animated almost exclusively by their passions.[5]

It would be much easier to sustain this view were it not for the
extraordinary scene that follows immediately upon Shahriyar's discovery of his wife's treachery. Only after his encounter with the jinn
and the captive bride does Shahriyar execute his wife for her infidelity and institute the draconian policy by which he hopes to prevent another such shattering and humiliating betrayal. And this scene
ought to be read, not as confirmation of the wickedness of women,
but as a rather surprising evidence that Shahriyar's wife is not a monster but a woman with a real and legitimate grievance.

The jinn is a gigantic, powerful being before whom Shahriyar,
though monarch of a great realm, is as humble as his wife's lover, the
black slave Mas'ood, is before him. Yet Shahriyar sees the jinn as
essentially like him and his brother in his vulnerability to female
treachery. And since this kind of humiliation is proportionate to one's
greatness, he feels indeed that the jinn has suffered a worse indignity
than he and his brother have.

By identifying himself with the jinn, Shahriyar invites us to see in
this incident a dramatization of how he himself perceives what has
happened to him. How telling it is then to realize that he sees the jinn

as the aggrieved party in this drama. In doing this, he overlooks, or gives no value to, the great injustice that the woman has endured. The jinn stole her away from her husband on her wedding night and has since kept her locked up at the bottom of the sea, releasing her temporarily only when it suits him to do so. Surely, she is the one who has suffered injustice. And if she has, like Shahriyar's wife, taken her vengeance on the jinn in a way that is most damaging to his sense of himself, she has done so because that is virtually the only means left open to her of expressing her very justified anger against him. She cannot physically oppose the jinn. He is too strong. She cannot flee him. He would find her wherever she went. She cannot plead with him. Had he any regard for her wishes, he would not have kidnapped her in the first place. And were she somehow to escape, the bridegroom and her family would not welcome her back after so long and problematic an absence.[6]

If the jinn is playing Shahriyar's role in this drama, then the bride is playing his wife's. Like the bride, she is a woman coveted as a precious object and stored away to be enjoyed as her husband wills. Her humanity is ignored or denied. The jinn's theft of the bride thus becomes a metaphor for a young woman's sense of betrayal when the romantic connection she had hoped would begin with her wedding is never formed. And she awakes to find herself bound inescapably to a man whose principal interest in her is a desire to protect his exclusive sexual access to her. She had hoped to marry a man and finds herself instead the prisoner of a monster whose vastly greater power is vulnerable in only one place.

Perhaps we should explain Shahriyar's lapse in justice here as a temporary aberration. After all, he has endured a great deal and is not in his right mind. He has been obliged by the threat of a painful death to cuckold the jinn after just having endured the experience of being himself cuckolded. The woman who has compelled him to this humiliating and frightening act has also just taken his signet ring, a symbol both of wholeness and of identity, and strung it like a bead on a necklace along with hundreds of others. Symbolically, he has been transformed from monarch of a vast realm to a mere cypher. Yet such moments of stress only release what has been in the unconscious all along. The jinn and the bride rise to view from the depths of the sea, but they come out of Shahriyar's psyche as much as they come out of the sea. For Shahriyar the injustice lies not in kidnapping a bride or in keeping her locked away against her will but only in that bride's violation of her captor's exclusive sexual control of her.

The exercise of justice requires the recognition and acceptance of the humanity of those subjected to judgment. Commerce with those who are more or less than human requires different protocols. Shahriyar's sphere of humanity includes only males. He sees the jinn as human, although he is not, but cannot see the bride as human, although she is. Her power, like that of all women, seems superhuman to him, and more than he can defend himself from by ordinary means. He does not see that he is largely to blame for the fact that their power is directed against him. The jinn has created an enemy for himself by his injustice. In his madness, Shahriyar cannot accept that, or the responsibility for his wife's infidelity that such acceptance would imply. Instead, he interprets what has occurred as final and unarguable proof that all women are evil and bent on the betrayal of men, and that all men are, like him, vulnerable to their power. The vision that might have cured him only feeds his psychosis. He returns to the palace, takes vengeance on his wife and her servants, and institutes his war on women, putting boxes around them from which no amount of determination and cunning will allow them to escape.

Why should his wife's infidelity, however flagrant, shatter Shahriyar so completely? The trauma he has endured is surely enough to explain a serious and disabling neurosis, but not the murderous and violent psychosis into which he falls. Shahzaman's deep depression was cured because he saw that his older, more powerful brother had suffered an even worse humiliation than he had. Shahriyar's encounter with the jinn parallels the experience of his younger brother in exactly those terms, yet he is, if anything, made worse by it. There is an apparent alleviation of his symptoms in that he is able to return to the palace and resume his responsibilities as king. But as we see, this is really a deeper madness masquerading as cure. Why?

Shahriyar's madness bespeaks not simply an inability to treat women as his equals but a deep-seated fear of and rage against them. Any analyst, whether Freudian or Jungian, would assume that the source of this fear and rage was a childhood trauma, and, probably, that it both involved his mother and included the essential elements of the later trauma that so disordered his wits. That is, his mother, like his wife, used her intimate bond with him to betray him cruelly at the very center of his being. It is impossible to know much more than this.

When we look at the beginning of the story to discover what the relation of Shahriyar to his mother was like, the only evidence we find is negative. There is the old king and his two sons, but no mention of the queen, nor even of daughters, for that matter. There is no evidence of any feminine presence at the court at all. Moreover, this complete absence of the feminine at their father's court is true for the courts of the two sons as well. The wives of Shahriyar and Shahzaman play no active role in the life of either court. Shahzaman's wife neither makes the journey to visit Shahriyar with her husband nor is there to bid him farewell. Shahriyar's wife neither welcomes Shahzaman on his arrival nor takes responsibility for his entertainment. Yet in other stories of the collection, wives and daughters play just such active roles in the court. Indeed, neither wife is allowed to identify herself except by the negative act of her adultery. The failure to give them their own identities both reduces their status within the story and indicates a general denigration of women on the part of Shahriyar and Shahzaman. If royal wives are treated thus, what can the lot of other women be?

In short, the evidence of the story, though meagre and negative, suggests that Shahriyar and Shahzaman are men who have grown up entirely in a context that gives women no importance. As a consequence, neither has been able to form a positive bond either with women or with those feminine qualities in themselves which are called the anima in Jungian psychology.[7] While this need not affect a man's performance in an essentially masculine society, particularly during the years of his early manhood, when his principal need is to establish himself in a man's world, it can have a devastating effect on his psyche when he reaches middle age. As Jung puts it in the essay referred to above:

After the middle of life, however, permanent loss of the anima means a diminution of vitality, of flexibility and of human kindness. The result, as a rule, is premature rigidity, crustiness, stereotypy, fanatical one-sidedness, obstinacy, pedantry.[8]

When one adds to this, as I think one should for Shahriyar but not Shahzaman, both a childhood trauma like that I have suggested and the burden of ruling a vast kingdom, the result is a personality of great fragility and instability. Such a personality would also be unusually vulnerable to attack from the feminine.

Shahriyar's traumatic confrontation with his wife's infidelity would have been difficult for him to endure with a healthy ego. As it is, it drives him into a dramatic flight from reality. The captive bride compounds this trauma by making him live through it again and then takes from him symbolically what she and Shahriyar's wife have already deprived him of, his identity and sense of wholeness. When he returns to the court he initiates a compulsive, psychotic behavior that is particularly suited to the wound he has suffered. He attempts to form that positive bond with the feminine that he lacks by marrying a new bride each night, but then he destroys her before she can use that bond of intimacy to wound him further.

There is an ambiguity in Shahriyar's continuing to seek at least sexual connection with women. It provides him with an opportunity to exercise his control over them and, not incidentally, to punish the courtiers who knew of his humiliation. Their daughters are the first murdered. But it also indicates that he still desires, somehow, to form a bond with the feminine.

The Cure

Enter Shahrizad. She is both the first woman in the story to have a name, and with it an individual personality, and the first to exercise a deciding measure of control over her own life. No explanation is offered for her uncharacteristic independence. Since there is no mention of either her mother or of any brothers, perhaps we are to assume that the vizir has raised his daughter exclusively himself, and raised her somewhat as a son, that is, as a person of value and importance. Whatever the reason, she has acquired what was a rare accomplishment in a woman, a solid knowledge of poetry and of history, particularly of the kings of other nations and times. We know that such historical works were characteristically composed in the form of stories and incidents from the lives of individual rulers, accompanied by comments on their virtues and failings. That is, Shahrizad is a learned student of royal, male behavior and has a rich store of tales at her disposal. By implication, it is upon the basis of this knowledge that she has discovered a remedy for the shah's madness and a solution for the dilemma it poses for the court and populace.

It is worth noting here that the cure for his madness comes not from the diligent, loyal vizir as one would expect, but from his daughter. The logic of this is that since the wounding to the king's psyche that is the cause of his psychosis comes from the feminine side, the cure for it must come from there as well.

Stories, however, must provide their own narrative logic. Shahrizad's aptitude for the task and her superiority to her father as a physician for this particular ill in the body politic is made plain in their brief discourse and the two tales that are embedded in it. The vizir has returned home feeling angry, oppressed, and fearful after unsuccessfully scouring the community for another maid to sacrifice to the shah. It is hard to feel much sympathy for him. He is, to begin with, the instrument of the shah's cruel policy. Moreover, he has not succeeded either in opposing that policy or in dissuading him from it during the preceding three years. As a result, the kingdom is on the verge of dissolution. Finally, if he was Shahriyar's vizir before the trauma that engendered this policy, he has also failed to protect the king from that trauma, by warning him of the queen's infidelity before it had become common knowledge. He is not, in short, a very skillful, effective, or virtuous vizir. All that one can say in his favor is that he has used his position to protect his own daughters.

When she learns of his dilemma, Shahrizad, whom we know to be a learned and thoughtful young woman, makes a remarkable suggestion. She will marry the king and be either a sacrifice for Muslim women or the cause of their deliverance. Shahrizad is not offering simply to buy her father a little time with her life. She hopes to rescue all the women of the kingdom by her action. She has a plan. Her father does not ask her about that but tries to dissuade her from risking her life. When she is adamant in her resolve, he tells her two stories intended to exemplify the unhappy consequences of her decision. Despite having allowed and encouraged the development of her abilities it appears that he does not really believe in them. Not only has he failed to discover a cure himself, but he is unable even to ally himself with the one who has found a cure. Shahrizad must look for help to the only other woman in the family, her younger sister, Dinazad.

In the first of the vizir's stories, a farmer uses his secret knowledge of the speech of animals to punish the ass who has encouraged the ox to feign illness in order to escape the heavy labor of plowing. At the conclusion of this story the ox, having been told by the ass that if he continues to avoid labor in this way he will wind up at the butcher's shop, frisks about to show the farmer how eager for the yoke he now is. When the farmer laughs at this, his wife asks why. And when he will not tell her — for to do so would be to forfeit his life — she effects the transition to the second story by insisting that he do so.

In the second story, the farmer is on the point of yielding to his wife's foolish insistence that he reveal his secret, even if it kills him, when his secret knowledge allows him to learn from the cock how to deal with such a headstrong wife. He beats her out of her lethal whim, and peace is restored.[9]

These are amusing but undistinguished stories. What strikes one most on reading them is how poorly they fit the occasion. It is hard to find the vizir or Shahrizad or Shahriyar in them, and harder still to see how the moral of either applies to Shahrizad's decision to marry Shahriyar. The ass is punished for not minding his own business, but very lightly. He must plow in the ox's place for two days. The ox takes poor advice but is rewarded with two day's rest and learns as well the valuable lesson that there are worse fates than hard labor. In the second story the wife is punished for her selfishness, for being willing to sacrifice her husband's life only to learn the secret of what makes him laugh. The only moral that the vizir draws from this story, or from both of the stories, is that he should perhaps beat Shahrizad for her disobedience as the farmer did his wife. But this is based on the most superficial comparison. Although both are disobedient, Shahrizad's motive is the opposite of that of the farmer's wife. She would disobey her father in order to save his life and those of all young women in the kingdom. Moreover, she would do so at the risk of her own life.

Whatever their virtues as tales, in this context they function principally to demonstrate what we have already suspected, that the vizir is inept and will be unable to cure the king and save the realm on his own. The tales are worse than irrelevant, they undermine the very point he wishes to make. In the first, special knowledge — magic — allows the farmer to manipulate his animals for their own good, as Shahrizad would use her special knowledge to manipulate or instruct the king for his. In the second, the farmer learns that his magic can cause him harm unless he has the wisdom to understand human nature as well. Shahrizad must be both clever and wise if she is to succeed.

Both tales teach one to consider very carefully the motives of those who offer advice and to distrust those who, like the vizir, act out of self-interest. There is another message in these tales, and one that bears on Shahrizad's mode of curing the king. It is that a dull tale, and one that is not to the point, convinces no one.

Naturally, Shahrizad is unmoved by these tales and repeats the very phrase with which she met her father's first attempt to dissuade her, "There is no escape from this [course]." She understands what is at stake and what is required, as her father does not. He is no more able to stop her than he is able to stop the king.

Shahrizad has grasped why the king has gone mad, and she has seen the significance of his continuing to seek a bond with women. Were he completely lacking in compassion she would have no hope of initiating her plan. She has wagered everything on his agreeing to her request for permission to say farewell to her sister. The solution Shahrizad has chosen assumes that there is a sane and reasonable Shahriyar trying to get out of the mad and murderous one. It is also a very feminine one. Not armed rebellion, not assassination, not elimination or defeat of the king by any means. She has chosen instead to educate him in the variety and complexity of human personality, both male and, in particular, female. In doing this she will help him develop the anima he lacks, to provide him with that part of his education that he missed because the feminine presence was missing or negative in his childhood. She will become for him that positive, developed anima he lacks. And she will do this by means of a talking cure — although it is one that conforms to the expectations of Baghdad, not Vienna. That is, the doctor does the talking, not the patient, and tells tales that address the patient's concerns.[10]

Shahrizad's first sequence of tales makes the ends of her method implicit and adumbrates the message she principally wishes to convey. The frame of the sequence is provided by the story of the merchant who accidentally kills the son of a jinn. The jinn plans to kill the merchant in retaliation but is persuaded to delay his execution for a year so that the merchant can settle his affairs at home. When the merchant, true to his word, returns at the end of the year to meet his fate, his sad plight attracts the interest of three passersby who are merchants like him, and who are moved to pity by his story. When the jinn returns they offer to barter their own strange adventures for their colleague's life, and the jinn accepts their proposal. The tale to this point has two clear messages, or, one moral and one message. The moral is that a harsh, retributive justice that takes no account of individual guilt is monstrous. While the merchant is, however accidentally, responsible for the death of the jinn's child, the jinn's exaction of his life for his son's seems excessive to three chance passersby — all of whom are men of experience, and possibly learned as well. How much crueler would they find Shahriyar's decision to punish the women of his kingdom as he has. He is murdering innocent young women for no greater crime than being female.

The message is as important as the moral and is symmetrical with the earlier message that a dull, irrelevant tale has no value. It is that a good tale is a fair exchange for at least a portion of the price on one's head. When the king agrees to delay Shahrizad's death one night in order to hear the end of the tale, he implicitly accepts the same bargain that the jinn has. If the stories are good enough, he will release his victim, Shahrizad, and, by extension, all the young women of his kingdom. At the same time, he is making clear, whether consciously or not, that he is willing to listen to tales that touch on the sensitive issue of his madness.

At least one commentator finds Shahrizad's choice of these tales tactless and painful to the king.[11] Bruno Bettelheim has shown, however, that children troubled by a particularly painful problem, such as the death of a parent, prefer stories that deal directly with the problem, especially when they suggest that there is a means of resolving it successfully. And this, as we shall see, is precisely what Shahrizad's tales do. We should also keep in mind that Shahrizad has begun by accepting the king's psychosis and putting herself physically in his power. It is unlikely that he would perceive her as a threat when he has already dispatched so many young women like her in the preceding three years.

Having first addressed the question of the absolute injustice of

Shahriyar's war on women, Shahrizad turns in the three stories to
that of the innate character of women and its relation to their power.
The narration of each of the travelers presents a different portion of
her lesson. In the first, the bad wife is a witch who, out of malice and
jealousy, enchants her husband's concubine and his son and then tries
to wreak vengeance on him by tricking him into having them slaugh-
tered. Could a woman be more evil? Yet it is another woman, the
daughter of the husband's herdsman, who helps him to defeat his
wife's evil scheme and rescue his son by putting her white magic at his
disposal.

Women clearly come in at least two kinds, good and evil. Both
kinds have that great power that Shahriyar fears—here given the
form of witchcraft, as it so often is both in and out of folktales. Yet
how they use that power depends on their character. We and Shahriyar
are surely meant to see Shahrizad as like the herdsman's daughter in
this tale since she and her father stand to Shahriyar very much as the
daughter and her father stand to the merchant. We are meant to assume that she, like that daughter, is a virtuous woman. And even if
her abilities seem at times magical to Shahriyar, he need not fear
them, for she intends to use them only for his benefit, to undo the evil
his wife has done him. Indeed, the message here, and it is one that is
repeated in the tales that follow, is that given reasonable security and
protection women are quite happy to be guided by men in the exercise of their powers. There is no quarrel here with the Islamic belief
that women ought to be subordinated to men, only an insistence that
with that subordination come respect and protection.

In the second story, two evil brothers conspire to murder their good
and prosperous brother. He is saved by a female jinn—jinniyya—
to whom he has given protection and shown kindness when she, in
human form, asked it of him. The evil brothers are punished by being
changed into dogs for ten years, but their brother forgives them their
crimes against him. The good merchant is not only a master of worldly
matters, witness his repeated assistance to his feckless brothers, but is
capable of kindness and a deep loving bond with a woman. He does
not exclude his wife from his life but gives her so central a place in it
that he neglects his brothers and they grow murderously jealous. The
reward this second merchant receives for granting his wife the kindness and love she has asked for is his own salvation. When she reveals
her great and unsuspected power, she uses it to save him from certain
death and to transport him swiftly and safely home. The good merchant's wicked brothers also remind us, and Shahriyar, that it is not
only women who are capable of great evil.

There is another message here as well. The good brother would forgive his evil siblings completely, despite the grossness of their crime. The jinniyya wishes to punish them with death, which indeed they deserve by the standards of strict justice, even though they are her husband's brothers. The husband and wife err in opposite directions. A more reasonable punishment is the one that the evil brothers receive at last. Having behaved metaphorically like dogs to their brother, they are made to suffer for ten years as actual dogs. This is a punishment more merciful than death, yet commensurate with their crime.

The story of the third passerby comes to the nub of Shahriyar's psychosis and obliges him to relive vicariously the trauma that engendered it. When this merchant returns home from his travels, he not only discovers his wife in bed with a black slave, but, like Shahriyar, he must witness her relishing the experience. Then, before he can gather his wits to act, she turns him into a dog.

In turning the merchant literally into a dog, the wife has here accomplished in real, if fantastic, fact, what the wives of Shahzaman and Shahriyar have done psychologically — turned them into what are, in Islamic terms, the vilest of creatures. Here again the device of giving flesh to metaphor has been used, and to surprisingly similar ends. The brothers have been made into dogs in order to force upon them the realization that they have committed a grave crime in attempting to murder their brother. Surely, they ought to have realized this without any such extraordinary admonition, but as their brother said, "Satan made their actions seem good to them." When the third traveler is obliged to suffer the same punishment, it suggests that he, too, has committed some grave crime of which he is himself not aware. However much he is made to suffer, the merchant is not an altogether innocent victim. Or put another way, his wife is not wholly unjustified in her betrayal of him. And since the situation of the third traveler so closely parallels that of Shahriyar, it is hard not to see here a subtle suggestion on Shahrizad's part that Shahriyar consider the measure of his responsibility for his own wife's infidelity.

The close parallels between the king and the merchant continue with further telling implications for Shahriyar. The traveler-turned-dog then runs into a butcher's shop, and there begins to devour bones indiscriminately. The butcher's shop is an apt metaphor for Shahriyar's kingdom as it has become during the preceding three years, as the dog's indiscriminate consumption of bones is a metaphor for Shahriyar's "devouring" of his kingdom's young women. In the shop, again it is not the butcher but his daughter who releases the victim from his spell. But she goes a step further than the herdsman's daughter and teaches him how to punish his wife not by killing her but by working on her a transformation like that she has inflicted on him. Since she was eager to bear an inappropriate burden, a man not her husband, her husband now turns her into a beast of burden who must bear whoever wishes to ride her, but at no pleasure to herself. Again, vengeance is acceptable, but it should fit the crime. The third merchant is a man of healthy ego, and he finds the appropriate punishment at once, but he is able to accomplish it only with the aid of the butcher's daughter. The vizir's daughter will guide Shahriyar back to that mastery of justice that he formerly enjoyed.

The third tale is only a fraction as long as the other two. Yet the jinn is delighted with it and accepts it as equal in value to the other two. He is right to do so, for the tale is a treasure. It recapitulates the themes of the first two, presents an analysis of Shahriyar's affliction, and, like the conclusion of this sequence, foreshadows the successful resolution of the therapy. Once Shahrizad has returned Shahriyar to his normal self by means of her tales, he, like the jinn, will release all those whom he now holds under threat of death — the young women of his kingdom.

Framing the Thousand and One Nights

My interpretation of the tale of Shahriyar and Shahrizad has important implications for understanding how the tale functions as a frame tale for the *Thousand and One Nights.* Some commentators have characterized the tale as an inferior example of the framing tale. The tale is told by a single narrator, a technique that is monotonous in itself. Moreover, it lacks the surface links between narrator and tale or tales that are to be found in Chaucer and Boccaccio.[12] One need not look so far afield. There are well-framed sequences of tales included in the *Nights* themselves that have those very features which the tale of Shahriyar and Shahrizad lacks. In "The Barber of Baghdad," for instance, or even in the sequence we have just looked at, there is a lively, many-sided interplay between the narrators and the tales they tell. Once Shahrizad has been launched on her narration, however, the personalities of the frame tale essentially vanish from view for some three years, reappearing only to provide the happy ending that concludes at least some manuscripts.

These criticisms may be off the point. The problem is not with the tale but with the criteria used to judge it. The linkages between the tale of Shahriyar and Shahrizad and those which follow are not narrative and superficial but thematic and psychological. The themes articulated here recur throughout the *Nights* in ways that have not yet been explored in any detail. For example, in the next sequence of tales, although most of the tales that compose it display nothing like the close thematic relation to the tale of Shahriyar and Shahrizad that those just analyzed do, the last tale returns us to their world once more. Here, again, we have the familiar triangle of a faithless queen, her black slave lover, and a king who has been cruelly damaged by her. There is also a kingdom that has been put at risk, albeit in a way very different from that of Shahriyar. The protagonist, a king from outside the enchanted realm, slays the slave, tricks the evil queen into releasing her husband and the people of his realm from her spell, and restores order and tranquility to the realm. In short, this tale provides another teaching for Shahriyar that continues the lessons of the earlier stories and seems to be intended to remind the audience of the special context in which these tales are being told.

The exploration of these questions is the subject for another study. My only intention in raising them here is to point out that the psychological realities of the tales in the *Thousand and One Nights* form an essential dimension both of their appeal and of the narrative unity into which they have been formed.

Notes

1. *Alf Laila wa Laila,* Bulaq edition of A.H. 1252, offset in Baghdad by Qasim Muhammad al-Rajab, p. 2.

2. The tale is here presented in a context that unites Islamic Iran with its pre-Islamic past. E. Cosquin has found a Sanskrit analogue for its principal theme — the betrayal of the monarch by his queen in the palace garden — which he considers its original. *Le prologue-cadre des 1001 Nuits. Etudes folkloriques* (Paris, 1922), pp. 265–347.

3. The palace garden, which was often given a celestial name, provided a paradisial setting for a monarch who was perceived as the brother of the sun and moon, and the shah often held court there during major festivals of the year. (Cf. J. W. Clinton, *The Divan of Manuchihri Damghani* [Minneapolis, 1972], chaps. 1, 5, and 6.) An ideal monarch was one who made the whole of his kingdom just such a paradisial garden. In the *Shahnamah* the justice of Faridun is described thus: "By his goodness he protected everyone from evil, as padishahs ought to do. / He adorned the world like paradise, planting cypresses and rose bushes instead of [ordinary] plants." (Abul-Qasim Firdausi, *Shahnamah,* ed. Ye. E. Bertels [Moscow, 1960], 1:81.) It also symbolized his state as well as that of the kingdom. When Faridun receives back the body of his son, Iraj, who has been murdered by his two brothers, he manifests his grief by weeping, tearing his hair, and laying the palace garden waste (1:106).

4. I have in mind those of Mia I. Gerhardt (*The Art of Storytelling* [Leiden: E. J. Brill, 1963], p. 398), and of the earlier translators such as Lane and Burton, in particular. See, for example, Lane's n. 27, 1:38, of the 3-vol. edition of his work (London, 1859). M. Mahdy sees the wives as rebellious, though not actually depraved. "Remarks on the 1001 Nights," *Interpretation* 2/2–3 (Winter 1973): 157–68.

5. As one of the poems in the text puts it, "Never trust in women, nor rely upon

3. To Spin a Yarn: The Female Voice in Folklore and Fairy Tale

KAREN E. ROWE

I begin not, as one might expect, with a *conte de fées* or a *Märchen* but instead with a story, which provides us with a more ancient paradigm for understanding the female voice in folklore and fairy tale. But to speak about voice in a tale so singularly about the voiceless is immediately to recognize that to tell a tale for women may be a way of breaking enforced silences. I refer to Ovid's account in the *Metamorphoses* of Philomela and Procne, which in Western tradition can serve as a type for the narrative power of the female, capable of weaving in tapestry the brutal story of rape that leads to the enactment of a terrible revenge.[1] Since the image of Philomela as weaver and nightingale becomes the quintessential type of the woman as tale-teller, it is best to review the story, noticing Ovid's preoccupation with the varieties of utterance and silence and the analogy that can be drawn between the story of Philomela and the art of creating a tale itself. Based upon this paradigm we can begin to explore the lineage of women as tale-tellers in a history that stretches from Philomela and Scheherazade to the raconteurs of French *veillées* and salons, to English peasants, governesses, and novelists, and to the German *Spin-*

I am grateful for support provided by a Fellowship for Independent Study and Research from the National Endowment for the Humanities, which enabled me to undertake research for this essay while a resident fellow of the Mary Ingraham Bunting Institute, Cambridge, Massachusetts.

nerinnen and the Brothers Grimm. It is a complex history, which I can only highlight in this essay.

To return to Ovid. With "flame bursting out of his breast," Tereus, as Ovid recounts, in his "unbridled passion" is granted a perverse eloquence (p. 144). Although he disguises them as the pleadings of a "most devoted husband," the "crime-contriver" Tereus speaks only false reassurances of protection, honor, and kinship (p. 144). The voyage to Thrace accomplished, Tereus violently seizes Philomela and

> told her then
> What he was going to do, and straightway did it,
> Raped her, a virgin, all alone, and calling
> For her father, for her sister, but most often
> For the great gods. In vain.
>
> (p. 146)

Trembling "as a frightened lamb which a gray wolf has mangled," she vows to "proclaim" the vile ravishment, to "go where people are / Tell everybody," and "if there is any god in Heaven, [He] will hear me" (pp. 146, 147). Fearing already the potency of Philomela's voice, the cruel king Tereus

> seized her tongue
> With pincers, though it cried against the outrage,
> Babbled and made a sound something like *Father*,
> Till the sword cut it off. The mangled root
> Quivered, the severed tongue along the ground
> Lay quivering, making a little murmur,
> Jerking and twitching . . .
>   . . . [and] even then, Tereus
> Took her, and took her again, the injured body
> Still giving satisfaction to his lust.
>
> (p. 147)

What Tereus has injured, we might keep in mind, is not only the organ of speech, but the orifice of sexuality itself—and when the ravaged Philomela speaks later through another medium, it is on behalf of a body and spirit doubly mutilated. Philomela, who supposedly lacks the "power of speech / To help her tell her wrongs," discovers that

> grief has taught her
> Sharpness of wit, and cunning comes in trouble.
> She had a loom to work with, and with purple

On a white background, wove her story in,
Her story in and out, and when it was finished,
Gave it to one old woman, with signs and gestures
To take it to the queen, so it was taken,
Unrolled and understood.

(p. 148)

Remember too this old woman, whose servant status belies her importance as a conveyor of the tale. Having comprehended her sister's woven story, Procne enacts a dreadful punishment. She slaughters, stews, and skewers her beloved son Itys as a fitting banquet for the lustful defiler of flesh, Tereus, doomed to feast greedily "on the flesh of his own flesh" (p. 150). As we know, the gods intervene to thwart a further cycle of vengeance by transforming Tereus into a bird of prey (the hoopoe or a hawk), Philomela into the onomatopoetic image of the quivering tongue as a twittering swallow, and Procne into the nightingale. The Romans (with greater sense of poetic justice) transposed the names, making Philomela into the nightingale who sings eternally the melancholy tale of betrayal, rape, and maternal sorrow. As such, she comes down to us as the archetypal tale-teller, one who not only weaves the revelatory tapestry but also sings the song which Ovid appropriates as his myth.[2]

Ovid's account forces upon us the analogy between weaving or spinning and tale-telling. Classicist Edith Hamilton elaborates upon this connection by noting that "Philomela's case looked hopeless. She was shut up; she could not speak; in those days there was no writing. . . . However, although people then could not write, they could tell a story without speaking because they were marvelous craftsmen. . . . The women . . . could weave, into the lovely stuffs they made, forms so life-like anyone could see what tale they illustrated. Philomela accordingly turned to her loom. She had a greater motive to make clear the story she wove than any artist ever had."[3] And when Procne "unrolled the web . . . with horror she read what had happened, all as plain to her as if in print." What is notable about Hamilton's account is the ease with which she elides the acts of weaving or spinning, narrating a tale in pictorial or "graphic" terms, and writing that is to be read and understood by the comprehending audience. But Hamilton's elisions find their basis in the semiotics of Greek itself, which Ann Bergren brilliantly analyzes in her study "Language and the Female in Early Greek Thought."[4] Bergren argues cogently that "the semiotic activity peculiar to women throughout Greek tradition is not linguistic. Greek women do not speak, they weave. Semiotic woman is a weaver. Penelope is, of course, the paradigm," to which we might add, among others, Helen, Circe, the Fates, and Philomela. But the semiotic relationships are far more complicated. For if women weave and use the woven object, be it tapestry or robe, as a medium for narrating the truth, it must also be recalled that Greek culture inherited from Indo-European culture a tradition in which poets metaphorically defined their art as "weaving" or "sewing" words. Having appropriated the terms of what was "originally and literally woman's work par excellence," as Bergren illustrates, Greek poets "call their product, in effect, a 'metaphorical web.'" Bergren's emphasis falls upon the male appropriation of women's peculiar craft of spinning as a semiotic equivalent for the art of creating Greek poetry itself. For my purposes, the intimate connection, both literal and metaphoric, between weaving and telling a story also establishes the cultural and literary frameworks within which women transmit not only tapestries that tell stories, but also later folklore and fairy tales. In this respect, Bergren's analysis of Philomela again becomes germane, for she writes: "Philomela, according to Apollodorus (3.14.8), *huphēnasa en peplōi grammata* 'wove pictures / writing (*grammata* can mean either) in a robe' which she sent to her sister. Philomela's trick reflects the 'trickiness' of weaving, its uncanny ability to make meaning out of inarticulate matter, to make silent material speak. In this way, women's weaving is, as *grammata* implies, a 'writing' or graphic art, a silent, material representation of audible, immaterial speech." Similarly, when later women become tale-tellers or *sages femmes*, their "audible" art is likewise associated with their cultural function as silent spinners or weavers, and they employ the folk or fairy tale as a "speaking" (whether oral or literary) representation of the silent matter of their lives, which is culture itself.

What then are the multiple levels through which Philomela's tale is told, that is, in which the silent tapestry is made to speak so graphically? First, we might acknowledge the actuality of Tereus' rape itself, the truth of an act which is re-presented to us in various forms. When Philomela threatens to seek an audience to whom she will tell her story, Tereus belatedly recognizes the terrible power of the woman's voice to speak, and by a possible psychological displacement, of the fear he harbors that the woman's body will reveal the foul ravishment by generating illegitimate offspring. This double recognition that both tongue and body may speak of his unspeakable act explains why Tereus must not only sever Philomela's tongue but imprison her in the woods as well, removed from society and unable to communicate her sorry fate in either way.

Second, Philomela turns in her agony to the mainstay of women's domestic life, the spinning enjoined upon women both by ancient practice and by the later biblical portrait in Proverbs (31:10–31) of the virtuous woman. She who spins is the model of the good woman and wife and, presumably, in many cultures of the subservient woman who knows her duty — that is, to remain silent and betray no secrets. Philomela, tongueless though she may be, creates a tapestry that becomes her voice. Ironically, Philomela, the innocent woman who spins, becomes the avenging woman who breaks her enforced silence by simply speaking in another mode — through a craft presumed to be harmlessly domestic, as fairy tales would also be regarded in later centuries. What is significant, however, is that Philomela's tapestry becomes the first "telling," a *grammata* (woven picture/writing) that fulfills the verbal threat previously uttered, yet so cruelly foreshortened. It is the first remove from the actual rape as an event, done this time through a medium which "writes" (*graphein*) that truth in a style governed by the conventions of pictorial narration.

Third, the tapestry, woven strand by strand, becomes itself a metaphor for Ovid's patiently detailed rendering of the myth in words. Ovid, the skilled craftsman of Roman storytelling, in a sense semiotically resembles Philomela, whose distinctive female craft is weaving. Ovid further stylizes the tale in one further remove from the act when he attaches the transformation or metamorphosis of Philomela into a swallow and Procne into a nightingale. That metamorphosis presents us with another way of envisioning the relationship of Philomela's story to Ovid's. We might conclude that Ovid himself has heard the nightingale's singing (as the emperor would later do in Hans Christian Andersen's "The Nightingale") and has articulated it for us, as part of his sequence of tales which comprise the *Metamorphoses*. Nonetheless, the event and threatened telling, the tapestry that speaks, and the eternal song of lament that retells all originate with Philomela, though we know them only through the crafted version of Ovid's poetic art.

The paradigm that I envision is, therefore, twofold. First, Philomela as a woman who weaves tales and sings songs becomes the prototype for the female storytellers of later tradition, those *sages femmes* whose role is to transmit the secret truths of culture itself. It is critical to note, as I hinted earlier, that the conveyor of the tapestry is herself an old and trusted servant woman, who takes the tapestry through which the voiceless Philomela speaks to the sister, Procne, who reads and understands the depiction. Similarly, I might suggest that in the history of folktale and fairy tale, women as storytellers have woven or spun their yarns, speaking at one level to a total culture, but at another to a sisterhood of readers who will understand the hidden language, the secret revelations of the tale. Second, Ovid, the male poet, by appropriating Philomela's story as the subject of his myth also metaphorically reinforces the connection between weaving and the art of storytelling. Through his appropriation, he lays claim to or attempts to imitate the semiotic activity of woman par excellence—weaving, by making his linguistic recounting an equivalent, or perhaps implicitly superior version of the original graphic tapestry. Like Zeus, as Ann Bergren details, who incorporates his wife, Metis, and gives birth to the virgin Athena, so too Ovid seeks to control the female power of transformative intelligence, that power which enabled Metis to shift and change shapes. Despite its primacy as a literary text, Ovid's account is nonetheless a retold version, having already been truthfully represented through the peculiarly female medium of weaving, and only imitatively represented to us through the creative, transformative power of poetic art—the weaving of a tale in a second sense. In Ovid's tale itself, Tereus more brutally attempts to usurp speech, not only by cutting out the female tongue with which Philomela threatens to "speak" of his crimes, but also by contriving a false story of her death in a duplicitous and ultimately fatal misrepresentation of reality. To appropriate the tongue/text and the fictive-making function, for both Tereus and Ovid, is fraught with triumph *and* terror, for both only approximate the truth and can do no more than render a twice-old tale.

When the French scholar Antoine Galland first translated *The Book of the Thousand Nights and a Night* from Arabic into French (1704–17), he retitled them *Arabian Nights Entertainments,* no doubt heightening the appeal to the French court's sophisticated taste for exotic delights.[5] When we conjure up *The Arabian Nights,* we are also likely to think first of discrete tales, primarily masculine adventures ("Ali Baba and the Forty Thieves," "Aladdin; or, The Wonderful Lamp," or "Sinbad"), recalling neither the narrative framework nor the stated function which is not only to entertain but also to instruct. But who tells the tales? And for what reason? The frame story identifies Scheherazade as the tale-spinner and the purpose as a double deliverance, of virgins from slaughter and of an aggrieved king from his mania.[6]

The frame plot of *The Arabian Nights* may thus seem straightforward. King Shahryar of India surprises his adulterous wife as she torridly copulates with a blackamoor slave. He executes his wife and swears "himself by a binding oath that whatever wife he married he would abate her maidenhead at night and slay her next morning to make sure of his honour; 'For,' said he, 'there never was nor is there one chaste woman upon face of earth'" (p. 14). Scheherazade, the "wise and witty" daughter of the King's Wazir, steps in to break this cycle of silent sacrifice by offering herself as a "ransom for the virgin daughters of Moslems [*sic*] and the cause of their deliverance" (p. 15). Her counterplot requires, however, the complicity of her sister. Admitted to the bedchamber, Dunyazad, foreshadowing each evening's formulaic plea, appeals, "Allah upon thee, O my sister, recite to us some new story, delightsome and delectable, wherewith to while away the waking hours of our latter night," so that Scheherazade in turn might "'tell thee a tale which shall be our deliverance, if so Allah please, and which shall turn the King from his blood-thirsty custom'" (p. 24). Tale after tale, Scheherazade ceases just before "the dawn of day . . . to say her permitted say," thereby cannily suspending each tale mid-way and luring the King into a three-year reprieve — or a thousand and one Arabian nights (p. 29).

Historia interrupta may be sufficient to stave off execution, but it is clearly not to be recommended as a contraceptive, for within three years' time Scheherazade has "borne the King three boy children" (p. 508). Craving release "from the doom of death, as a dole to these infants," Scheherazade elicits repentant tears from the king, who readily responds: "I had pardoned thee before the coming of these children, for that I found thee chaste, pure, ingenuous and pious!" (p. 508). Sexuality and marital fidelity are here intimately linked with the act of tale-telling, strikingly resembling the same motifs in the story of Procne and Philomela. Whereas in Ovid's myth, the tapestry becomes a medium for communicating Tereus' adulterous rape and instigating a proper vengeance, in *The Arabian Nights* the two sisters conspire together to cure King Shahryar by telling admonitory stories of past times and by demonstrating Scheherazade's chaste fidelity. Scheherazade's purity, signified by the legitimate product of her womb, converts the king from his "blood-thirsty custom." But it is likewise Scheherazade's wise telling of tales that instructs the king in precisely how to interpret his good fortune: "'Thou marvelledst at that which befel thee on the part of women,'" Scheherazade allows, "'and indeed I have set forth unto thee that which happened to Caliphs and Kings and others with their women . . . and in this is all-sufficient warning for the man of wits and admonishment for the wise'" (pp. 508–9). Like an analyst upon whom the patient projects his murderous jealousy, so Scheherazade's stories function for King Shahryar, who with reasoning powers restored and heart cleansed returns from mania to sanity.

Scheherazade's power to instruct derives from three kinds of special knowledge attributed to women: the knowledge of sexual passion, the knowledge of healing, and the wisdom to spin tales. More a model of the intellectual and literate storyteller than, like Philomela, of the domestic spinner and singer, Scheherazade, it is written, "had perused the books, annals and legends of preceding Kings, and the stories, examples and instances of by-gone men and things; indeed it was said that she had collected a thousand books of histories relating to antique races and departed rulers. She had perused the works of the poets and knew them by heart; she had studied philosophy and the sciences, arts and accomplishments; and she was pleasant and polite, wise and witty, well read and well bred" (p. 15). The description might apply as well to those later "learned Ladies" of the French court, Madame d'Aulnoy and Mlle. L'Héritier, or to well-bred English governesses (Madame de Beaumont, Charlotte Brontë, Jane Eyre). And one stands amazed at the immense repertoire of Scheherazade's stories, sufficient we might imagine for another one thousand and one nights of delectation and delight. Scheherazade paradigmatically reinforces our concept of female storytellers as transmitters of ancient tales, told and remolded in such a way as to meet the special needs of the listener — in this case, King Shahryar and all men who harbor deep fears of the sexual woman and the dual power of her body and voice. As readers of *The Arabian Nights*, we participate as eavesdroppers in the bedchamber, together with the King and Dunyazad, whom Scheherazade initiates into the mysterious truths of sexuality and folklore. Similar to Procne, who unrolled the tapestry and understood its *grammata*, Dunyazad comes to signify the community of all women to whom the female narrator tells tales.

The voice to tell "marvellous stories and wondrous histories," the wisdom to shape them rightly, the procreative and imaginative generativity belong to Scheherazade. But in *The Arabian Nights* we find another instance of male appropriation (p. 515). No doubt a remarkably quick student, King Shahryar retells "what he had heard from" Scheherazade during three years' time to his brother Shah Zaman, who is afflicted with the same jealous mania (p. 510). He is also miraculously redeemed and conveniently wed to Dunyazad. Having usurped the storytelling and curative power originally possessed by Scheherazade, the King further summons "chroniclers and copyists and bade them write all that had betided him with his wife, first and last; so they wrote this and named it '*The Stories of the Thousand Nights and a Night*'" (p. 515). A succeeding, equally "wise ruler," who "keen-witted and accomplished . . . loved tales and legends, especially those which chronicle the doings of Sovrans and Sultans," promptly "bade the folk copy them and dispread them over all lands and climes; wherefore their report was bruited abroad" (pp. 515–16). As the basis for a theory of the origin and dissemination of *The Arabian Nights*, this account may be as fictional as the frame story of Scheherazade; nevertheless, it usefully suggests the manner in which tales told by a woman found their way into royal circles, then were dispersed to the "folk," where presumably oral recountings insured their descent to the present day. Even the narrator hesitates to push this theory too hard, disclaiming that "this is all that hath come down to us of the origin of this book, and Allah is All-knowing" (p. 516).

Beyond this intratextual story that establishes Scheherazade as the frame tale-teller, the question of authorial identity becomes yet murkier. Scholars have suggested that Scheherazade's story appeared in the tenth-century *Hezar Afsane,* attributed to the Persian Princess Homai, daughter of Artaxerxes I, whose female authorship I would like to believe. But the alternative of a fifteenth-century Arabian collection, compiled by a professional storyteller in Cairo, sex unspecified, leaves us with no firm indication. We do know that in later centuries *The Arabian Nights* have come down to us (the folk) through French and English translations by savants, such as Galland, Henry Torrens (1838), E. W. Lane, John Payne (1882–84), and Richard Burton (1885–88), whose sixteen-volume English edition has been praised for its "exceptional accuracy, *masculine vitality,* and literary discernment" (emphasis added). Reinforcing the paradigm set by Ovid's *Metamorphoses,* Scheherazade's story and *The Arabian Nights* exemplify further the appropriation of text by a double narration in which a presumably male author or collector attributes to a female the original power of articulating silent matter. But having attributed this transformative artistic intelligence and voice to a woman, the narrator then reclaims for himself (much as Tereus and the King assert dominion over body and voice within the tales) the controlling power of retelling, of literary recasting, and of dissemination to the folk—a folk that includes the female community of tale-tellers from which the stories would seem to have originated.

Subsequent European collections of folk and fairy tales often assert a similarly double control over voice and text, whether as a mere literary convention or as a reflection of the actual informants and contexts of tale-telling. *The Book of the Seven Wise Masters,* or *Seven Sages,* probably of ninth-century Persian origin, but known in Europe, practically inverts the frame story of *The Arabian Nights Entertainments.*[7] Not a wazir's daughter, but instead a king's son, under notice of death, is saved from execution by the tales of seven philosophers, who tell stories of female deceptions, while a woman vehemently defends her sex from these slanders. Gianfrancesco Straparola (c. 1480–c. 1557), in his sixteenth-century Italian collection, *Le piacevoli Notti* or *The Delightful Nights* (1550–53), excuses the crude jests and earthy telling of tales by claiming (perhaps falsely?) to have heard them "from the lips of ten young girls." And Giambattista Basile's

(1575–1632) famous *Lo Cunto de li Cunti* (1634–36) or the *Pentamerone* (1674) contains a frame story attributing the fifty tales to common townswomen. Charles Perrault, borrowing perhaps from *les contes de vieilles* told by his son's nurse or repeated by his son Pierre, creates in *Histoires ou Contes du tems passé: Avec des Moralitez* (1697) the style of restrained simplicity that set the literary standard for subsequent fairy tale collections and *Kunstmärchen*.

Madame d'Aulnoy (c. 1650–1705) may be the female exception that proves the rule of male appropriation, for as the author of eleven volumes she becomes notable for her elegantly ornamented fairy tales, designed to delight the adult aristocratic tastes of Louis XIV's court. As Dorothy R. Thelander establishes in "Mother Goose and Her Goslings: The France of Louis XIV as Seen through the Fairy Tale," these "fairy tales formed a distinct socioliterary genre," whose "roots lay in stories that peasant nursemaids and servants told children left in their charge, yet they were shaped for an adult and relatively sophisticated audience," that "shared the ideals of, the Paris salons, particularly those which cultivated the refinement of language and manners associated with the précieux."[8] It is perhaps a sign of how removed Madame d'Aulnoy is from *les vieilles* as hearth-side taletellers that in one volume of her *contes de fées*, she imagines them to be narrated by some women during a short carriage trip. I do not intend to dispute the issues of the Ancien Régime and salon tales, or of Perrault's authorship, or of his style. My argument underscores, however, the observation of how regularly the tales are assumed and asserted to have their origins in a province definably female, and how the literary *contes de fées* become geared to an increasingly large circle of women readers — aristocratic ladies, mothers and nursemaids, governesses, young girls, and ironically the folk.

What surfaces during the period of the seventeenth century in which fairy tales become part of Western Europe's literary as well as oral tradition are "tell-tale" signs of a twofold legacy. First, we have noted already how insistently literary raconteurs, both male and female, validated the authenticity of their folk stories by claiming to have heard them from young girls, nurses, gossips, townswomen, old crones, and wise women. The female frame narrator is a particularly significant indicator, because it converts into literary convention the belief in women as truth-sayers, those gifted with memory and voice to transmit the culture's wisdom — the silent matter of life itself. Consider, for example, the term *conte de fées*. The terms *fées* and *faerie* derive originally from the Latin *Fatum*, the thing spoken, and *Fata*, the Fates who speak it. According to Andrew Lang, in his "Introduction" to *Perrault's Popular Fairy Tales* (1888), "the *Fées* answered, as in Sleeping Beauty, to Greek *Moirai* or Egyptian *Hathors*. They nursed women in labour: they foretold the fate of children."[9] And Katherine Briggs, in *An Encyclopedia of Fairies*, cites the derivation from "the Italian *fatae*, the fairy ladies who visited the household of births and pronounced on the future of the baby."[10] These Italian, French, and English derivatives from the Greek and Latin, compel us to see the origin of fairy as closely related to female acts of birthing, nursing, prophesying, and spinning — as ancient myth makes plain. Recall the three Fates: Klōthō, the spinner, spins the thread of life; Lachēsis, draws it out, thereby apportioning one's lifespan and destiny; and the dread Atropos, she who cannot be kept from turning the spindle, is "the blind *Fury* with th'abhorred shears," who "slits the thin-spun life."[11] *Contes de fées* are, therefore, not simply tales told about fairies; implicitly they are tales told by women, descendents of those ancestral Fates, who link once again the craft of spinning with the art of telling fated truths. In these women's hands, literally and metaphorically, rests the power of birthing, dying, and tale-spinning.

Second, it is not just the nature of the female raconteur, but also the context within which she tells tales in France, Germany, and England that reinforces associations between the literal and metaphorical spinning of yarns. Edward Shorter, among other historians of French popular culture, documents how in the *veillées*, those weekly gatherings of farm families, the women would "gather closely about the light of the nut-oil lamp," not only to "spin, knit, or darn to keep their own family's clothes in shape," but also to "tell stories and recite the old tales. Or maybe, as one disgusted observer reported of the late-nineteenth century, they just 'gossip.'"[12] The *veillée* in some parts of France became sex segregated, often a gathering exclusively of women with their marriageable daughters, in which both generations carded wool, spun, knitted, or stitched, thus enacting the age-old female rituals. As Abel Hugo, one of Shorter's nineteenth-century antiquarians, portrays it, "the women, because of the inferiority of their sex, are not admitted at all to conversation with their lords and masters. But after the men have retired, the women's reign begins. . . ."[13] Within the shared esprit of these late-evening communes, women not only practiced their domestic crafts, they also fulfilled their role as transmitters of culture through the vehicle of "old tales," inherited from oral tradition or the filtered down versions from the *Bibliothèque bleue*, those cheaply printed, blue-covered penny dreadfuls sold by traveling colporteurs.

Moreover, women not only set social rules by way of tale-telling but also actively presided over courtship rituals. In the Gâtine district, where the evening's spinning often turned to dancing, it was reported that "'the fellows . . . show up to visit their girlfriends [*maîtresses*]. The young shepherdess lets her spindle fall to the ground in order to see who's interested. The boys all leap to pick it up,'" thereby signaling their matrimonial interest.[14] This rural version of Sleeping Beauty implies traditional expectations of women — that they be expert spinsters, judged suitably marriageable by virtue of their skill. The complex relationship among spinning, tale-telling, and courtship explains why women (*les vieilles*), as figures within fairy tales, as frame narrators of them, or as actual raconteurs, are often considered *les sages femmes*. In medieval French, the phrase means midwife, one who literally presides at births.[15] But in its extended meaning, the term comes to signify wise women who transmit culture, whether by presiding over the rites of passage through which young persons pass, as in the Gâtine courtship rituals, or by spinning tales that counsel the young through a combination of entertaining story with moral and social instruction.

Similarly, Ruth B. Bottigheimer finds that "in the German tradition," "Jacob Grimm asserted that 'the spindle is an essential characteristic of wise women.' The spindle is, as the tales themselves demonstrate, not only the identifying mark of wise women, but of all women, and especially — in the Germanies from the Middle Ages to the 19th century — of diligent, well-ordered womanhood," precisely the ideal which French *vieilles* and German *Spinnerinnen* seek to inculcate.[16] In German the verb *spinnen* means also to fantasize, an apt talent for the one who spins not only cloth but tales as well. And as in the French *veillées*, so too German folk tales, according to Bottigheimer, "were assumed to have originated in or to have passed through in many cases the *Spinnstube*, for it was there that women gathered in the evening and told tales to keep themselves and their company awake as they spun. And it was from informants privy to this oral tradition that Wilhelm and Jacob Grimm gathered many of their folk tales." These links between tale-spinning and yarn-spinnng may be so well-established as to be taken for granted. But what should strike us is the sexually segregated privacy of the *veillée* or the *Spinnstube*. While engaged in the female craft par excellence, these women full of knowledge found an arena and form through which to articulate the silent matter of life. If not through graphically woven tapestries from Philomela's loom, then through the mesmerizing voice, wise women (like Metis, Athena, the Fates, Scheherazade) passed on the secret lore — of birthing, dying, destiny, courtship, marriage, sexuality — from generation to generation.

The annals documented the actual circumstances in which women practiced their weaving of yarns, but in addition an increasing pleni-

tude of illustrations, particularly frontispieces, for published collections of fairy tales testified to the perceived position of female
storytellers in European cultures. If pictures speak, as Philomela's
tapestry counsels us to believe, so too the deliberately pictorial representations embedded in the popular consciousness images of grand-
mothers, mothers, nursemaids, and governesses gathered at homely
hearths, attended by an audience frequently of children, as the raconteur tells or later reads the tales. Such illustrations both reflected and
fostered the identification of fairy tales with the predominantly female realm of domesticity. The concept of the tale-teller as a wise
woman who reigns over the female world of the *veillée* or *Spinnstube* is
immortalized by the Clouzier frontispiece (Figure 3.1) for Perrault's
Histoires ou Contes du tems passé, which etches indelibly the archetype
of Mother Goose in the popular imagination. This famous engraving
for Barbin's 1697 edition shows an old woman, seated by the hearth-
side, who, with distaff prominently displayed, hand-spins, while she
tells tales to a cluster of three children, or rather adolescents, and one
smug cat, perhaps the enigmatic yet intelligent breed of Cheshire.
Hardly a picture of the village cowbarn, this frontispiece already
commemorates the movement of tales into upper class or bourgeois
kitchens and parlors, where old servants or nurses might tell tales *en
famille* by candle and firelight. The now famous placard, "contes de
ma mere loye," translated here in Robert Samber's 1729 edition as
"Mother Goose's Tales," marks the arrival in Britain of this quintessential spinner of yarns.[17] As Margaret Spufford points out in *Small
Books and Pleasant Histories*, fairy tales in England also descended
from oral tradition, but as with Perrault's tales in France, they found
their way during the seventeenth through the nineteenth centuries
into chapbooks hawked throughout the countryside by peddlers.[18]
Although the phrase "contes de la Mère Oye" had appeared as early
as 1650 in *La Muse Historique*, its popularity owes far more to the dissemination of Perrault's collection and reproductions of Clouzier's
design in numerous later French and English editions of Mother
Goose's tales.[19]

Gustave Doré's frontispiece (Figure 3.2) for *Les Contes de Perrault*
(1862) may come to rival Clouzier's in the nineteenth century, when it
replaces the ruddy servant with a grandmotherly figure who reads
the *contes naïfs*, while an apparently younger governess or nanny
hovers above and a passel of engrossed children huddle at her knees.[20]
The spinning stool gives way to a comfortable, highbacked chair; the
cat to a woolly stuffed lamb; the placard to a framed picture, presumably of the giant ogre in *Le Petit Poucet*, about to be stripped of his
seven league boots by the intrepidly clever Hop o' my Thumb. How-

Figure 3.1. Frontispiece. *Histories; or, Tales of past times . . . With Morals* (London, 1729), which was copied from Clouzier's now very rare "Frontispiece" for the 1697 edition of Perrault.

Figure 3.2. Frontispiece. *Les Contes de Perrault. Dessins par Gustave Doré* (Paris, 1862). Used by courtesy of Shirley Arora.

ever, the Grimm brothers' *Kinder- und Hausmärchen,* not published until 1812–15, may best memorialize the segregated sources of tales from the *veillées,* if the frontispieces by George Cruikshank for the English translation (1823–26) are indicative.[21] In the ribald environment of a hearthside scene (Figure 3.3) for volume 1, men predominate. For Volume 2, the scene (Figure 3.4) changes to a domestic gathering, where a woman, her spinning wheel momentarily abandoned, tells, one may suppose, the tales that Jacob and Wilhelm so assiduously recorded. Notably, the man reads, while the woman tells tales, perhaps an indication of a disparity in literacy, but also a subtle testament to the literary appropriation of the female voice practiced by the Brothers Grimm and Perrault. With less impact than Perrault's, Madame d'Aulnoy's *contes de fées,* including "The Blue Bird," "Graçioca and Percinet," and "The White Cat," also crossed the channel (1699–1722) to become known as Mother Bunche tales, a cognomen that recurs, for example, in the extended title for Benjamin Tabart's *Popular Fairy Tales; or, a Liliputian Library* (1818).[22] The title "Mother" reminds us not only of the female lineage, the French roots in *la vieille,* and the common meaning as an address for elderly women of the lower class; it also reinforces the association between taletelling and women as *les sages femmes,* the midwives who assist at births *and* ease the cultural rites of passage for children as they mature. The figure who both mediates between men and natural forces *and* protects spinners in Germany is Frau Holle, who perhaps also represents metaphorically the Grimms' peasant informants from Hesse-Cassel and all women whose voices emerge from the *Spinnstube,* as Bottigheimer illustrates in her essay, "Tale Spinners: Submerged Voices in Grimms' Fairy Tales."[23] The durability of the appellations, "Mother Goose," "Mother Bunch," "Frau Holle," and of their pictorial representations suggests how deeply embedded in our cultural consciousness are the intricately woven threads which bind together the concept of wisdom presiding over the hearth, the art of spinning literally and figuratively, and the imaginative telling of cultural truths through fairy tales as powers vested in the hands, voices, and domestic province of women.

To have the antiquarian Grimm Brothers regarded as the fathers of modern folklore is perhaps to forget the maternal lineage, the "mothers" who in the French *veillées* and English nurseries, in court salons and the German *Spinnstube,* in Paris and on the Yorkshire moors, passed on their wisdom. The Grimm brothers, like Tereus, Ovid, King Shahryar, Basile, Perrault, and others reshaped what they could not precisely comprehend, because only for women does the thread, which spins out the lore of life itself, create a tapestry to

GERMAN POPULAR STORIES,
Translated from the
Kinder und Haus-Märchen,
COLLECTED BY
M. M. GRIMM,
From Oral Tradition.

Published by C. Baldwyn, Newgate Street.
LONDON,
1823.

Figure 3.3. Title page. *German Popular Stories*, vol. 1 (London, 1823). Illustrated by George Cruikshank.

GERMAN POPULAR STORIES,

Translated from the

Kinder und Haus-Märchen,

COLLECTED BY

M. M. GRIMM,

From Oral Tradition.

VOL. II.

G. Cruikshank fecit

JAMES ROBINS & Co LONDON.

AND

JOSEPH ROBINS JUNr & Co DUBLIN.

MDCCCXXVI.

Figure 3.4. Title page. *German Popular Stories,* vol. 2 (London and Dublin, 1826). Illustrated by George Cruikshank.

be fully read and understood. Strand by strand weaving, like the craft practiced on Philomela's loom or in the hand-spinning of Mother Goose, is the true art of the fairy tale—and it is, I would submit, semiotically a female art. If we then recognize the continuity of this community of female storytellers, then perhaps Madame d'Aulnoy or her carriage trade ladies differ only in status and style from Basile's townswomen, the French *vieilles*, or English old wives and middle-class governesses. We may also wish to reconceptualize Madame d'Aulnoy, Mlle. L'Héritier, and Madame de Beaumont, not as pesudo-masculine appropriators of a folkloric tradition, but as reappropria-tors of a female art of tale-telling that dates back to Philomela and Scheherazade. As such, they foreshadow, indeed perhaps foster, the eighteenth- and nineteenth-century emergence of a passion for ro-mantic fictions, particularly among women writers and readers.[24] Moreover, the "curious" socio-literary genres of the salon tale and Perrault's nursery tales (*contes naïfs*) may be reperceived as a mid-stage, linking the ancient oral repertoire of folktales to the later, dis-tinctively literary canon that embraces collections of folk and fairy tales as well as *Kunstmärchen*, moral and didactic stories, and roman-tic novels in which fairy tale motifs, structures, and frame narrators exert a shaping influence.

Notes

1. Ovid, *Metamorphoses*, trans. Rolfe Humphries (Bloomington: Indiana University Press, 1963), bk. 6, pp. 143–51. All future references from book 6 will be cited paren-thetically in the text by page.

2. See also Cheryl Walker, *The Nightingale's Burden: Women Poets and American Culture Before 1900* (Bloomington: Indiana University Press, 1982), pp. 21–22.

3. Edith Hamilton, *Mythology: Timeless Tales of Gods and Heroes* (New York: New American Library, 1940), pp. 270–71.

4. Ann L. T. Bergren, "Language and the Female in Early Greek Thought," *Arethusa* 16, nos. 1 and 2 (Spring and Fall 1983): 71. See also Ann L. T. Bergren, "Helen's Web: Time and Tableau in the Iliad," *Helios*, n.s. 7, no. 1 (1980): 19–34. For discussions of the shifting aesthetic theories of the relationship between art and literature, picture and poesy, see Wendy Steiner, *The Colors of Rhetoric: Problems in the Relation between Modern Literature and Painting* (Chicago: University of Chicago Press, 1982); and Richard Wendorf, ed., *Articu-lated Images: The Sister Arts from Hogarth to Tennyson* (Minneapolis: University of Minnesota Press, 1983).

5. *Tales from the Arabian Nights Selected from "The Book of the Thousand Nights and a Night,"* trans. Richard F. Burton, ed. David Shumaker (New York: Avenel Books, 1978). See David Shumaker's "Introduction" for comments on the presumed authorship that follow.

6. The relationship between tale-telling and healing is addressed at greater length in chap. 2, "Madness and Cure in the *Thousand and One Nights*," by Jerome Clinton.

7. Peter Opie and Iona Opie, "Introduction," *The Classic Fairy Tales* (London: Oxford University Press, 1974), pp. 20–21.

8. Dorothy R. Thelander, "Mother Goose and Her Goslings: The France of Louis XIV as Seen Through the Fairy Tale," *The Journal of Modern History* 54 (1982): 467–96.

9. Andrew Lang, ed., *Perrault's Popular Tales* (Oxford: Clarendon Press, 1888; repr. New York: Arno, 1977).

10. Katherine Briggs, *An Encyclopedia of Fairies* (New York: Pantheon, 1976), p. xi, as quoted in Thelander, "Mother Goose," p. 487.

11. Bergren, "Language and the Female in Early Greek Thought," p. 87, n. 5, suggests this provocative emphasis on Atropos, who otherwise might be translated "she who does not turn." Bergren cites Thompson as the source of "she who cannot be kept from turning," the spindle itself.

12. Edward Shorter, "The 'Veillée' and the Great Transformation," in *The Wolf and the Lamb: Popular Culture in France from the Old Regime to the Twentieth Century*, ed. Jacques Beauroy, Marc Bertrand, and Edward T. Gargan (Saratoga, California: Anma Libri, 1977), pp. 127–40. The first long quotation is taken from p. 129.

13. Abel Hugo, from *La France pittoresque*, 3 vols. (Paris, 1835), 1 : 238, as quoted in Shorter, "The 'Veillée,'" p. 131. In *Ethnologie et langage: La parole chez les Dogon* (Paris: Gallimard, 1965), Geneviève Calame-Griaule similarly observes the "parole cachée" (concealed speech) among the Dogon women, who while spinning cotton whisper the stories of their men. It is also while mother and daughter spin that the mother teaches her daughter the necessary knowledge of marriage and sexual relations. These "confidences" are a mode dear to the Dogon women ("une parole féminine"), and as we have seen in European cultures, here too in an African tribe of the French Sudan the associations turn around the ideas of spinning yarn and of a secret, both skills and truths passed from mothers to daughters.

14. Cited from Dupin, *Mémoire statistique du département des Deux-Sevres* (Paris, 1804), p. 211. The author was departmental prefect. The Gâtine district is located in the province of Tourraine, north of the Loire and east of Tours, near Orléans.

15. See Marthe Roberts, "The Grimm Brothers," in *The Child's Part*, ed. Peter Brook (Boston: Beacon Press, 1969), pp. 44–56.

16. Ruth B. Bottigheimer, "Tale Spinners: Submerged Voices in Grimm's Fairy Tales," *New German Critique* 27 (1982): 141–50.

17. Charles Perrault, *Histories; or, Tales of past times . . . With Morals*, trans. Robert Samber (London: For J. Pote, 1729). The engraving copies Clouzier's frontispiece (done after the gouache illustrations in the 1695 dedication manuscript), which appeared first in *Histoires ou Contes du tems passé: Avec des Moralitez* (Paris: Claude Barbin, 1697). In fact, this first English edition is based upon a 1721 edition, *Histoires ou Contes du temps passé, Avec des Moralitez* (Amsterdam: La Veuve de Jaq. Desbordes, 1721), in which a copy of Clouzier's frontispiece also appeared. The 1721 edition, with the subtitle "Nouvelle Edition augmentée d'une nouvelle, à la fin, suivant la copie de Paris," added to Perrault's original eight tales "L'Adroite Princesse" ("The Discreet Princess; or, The Adventures of Finetta") by Mademoiselle L'Héritier, a tale that is likewise included in Samber's English translation.

18. Margaret Spufford, *Small Books and Pleasant Histories: Popular Fiction and Its Readership in Seventeenth-Century England* (London: Methuen, 1981).

19. Cited in Lang, "Perrault's Popular Tales," p. xxiv.

20. *Les Contes de Perrault. Dessins par Gustave Doré* (Paris: J. Hetzel, 1862).

21. See the title pages for vol. 1 of *German Popular Stories, Translated from the kinder und haus-Märchen* [by Edgar Taylor], *Collected by M. M. Grimm, From Oral Tradition* (London: C. Baldwyn, 1823), and for vol. 2 (London: James Robins, and Dublin: Joseph Robins, 1826).

22. Benjamin Tabart, *Popular Fairy Tales; or, a Liliputian Library; Containing Twenty-six Choice Pieces of Fancy and Fiction, by those Renown Personages King Oberon, Queen Mab, Mother Goose, Mother Bunch, Master Puck, and other distinguished Personages at the Court of the Fairies* (London: Sir Richard Phillips and Co., 1818?).

23. Bottigheimer, "Tale Spinners," *passim*.

24. See also Mary Elizabeth Storer, *La Mode des contes de fées (1685–1700)* (Paris: Champion, 1928); Jacques Barchillon, *Le Conte merveilleux français de 1690 à 1790* (Paris:

Campion, 1975); Marc Soriano, *Les Contes de Perrault, culture savante et traditions populaires* (Paris: Gallimard, 1968); and Robert Mandrou, *De la culture populaire aux XVIIe et XVIIIe siècles: La Bibliothèque bleue de Troyes* (Paris: Stock, 1964; new ed. 1975); G. Bolleme, *La bibliothèque bleue* (Paris, 1971).

Bibliography

Bergren, Ann L. T. "Language and the Female in Early Greek Thought." *Arethusa* 16.1 and 2 (1983): 69–95. A semiotic approach to the relation between "female" language and the sign-making activity of women in Greek, namely, weaving. Concludes that the power of languages ascribed to the female may be a reflex of the role she plays in the social process of marriage exchange.

Bottigheimer, Ruth B. "Tale Spinners: Submerged Voices in Grimms' Fairy Tales." *New German Critique* 27 (1982): 141–50. Focuses on thirteen "spinning tales" to study the work ethic surrounding this characteristically female occupation. Finds the narrative voice of Wilhelm Grimm which purports to render faithfully the folk material at odds with the second voice within the tales themselves.

Lieberman, Marcia R. "'Some Day My Prince Will Come': Female Acculturation Through the Fairy Tale." *College English* 34 (1972/73): 383–95. Analyzes Andrew Lang's *Blue Fairy Book* (1889), while contending that children learn behavior and associational patterns, value systems, and how to predict the consequences of actions from fairy tales. Details emphasis on beauty as a girl's most valuable asset, marriage as the fulcrum of female experience, and the passivity of heroines in contrast to heroes.

Roberts, Marthe. "The Grimm Brothers." In *The Child's Part*. Edited by Peter Brooks. Boston: Beacon Press, 1969. Approaches fairy tales as studies that account for the necessity for individuals to pass from one state to another, to be formed through pained metamorphoses which terminate only with accession to true maturity. Contends that the figure who presides over rites of passage is *la sage femme*, the wise woman, who like the Greek fates and Germanic Norns, oversees the fate of the human beings whose destiny she represents.

Rowe, Karen E. "Feminism and Fairy Tales." *Women's Studies: An Interdisciplinary Journal* 6 (1979): 237–57. Examines selected popular folktales from the perspective of modern feminism in order to revisualize those paradigms which shape romantic expectations and to illuminate psychic ambiguities which confound contemporary women.

Stone, Kay. "Things Walt Disney Never Told Us." *Journal of American Folklore* 88 (1975): 42–49. Points out the paucity of studies as of 1975 of heroines in the Grimm Brothers fairy tales and provides a survey based on popular and scholarly collections in English as well as interviews with dozens of women.

von Franz, Marie-Louise. *Problems of the Feminine in Fairytales*. New York: Spring Publications, 1972. Starting with the paradox in fairy tales that the feminine figures are the pattern neither of the anima nor of the real women, but of both, hypothesizes that in some fairy tales the feminine formative influence has been greater and in others the male.

Waelti-Walters, Jennifer. *Fairy Tales and the Female Imagination*. Montreal: Eden Press, 1982. Contends that fairy tales are subversive because of the detrimental role models they present to girls and the long-lasting influences these models have on the female imagination and the support given the fairy tale genre by child psychologists.

4. Telling Tales — Spreading Tales: Change in the Communicative Forms of a Popular Genre

RUDOLF SCHENDA

Posing Questions

The historian of European folk literature faces several complex and complicated questions in connection with the subject of change in and the dissemination of *Märchen*. I would like to raise a few of these questions and then try to find solutions. Is the *Märchen*° actually a genre clearly defined by ancient traditions, or has it taken shape only recently under quite specific historical conditions? May one actually accept the elevated position of the fairy tale which it occupies today within the confines of what is known about folk narrative? What relationships does the fairy tale bear to orality? Is it actually a form of oral communication or a form of printed communication, that is, reading material? And how do these two very different modes of communication relate to each other historically? Has the fairy tale, in one form or another, transmitted either orally or in print, always been

Translated by Ruth B. Bottigheimer.
° I shall use the German word *Märchen* when it means brief narratives in general, whether they be shaggy dog stories, fairy, folk, or animal tales, and otherwise I shall translate it in the sense of the text — TRANS.

a children's genre or is this orientation toward a young audience a development of more recent times? What intentions lie hidden behind such designations as fairy tales (*Kindermärchen*), tales for children (*Märchen für Kinder*), or even in the assertion, "Children need fairy tales."° Indeed, how is that complex creation, the fairy tale, put together? That is, who are its producers, its "tellers," and its consumers, now and in the past?

Narration as a Social Act

Unfortunately we have no history of narration or of narrative acts for European history in the last thousand years, although there is much evidence that gatherings of all kinds were accompanied by storytelling, which included not only factual reports but also unusual, fantastic, and comic occurrences. Storytelling is a social act, which presupposes a narrator, often highly gifted, and a public. The roles could even be reversed on occasion.

These social preconditions are necessarily accompanied by the verbal aspects of language itself as well as by nonverbal qualities, mimicry, and gesture. Narrative acts of this sort are not one-sided performances: the narrator needs the reactions of his or her public, its objections, questions, approval, protests, laughter and tears, and the interruptions and the change of pace occasioned by shifting from one storyteller to another. For example, the exchange of storytelling experiences between beginners and those who are more experienced brings out a relationship of dominance in addition to a collective exchange of narrative knowledge.[1] From the history of tale-telling we know that there are special occasions for storytelling as well as quite ordinary ones. Storytelling situations arising from the travel of artisans from one place to another, pilgrimages of the pious,[2] and coach trips of the well-to-do were uncommon occurrences; storytelling on a daily basis usually took place in conjunction with specific jobs, during or after work, or among people sitting together in a pub or a workroom, or in the sleeping quarters of farm workers. The usual locus for storytelling could be transformed by the arrival of a stranger coming from afar who recounted his experiences or told tales he had heard from others.

°*Kinder brauchen Märchen* (Children need fairy tales) is the title of the German edition (Stuttgart: Deutsche Verlagsanstalt, 1977) of Bruno Bettelheim's *Uses of Enchantment* (New York: Alfred Knopf, 1975) — TRANS.

The Problem of Genres

We have rich evidence for all these varieties of communicative acts. From this evidence, we can also conclude that tales of adventure, of piety, and of humor were also told. Genre designations before the eighteenth century hardly exist. In speaking of *Erzählungen, tales, contes, cuentos, racconti,* one encompasses everything which is later separated into fairy and folktale, legend, and jest. But we should be aware that the genre, which today we call fairy tale or folktale, always played only a minor role within the variety of narrative acts. The jest and the tale of adventure were more customary,[3] and recitals of sickness and dying were daily occurrences.[4] Only a fad at the end of the seventeenth and beginning of the eighteenth century, "la mode des fées," as well as forced examples of this genre elicited in the nineteenth century have lent the fairy tale a certain disproportionate importance.

In the beginning there were stories and narratives of all sorts. Who then introduced these genre distinctions?[5] The eighteenth century still did not recognize any difference between fairy tale and legend, a good example of which appears in the third volume of Christian Gotthilf Salzmann's *Unterhaltungen für Kinder und Kinderfreunde.* He introduces various tales of the Thuringian Kyffhäuser in his description of a trip from Dessau to Thuringia. First he calls them "adventurous tales that I had heard in my youth," and then he calls the history of The Emperor Barbarossa not a legend but a story. After two further stories, however, that include magic events in the vicinity of this magic mountain, his children shout: "Aha! Daddy's fooling us! Daddy's telling fairy tales," and Salzmann agrees: "And I said, I wasn't holding it up as anything but a fairy tale." The teacher thus rejoices that his children can distinguish reality from fantasy: he contrasts these new children of reason with his own youthful schoolmates of a previous generation, who "continually told these and also other stories of the Kyffhäuser, as well as stories about the Wild Hunt, black men and white ladies, all of which they believed."[6] Here we have every variety of genre thrown together: history (*Geschichte*), story (*Erzählung*), fairy tale (*Märchen*), and anecdote (*Histörchen*), except the one which we would use today, namely, legend (*Sage*). In connection with popular narratives the eighteenth century does not really have fixed genres; the chief aim is to distinguish between reason and superstition. Children have to learn to overcome their fear of ghosts, to rein in their fantasy, to look directly at reality, and to have rational control of their life.

The Discovery and the Invention of the Fairy Tale

Genre distinction is clearly guided by other interests. Deciding on philological categories and setting up genre subdivisions became both useful and necessary in the course of the Romantic appropriation of countless newly discovered medieval literary works, and during Achim von Arnim's and Clemens Brentano's[7] literary development of a new folk voice, the invention of new poetic genres became possible. As the fairy tale crystallized in a slow philological process after 1812,[*] it became a product of philological necessity and poetic possibility. Besides that, it fulfilled the political expectations of a broad literary public.

Even Wilhelm and Jacob Grimm were initially uncertain about using these genre subcategories. That is as evident in the fairy tale collections of 1812 and 1815[8] as it is in the foreword to the *German Legends* of 1816 and 1818[9] or from the way in which Jacob Grimm used material in his *German Mythology* of 1835. The well-known formulation of 1816: "The fairy tale [*Märchen*] is more poetic, the legend [*Sage*] more historic"[10] grows out of this uncertainty, which continues among their epigones until the middle of the nineteenth century.

Misunderstandings: "Oral" and "From the People"[**]

I have spoken of philologists' creation of genre and poets' invention of fairy tales, that is, of litterrateurs, and I think we should be aware of the content and the range of this process, which is, above all, German. Two misconceptions should be cleared up. The first is the orality of ancient fairy tales and legends, and the second is the folk or lower-class origin of both these genres. Nothing is more false than imagining the Grimms or their disciples in hiking boots and Loden coats with notebooks and pencils in the field. The great majority of the tales in the collection are literary in origin and were noted down in a bourgeois setting, namely, in Cassel at the Wilds and Hassenpflugs, or else copied out of books.[11] Frau Viehmann, about whom the Grimms write in the foreword to volume 2 in 1814, was indeed a "peasant" from Zwehrn near Cassel, but the Grimms report

---

[*] The date of the publication of the first volume of the first edition of the *Kinder- und Hausmärchen gesammelt durch die Brüder Grimm* — ED.
[**] "Aus dem Volke" — TRANS.

only on her looks ("was probably beautiful in her youth"!) and on her reliable way of reciting,[12] but not on her level of education or her social status. The *German Legends* were drawn completely from printed or written sources; wherever the Grimms note the origin as "oral," they only mean that a contributor had asserted in his letter containing the legend that such a legend had been told in his area somewhere at some time.[13] We certainly may have strong reservations about the orality of evidence from second or third hand. Every fascicle of the *Enzyklopädie des Märchens* indicates afresh that countless tale types and motifs were drawn from the treasure trove of medieval epics and lives of the saints, from Renaissance novellas and humanist compilations, from Baroque sermons and Enlightenment doctoral dissertations, from almanacs and chapbooks.[14] We have read far too little of the vast amount of these "lower" literary genres to be able to maintain that some form of "oral" tradition was not written down or printed and read or read aloud and thereby transported further along, either shortly before or at most two generations before the storytelling act.

I do not mean to deny the creativity or the feats of memory of the people, and I also perceive no opposition to theories developed from East German research in this field;[15] neither am I regurgitating Hans Naumann's thesis of the trickle down of cultural material (*gesunkenes Kulturgut*). I am instead questioning the very basis of the Romantic theories of an oral tradition unbroken since pagan times and of a lower-class origin of so-called folk narrative, and I am allowing myself to lose some respect for the genres "fairy tale" and "legend" as they were carved in stone following the Grimms and above all as they were celebrated by Ludwig Bechstein. Such a loss of respect is all the more necessary when one regards the total chaos of Romantic literary production before and accompanying Grimms' *Tales*, which attempted to elevate "folk" tales into the realm of literary fairy tales or into the kingdom of knightly horror stories.[16] And in line with this distancing I also regard some of the psychoanalytic and pedagogic reverence for the fairy tale as a kind of idolatry, as a veneration of a false deity, as a denial of what the folk really recounted and what the actual psycho-social requirements of the members of the lower class were.[17]

It would nonetheless be foolish if we imputed to the Grimms either literary dilettantism or an intent to defraud. In contrast to the oeuvre of Ludwig Bechstein, theirs is whole cloth and a great poetic accomplishment: as bourgeois citizens and intellectuals, they tried to recognize the inherent cultural values of speech patterns and the narrative tradition of country people and illiterates (whom they never once mention, however); they collaborated in what seemed necessary to them then — the reconstruction of a common national historical past for all members of petty German principalities by the creation of literary prose pieces, whose best examples delight every aficionado of Romantic literature. But — and this must also be said — they had a rather foggy notion of oral narrative forms in the context of daily life or of special forms of communication in the country among illiterate manual laborers.[18]

Social Preconditions for Telling Fairy Tales

Only more recently, since approximately the beginning of this century, have we begun to learn — little by little — what stories the "people" really told. Before this could happen, a shift in moral attitudes toward sexual propriety and other bourgeois virtues had to occur — Rapunzel suddenly has twins, but there had been no mention of sexual intercourse — while on the other hand scenes of murder and mayhem — mangling, dismemberment, and frenzy — were allowable anywhere.[19] Even the great collector, Richard Wossidlo from Mecklenburg, was still bent on hearing what he wanted and what he expected, namely, the remnants of myths. Ulrich Jahn (1891) and Gottfried Henssen (1935, 1953) got a little closer to the people; and a very strong impulse in this direction came from Mark Azadowskii's little volume, *Eine sibirische Märchenerzählerin* (A Siberian fairy tale teller) (1926)[20] and from Linda Dégh's work, *Märchen, Erzähler, und Erzählgemeinschaft* (English title: *Folk Tales and Society*) (1962).[21] Only after World War II, and probably because of wartime experiences, did researchers concern themselves more intensively with recitals of daily events and the storytelling milieu and what occasions it, as well as the course of the narrative act itself. In recent years publications that point in this new direction are those of Daniel Fabre, Linda Dégh, Aurora Milillo, Helmut Fischer, Emily Gerstner-Hirzel, and Ulrich Tolksdorf.[22]

From these and other studies we can perceive how storytelling as a social act is still proceeding in border zones or border situations and also how it evolved a hundred or a hundred and fifty years ago.[23] In particular we can imagine the social conditions in which even fairy tales were told. We are dealing with a narrative milieu composed of country people, the greater number of whom were illiterate and who were at home with direct forms of communication such as speaking, gesticulating, demonstrating, and imitating the model. Oral communication played a much greater role in this milieu than city dwellers can imagine today. For the sort of amusement that was distinguished culturally from the quotidian, they certainly had no salons as did the nobility or the haute bourgeoisie,[24] though they had at their disposal large community rooms with a hearth and a source of light. The absence of news printed daily made the exchange of information especially necessary; the long winter evenings left much time to share events and experiences, partly true and partly embellished, some up-to-date and some recalled from memory. The public consisted of the extended family, some of the neighbors, and even the animals; often there was one among them who could read, who could repeat something interesting from what he had read, or who could even read aloud from a broadside or pamphlet. Children were present at these *veillées, Nachtkarzen, veglie,*[25] but went to bed earlier than the adults; afterward story content shifted to themes that were not meant for young ears. Such storytelling groups were well aware of their low social status. For them, fairy tales, jests, and legends fulfilled secret desires for wealth and adventure, love and lust, a topsy-turvy world, and a different social existence at the level of fantasy. Even the fairy tale, which some hold to be timeless and ahistorical, builds in local color and references to social conditions, especially concerning children, and are full of peasant world views[26] and biographical bits; they are influenced, furthermore, by the norms and value judgments of bourgeois editors, for instance, with reference to paternal authority, acceptance of poverty, or the punishment of criminals.[27] In a word, fairy tales have their specific, historical frame of reference.[28] And because that is so, as one recognizes more and more today,[29] it is utterly incomprehensible why fairy tale texts from a specific historical framework, which deal with communal work and communal social facts of a particular milieu and which were once the cultural possession of the people, should be torn from their frame of reference and served up to children in every possible counterfeit form: romanticized and put into High German, expurgated and prettified, without gesticulation and miming, and to make up for that, illustrated for the most part by third-rate daubers and with not a single word of commentary about all the details that relate to the text. If children really need fairy tales, and doubt about that must be allowed,[30] then they should be given fairy tales that correspond to reality, and that means narrative texts with historical explanations about their development and dissemination.

Fairy Tales in the Service of Ideologies

One can certainly maintain that the Grimms lost control of their oeuvre, in particular Wilhelm, who was singly responsible for the editions of the *Kinder- und Hausmärchen* after 1819.[31] After the failed

bourgeois revolution of 1848, at the very latest, educators and pro-
tonationalists appropriated the Grimms' legacy. In 1851 Friedrich
August Wilhelm Diesterweg wrote about the meaning, the goals, and
the means of German national education, and about how important it
is to unearth all treasures of the German national language, because
German is "an aboriginal, a crystal clear language and at the same
time a language as hard as granite." Reckoned part of this linguistic
treasure were "the German folksong, the German fairy tale, the German folk epic, and the German proverb. I call 'German' the music
created by Germans, the cantos, the folk melodies, our tales, our
(principally Protestant) hymns, our proverbs." And a little later Diesterweg writes: "It is indeed with that that we will nourish, feed, and
quench the thirst of our youth."[32] Popular linguistic substance is thus
taken completely into the service of the ideology of Germanic primor-
diality and thus of the national unity of the German people in the
sense of Johannes Matthias Firmenich's *Germaniens Völkerstimmen*
(1843–66).[33] This ideology, which aimed at the constitution of a
powerful centrally governed German state, was to be fed to young
people in conjunction with fairy tales. One year later Ludwig Bechstein wrote in Ernst Moritz Arndt's *Germania*, a similarly patriotic
journal, about the fairy tale and its treatment in Germany, emphasizing — quite the accomplished pupil of Jacob Grimm — the close
relationship between the world of the fairy tale and of Germanic mythology. After presenting an overview of fairy tale literature from the
late Middle Ages to Grimms' *Fairy Tales*, Bechstein concluded that
the contemporary political situation was an earnest one which had no
need of fairy tales, "but *children* have need of them as of cool spring
water, for the fairy tale world is a Castalian poetic source full of in-
eradicable magic, the very best tonic for the hands and eyes of our
children." The best proof of this assertion might be Bechstein's own
German Fairy Tale Book (*Deutsches Märchenbuch*), which was published
in a total of 63,000 copies from 1845 on.[34] Bechstein, an archivist
from Meiningen, is shamelessly advertising his own book here and
also attempting to steer children away from politics with fairy tales by
emphasizing their timelessness and thus their apolitical nature. One
year later one once again reads a hymn to the depth and judiciousness
of the German people in the writings of the Hessian Catholic Johann
Wilhelm Wolf (whose pseudonym was "Laicus"). He contrasts "our
fairy tales" with "the refined novels of the modern French school:
these miscarriages of an impure fantasy and a rotten soul must appear
impoverished and repugnant, where our fairy tales reveal the pure
colorful flourishing of its fresh fragrant fantasy."[35] Fairy tales thus
possessed an outstanding pedagogical and — Bechstein's assertions to

the contrary notwithstanding — political value. Even then they were able to be mobilized behind every possible partisan banner. This ideological service of the fairy tale came into play particularly during the Wilhelmine age, as Ulrike Bastian has recently shown in her book about Grimms' *Fairy Tales* and the literary-pedagogical debate.[36]

The New Flood of Fairy Tale Books

Making use of books of fairy tales and legends became all the more necessary in schools and in homes with the addition of millions of newly literate children, youths, and adults,[37] for whom there was not enough suitable reading material. The bourgeois romances of the Restoration were seen as old fashioned; Christoph von Schmid was too piously Catholic, Christian Gottlob Barth too strictly pietistic, Gustav Nieritz too dry. Thus those publishers who were alert grasped eagerly at new "folk" reading materials, which the folktale and legend collectors were delivering to them in heaps and piles. Casting a broad bibliographical net, I have counted all the book and essay titles that include the word "legend" (*Sage*) for the twenty years between 1850 and 1869; there are at least ten book and twenty essay or article titles a year. At least a hundred authors were busy at this work, for approximately thirty of whom biographical information can be found: they are doctors, lawyers, journalists, and university and gymnasium professors, nearly without exception all with higher education; Catholics and Protestants appear in equal numbers.[38] I have not yet counted all the fairy tale titles themselves, of which there are fewer than there are books and articles about legends.

We do have a few bibliographical aids, however, in assessing the fairy tale book, at least in the twentieth century. In 1979, volume 83 of the *Gesamtverzeichnis deutschsprachigen Schrifttums* (GV) appeared, covering the years 1911- 65 and including the heading *"Märchen."*[39] For the fifty-five years that this bibliography encompasses there are no less than seven hundred titles, about twelve a year, of books, brochures, and pamphlets dealing with one aspect or another of this genre: African, Egyptian, Arabian, Baltic, Bavarian and Breton fairy tales straight through to "fairy tales from everywhere," for "fairy tales recognize no boundaries," especially not in bookstores.[40] Because they must be sold, publishers entitle these volumes *Neue Märchen* (New fairy tales), of which there are eight titles; *Schöne Märchen* (Beautiful fairy tales); even *Die schönsten Märchen* (The most beautiful fairy tales), of which there are thirty-four titles. Spurring sales was clearly the object of serial editions of which more than a dozen appear in the *Gesamtverzeichnis,* for example, the *Märchenborn* (The fountain of fairy tales), *Hausser's Märchenbücher* (Hausser's fairy tale books), or the *Deutsche Märchenbücherei* (German fairy tale library). One certainly may not assume that the same old folktales were printed again and again. Literary fairy tales here far outnumber those tales coaxed from "the mouth of the people." And naturally certain curiosities also show up: In Niederzwehrn (near Cassel) in 1955 there was a fairy tale festival at the Dorothea Viehmann School to mark the bicentennial of Viehmann's birth;° in the middle of World War I Schultze and Velhagen published *Ein Märchen und dennoch wahr! Ein Hoffnungsstrahl für alle Kämpfenden* (A Fairy tale and yet true! A glimmer of hope for all soldiers) (1915); and the Allgemeiner Deutsche Gewerkschaftsbund (General German Union Organization) published *Das Märchen vom Preisabbau* (The fairy tale of price reduction) (1925). The title *Märchenwelt* (Fairy tale world), which appeared eighteen times, was an all-purpose one. Let us take a different bibliographical reference book as a check: *Das Verzeichnis lieferbarer Bücher von 1975–76* (The catalog of available books 1975–76).[41] How many fairy tale books are currently on the market in Germany? For the year 1975 we have eighty titles which begin with the word "*Märchen . . . ,*" fifteen titles with "*Märchenbuch,*" fifty-five titles with compound words including "*Märchen*" such as "*Märchen-Fibel*" (fairy tale primer), "*Märchenposter*" (fairy tale posters), "*Märchentruhe*" (Fairy tale treasure chest), and "*Märchenwald*" (Fairy tale woods). There are 150 further cross references to books that have the word "*Märchen*" in the title, and finally the sixty titles of the *Märchen der Weltliteratur* (Fairy tales of world literature) from the publisher Diederichs. There are most certainly overlapping entries, but there are at least 200 fairy tale books listed for sale in those years as well as two dozen titles devoted to fairy tale research.

The Frankfurt Book Fair of 1978 took as its theme "Kind und Buch" (Children and books), and the special edition of the *Börsenblatt für den deutschen Buchhandel* published in connection with the fair offers us a few additional illustrations for the subject of the market situation for fairy tales. We find out that there is a Hans-im-Glück°° prize founded in 1977 by Hans-Christian Kirsch. We also learn that imprisoned juvenile delinquents prefer detective stories to fairy tales, and we get recommendations from publishing houses about which fairy tales are the right ones for which age group. We still get offered

---

° Dorothea Viehmann was the source of numerous tales in volume 2 of Grimms' collection — Trans.

°° The name of tale #83 in the Grimm collection — Ed.

Die Schönsten Märchen (The most beautiful fairy tales)[42] and *Die Schön-sten Sagen* (The most beautiful legends); the fairy tale books bear prices such as "from 3.95" like other cheap goods, and so on.[43]

Within the last hundred years the form in which the popular narrative genre, the fairy tale, is told has changed radically. It is no longer communicated in a direct teller-listener conversation but indirectly through the printed medium of the text. Telling fairy tales in this fashion diminishes to the vanishing point the spontaneous speech patterns of oral syntax,[44] gesticulation, and miming, but it gains the accompanying illustrations with their capacity to stimulate the fantasy. The text of the fairy tale becomes fixed into an invariable, an archaic, artifact. But it also becomes generally available, by escaping far beyond the limited circle of the primary communicators not only to bourgeois children but gradually to lower-class children as well, and thus it is returned to the people — as it were — by means of books. The reading (as opposed to the listening) reception of fairy tales is meanwhile no longer a social act but the isolated occupation of an individual;[45] buying and giving fairy tale books as presents have become the social acts associated with fairy tales. The channel that produces the fairy tale is no longer a living individual but a production team of anonymous authors, editors, and unknowable publishing houses. Exchanging ideas with the producer, asking questions during the telling, or revealing one's emotional responses to the narrator cannot take place in this environment. The fairy tale reader can at most toss the book into the corner or write the publisher a letter which will not be answered. Fairy tale communication in the age of the book is thus nearly completely depersonalized and objectified. Even at public fairy tale readings the fairy tale texts are reduced to and cast into standard literary forms. The fairy tale has become a museum piece, like most of the daily activities of the traditional folk culture from bread baking to singing songs. Achim von Arnim was right in the end. In a letter to Jacob Grimm (22 October 1812) he prophesied that writing fairy tales down would hasten the "death of the entire fairy tale corpus."[46]

Total Exploitation of Fairy Tales

Subjugating the previously oral tales of the people to the laws of bourgeois literary scholarship and industrialized production of reading materials has led to numerous further adaptations of the form of the fairy tale itself. I would like to remind the reader of just a few facts. The *reading* of fairy tales has itself been overtaken by new forms of fairy tale communication. In the economic year 1971–72, 146 records from 19 publishers of 71 different Grimms' fairy tales were offered for sale.[47] The texts preserving fairy tales have thus been joined by the "sound-preserving" texts;[48] the texts read aloud by professionals in front of a microphone lend themselves to repetitions of great frequency and intensity; listeners are in particular delivered up helplessly to those sound effects generating a special mood.[49] In the fifties, films of fairy tales dominated German children's television as fairy tale plays did the radio; since then better materials for amusement and education have been found.[50] Fairy tales on stage are above all the most welcomed Christmas fare of the city theaters; in 1977–78, 51 fairy tale plays appeared among the 171 theater performances for children, that is, 30 percent of the repertoire and 40 percent of all performances.[51] Other forms of fairy tales are aimed at adults. I will only mention fairy tales in advertising, which are used for furthering the sales of chocolate, vitamin preparations,[52] noodles,[53] or cleaning materials;[54] fairy tale caricatures, often cloaked in erotic ambiguity,[55] and sexy fairy tales with straightforward erotic content, among which Snow White, Little Red Riding Hood, or Sleeping Beauty present themselves as objects of desire. Further we are aware of fairy tale parodies, with which one could fill volumes,[56] and political fairy tale pamphlets[57] and broadsides.[58]

Let us return to "our dear little ones." I have seen the following things: fairy tale gardens,[59] fairy tale picture books,[60] fairy tale pop-ups, Leporellos (folding books for children), fairy tale toy theaters, fairy tale shop windows, fairy tale playing cards and pictures for album collections, fairy tale posters, fairy tale dolls, fairy tale coloring books, a paper doll cut-out outfit for the naked emperor and a thumb puppet theater with Puss in Boots,[61] and naturally, numberless gingerbread houses at Christmas. Those, too, are forms of communicating fairy tales, products of the culture industry, which exploits anything recognizable to sell new goods in old wrappers, no matter how limited their utility: paper goods, toys, food, consumer items for leisure time. In line with passing on fairy tale terms frozen into fairy tale literature, one feeds children with fairy tale consumables, in such a manner — a chocolate Red Riding Hood you can devour yourself — that Friedrich Diesterweg, if he could see the realization of his ideas, would distance himself with horror from his "menu" for youth.[62]

---

* This word refers not only to the shape of a particular Franconian bottle but sometimes to the wine itself — TRANS.

And Finally: Fairy Tales for Children?

I will not enter the vexatious discussion about the value or value-lessness of fairy tales for children,[63] but I will say something about children. Were fairy tales actually told to children in former times? Of course they were! One of my oldest pieces of evidence comes from a dissertation in the year 1726 on the concept of the *Bocksbeutel,*° the tenacious retention of old customs. The author, Ernst Joachim West-phalen, writes about nursemaids and old women who frighten little girls in order to force their spirit and their common sense under the yoke of blind obedience. As soon as little girls started to say their first words, these old women had nothing better to do than to stuff their charges with superstition:

Narrant multo verborum apparatu historiolas about the Block Mountain, about the black witch, about the fellow who sticks children in his sack, about Tom Thumb, about Blue Beard, about the cuckoo soup and Witch's Foot and old lady Eten Inne, about the princess in the blue tower, etc. et infinitas fabulas.[64]

Here we are encountering scare stories known internationally; En-lightenment thinkers were definitely not of the opinion that one should educate children using such old wives' tales. Even Jacob Grimm in his letter to Achim von Arnim (28 January 1813)[65] was quite uncer-tain whether the *Kinder- und Hausmärchen* (*Grimm's Fairy Tales*) should be put into young hands: "The book of fairy tales is not written for children at all, but it meets their needs and desires, and that pleases me immensely." Jacob Grimm's original reservations were abandoned in the process of Wilhelm Grimm's improvements of the texts.[66] The pre-1848 discussions about the appropriateness of fairy tales for chil-dren as well as their misopedia[67] were forgotten after the Revolution: in 1850 Hans Christian Andersen's fairy tales chosen "for young people"[68] appeared; in 1835 Johann Wilhelm Wolf (mentioned above) could assert that the Grimm collection and its imitations "had already been of inestimable influence on the rearing of thousands" and that they had saved young people from the "confused and perverse fab-rications" of writers for young people.[69] In the same year Heinrich Pröhle, the most important folktale researcher at the time in north Germany, was anxious about the prospective reception of his collec-ton of fairy tales:

How will you tales with your north German spirit and north German folktale jokiness stand up under the scrutiny of the whole German people? Will people find wrinkles on your forehead or will you be a child among children? How wonderful, oh how wonderful, if you could help in the sense of the ancients, who told stories to children to terrify them away from evil and to teach them to love goodness! How wonderful, oh how wonderful, if you could teach them to play, to love their fatherland, to hold its boundaries sacred, to honor its people, never to forget the heroic deeds of their forefathers, but not to join in the celebrations of impertinent rabble.[70]

This quotation contains the new trends in a nutshell: the metamorphosis of the genre, children's literature, the emphasis on its pedagogical utility, and its political applicability particularly in its use against everything French.

Finally I would like to pull one more example from the Restoration period, one that shows how fairy tales had not yet been recast as children's literature at that point. In the foreword to Carl and Theodor Colshorn's Hannoverian collection of 1854, a father takes a walk with little Augusta, a "sweet little girl of seven or eight," and he hides something white in the grass, while the child picks flowers. Then

She came skipping up to him and said: "Papa, can I look for rabbits' nests now?" Then her papa nodded and his eyes twinkled; and she looked and looked. "Oh, what's that!" she suddenly called out, "What can be in there?" She quickly tore the paper aside and shouted with joy. "O Papa, what's the rabbit brought me today! Grimm's *Fairy Tales*, bound in blue velvet, with gold edges on the pages and a golden title!" And she took the book home with her, was delighted at its precious fairy tales and held it dear. Augusta has now grown up and is a mother herself; but the book is dear to her as it was then and will be dear to her until she dies.[71]

A literary genre, which for Giambattista Basile first served as courtly amusement, which then for more than a century supplied material for bourgeois hack literature, became transformed into children's literature around the middle of the last century for pedagogical, political, and book-trade reasons. In dozens of different outward shapes, in thousands of text transformations, the fairy tale clearly remains dear to children to the present day — to the extent that appearances do not deceive, and to the extent that the whole fairy tale hullabaloo is not a bugbear of bibliographies and pedagogical journals! Today's observer of the contemporary child should really expect that it is not only juvenile delinquents who reject fairy tales because they no longer have anything to say to them. One could at least argue that a modern child can hardly identify with suffering heroes and rescues by magical helpers in these old stories. Their problems lie on a different plane and are far more complex. Fairy tales offer children instead such a thick packet of long outdated familial, social, and conjugal norms that their divergence from actual patterns of living can lead to powerful disorientation. In contemporary reality more and more children deal not with happy weddings but with marriages gone to pieces and unmarried siblings. Children of today hear and read about emancipated women and about feminist ideas, and they see the old patriarchal roles falling apart. Even more discrepancies between fairy tale reality and children's daily lives could be added to the recent anti-Bettelheim theses of the French psychologist Pierre Péju.[72] But here I am entering a territory that rightfully belongs to pedagogues and psychologists, and they will wave the good old banners of fantasy and dreams in their land and overawe me, especially since I am myself defending not only the Enlightenment but also the Romantic point of view. I would like to add just one question to my pedagogical suggestions: Why should one draw dream and fantasy prototypes from old fairy tale materials, which, as I have shown, are so heavily freighted by many historically conditioned falsifications and ideologizations? Do we not really have enough untainted evidence concerning human hopes and daring, dreaming conquest, and fantastic mastery of this world?

I will summarize my main points:

1. The fairy tale has developed into the dominant genre among the varied forms of folk narratives for historical reasons. Because of this development, attention to other genres of folk narrative, especially the legend, the jest, and the recital of daily events, has been held back.

2. It may be true that in the course of the development of the mass media there has been a loss of true storytelling. Even truer, however, is that countless narrative acts of this kind still take place; since they do not fit into the available philological genre categories, they are hardly noticed.

3. It is useful to remove the fairy tale from its pedestal, to set it on the floor, not so that one can look at it from top to bottom, but so that one can look it directly in the face. The effect is twofold: the countenance of the fairy tale reveals many flaws and the other monuments of folk poesie seem of greater stature.

4. We should try to re-historicize the fairy tale, to reintegrate it into its cultural environment, and to revive the texts socially.

5. We will thereby recognize that fairy tales transport social norms and values that principally belong to the courtly absolutistic or to predemocratic-bourgeois ages. Whoever does not question these norms is likely to be suspected of being reactionary.

6. We should also try to tease out the mentality of the lower

classes from fairy tale and legend texts gathered later, which can perhaps be regarded as genuine. But in seeking such information about the folk, we should remember that there are also other historical sources, which inform us about the life and thought of the people.

7. The passive reception of narrative texts, no matter what their quality, is in the long run a sterile affair; the active production of stories, which naturally is not given to every individual, should be practiced more frequently. In addition to the criticism of the brand of fairy tale which I have introduced here, there must be an alternative form of fairy tale pedagogy, an "environmentally sound" narrative policy.°

8. Whoever looks squarely at the development of the capacity for fantasy and dealing with reality through daydreams might consider that there are also other forms of children's literature than fairy tales through which children can achieve these goals.

9. Changes in the forms of communicating fairy tales show that this genre, far more than others, has been subject to overuse and fatigue. It is to be heartily desired, perhaps even to be publicly demanded, that the production of culturally related consumer goods based on the seven dwarves, the seven kids, and the seven league boots be given a long rest.

10. If one must bring older children together with fairy tales, then one should leave the texts in their unbowdlerized, original form, as they were at the time they were originally written down, to the extent that that can still be determined. If children alone or together with their teachers do not know what to make of such authentic texts, then one should consider whether or not the entire secondary production of fairy tales in books and on tapes, for example, as well as fairy tale pedagogy, should not be given a decent burial.

But I am certain that the fairy tale pedagogues will find some means to keep children of today in close contact with fairy tales.

Notes

1. See also R. Schenda, "Witze, die selten zum Lachen sind: Bemerkungen zur gegenwärtigen französischen Witzblatt-Produktion," *Zeitschrift für Volkskunde* 74 (1978): 58–75, esp. 58–61.

2. Very early examples of pilgrims' storytelling can be found in old collections of *exempla*. See, for example, E. J. Arnould, *Le Manuel des péchés: Etude de littérature religieuse anglo-normande (XIIIᵉ siècle)* (Paris, 1940), pp. 117–18, 123, and 186 n. 3.

° Schenda is here referring to the environmental political party in Germany, the Greens, as well as to the fact that fairy tales have been integrated into German pedagogical theory since the last third of the nineteenth century — TRANS.

3. See Hermann Hubert Wetzel, *Märchen in den französischen Novellensammlungen der Renaissance* (Berlin, 1974).

4. Several of the fairy tale and legend collectors had already determined by 1850 that the fairy tale tellers had "almost completely died out." See, for example, G. Schambach and W. Müller, *Niedersächsische Sagen und Märchen* (Göttingen, 1855), p. vii.

5. For a genre discussion see the report of the congress, *Folk Narrative Research: Some Papers Presented at the Sixth Congress of the International Society for Folk Narrative Research*, Studia Fennica, no. 20 (Helsinki, 1976), pp. 13–74.

6. Christian Gotthelf Salzmann, *Unterhaltungen für Kinder und Kinderfreunde*, vol. 3, new improved ed. (Leipzig, 1812), pp. 168–71.

7. Wolfgang Frühwald, "Leben im Zitat: Anmerkungen zum Werk Clemens Brentanos," *Zeitwende (Die neue Furche)* 50 (1979): 80.

8. What is meant is the fact that a clear differentiation is not always made between fairy tale (*Märchen*) and religious tale (*Legende*), fable (*Fabel*) or jest (*Schwank*); it is striking that the fairy tales of Frau Viehmann are designated as "old legends" (*alte Sagen*) in the foreword to vol. 2 of the *Kinder- und Hausmärchen* (1815).

9. *Die deutschen Sagen der Brüder Grimm*, vols. 1–2, ed. Hermann Schneider (Berlin, Leipzig, Vienna, and Stuttgart, n.d.).

10. Ibid., 1:17.

11. See, above all, the works of Heinz Rölleke such as "Die 'stockhessischen' Märchen der 'Alten Marie': Das Ende eines Mythos um die frühesten KHM-Aufzeichnungen der Brüder Grimm," *Germanisch-Romanische Monatsschrift* 25 (1975): 74–86. Also "Die Marburger Märchenfrau: Herkunft der KHM 21 und 57," *Fabula* 15 (1974): 87–94.

12. If the Grimms were astonished, "wie genau sie [die Viehmännin] immer bei derselben Erzählung bleibt und auf ihre Richtigkeit eifrig ist," then they could have also asked themselves, what (literary?) authority she was following. Ordinary oral tradition has no authority at all (though it may be different with piously kept family traditions), indeed joy in varying the version is recognized as a characteristic of the creative accomplishment of the lower classes.

13. Fritz Erfurth, "Die Deutschen Sagen der Brüder Grimm" (diss., Münster, 1938), pp. 103–4, gives a preliminary overview of the sources for *Die deutschen Sagen*.

14. The influence of printed material on what is told orally has been stressed again and again in recent years. See Erna Pomeranceva "I. F. Kovalev, ein belesener russischer Märchenerzähler," *Deutsches Jahrbuch für Volkskunde* 11 (1965): 265–74; Elfriede Moser-Rath, "'Calembourg': Zur Mobilität populärer Lesestoffe," in *Volkskundliche Fakten und Analysen: Festschrift Leopold Schmidt* (Vienna, 1972), pp. 470–81; Matthias Zender, "Volkserzählungen als Quelle für Lebensverhältnisse vergangener Zeiten," *Rheinisches Jahrbuch für Volkskunde* 21 (1973): 120; Johannes Künzig and Waltraud Werner, eds., *Schwänke aus mündlicher Ueberlieferung* (Freiburg, 1973), vols. 7–8, and Hermann Bausinger, "Buchmärchen," *Enzyklopädie des Märchens*, vol. 2 (1981), col. 974–77.

15. See Hermann Strobach, ed., *Deutsche Volksdichtung: Eine Einführung* (Frankfurt, 1979). See my review in *Fabula*, vol. 23 (1982).

16. A dissertation about fairy tales before the KHM will soon be completed in Göttingen in the Seminar für Volkskunde by Manfred Grätz. See also the excerpt, which Grätz contributed to the *Enzyklopädie des Märchens* as an article, "Deutschland," (1981).

17. Excursus: I feel confirmed in this by no means heretical but thoroughly orthodox attitude by two marginal notes in a copy of a fairy tale book in the State and University Library of Lower Saxony in Göttingen. Known to be by Christian Ernst Benzel-Sternau, the book bears the title, *Titania oder das Reich der Mährchen, aus dem Klarfeldischen Archive, vom Herausgeber des goldenen Kalbes* (Regensburg, 1807), and at a particularly unbearable fairy tale – poetic place on p. 247 one sees the commentary of a critical reader: "Das Buch ist beschissen." And another reader added the following comment to these marginalia: "Dummer Narr, schreib reinlicher." Exactly. In criticizing our predecessors we must proceed more honorably, more carefully.

18. Charles Perrault makes fewer difficulties for us, because while he uses folk elements in great number, he does not claim to have gotten them from the people. Perrault's problem consisted of hardly daring to bring such secular material either to the academy or to court.

19. For the section on juvenile reading materials see R. Schenda, "Schundliteratur und Kriegsliteratur: Ein kritischer Forschungsbericht zur Sozialgeschichte der Jugendlesestoffe im Wilhelminischen Zeitalter." Now in R. Schenda, *Die Lesestoffe der kleinen Leute: Studien zur populären Literatur im 19. und 20. Jahrhundert* (Munich, 1976), pp. 78–104, 159–78.

20. M. Asadowskij, *Eine sibirische Märchenerzählerin*, FFC 68 (Helsinki, 1926). See the article by Linda Dégh, "Biologie des Erzählens," *Enzyklopädie des Märchens*, vol. 2 (1979), cols. 386–406, esp. 393–94.

21. Linda Dégh, *Erzähler und Erzählgemeinschaft* (Berlin, 1962).

22. Daniel Fabre and Jacques Lacroix, *La Tradition orale du conte occitan*, Les Pyrénées Audoises, vols. 1–2 (Paris, 1974, 1973) (*sic*). Linda Dégh: *People in the Tobacco Belt: Four Lives* (Ottawa, 1975). Aurora Milillo, *Narrativa di tradizione orale: Studi e ricerche* (Rome, 1977). Helmut Fischer, *Erzählgut der Gegenwart: Mündliche Texte aus dem Siegraum* (Cologne, 1978). Emily Gerstner-Hirzel, *Aus der Volksüberlieferung von Bosco Gurín* (Basel, 1979). Ulrich Tolksdorf, *Eine ostpreussische Volkserzählerin: Geschichten — Geschichte — Lebensgeschichte* (Marburg, 1980).

23. Much other evidence for the social conditions of narrative acts can be found in autobiographical literature. I cite, as a little-known example, Jurij Brezan, "Eine Geschichte in tausend Varianten," in *Das schönste Buch der Welt: Wie ich lesen lernte* (Berlin: Aufbau Verlag, 1977), pp. 66–67. See also R. Schenda, "Autobiographen erzählen Geschichten," *Zeitschrift für Volkskunde* 77 (1981): 71–72, n. 15.

24. One should note the narrative frames for the collections of Giovanni Boccaccio, Giambattista Basile, and *A Thousand and One Nights*, and also the narrative milieu, which is hinted at or introduced in the French novelists of the sixteenth century.

25. See Hans Medick, "Spinnstuben auf dem Dorf: Jugendliche Sexualkultur und Feierabendbrauch in der ländlichen Gesellschaft der frühen Neuzeit," in Gerhard Huck, ed., *Sozialgeschichte der Freizeit* (Wuppertal, 1980), pp. 19–49.

26. See Charles Joisten, *Contes populaires de l'Ariège* (Paris, 1965), p. 9.

27. Klaus Doderer, *Klassische Kinder- und Jugendbücher* (Weinheim and Basel, 1969), pp. 137–51 ("Das bedrückende Leben der Kindergestalten in den Grimmschen Märchen.") See also my bibliographical note with reference to the Bechstein edition by Walter Scherf in *Fabula* 21 (1980): 353.

28. Linda Dégh, "Biologie" (see n. 21).

29. See also R. Schenda and Susanne Schenda: "La donna e il concetto di lavoro nei racconti popolari siciliani della Gonzenbach e del Pitrè," in *La Cultura materiale in Sicilia*, Quaderni del Circolo Semiologico Siciliano, nos. 12–13 (Palermo, 1980), pp. 457–64. Helmut Brackert, ed., *Und wenn sie nicht gestorben sind . . . : Perspektiven auf das Märchen* (Frankfurt, 1980) (=es, p. 973). In this volume see especially Iring Fetschers contribution, "Von einem tapferen Schneider: Versuch einer soziologisch-sozial-historischen Deutung," pp. 120–36.

30. For criticism of Bettelheim see Pierre Péju, *La Petite Fille dans la forêt des contes* (Paris: R. Laffont, 1981).

31. A rejoinder in connection with this is a little-known review by Felix Liebrecht: "Grimm, Wilhelm: Zu den *Kinder- und Hausmärchen*," in *Literarisches Centralblatt für Deutschland*, ed. F. Zarncke (Leipzig, 1857), cols. 335–36.

32. F. A. W. Diesterweg, "Deutsche Nationalerziehung, ihre Bedeutung, ihr Zweck, ihre Mittel," in *Germania: Die Vergangenheit, Gegenwart und Zukunft der deutschen Nation*, ed. E. M. Arndt (Leipzig, 1851), 1 : 64–72, esp. 69–70.

33. With reference to this see Helmut Plessner, *Die verspätete Nation: Ueber die politische Verführbarkeit bürgerlichen Geistes* (Stuttgart, 1962); Klaus von See, *Germanen-Ideologie vom Humanismus bis zur Gegenwart* (Frankfurt, 1970).

34. Ludwig Bechstein, "Das Märchen und seine Behandlung in Deutschland," in *Germania*, ed. Arndt (see n. 32), 2 : 316–28, esp. 326–27.

35. J. W. Wolf, *Hessische Sagen* (Göttingen and Leipzig, 1853), p. vii.

36. Ulrike Bastian, *Die Kinder- und Hausmärchen der Brüder Grimm in der literaturpädagogischen Diskussion des 19. und 20. Jahrhunderts*, Studien zur Kinder- und Jugendforschung, no. 8 (Frankfurt: Haag and Herchen, 1981), pp. 45–100.

37. With a roughly rounded-off population of 50 million over six years of age and with a literacy rate of 30 percent in 1830, 50 percent in 1850, 70 percent in 1870, and 90 percent in 1890, an annual growth rate of approximately one-half million new readers a year results. For a history of literacy see R. Schenda, "Alphabetisierung und Literarisierungsprozesse in Westeuropa im 18. und 19. Jahrhundert," in *Soziale Innovationen in der ländlichen Welt*, Wolfenbütteler Forschungen (1982).

38. R. Schenda, "Mären von deutschen Sagen: Bemerkungen zur Produktion von 'Volkserzählungen' zwischen 1850 und 1870," in *Geschichte und Gesellschaft* (Göttingen: Vandenhoeck & Ruprecht, 1982).

39. Reinhard Oberschelp and Willi Gorzny, eds., *Gesamtverzeichnis deutschsprachigen Schrifttums (GV) 1911–1965*, vol. 83 (M–Mal) (Munich, New York, London, and Paris: K. G. Saur, 1979), pp. 175–93.

40. *Märchen von überall her* (Cologne: Benziger, 1962; 2d ed., 1964); *Märchen kennen keine Grenzen* (Cologne: Europa-Union-Verlag, 1965).

41. *Verzeichnis lieferbarer Bücher 1975–76*, vol. 2 (Frankfurt: Verlag der Buchhändler-Vereinigung GmbH, 1975), pp. 2525–2528. See also my bibliographical note in: *Fabula* 20 (1979): 360–61.

42. Bertelsmann offers as examples "Die schönsten Märchen in einer schönen Reihe" (publisher's advertisement): *Die schönsten Märchen der Brüder Grimm, . . . von Wilhelm Hauff, . . . von H. C. Andersen, . . . aus 1001 Nacht, . . . aus aller Welt*, and *Die schönsten Tiermärchen aus aller Welt*. The precision of the nameless editors is notable: each volume consists of exactly 287–88 pages and costs exactly DM16.80!

43. See R. Schenda, "Kinder- und Märchenbücher, Märchenforschung und Geschichte," *Börsenblatt für den deutschen Buchhandel*, 4 Oct. 1978 (*Kind und Buch*), pp. 25–29.

44. See Ernst Bloch, "Gesprochene und geschriebene Syntax: Das Anakoluth," in Ernst Bloch, *Literarische Aufsätze*, Gesamtausgabe, no. 9 (Frankfurt, 1965), pp. 560–67.

45. In this connection, the text of an advertisement from the Schneider publishing house is noteworthy: "Die Kinder kennen [Grimms Märchen] schon alle vom Erzählen und vom Vorlesen. Jetzt können sie die Geschichten [in Schreibschrift gedruckt] als Leseanfänger selber [d.h. alleine] lesen. Das Lesen wird durch die Schreibschrift erleichtert und zum Erfolgserlebnis [!]. Viele Schwarzweissillustrationen und eine ganzseitige Farbillustration zu jedem Märchen sorgen noch zusätzlich [!] für Auflockerung und Abwechslung." From *buch aktuell* Sonderteil, 1981, p. 43.

46. Reinhold Steig and Herman Grimm, eds., *Achim von Arnim und die ihm nahestanden*, vol. 3, *Achim von Arnim und Jacob Grimm*, ed. Reinhold Steig (Stuttgart and Berlin, 1904), pp. 223: "Fixierte Märchen würden endlich der Tod der gesamten Märchenwelt sein. Das hat aber auch nichts auf sich; jedes Kind erzählt schon anders, als es im selben Augenblicke von der Mutter gehört. . . . Die Hauptsache ist, dass das erfindende Talent immerfort geweckter werde; denn nur darin geht den Kindern eine freudige Selbstbeschäftigung auf."

47. Jürgen Janin, "Volksmärchen und Schallplatten," *Wirkendes Wort* 24 (1974): 178–93.

48. Helmut Fischer, "Märchen auf Schallplatten: Zur Problematik der unbegrenzten Reproduzierbarkeit stereotyper Hörbilder," *Das gute Jugendbuch* 25 (1975): 110–17.

49. See also Michael Czernich, "Kinderschallplatte," *Lexikon für Kinder- und Jugendliteratur* 2 (1977): 202–4.

50. Klaus Jensen and Jan-Uwe Rogge, *Der Medienmarkt für Kinder in der Bundesrepublik*, Untersuchungen des Ludwig Uhland-Instituts der Universität Tübingen, no. 50 (Tübingen, 1980), pp. 83, 87, 120–21, 129.

51. Ibid., pp. 96–99. See also Walter Israel, "Märchen und Bühnenmärchen im Zeitalter der Medien," *Jahrbuch des Arbeitskreises für Jugendliteratur* 3 (1976): 109–20. Manfred Jahnke, *Von der Komödie für Kinder zum Weihnachtsmärchen*, Hochschulschriften Literaturwissenschaft, no. 25 (Meisenheim am Glan, 1977).

52. Tycho Jaresmil, "MUL-GA-TOL oder wie erzieht man Kinder zu magischem Denken," *Ethnomedizin* 1 (1971): 134–35.

53. Luigi Maria Lombardi-Satriani, *Folklore e profitto: Techniche di distruzione di una cultura* (Rimini: Guaraldi, 1973), pp. 139–65.

54. Tom E. Sullenberger, "Ajax Meets the Jolly Green Giant: Some observations on

the Use of Folklore and Myth in American Mass Marketing," *Journal of American Folklore* 87 (1974): 53–65.

55. Lutz Röhrich, "Der Froschkönig und seine Wandlungen," *Fabula* 20 (1979): 170–92. See also Lutz Röhrich, "Märchen für Kinder und Erwachsene," in Dieter Pesch, ed., *Bilderbücher* (Cologne: Rheinland Verlag, 1980), pp. 19–25.

56. Hans Joachim Gelberg, ed., *Neues vom Rumpelstilzchen und andere Hausmärchen von 43 Autoren* (Weinheim and Basel, 1976). See also Gelberg, "Grimms Märchen für Kinder von Heute? Betrachtungen zu Janoschs Märchenbuch," in D. Pesch, *Bilderbücher* (see n. 55), pp. 27–39. Wolfgang Mieder, ed., *Grimms Märchen Modern: Prosa, Gedichte, Karikaturen*, UB 9554 (Stuttgart: Reclam, 1979).

57. Fredi Hänni, "Ein helvetisches Märchen: Hans-Franz im Glück," *das konzept* 9, no. 10 (Zurich, Oct. 1980): 18. The article refers to Representative Jean-François Bourgknecht from the canton of Freiburg.

58. "Tanz der Tiere: Ein alternatives Märchen von F. S. Pri 1981." Handout at the University of Freiburg, distributed 15 March 1981.

59. Helga Stein, "Einige Bemerkungen über die Märchengärten," lecture at the Folk Narrative Congress, Helsinki 1974. Mimeographed paper and related materials are available in the archive of the *Enzyklopädie des Märchens*, Göttingen.

60. Hartmut Euler, "Hasen, Zwerge, Puppenmuttis: Einige Bemerkungen zum 'trivialen' Bilderbuch," *Informationen Jugendliteratur und Medien*, Jugendschriften-Warte, no. 28/4 (August 1976), pp. 49–54.

61. See my bibliographical note with reference to *Die schönsten Märchen der Welt zum Sammeln* (Hamburg 1976), *Fabula* 19 (1978): 181.

62. See n. 32.

63. A good summary of the pros and cons can be found in Horst Künnemann, *Kinder und Kulturkonsum: Ueberlegungen zu bewältigten und unbewältigten Massenmedien unserer Zeit* (Weinheim and Basel, 1974), pp. 99–109: "Märchen—gestern und heute: Was spricht für die Märchen?" Powerful criticism related to this theme can be found in Melchior Schedler, "Erziehung durch den Mythos: Das Märchen," *Schlachtet die blauen Elefanten: Bermerkungen über das Kinderstück* (Weinheim and Basel, 1973), pp. 170–92.

64. Ernst Joachim Westphal(en), *De consuetudine ex sacco et libro in Germania sigillatim in Magapoli: Tractatio historica, etymologica et civilis* (Rostock and Leipzig, 1726), pp. 222–25. The author refers to the Gestriegelte Rockenphilosophie (appeared first in 1718; the anonymous author was J. G. Schmidt).

65. Steig and Grimm, *Achim von Arnim* (see n. 46), p. 271. See also p. 269: "Sind denn diese Kindermärchen für Kinder erdacht und erfunden? ich glaube dies so wenig als ich die allgemeinere Frage nicht bejahen werde: ob man überhaupt für Kinder etwas eigenes einrichten müsse? Was wir an offenbarten und traditionellen Lehren und Vorschriften besitzen, das ertragen Alte wie Junge, und was diese daran nicht begreifen, über das gleitet ihr Gemüth weg, bis dass sie es lernen."

66. Heinz Rölleke, ed., *Die älteste Märchensammlung der Brüder Grimm: Synopse der handschriftlichen Urfassung von 1810 und der Erstdrucke von 1812* (Cologny-Geneva: Fondation Martin Bodmer, 1975).

67. References can be found in George Wilhelm Hopf, *Ueber Jugendschriften: Mittheilungen an Aeltern und Lehrer* (Fürth, 1850), pp. 22–25. Hopf quotes from Jean Paul, Schleiermacher, Gervinus, Rosenkranz, and F. Kapp. I have not been able to locate the texts of the last three.

68. See *Das literarische Centralblatt*, vol. 1 (1850), cols. 131, 181. One should take special note of the book prices!

69. J. W. Wolf, *Hessische Sagen* (see n. 35), p. vii.

70. H. Pröhle, *Kinder- und Volksmärchen* (Leipzig 1853), p. vii.

71. C. Colshorn and Th. Colshorn, *Märchen und Sagen aus Hannover* (Hannover, 1854), p. viii.

72. Péju, "La Petite Fille" (see n. 30), pp. 63–67: "Les contes sont-ils 'pour enfants'?"

5. Born Yesterday: Heroes in the Grimms' Fairy Tales

MARIA M. TATAR

There comes an old man with his three sons —
I could match this beginning with an old tale.

— Shakespeare, As You Like It

Identifying fairy tale heroes by name is no mean feat. In the Grimms' collection, only one in every ten actually has a name. But it is also no secret that the most celebrated characters in fairy tales are female. Cinderella, Snow White, Little Red Riding Hood, and Sleeping Beauty: these are the names that have left so vivid an imprint on childhood memories. With the exception of Hansel, who shares top billing with his sister, male protagonists are exceptionally unmemorable in name, if not in deed. Lacking the colorful descriptive sobriquets that accord their female counterparts a distinctive identity, these figures are presented as types and defined by their parentage (the miller's son), by their station in life (the prince), by their relationship to siblings (the youngest brother), by their level of intelligence (the simpleton), or by physical deformities ("Thumbling").[1]

Most people may be at a loss when it comes to naming fairy tale heroes, but few have trouble characterizing them. "In song and story," writes Simone de Beauvoir, "the young man is seen departing adventurously in search of woman; he slays the dragon, he battles

This article is an expanded and revised version of "Tests, Tasks, and Trials in the Grimms' Fairy Tales," presented at the conference "Fairy Tales and Society" and subsequently published in *Children's Literature* 13 (1985): 31–48 (New Haven: Yale University Press, 1985). It appears with the permission of Yale University Press.

giants." And what are this young man's attributes? One commentator on the Grimms' collection describes him as "active, competitive, handsome, industrious, cunning, acquisitive." That list sums up the conventional wisdom on the dragon-slayers and giant-killers of fairy tale lore.[2]

That conventional wisdom proves, however, to be a fairy tale so far as German folklore is concerned. A reading of the first edition of the *Nursery and Household Tales* reveals that there are exactly two dragon-slayers and only one giant-killer in the entire collection of more than 150 tales.[3] One of those stories, "Johannes-Wassersprung and Caspar-Wassersprung" rehearses the classic story of the slaying of a seven-headed dragon and the liberation of a princess, but (for unknown reasons) that tale never did make it to the second edition of the *Nursery and Household Tales*. The other dragon-slaying hero bears the distinctly unheroic name "Stupid Hans" ("Dummhans"), and the contest in which he dispatches three dragons, each with a different number of heads, is less than gripping. As for the one giant-killer, he succeeds in decapitating three giants, but only because the proper sword is placed directly in his path. If there is any attribute that these heroes share, it is naiveté. Like so many other heroes in the Grimms' collection, they are decidedly unworldly figures. "Innocent," "silly," "useless," "foolish," "simple," and "guileless": these are the actual adjectives applied again and again to fairy tale heroes in the Grimms' collection.

Among folklorists, it is the fashion to divide heroes into two separate and distinct classes. There are active heroes and passive heroes, "formal heroes" and "ideal heroes," dragon-slayers and male Cinderellas, tricksters and simpletons.[4] In theory, the oppositions active/passive, seeker/victim, and naive/cunning seem to serve as useful guides for classifying fairy tale heroes. But in practice it is not always easy to determine whether a hero relies on his own resources or depends on helpers. Does he have a zest for danger or does he simply weather the various adventures that befall him? Just what is his level of intelligence? What at first blush appear to be perfectly straightforward choices are in the end fraught with complexities. The happy-go-lucky simpleton who appears to succeed without trying is, for example, not always as doltish as his name or his reputation in the village would lead us to believe, and the roguish trickster does not always live up to his reputation for shrewd reasoning.

There is a further complication. Despite their seeming artlessness, fairy tales are not without occasional ironic touches that subvert surface meanings. In particular, the epithets and predicates reserved for their protagonists can highlight utterly uncharacteristic traits. The eponymous heroine of "Clever Else" ranks high on the list of dull-witted characters; the tale "Hans in Luck" charts a steady decline in its hero's fortunes; and the courageous tailor in the tale of that title displays more bravado than bravery.[5] In the world of fairy tales, a simpleton can easily slip into the role of the cunning trickster; a humble miller's son can become a king; and a cowardly fool can emerge as a stout-hearted hero. Character traits display an astonishing lack of stability, shifting almost imperceptibly into their opposites as the tale unfolds. Bearing this in mind, let us take the measure of male protagonists in the Grimms' collection to determine what character traits they share and to assess the extent to which the plots of their adventures possess a degree of predictability.

If the female protagonists of fairy tales are often as good as they are beautiful, their male counterparts generally appear to be as young and naive as they are stupid. Snow White's stepmother may be enraged by her stepdaughter's superior beauty, but the fathers of male heroes are eternally exasperated by the unrivaled obtuseness of their sons. To the question, Who is the stupidest of them all? most fairy-tale fathers would reply: my youngest son. Yet that son is also the chosen son, the son who ultimately outdoes his older and wiser siblings. In an almost perverse fashion, fairy tales featuring male protagonists chart the success story of adolescents who do not even have the good sense to heed the instructions of the many helpers and donors who rush to their aid in an attempt to avert catastrophes and to ensure a happy ending. "You don't really deserve my help," declares one such helper in frustration after his sage advice has been disregarded on no less than three occasions.[6]

In fairy tales the world over, the least likely to succeed paradoxically becomes the most likely to succeed. Merit rarely counts; luck seems to be everything. Aladdin, the prototype of the undeserving hero who succeeds in living happily ever after, begins his rise to wealth and power under less than auspicious circumstances. The introductory paragraphs of his tale give the lie to the view that classical fairy tales reward virtue and punish evil. "Once upon a time," so the story of "Aladdin and the Enchanted Lamp" begins, "there lived in a certain city of China an impoverished tailor who had a son called Aladdin. From his earliest years this Aladdin was a headstrong and incorrigible good-for-nothing." When he grows older, he refuses to learn a trade and persists in his idle ways until his father, "grieving over the perverseness of his son," falls ill and dies. Yet this same Aladdin, who becomes ever more wayward after sending his father to the grave, ultimately inherits a sultan's throne. As one critic correctly points out, the story of Aladdin and his enchanted lamp exalts and glorifies a figure who stands as "one of the most undeserving characters imaginable." It is telling that Aladdin could make his way easily from the pages of German translations of the *Thousand and One Nights* into the oral narratives of one region in Germany. Once his exotic name was changed to "Dummhans," he was quickly assimilated into Pomeranian folklore — so much so that it was difficult to distinguish him from native sons.[7]

The heroes of the *Nursery and Household Tales* may, for the most part, be unlikely to win prizes for intelligence and good behavior, but they are even less likely to earn awards for courage. Their stories chronicle perilous adventures, but they themselves often remain both cowardly and passive. When summoned to discharge the first in a series of three tasks, the simpleton in the tale known as "The Queen Bee" simply sits down and has a good cry. In "The Three Feathers," the hero sits down and "feels sad" instead of rising to the challenges posed by his father. Fairy tale heroines have never stood as models of an enterprising spirit, but it is also not rare for fairy tale heroes to suffer silently and to endure hardships in a hopelessly passive fashion.

For all their shortcomings, the simpletons in the Grimms' fairy tales do possess one character trait that sets them apart from their fraternal rivals: compassion. That compassion is typically reserved for the natural allies and benefactors of fairy tale heroes: the animals that inhabit the earth, the waters, and the sky.[8] Even before the simpleton embarks on a journey to foreign kingdoms or undertakes various tasks to liberate a princess, he must prove himself worthy of assistance from nature or from supernatural powers by displaying compassion. Of the various tests, tasks, and trials imposed on the hero, this first test figures as the most important, for it establishes the privileged status of the young simpleton. Once he exhibits the virtue of compassion — with its logical concomitant of humility — he can do virtually no wrong, even when he violates interdictions, disregards warnings, and ignores instructions. This preliminary test, a test of the hero's character, comes to serve the dual function of singling out the hero from his brothers and of furnishing him with potential helpers for the tasks that lie ahead.

Two fairy tales from the Grimms' collection illustrate the extent to which compassion is rewarded. In "The Queen Bee," the youngest of three sons defends an ant hill, a bevy of ducks, and a beehive from the assaults of his mischievous brothers. "Leave the animals alone," he admonishes his elders on three occasions. Compassion pays off in the end, for this youngest of three sons is also the only one to escape being turned to stone — a punishment that perfectly suits the crimes of his callous siblings. With the help of his newly won allies, the simpleton of the family discharges three "impossible" tasks spelled out for him on a stone slab. He gathers a thousand pearls that lie strewn about the forest; he fetches a bedroom key from the sea's depths; and he succeeds in identifying the youngest of three "completely identical" sisters. Or, to be more precise, the ants gather the pearls, the ducks fetch the key, and the bees identify the youngest sister. Yet the simpleton is credited with disenchanting the palace in which the trio of princesses resides, and he thereby wins the hand of the youngest and earns the right to give the two other sisters in marriage to his brothers.

The hero of "The White Snake," like the simpleton of "The Queen Bee," hardly lifts a finger to win his bride. Once he displays compassion for wildlife by coming to the rescue of three fish, a colony of ants, and three ravens, he joins the ranks of the "chosen" heroes who receive assistance from helpers as soon as they are charged with carrying out tasks. Although male fairy tale figures have customarily been celebrated for their heroic exploits and feats, their greatest achievement actually rests on the successful passing of a character test. By enshrining compassion and humility, which — unlike intelligence and brute strength — are acquired characteristics rather than innate traits, the Grimms' tales make it clear to their implied audience (which gradually came to be adolescents) that even the least talented of youths is equipped with the potential to rise to the top.[9]

Once the hero has succeeded in passing the preliminary character test, he is braced for the tasks that lie ahead. The grateful beneficiaries of his compassionate acts and humble deeds are quick to even out the balance sheets. As soon as the hero finds himself faced with an impossible task — emptying a lake with a perforated spoon, building and furnishing a castle overnight, devouring a mountain of bread in twenty-four hours — help is at hand. For every task that requires wisdom, courage, endurance, strength, or simply an appetite and thirst of gargantuan proportions, there is a helper — or a group of helpers — possessing the requisite attributes. And ultimately the achievements of the helper redound to the hero, for he is credited with having drained the lake, built the castle, and consumed the bread.

Passing the preliminary test and carrying out the basic tasks are in themselves sufficient to secure a princess and her kingdom. Nonetheless, a number of fairy tales mount a third act in keeping with the ternary principle governing their plots.[10] This final trial which the hero must endure is motivated by the reappearance of the fraternal rivals who vexed the hero in his earlier, preheroic days. The brothers seize the earliest opportunity to pilfer the hero's riches, alienate him from his beloved, malign his good name, or banish him from the land.

Yet they are no match for the hero, who deftly succeeds in outwitting them and in surviving their murderous assaults. Although the hero is rarely instrumental in carrying out the tasks imposed on him, in the end he acquires the attributes of his helpers and possesses the strength, courage, and wit needed to defeat his rivals.

Just as the humble male protagonist matures and is elevated to a higher station in life, so his antagonists are demeaned and demoted in the final, optional segment of the tale. If the hero distinguishes himself from the start by showing mercy and compassion for animals, he remains singularly uncharitable when it comes to dealing with human rivals. "Off with everyone's head but my own," proclaims the hero of "The King of the Golden Mountain." And he makes good on that threat. Even brothers and brides are dispatched by fairy tale heroes without a moment's hesitation once their deceit comes to light. Treachery is punished as swiftly and as predictably as compassion is rewarded. This third phase of the hero's career endows his story with a kind of symmetry and balance for which all tales strive. Like the first two acts, the final act stages a contest between a youth and his two older but morally inferior brothers. Both dramatic conflicts culminate in the rewarding of good will and the punishment of treachery; the last act simply intensifies the reward (a princess and a kingdom) and the punishment (death). In doing so, it gives not only added moral resonance but also a measure of finality to the tale. The hero has not only attained the highest office in the land but also eliminated his every competitor. For that office, he was singled out in the tale's first episode, made singular in the tale's second part, and celebrated as the sole and single heir to the throne in the tale's coda.

The trajectory of the hero's path leads him to the goal shared by all fairy tales, whether they chart the fortunes of downtrodden male or downtrodden female protagonists. In keeping with the fundamental law requiring the reversal of all conditions prevailing in its introductory paragraphs, the fairy tale ends by enthroning the humble and enriching the impoverished. The male heroes of fairy tales are humble in at least one, and often in both, senses of the term. More often than not they are low men on the totem pole in families of common origins. But whether born to the crown or raised on a farm, they are also humble in character: without this special quality they would fail to qualify for the munificence of helpers and donors. Humility therefore seems to be the badge of the fairy tale hero. And since humbleness, in one of its shades of meaning, can inhere in members of any social class, both princes and peasants are eligible to assume the role of hero in fairy tales.

Humility may be an innate characteristic of fairy tale heroes, but it also comes to color the psychological makeup of fairy tale heroines. Female protagonists are by nature just as humble as their male counterparts, but they display that virtue in a strikingly different fashion. Fairy tales often highlight psychological characteristics by translating them into elements of plot, and with female heroines, this proves especially true. Daughters of millers and daughters of kings alike are not merely designated as humble; they are actually humbled in the course of their stories. In fact, "humbled" is perhaps too mild a term to use for the many humiliations to which female protagonists must submit.

Since most fairy tales end with marriage, it seems logical to assume that a single tale suffices to illustrate the contrasting fates of male and female protagonists. Yet though there is often a happy couple at the end of a fairy tale, the fate of only one single, central character is at stake as the tale unfolds. That pivotal figure stands so firmly rooted at the center of events that all other characters are defined solely by their relationship to him or her and thereby lack an autonomous sphere of action. Note that in "Cinderella," for instance, even the bridegroom, for all the dashing chivalry attributed to him by Walt Disney and others, remains a colorless figure. The tale tells us nothing more about him than that he is the son of a king. Lacking a history, a story, and even a name, he is reduced to the mere function of prince-rescuer waiting in the wings for his cue. The brides in stories of male heroes fare little better. Relegated to subordinate roles, they too fail to command our attention and to engage our interest. Still, there are exceptions to every rule, and the Grimms' collection provides one noteworthy exception to the rule that only one character can occupy center stage in fairy tales. "The Goose Girl at the Spring" weaves together the fates of both partners in the marriage with which it concludes. To be sure, there are signs that the tale is not of one piece, that at some historical juncture it occurred to one teller of tales to fuse two separate and distinct plots.[11] Nonetheless those two plots conveniently dovetail to create a single narrative. The story of the humble count and of the humbled princess who marries him offers an exemplary study in contrasts between the lot of males and females in fairy tales culminating in marriage ceremonies.

"The Goose Girl at the Spring" commences with an account of the heroine's future bridegroom. Although this young man is handsome, rich, and noble, he must—like the most lowly fairy tale heroes—prove his mettle by displaying the virtues of compassion and humility. Without these twin virtues, his otherwise impeccable credentials would prove utterly worthless. And indeed, we learn not only that the young count is able to "feel compassion" but also that he is, despite his noble station in life, not too proud to translate compassion into action. Once he demonstrates his humility by easing the burdens of a feeble old hag, shunned by everyone but him, he earns himself a passport to luck and success. Like his many artlessly benevolent folkloric kinsmen, the count becomes the recipient of a gift that accords him a privileged status among potential suitors of a princess. The emerald etui he receives from the old hag ultimately leads him to his bride, a princess masquerading as a shepherdess.

Neither the count nor his rustic bride can boast humble origins. The unsightly girl tending geese at the beginning of the tale is not at all what she seems. At the well, she peels off her rural costume along with her rough skin to reveal that she must be a princess. Despite her aristocratic origins, she too can in the end ascend to a higher position, for her fairy tale days are spent in the most modest of circumstances. Unlike her groom, however, she was pressed into assuming a humble position when her own father exiled her from the household. Like countless folkloric heroines, she suffers a humiliating fall that reduces her from a princess to a peasant, from a privileged daughter to an impoverished menial. Fairy tale heroes receive gifts and assistance once they actively prove their compassion and humility; heroines, by contrast, become the beneficiaries of helpers and rescuers only after they have been abased and forced to learn humility.

There are many well-known tales of victimized female heroines who rise to or return to the ranks of royalty once they have been humbled and humiliated.[12] But no tales spell out more explicitly that humiliation figures as a prerequisite for a happy ending than "King Thrushbeard," "The Mongoose," and "The Six Servants." The bride of King Thrushbeard furnishes the classic example of the heroine who earns a king and a crown as soon as straitened circumstances break her arrogance and pride. It is not enough that she curses the false pride that led to her downfall; her husband must also solemnly state: "All of this was done to crush your pride and to punish you for the haughty way in which you treated me." When King Thrushbeard generously offers to reinstate her to a royal position, she feels so deeply mortified that she declares herself unworthy to become his bride. The princess in the tale known as "The Mongoose" also finds herself humbled by her prospective husband. Nonetheless, she takes the defeat in stride and declares to herself with more than a touch of satisfaction: "He is cleverer than you!" The princess-heroine of "The Six Servants" is also cheerfully repentant and resigned to her fate by the end of her story. Reduced to tending swine with her husband (a prince who has duped her into believing that he is a peasant), she is prepared to accept her lot: "I've only got what I deserved for being so haughty and proud." After revealing his true station in life, her husband justifies the deception by declaring: "I suffered so much for you, it was only right that you should suffer for me."

As the tale "The Six Servants" makes clear, young men "suffer" by taking the credit for tasks carried out by animal helpers, human servants, or supernatural assistants. Women suffer by being forced into a lowly social position. Male heroes demonstrate from the start a meekness and humility that qualify them for an ascent to wealth, the exercise of power, and happiness crowned by wedded bliss; their female counterparts undergo a process of humiliation and defeat that ends with a rapid rise in social status through marriage, but that also signals a loss of pride and the abdication of power.

Before we move on to another category of heroes, a quick review of our first class is in order. The naive hero in tales of three sons lacks the brains and brawn conventionally associated with heroic figures; he must rely on helpers with superhuman or supernatural powers to carry out every task demanded by a king in return for the hand of a princess. Instead of slaying dragons, he offers to louse them; instead of killing giants, he befriends them and makes himself at home in their dwellings. His demonstrations of compassion set the stage for the reversal of fortunes characteristic of fairy tale plots. Only from a position of humility can he be elevated to the loftiest office in the land. Just as this hero works his way up the social ladder by climbing down it, so too he acquires intelligence and power by putting obtuseness and vulnerability on display. Although it is never explicitly stated that he becomes smart and strong in the end, most fairy tales imply that their heroes have acquired the attributes of royalty right along with the office of king.

The youngest of three sons makes his way through magical kingdoms where an ant might plead for a favor, an enchanted princess could call on his services, or a dwarf might suddenly demand a crust of bread. But a second group of heroes in the Grimms' tales moves in what appears to be a more realistic setting: villages and the roads connecting them. The cast of characters in tales with those heroes includes kings and princesses. But the tales themselves lack the supernatural dimension of fairy tales and tend to be more down-to-earth in tone and more earthy in humor. The heroes are often far enough along in life to have a profession: many are apprentices, but some are tailors, foresters, tradesmen, or mercenaries. Many are "men" and not "boys." (One is so old that he finds himself obliged to choose the eldest of twelve princesses when a king offers him one of his daughters in marriage.) Still, these heroes do not seem equipped with much more intelligence, strength, or valor than the young simpletons of fairy tales. They may not be village idiots, but in accordance with the general tendency of German folklore to avoid endowing male protagonists with heroic traits, their strengths are rarely spelled out.

Naiveté also appears to be the principal hallmark of village boys and men. But what appears to be a character defect is in fact turned to good account once the protagonist determines to seek his fortunes in the world. Nietzsche once observed that fear is an index of intelligence, thus confirming the old saw that fools rush in where wise men fear to tread.[13] The more naive the hero, the more foolhardy and fearless he is, and the more likely he is to rise to the challenges of various tasks devised to foil the suitors of a princess. Naiveté implies fearlessness, which in turn can take on the character of courage.

In much the same way that naiveté can shade into courage, it can also translate into cunning. A hero's stupidity can take such extreme forms that it utterly disarms his antagonists. A young man who starts out handicapped by his boundless naiveté may in the end triumph over his adversaries by outwitting them. The protagonist unwise to the ways of the world can therefore be in the best possible position to exhibit heroic qualities by the close of his story.

Heroic feats performed by figures with clear character defects — lack of wisdom and wit — can, however, end by producing comic effects. "Blockhead," "Numbskull," or "Simpleton" rush into one hazardous situation after another, simply because they are too naive to know better; they get the upper hand by putting their dimwittedness on display, taking every word of advice that they hear literally; but they also escape harm because they are so naive that they confound their opponents. It may be true that they succeed in accomplishing the tasks laid out for them, but there is more than a touch of vaudeville to their every move.

The burlesque effect produced by tales chronicling the deeds of fearless heroes is perhaps most pronounced in "The Fairy Tale of One Who Went Forth to Learn Fear." The hero of that tale tries in vain to learn to be afraid, or more precisely, to shudder. Through one hair-raising episode after another he preserves his equanimity and coolly turns the tables on his would-be terrorizers. In one last desperate attempt to discover what it is to feel fear, he spends three nights warding off and ultimately exorcising the demons haunting a castle. His reward is the hand of a princess, but still he feels no fear. Only in his marriage bed does he finally learn to shudder, when his resourceful wife pulls off his covers and pours a bucket of live minnows on him. Bruno Bettelheim is surely right to read psycho-sexual implications into this final act of the fairy tale, particularly since the art of shuddering rather than the actual experience of fear constitutes the overt tale value. But the hero's inability to feel fear ought not to be construed as a negative trait: Bettelheim asserts that "the hero of this story could not shudder due to repression of all sexual feelings."[14] It is precisely the absence of the capacity to fear that enables the sprightly hero to withstand the horrors of a haunted castle and consequently to win the hand of his bride. Indeed, the ability to fear comes so close to courage in this tale that the protagonist begins to take on, for all his unflinching artlessness, heroic attributes. Unlike his humble and helpless kinsmen in classical fairy tales of three sons, he breezily accomplishes one task after another without resorting to aid from friendly foreign agents. Were it not for the comic overtones to the adventures of this fairy tale hero, it would seem entirely appropriate to place him in the class of heroes who live by their courage and wits.

If naiveté and courage are virtually synonyms in the folkloric lexicon, naiveté and cunning are also not far apart in meaning.[15] Indeed the more hopelessly naive and obtuse the hero of a tale, the more likely it is that he will triumph over his adversaries and that his adventures will be crowned with success. "The Courageous Tailor," who decorates himself for having dispatched seven flies with one blow, seems to stand as the very incarnation of fatuous vanity. Yet his bravado endows him with the power to outwit giants, to accomplish the tasks posed by his bride's belligerent father, and to subdue a blue-blooded wife who is repelled by the thought of a marriage below her own social station. In this tale, the line dividing naiveté from shrewdness and bravado from bravery has been effaced. The naive hero without fear and brains is virtually indistinguishable from the trickster.

By now it should be clear that the humble and naive youngest of three sons is a not so distant cousin of the fearless and naive hero. In fact, the hero of the Grimms' "Crystall Ball" combines the attributes of humble heroes and fearless fools: he possesses the simplicity and humility that go hand-in-hand with his familial status as the youngest of three sons, and he is also said to have "a heart without fear." It is above all his foolishly dauntless spirit that gives him the audacity to line up as the twenty-fourth suitor to seek out a princess imprisoned in the "Castle of the Golden Sun" and to undertake her liberation. And it is solely his slow-wittedness that provides him with the means for arriving in the kingdom inhabited by the princess. He "forgets" to return a magical hat to two giants and thereby receives just the right means for transporting himself to that kingdom. In fairy tales, brashness can clearly accomplish as much as bravery; naiveté is as effective as craft. The manifest lack of a virtue often translates into its possession. Just as Cinderella proves to be the fairest and the noblest of them all despite her shabby attire and her station at the hearth, so the simpleton of the family ultimately prevails over his older and wiser antagonists.

As noted, the rigors of a fairy tale hero's life endow him in the end with the attributes commonly associated with royalty. Even if the humble simpleton never lifts a sword and is incapable of answering a single question, let alone a riddle, he becomes a prince in more than just name. The feats of every woodland helper become his own deeds and accomplishments, and he becomes a figure with all the heroic qualities of dragon-slayers and giant-killers. Since our other class of tales, those featuring the comic adventures of heroes without fear, generally dispenses with tests of compassion, it also does away with the helpers who are responsible for elevating humble protagonists to heroic stature. Fear-less heroes must instead rely wholly on their own mental and physical resources — however modest they may be. It is those resources that are put to the test in the opening paragraphs of the tale, where brashness achieves more than bravery and artlessness proves more effective than artifice.

Since the hero without fear displays a greater measure of self-reliance than his humble kinsmen, the plot of his adventures contains the potential for greater realism. Gone are encounters with talking animals, supernatural counselors, and other exotic agents. Instead the hero meets hunters, locksmiths, sextons, innkeepers, and other such folk. He may not marry a peasant's daughter, but the castle in which he finally takes up residence has the distinct odor of the barnyard. Again, we are in the village rather than in an enchanted forest. Yet it would be misleading to label these tales realistic. They do not strive to hold a mirror up to the social conditions of the age or culture in which they were told. These are tall tales, stories that take advantage of exaggeration, punning, parody, and literalism to produce comic effects.

The many realistic touches in these folktales, in tandem with their farcical aspect, point to their basic affinity with tales of tricksters, where professional fools, tradesmen, retired soldiers, and youths of various other callings conspire to thwart their masters, creditors, or any of the other overprivileged. Through ingenious disingenuousness they succeed in coming out on top. An open-ended episodic principle organizes the plot of both tall tales featuring heroes without fear and trickster stories. One absurd skirmish follows another, with no distinctive growth, development, or maturity after one episode or another. By contrast, the humble hero's adventures take the form of a three-act drama, with a test in the first act, tasks in the second, and a final trial crowned by success in the third. The goal may be the same for both types of heroes, but the paths bear little resemblance to each other.[16]

Fairy tales charting the adventures of male protagonists posit from the start one dominant character trait that establishes a well-defined identity for the hero even as it proclaims his membership in the class of heroic figures. The verbal tag attached to the character ("Dummy," "the youngest of three sons," "Blockhead") ensures that he is recognized as the central character of the narrative. But in the course of the hero's odyssey, his dominant character trait begins to shade into its opposite through a process that can be termed inversion. The humble hero weds a woman of royal blood; the brazen fool proves his mettle; and the naive simpleton outwits just about anyone. In fairy tales, the youth lacking a good pedigree, a stout heart, and a sharp wit is precisely the one who wins himself a princess and a kingdom.

Inversion of character traits is a common occurrence in fairy tales. A reversal of the conditions prevailing at the start is, after all, manifestly the goal of every tale. The folktale in general, as Max Lüthi has observed, has "a liking for all extremes, extreme contrasts in particular." Its characters, he further notes, are either beautiful or ugly, good or bad, poor or rich, industrious or lazy, and humble or noble.[17] Yet much as readers and critics insist on the fairy tale's low tolerance for ambiguity and stress the inflexibility of the attributes assigned to heroes and villains, the frequency with which inversion appears suggests that they overstate their case. Just as "Beast" can be at once savage and civilized, so the youngest of three sons can be both a simpleton and a sage, a humble lad and a prince, a coward and a hero. Both character attributes and social conditions rapidly shift from one extreme to the other in fairy tales.

That character traits are not as standardized or programmed as would appear becomes evident if we analyze the fate of one character who does not figure prominently in the pantheon of fairy tale heroes. The eponymous protagonist of "Hans in Luck" might, in fact, well be called an antihero. In the course of his travels, he outwits no one — instead he becomes the victim of numerous transparently fraudulent transactions. His fortunes, rather than rising, steadily decline. And at the end of his journey, he seems no wiser and is decidedly less prosperous than he was at its beginning. Still, Hans is said to be lucky, and he feels himself to be among the happiest men on earth. The steps of Hans's journey to felicity are easy enough to retrace. After serving his master loyally and diligently for a period of seven years, Hans winds his way home with a weighty emolument: a chunk of gold the size of his head. Hans happily barters this monetary burden for a horse that will speed him on his way home. In the further course of his journey, he exchanges the horse for a cow, the cow for a pig, the pig for a goose, and the goose for a grindstone and rock. Even after these two worthless rocks land at the bottom of a well leaving him nothing to show for his labors of seven years, Hans remains undaunted. He literally jumps for joy and praises God for liberating him from the burdens that slowed his journey homeward. Unencumbered by earthly possessions and with a light heart, Hans heads for his mother's home.

Conventional wisdom has it that the happy-go-lucky hero of this tale stands as the archetypal benighted fool. The very title of the tale, "Hans in Luck," is charged with irony: only a fool would delight in parting with the hefty wages Hans receives from his master. Yet on closer inspection, it becomes clear that the story of lucky Hans may also celebrate freedom from the burden of labor. On the last leg of his journey, Hans jettisons grindstone and rock—the tools of the trade that was to secure for him a steady flow of cash; at the outset of his journey, he rids himself of the gold with which his labor was compensated. In a stunning reversal of the value system espoused in fairy tales, Hans's story not only substitutes rags for riches but also supplants marriage to a princess in a foreign land with a return home to mother. In short, it ends where most tales begin. Instead of charting the course of an odyssey toward wealth and marriage, it depicts the stations of a journey toward poverty and dependence. But in remaining wholly indifferent to the wages of labor and freeing himself from its drudgery, Hans displays a kind of wisdom that invalidates ironic readings of his tale's title. Bereft of material possessions yet rich in spirit, he turns his back on the world of commerce to embrace his mother.[18]

The story of lucky Hans dramatically demonstrates the impossibility of establishing a fixed set of character traits shared by male heroes. Like Hans, who is both foolish and wise, poor and rich, lucky and unfortunate, the heroes of numerous fairy tales possess attributes that imperceptibly shift into their opposites. All the same, it is clear that certain oppositions (humble/noble, naive/cunning, timid/courageous, compassionate/ruthless) are encoded on virtually every fairy tale with a male hero. It is, then, difficult to draw up an inventory of immutable character traits largely because a single figure within a tale can—and usually does—have one character trait and its opposite. But it is also equally difficult, if for different reasons, to establish precise models for the plots of tales featuring male heroes. For every score of heroes who wed princesses and inherit kingdoms, there is one who returns home as an impoverished bachelor. For ten heroes who receive assistance and magical gifts by demonstrating compassion, there is one who acquires aid and magical objects through an act of violence. For every animal bridegroom who is released from a curse through the love and devotion of a woman, there is one who is disenchanted by the callous treatment he receives at the hands of his bride. To be sure, there is a measure of predictability in these plots, but only if we bear in mind that every narrative norm established can be violated by its opposite. Thus the preliminary test of good character at the start of tales with a ternary plot structure can be replaced by a demonstration of the hero's ruthlessness. The story of a hero dependent on magical helpers in carrying out appointed tasks can exist side by side with the tale of a hero who acts autonomously and takes on the characteristics of helpers.[19]

Recognizing and appreciating the fairy tale's instability—its penchant for moving from one extreme to another—is vital for understanding its characters, plots, and thematic orientation. Fairy tale figures have few fixed traits; they are totally re-formed once they reach the goals of their journeys, when they become endowed with the very qualities in which they were once found wanting. Male protagonists may adhere slavishly to the ground rules of heroic decorum, or they may break every rule in the book; either way, their stories end with the accession to a throne. And finally, the conditions prevailing at the start of tales are utterly reversed by the end. The fairy tale, in sum, knows no stable middle ground. Inversion of character traits, violation of narrative norms, and reversal of initial conditions are just a few of the ways in which it overturns notions of immutability and creates a fictional world in which the one constant value is change.

In this context, it is worth emphasizing once again some of the disparities between folkloric fantasies and social realities. The radical reversals that lift fairy tale heroes from humble circumstances to a royal station in life were virtually unknown during the age in which fairy tales developed and flourished, but they undeniably correspond to childhood fantasies of past ages and of our own day. If in real life the youngest of three sons rarely had the wherewithall to succeed in life or to transcend his station in life, fairy tales held out the promise that humility and other virtues might well outweigh the benefits of an inheritance. But beyond offering consolation to underprivileged sons who lived in an era when primogeniture was custom or law, fairy tales more generally respond to the insecurities of every child. Even the eldest child is likely to perceive himself as the least gifted or least favored among his siblings and can thereby readily identify with simpleton heroes. Fundamental psychological truths, rather than specific social realities, appear to have given rise to the general plot structure of those tales.

A stable plot still leaves room for much variation. Skillful raconteurs can take the same story line and give it unique twists and turns. The tone may vary from one tale to the next, and the hero may also be presented in different lights. As Robert Darnton has shown, comparing different national versions of a single tale type can be a revealing exercise. Reading through various tellings of "Jack the Giant Killer," one can register the changes from "English fantasy to French cunning and Italian burlesque." More important, there are subtle shifts in the character of the protagonist as he slips from one culture into another. Darnton has observed that the trickster figure is especially prevalent in French folklore and literature.[20] By contrast, as we have seen, the simpleton (or to put it in more flattering terms) the guileless youth figures prominently in the Grimms' collection. These differences between the folkloric heroes of the two cultures may, however, be more apparent than real, for the roguish Gallic trickster and his naive Teutonic counterpart have more in common than one would suspect. Even the names most frequently bestowed in the *Nursery and Household Tales* on the types ("Dummling" for the simpleton and "Daumerling" for the trickster) suggest that they are kindred spirits. Both the simpleton and the trickster ultimately make good by outwitting or outdoing their seemingly superior adversaries. Still, the shift in emphasis from cunning to naiveté as one moves across the Rhine is telling, suggesting as it does that the French celebrate cleverness and audacity while the Germans enshrine the virtues of naiveté and guilelessness.

If we take a closer look at German literary traditions — both oral and written — it becomes clear that the naive hero is by no means a folkloristic aberration. He fits squarely into a long line of such figures. Wolfram von Eschenbach's Parzival, who comes to incarnate the highest chivalric ideals, is described as "der tumme" ("the young and inexperienced one"). Dressed by his mother in the costume of a fool, he mounts a wretched nag to seek his fortune in the world. Although there are hints that he is something of a dragon-slayer (he arrives at Munsalvæsche at Michaelmas, the Feast of St. Michael, the vanquisher of Satan as dragon), the only dragons he slays are emblazoned on his opponent's helmet. But like folkloric heroes, Parzival knows no fear and consequently displays valor on the battlefield. Although he fails the initial test of compassion put to him, in the course of his adventures he learns humility and demonstrates compassion.

Remaining in the same poetic climate but moving to another era, we find that Richard Wagner's Siegfried also launches his heroic career as a naive youth without fear. The resemblances between his story and the "Fairy Tale of One Who Went Forth to Learn Fear" are unmistakable. To his cantankerous guardian, Mime, Siegfried confides that he wishes to learn what it is to fear — to which Mime responds that the wise learn fear quickly, the stupid have a harder time of it.[21] Siegfried clearly belongs in the latter category. Like the "one who went forth to learn fear," he discovers that emotion in the experience of love. As he sets eyes on the sleeping Brünnhilde, he feels a mystifying quickening of emotions:

> How cowardly I feel.
> Is this what they call fear?
> Oh mother! mother!
> Your fearless child!
> A woman lies in sleep:
> She has taught him to be afraid!
>
> (*Siegfried*, Act III)

No one was more surprised by the resemblances between the Grimms' fairy tale character and the heroic Siegfried than Richard Wagner. In a letter to his friend Theodor Uhlig, he wrote: "Haven't I ever told you this amusing story? It's the tale of the lad who ventures forth to learn what fear is and who is so dumb that he just can't do it. Imagine my amazement when I suddenly realized that that lad is no one else but — young Siegfried."[22]

It would not be a difficult task to identify countless other guileless fools and lads without fear in German literature. From the Baroque era through the Romantic period up to the present, naiveté is the signature of many a literary hero. The protagonist of Grimmelshausen's *Simplicius Simplicissimus* may be a clever rogue, but his name is telling. Like Parzival, he moves from foolish innocence to an understanding of the ways of the world, though his story ends in disillusion. Goethe's *Wilhelm Meister's Apprenticeship*, perhaps the finest exemplar of the *Bildungsroman* — that most hallowed of German literary traditions — gives us a naive innocent who happens to be fortunate enough to stumble into the right circles. We do not have to look far in the Romantic era for heroes pure in heart and innocent in spirit. Every one of them — from Novalis's Heinrich von Ofterdingen to Josef von Eichendorff's Florio — begins the first leg of his journey into the wild blue yonder as a charmingly naive young man wholly untutored in worldly matters.

In an introduction to the *Magic Mountain*, Thomas Mann made a point of bowing in the direction of Hans Castorp's literary antecedents.

Mystified by the way in which the weight of literary tradition had — without his knowing it — determined his protagonist's character, he was also flattered by the company in which his hero was placed. Both Parzival and Wilhelm Meister, he noted, belong to the class of "guileless fools," and his Hans Castorp is no different. His "simplicity and artlessness" make him a legitimate literary cousin of those two quester figures. Yet Hans Castorp can also display all the wisdom of an innocent: when he wants something, he can be "clever," "crafty," and "shrewd." That Mann further emphasized resemblances "here and there" between Hans Castorp's story and fairy tales comes as no surprise.[23]

It may seem to be stretching a point to suggest that fairy tales can tell us something about what French historians call "mentalités." Yet storytellers have, throughout the ages, embroidered the narratives passed on to them with the cultural values as well as with the facts of their own contemporary milieu. Every subtle change can be significant, so long as it takes place on a large scale and does not simply represent one idiosyncratic telling of a tale. What the Grimms' collection tells us about fairy tales does not deviate fundamentally from what other German folkloric and literary sources declare. Naiveté has a special charm and magic of its own.

Notes

1. Max Lüthi asserts that the disproportionately large number of female heroines in fairy tales can be traced to the prominent role played by women in shaping the plots. See "The Fairy-Tale Hero," in *Once upon a Time: On the Nature of Fairy Tales*, trans. Lee Chadeayne and Paul Gottwald (Bloomington: Indiana University Press, 1976), pp. 135–46. By contrast Ralph S. Boggs asserts that 80 percent of German tales have a hero, and that only 20 percent have a heroine ("The Hero in the Folk Tales of Spain, Germany and Russia," *Journal of American Folklore* 44 [1931]: 27–42). Neither Lüthi nor Boggs identifies his statistical sample.

2. Simone de Beauvoir's characterization appears in *The Second Sex*, trans. H. M. Parshley (New York: Bantam, 1952), pp. 271–72. For the list of heroic attributes, see Jack Zipes, *Fairy Tales and the Art of Subversion: The Classical Genre for Children and the Process of Civilization* (New York: Wildman Press, 1983), p. 57.

3. The first edition is reprinted in *Die Kinder- und Hausmärchen der Brüder Grimm: Vollständige Ausgabe in der Urfassung*, ed. Friedrich Panzer (Wiesbaden: Emil Vollmer, 1953).

4. On the various types of heroes, see Katalin Horn, *Der aktive und der passive Märchenheld* (Basel: Schweizerische Gesellschaft für Volkskunde, 1983); August von Löwis of Menar, *Der Held im deutschen und russischen Märchen* (Jena: Eugen Diederichs, 1912); Ralph S. Boggs, "The Hero in the Folk Tales of Spain, Germany and Russia," pp. 27–42; Vincent Brun, "The German Fairy Tale," *Menorah Journal* 27 (1939): 147–55; and Louis L. Snyder, "Cultural Nationalism: The Grimm Brothers' Fairy Tales," in *Roots of German Nationalism* (Bloomington: Indiana University Press, 1978), pp. 35–54.

5. Constance Spender makes this point. See "Grimms' Fairy Tales," *The Contemporary Review* 102 (1912): 673–79.

6. These are the words of the fox in the Grimms' version of "The Golden Bird."

7. *Tales from the Thousand and One Nights*, trans. N. J. Dawood (Harmondsworth: Penguin, 1973), p. 165. Robert Crossley makes the point about Aladdin's lack of merit ("Pure and Applied Fantasy; or, From Faerie to Utopia," in *The Aesthetics of Fantasy Literature and Art*, ed. Roger C. Schlobin [Notre Dame, Ind.: University of Notre Dame Press, 1982], pp. 176–91). On Aladdin's fortunes in Germany, see Erich Sielaff, "Bemerkungen zur kritischen Aneignung der deutschen Volksmärchen," *Wissenschaftliche Zeitschrift der Universität Rostock* 2 (1952/53): 241–301.

8. On the ethnographic significance of animals in fairy tales, see Lutz Röhrich, "Mensch und Tier im Märchen," *Schweizerisches Archiv für Volkskunde* 49 (1953): 165–93.

9. Eugen Weber finds that the celebration of compassion in fairy tales reflects the rareness of that virtue during the age in which the tales flourished: "Kindness, selflessness is the greatest virtue (perhaps because there is so little to give, perhaps precisely because it is so rare)." See "Fairies and Hard Facts: The Reality of Folktales," *Journal of the History of Ideas* 42 (1981): 93–113.

10. On the three phases of action in classical fairy tales, see E. Meletinsky, S. Nekludov, E. Novik, and D. Segal, "Problems of the Structural Analysis of Fairytales," in *Soviet Structural Folkloristics*, ed. P. Maranda (The Hague: Mouton, 1974), pp. 73–139. The authors divide the action of fairy tales into a preliminary test, a basic test, and an additional final test.

11. Note the use in the tale of such heavy-handed transitions as "But now I must tell more about the king and the queen, who had left with the count." On the presence of only one single sharply defined plot in classical fairy tales, see Max Lüthi, *The European Folktale: Form and Nature*, trans. John D. Niles (Philadelphia: Institute for the Study of Human Issues, 1982), p. 34. Lüthi uses the term *Einsträngigkeit* (single-strandedness) to designate the absence of digressive plot lines in fairy tales. *Einsträngigkeit* is the term that Walter A. Berendsohn also uses to characterize the fairy tale's single-track plot structure in *Grundformen volkstümlicher Erzählkunst in den Kinder- und Hausmärchen der Brüder Grimm: Ein stilkritischer Versuch* (Hamburg: W. Gente, 1921), p. 33. The term has its origins in Axel Olrik's essay of 1919, which has been translated and printed as "Epic Laws of Folk Narrative," in *The Study of Folklore*, ed. Alan Dundes (Englewood Cliffs, NJ: Prentice-Hall, 1965), pp. 129–41.

12. On abasement as "a prelude to and precondition of *affiliation*" in "Cinderella," see Madonna Kolbenschlag, *Kiss Sleeping Beauty Good-Bye: Breaking the Spell of Feminine Myths and Models* (New York: Doubleday, 1979), p. 72.

13. Friedrich Nietzsche, "Morgenröte," 4:241, in *Friedrich Nietzsche: Werke in drei Bänden*, ed. Karl Schlechta (Munich: Hanser, 1954), 3:1172.

14. Bruno Bettelheim, *The Uses of Enchantment: The Meaning and Importance of Fairy Tales* (New York: Random House, Vintage Books, 1977), p. 281.

15. Stith Thompson emphasizes the ambiguous nature of the trickster's intellect: "The adventures of the Trickster, even when considered by themselves, are inconsistent. Part are the result of his stupidity, and about an equal number show him overcoming his enemies through cleverness." See *The Folktale* (1946; repr. Berkeley: University of California Press, 1977), p. 319. In *World Folktales: A Scribner Resource Collection* (New York: Charles Scribner's Sons, 1980), Atelia Clarkson and Gilbert B. Cross confirm the ambiguity when they point out that "the most incongruous feature of the American Indian trickster is his tendency to become a dupe or play the buffoon even though he was the wily, clever trickster in a story told the day before" (p. 285).

16. Variants of the tale of the courageous tailor demonstrate that a single core theme can lend itself to two different types of narratives: a biographical tale that focuses on the life of the hero and on his attempt to win the hand of a princess and an episodic tale that focuses on the various pranks played by a trickster. See the seven variants of "Das tapfere Schneiderlein," in Leander Petzoldt, *Volksmärchen mit Materialien* (Stuttgart: Ernst Klett, 1982), pp. 42–72.

17. Max Lüthi, *The European Folktale*, pp. 34–35.

18. For a reading of the story along similar lines, see Roderick McGillis, "Criticism in the Woods: Fairy Tales as Poetry," *Children's Literature Association Quarterly* 7 (1982): 2–8.

19. As Vladimir Propp put it, "when a helper is absent from a tale, this quality is

transferred to the hero." See *Morphology of the Folktale*, trans. Laurence Scott (Austin: University of Texas Press, 1968), p. 83.

20. Robert Darnton, "Peasants Tell Tales: The Meaning of Mother Goose," in his *The Great Cat Massacre and Other Episodes in French Cultural History* (New York: Basic Books, 1984), pp. 9–72. The quoted phrase appears on p. 44.

21. The retort is in Wagner's first version of *Siegfried* (Richard Wagner, *Skizzen und Entwürfe zur Ring-Dichtung*, ed. Otto Strobel [Munich: F. Bruckmann, 1930], p. 113).

22. The letter, dated 10 May 1851, appears in Richard Wagner, *Sämtliche Briefe*, ed. Gertrud Strobel and Werner Wolf (Leipzig: VEB Deutscher Verlag für Musik, 1979), 4:42–44. Heinz Rölleke discusses Wagner's dependence on the Grimms' fairy tale in "Märchen von einem, der auszog, das Fürchten zu lernen: Zu Überlieferung und Bedeutung des *KHM 4*," *Fabula* 20 (1979): 193–204.

23. Thomas Mann, *The Magic Mountain*, trans. H. T. Lowe-Porter (New York: Alfred A. Knopf, 1964), pp. 719–29. Castorp is described, in German, as a "Schalk"; he is "verschmitzt" and "verschlagen." Mann's remarks on the fairy tale quality of Castorp's story appear on p. v. Unfortunately Lowe-Porter translated Mann's term *Märchen* (fairy tale) as "legend."

Bibliography

Bettelheim, Bruno. *The Uses of Enchantment: The Meaning and Importance of Fairy Tales*. New York: Random House, Vintage Books, 1977. A sensitive and intelligent (if occasionally wrong-headed) psychoanalytic study of fairy tales and their therapeutic value for children.

Darnton, Robert. "Peasants Tell Tales: The Meaning of Mother Goose." In *The Great Cat Massacre and Other Episodes in French Cultural History*. New York: Basic Books, 1984. An astute reading of French folktales as cultural documents affording insight into the mental world of peasants.

Ellis, John. *One Fairy Story Too Many: The Brothers Grimm and Their Tales*. Chicago: University of Chicago Press, 1983. A polemical essay proposing to demonstrate that the Grimms' collection of tales constitutes literature rather than folklore.

Lüthi, Max. *The European Folktale: Form and Nature*. Translated by John D. Niles. Philadelphia: Institute for the Study of Human Issues, 1982. A lucid analysis of the form, style, and function of folktales by a renowned Swiss folklorist.

Maranda, P., ed. *Soviet Structural Folkloristics*. The Hague: Mouton, 1974. Key essays on thematic, structural, and typological features of fairy tales by Soviet scholars, most notable among them Eleazar Meletinsky.

Propp, Vladimir. *Morphology of the Folktale*. Translated by Laurence Scott. Austin: University of Texas Press, 1975. First published in 1928, this formalist analysis of the Russian folktale radically changed the face of folkloristic scholarship.

6. Silenced Women in the Grimms' Tales: The "Fit" Between Fairy Tales and Society in Their Historical Context

RUTH B. BOTTIGHEIMER

Mid-nineteenth-century Germany shared to a very large extent in European culture as a whole but differed from it in significant ways. A vigorously championed German ethic at that time was that of the silent woman.[1] Yet the years 1770–1830 in non-German Europe provide a very different pattern. Furnishing a pattern admired and imitated in the numerous courts and large cities of the Germanies, France of the ancien régime was a place where the privileged and educated could expect to be surrounded by articulate and eloquent women of letters. In Germany, a few women — Germaine Necker de Staël, Bettina Brentano von Arnim, and Charlotte von Stein — struggled to carry on this tradition, which culminated in the 1820s and 1830s in Berlin, where, briefly and uncharacteristically, several women led literary salons. Rahel Varnhagen, Dorothea Veit, and Henriette Herz provided forums for, and examples of, female wit and erudition. Far from typical, each lived a good part of her life in capital cities and was the daughter of Jewish parents, socially and sometimes even legally outside "society," unless converted to Christianity.

A very different ethic guided bourgeois families scattered in small towns throughout the Germanies. Their daughters, as described by

Theodore von Hippel in his long essay *Über die bürgerliche Verbesserung der Weiber* (1772), spent their youth simpering and primping their way to the altar. Exposure to good literature, von Hippel pleaded, would improve their minds and redirect their energy toward calm rationality. Von Hippel was not heeded by the authors of child-rearing books in the following decades, who incorporated and affirmed antifeminist leanings extracted from Rousseau, as quintessentially feminine the very traits deplored by von Hippel.[2]

Evidence from diaries and letters suggests that by the 1830s, silence as a positive feminine attribute had gained wide acceptance in all social classes in the dukedoms, principalities, and free cities that made up the Germanies, and that the 1860s and 1870s marked the extreme point for "the silent woman" in Germany. Gone were the animated literary salons led by women. When Fanny Lewald tried to follow the example set by Rahel Varnhagen in the 1850s, it was too late. Even if a woman were a genius, she complained, she would be told to sit quietly and knit.[3] A verse narrative in a children's annual of 1855 reformulates the punishment of being burned at the stake, one of the principal threats against silenced women found in numerous German tales of Grimms' *Fairy Tales* (*Kinder- und Hausmärchen*) by declaring that too much chatter could be punished, and severely:

The Huckster Chatterbox

"Finally, Miz Greta, be sensible!"
Nante says, laughing maliciously.
I well know that in olden times
Many witches were burned,
But you are burning yourself, by George!
This punishment seems really new
    For chattering.

Now, before you burn up completely
Do me one favor,
A little glowing ember for my pipe
Save me from your gown."
Miz Greta was almost petrified by shock
But she still doesn't leave off
    Her chattering.

Die Schwatzhafte Hökerin

"Zuletzt! Frau Grete, seid gescheidt!"
Spricht boshaft lachend Nante
"Ich weiß wohl daß in alter Zeit
Man viele Hexen verbrannte,

Ihr aber verbrennt euch selber gar!
Die Strafe scheint mir neu fürwahr
Für's Schwatzen.

Nun, eh' ihr ganz verbrennen thut
Mach mir noch eine Freude,
Für meine Pfeif' ein Fünkchen Glute
Schont mir von eurem Kleide." —
Die Grete ward vor Schreck fast Stein,
— Doch läßt sie es auch jetzt nicht sein,
Das Schwatzen![4]

Here too much talk is associated with witches and the grim punishment they met at the stake, although a very different situation occasions this verse: Frau Grete's footwarmer ignites her hem, which goes
unnoticed as she continues to chatter volubly.

One aspect of Grimms' *Fairy Tales* is arguably related to this
larger social phenomenon as well as to the history of German literature. Despite the ancient and international lineage of many of the
tales, the process of editing, codifying, and translating them produced
a distinctly nineteenth-century text, incorporating the gender-related
assumptions of Grimms' informants and of Wilhelm Grimm himself.
The question of language and speech taps into the very origin and
existence of oral and written literature. When J. H. Campe and other
child-rearing pundits of the turn of the nineteenth century were ad-
vocating the propriety of girlish and womanly silent repose, they
effectively reanimated a hoary German folk and literary tradition, a
misogynistic strain epitomized by the anonymous *Spiegel der regier-
sichtigen bösen Weibern*, which emphasized the hatefulness of nagging,
the only category of female speech it recognized.[5] The image of silent
women and of silent repose as the most praiseworthy female character trait emerges consistently in disparate areas of German life. One
is the subscript for one of the twelve scenes of human life printed on a
cotton kerchief of approximately 1880:

The boy's imagination soars abroad,
The girl walks at his side quietly.

Des Knaben Sinn schweift in die Weite,
Still geht das Mädchen ihm zur Seite.[6]

Another is Cosima Wagner's advice to her daughter, Daniela von
Bülow, before her marriage in 1885:

"You are [my] repose" is probably the highest accolade that can be addressed to a
woman. It is that above all which men seek as a foil to the clamor of the world.

Let it blossom beautifully in you, my dear child; let us women not join the crazy dance and let us instead represent quiescence, at which the poor persecuted men refresh themselves.

"Du bist die Ruhe" ist wohl das höchste Lob, welches einer Frau gesungen werden kann, das was der Mann vor Allem sucht, gegenüber der Unruhe der Welt; laß sie schön in Dir aufblühen, mein gutes Kind; machen wir Frauen den tollen Tanz nicht mit, und den Hast gegenüber stellen wir die Rast vor, an welcher die armen Gehetzten sich laben.[7]

Similarly the adumbration of silence moves through German literature like a leitmotiv. Whether removed from the turmoil of political affairs or relieved of care after questing after the Grail, fictional and epic figures, mostly male, have seemed ready to retire from the world to the reward of a silent solitude, whereas women *were* silent, as part of their basic identity, for example, as epitomized by the name of a prominent female character in Thomas Mann's *Dr. Faustus*, Schweigestill, an appellation which incorporates the imperative mode to be silent.

To be sure, silence can perform a narrative function. By retarding resolution a silent character can provide an opening for narrative elaboration by the authorial voice. This is as true of folk and fairy tales as it is of novels and dramas. What has always differentiated male from female repose and silence in the German oral and literary tradition, however, was the generally accepted understanding that it rewarded men for a life of striving but was enjoined upon women as comely and decent behavior. Men could be silent, but women were silenced.

This gender distinction is congruent with the distribution of power in most ages, a point Jean Bethke Elshtain makes in "Feminist Discourse and Its Discontent: Language, Power, and Meaning."[8] There she explores the relationship of language to power, seeing discourse as domination. In German-speaking countries even the vocabulary of legal personhood has long been grounded in the concept of language use. Knowing that *mündig* means "of age" and that *mundtot* means "dead in law" as well as "silenced" sharpens the reader's awareness of the possible extended meaning of "for she could not open her mouth" (*denn es konnte seinen Mund nicht auftun*) in "The Virgin's Child" (#3: "Marienkind").

We can infer that Wilhelm Grimm himself also understood discourse as domination by turning for a moment from silence to a consideration of speech at its most powerful: its use in casting spells. How and in what association these powers are distributed is a litmus test for otherwise invisible assumptions in the *Fairy Tales*. Of the many verses in the text, only a few represent true conjuring, and of these, the overwhelming majority are spoken by female figures. Casting spells, or conjuring, is here understood as an imperative addressed to natural powers (to appear, to intervene, or to assist) in contradistinction to rhymes which perform mere narrative functions. Certain powers realizable through speech were ascribed to women in the *Fairy Tales*, a belief Tacitus attributed to German tribes in the first century A.D. These powers appear in Grimms' *Fairy Tales* in the figures of Cinderella (*Aschenputtel*), Gretel, the goosegirl (*die Gänsemagd*), and the girl in "Tales of the Paddock" ("Märchen von der Unke") among others. Each of these female characters successfully invokes natural forces exemplifying what Elshtain calls "discourse as domination." All of this, taken together, offers a glimpse backward to the ancient Germanic folk belief in women's inherent power over nature expressed through words. It exists in certain of these tales as an integral part of the plot and cannot be removed without gross distortion of the tale itself.

But powerful verbalizing women represented something Germans in general and Wilhelm Grimm in particular were not at all comfortable with in the nineteenth century. In a society which prized silent retiring women one would expect female speech — which in conjuring potently bears woman's will or intention — to be curtailed or even condemned in that society's literary productions, whether "folk" or canonical, and that is precisely what happened in Germany. Completely absent from the German fairy tale tradition, which otherwise borrowed so heavily from France, is any version of Perrault's tale of "Riquet à la Houppe," whose ravishing but inarticulate princess is perfected by the conferral of eloquence.

Commonplaces of culture such as the desire for silence in women determine the events of fairy tales, which as a stripped-down genre must negotiate with social realities in order to make sense to their readers or hearers. Without subplots and a large cast of characters who can explore gradations of meaning and nuances of social practices, fairy tales and their plots achieve validity in their own cultures by alluding to generally held beliefs, even if these beliefs themselves are an illusion, an illusion which provides for its own survival by functioning as a paradigm for subsequent generations.

Silence in Grimms' Fairy Tales

Silence appears at several levels in Grimms' *Fairy Tales*.[9] Most conspicuous is the muteness which grows out of the narrative itself, when a character is cursed with or condemned to silence for a period of time. Next are the silences within the text resulting from the author or editor's distribution of direct and indirect speech. And finally — and least noticeable at first reading — is the manner in which the lexical context colors what is said. In Grimms' *Fairy Tales* the verbs "speak" (*sprechen*), "say" (*sagen*), "ask" (*fragen*), "answer" (*antworten*), and "cry out" (*rufen*) provide a hierarchical gradation for characters by marking their speech as licit or illicit. Gender considerations play a large part in these three categories, each of which is confirmed in numerous tales in the collection.

The salient example of language use or its prohibition as a narrative element occurs in "The Virgin's Child" (#3: "Marienkind"). Although never achieving the prominence of "Little Snow-White" (#53: "Sneewittchen") or "Little Red-Cap" (#26: "Rotkäppchen") in Germany and generally omitted from American and English editions of the *Fairy Tales*, it was nearly always included in children's editions of ten or more selections in Germany in the nineteenth century. The tale begins where most others end, with the sudden elevation from rags to riches, from grinding hunger to sweet plenty, from a woodcutter's hut to a divinely ordained palace, from earthbound companions to angelic playmates. But when the child stubbornly denies having opened a forbidden door, the Virgin Mary deprives her of speech and casts her out of heaven. After many miserable solitary years in the wilderness, a passing king discovers and marries her, but the girl/queen's muteness leaves her defenseless against accusations of cannibalism which arise when the Virgin Mary removes her infants one by one as a continuing punishment for her refractory denials. Condemned to the stake as a witch, she saves herself at the last moment by her sudden desire — fanned by the flames — to acknowledge her transgression.

In "The Twelve Brothers" (#9: "Die zwölf Brüder") the youngest sibling, a sister, must endure seven years' silence, neither speaking nor laughing. A single word will cause her brothers' instant death:

You must be dumb for seven years, and may not speak or laugh, and if you speak one single word, and only an hour of the seven years is wanting, all is in vain, and your brothers will be killed by the one word.

Du mußt sieben Jahre stumm sein, darfst nicht sprechen und nicht lachen, und sprichst du ein einziges Wort, und as fehlt nur eine Stunde an den sieben Jahren, so ist alles umsonst, und deine Brüder werden von dem einen Wort getötet.

She, too, stands bound to the stake on the verge of immolation when the last moment of the seven years passes, her fraternal deliverers appear, and she is rescued. In "The Six Swans" (#49: "Die sechs Schwäne") the sister accepts the condition of six years' silence to redeem her brothers—again neither laughter nor speech is allowed.[10] She too is powerless against the world, exposed first to clamorous pursuit by the king's huntsmen, then after marrying their king, to the lurking wickedness of her mother-in-law, who like the Virgin Mary spirits her children away one by one in order to bring her to the stake. There, bound and ready for grisly execution, she is released by her brothers as the last moment of the sixth year passes, and her mother-in-law is executed instead.

Silence is again enjoined in "The Iron Oven" (#127: "Der Eisenofen"). An enchanted prince imprisoned in an iron oven can be released only if the princess who discovers him maintains a complete silence during the journey back to her own realm. This injunction continues, until on her last visit home the princess is sternly warned that she must speak no more than three words with her family or else her prince will disappear. However, her joy at seeing her father is so great that she unintentionally violates the condition:

Then she related all that had befallen her, and how because she had transgressed the order which had been given her not to say more than three words, the stove, and the King's son also, had disappeared.

Da erzählte sie alles, wie es ihr gegangen wäre, und weil sie das Gebot übertreten hätte, nicht mehr als drei Worte zu sprechen, wäre der Ofen weg samt dem Königssohn.

And finally there is "The Glass Coffin" (#163: "Der gläserne Sarg"). Rather longer than the others, it more closely resembles a literary fairy tale, a *Kunstmärchen*. Psychological motivations are accounted for within the narrative; symbolic actions, self-consciously employed magic, the sophistication of a frame tale, and the particularity absent from most fairy tales all make their appearance. As in "The Virgin's Child," the girl is struck dumb in conjunction with her willful refusal to comply. In "The Virgin's Child" the punishment is justified by the nature of the transgression: Marienkind has opened a door forbidden her by no less a personage than the Virgin Mary herself, while in "The Glass Coffin," the female protagonist loses her voice at the appearance of the man who wishes to claim her hand in marriage. Although this tale is more a caricature than a genuine folktale, or even a literary fairy tale, its retention of the theme of silence in conjunction with marriage links it with a persistent folktale tradition that has surfaced in virtually every European country. The association of silence with marriage extends backward in two tales to the verge of womanhood and marriageability. Both Cinderella and Allerleirauh (#65) observe a strict silence in the ballroom to which they resort to establish their identity. Allerleirauh, in particular, exhibits ambivalent behavior; she coyly invites her own disclosure but denies her identity and womanly availability by her responses. Both flee the ballroom, never speaking, though their reasons differ.

Male silence exists, too, but it differs greatly from female silence, both in extent and in quality. For instance, in "The King of the Golden Mountain" (#92: "Der König vom goldenen Berge"), the merchant's son can break the magic spell binding the captive princess, if he silently endures the torments inflicted by twelve men for three nights running. Similarly the poor fisher's son in "The Three Black Princesses" (#137: "De Drei Schwatten Prinzessinnen") may not speak for the space of a year to the three princesses he has undertaken to redeem, but during that entire time no other proscription against speech binds him to silence.

They told him he must for a whole year not speak to them and also not look at them, and what he wanted to have he was just to ask for, and if they dared give him an answer they would do so.

He söll en gans Johr nig met en kühren un söll se auck nig anseihen; wat he gerne hebben wull, dat söll he men seggen, wann se Antwort giewen dröften, wullen se et dohn.

And finally in one of the ten legends appended to Grimms' *Fairy Tales*, "Poverty and Humility Lead to Heaven" (KL4: "Armut und Demut führen zum Himmel") the reader encounters a prince who, after renouncing speech as well as his position at court, spends seven years praying to God.

He took nothing but a little food, said nothing, but prayed to the Lord to take him into his heaven.

[Der Königssohn] nahm nichts als ein wenig Essen, sprach nichts, sondern betete zu dem Herrn, daß er ihn einmal in seinem Himmel aufnehmen wollte.

These examples clearly indicate gender-based differences in the imposition of speech loss by the teller of the tales. Male silence undertaken to redeem another person ("The Three Black Princesses") is neither total nor of long duration, while a male who wishes to redeem himself ("Poverty and Humility Lead to Heaven") takes on silence voluntarily. In clear contrast, the putative self-redemptive silence in "The Virgin's Child" is prescribed as a punishment, which generates the threat of graver punishment in secular society, that is, being burned at the stake. We further see that the two males on whom silence is imposed as a redemptive precondition both emerge from lower social orders, while females may be deprived of speech whether urchins or queens.

Finally it becomes clear through an examination of the editorial history of "The Virgin's Child" that the deprivation of speech provides an effective means of breaking the girl-queen's will, which completes the equation of speech with power. It is precisely the deprivation and transformation of power that seems to motivate the plot shifts evident in individual folk and many fairy tales during the Early Modern period in Europe. Either positive female folk figures with power were deprived of this power, or their power was transformed in the tales into the wickedness of witchcraft.[11]

The injunction to silence in these tales is paralleled in other tales by an actual silence. Many interpreters and critics of Grimms' *Fairy Tales* have discussed Wilhelm Grimm's preoccupation with substituting direct for indirect speech to enliven the tales stylistically, but none to date has posed the equally important questions: Who speaks? Whose voice is audible? In the enduringly popular "Frog-King; or, Iron Henry" (#1: "Der Froschkönig, oder der eiserne Heinrich"), the first tale in Grimm's collection, no one is struck dumb. Silence forms no part of the plot, and indeed we first meet the princess chatting up the frog, although he clearly occupies the rostrum. The same is true when the frog appears at the castle portal: both speak, but a good many of the princess's responses are described rather than uttered, while the frog freely articulates his thoughts.

She began to cry. . . . And as thus she lamented. . . .

Da fing sie an zu weinen. . . . Und wie sie so klagte. . . .

The frog's voice is clearly heard rebuking and silencing the princess:

"What ails you, King's daughter? You weep so that even a stone would show pity."

"Be quiet, and do not weep."

"Was hast du vor, Königstochter, du schreist ja, daß sich ein Stein erbarmen möchte."

"Sei still und weine nicht."

This pattern continues in "Rapunzel" (#12), where the sorceress occupies center stage, the prince is next in verbosity, and the titular protagonist, Rapunzel, lags far behind. Again, typically, Rapunzel's reactions are described, while the prince bursts out in plucky verbalization. For example, when the prince sees the sorceress gain swift admittance to the tower by calling:

"Rapunzel, Rapunzel, let down your hair,"

"Rapunzel, Rapunzel, Lass dein Haar herunter,"

he says:

"If that is the ladder which one mounts, I too will try my fortune."

"Ist das die Leiter, auf welcher man hinauf kommt, so will ich einmal mein Glück versuchen."

The reader learns that Rapunzel sings "a song . . . letting her sweet voice resound" ("ein Gesang . . . ihre süße Stimme"). The song's words remain a mystery.

When the prince climbs into the tower, we hear that "Rapunzel was terribly frightened" ("Rapunzel erschrak gewaltig"). Once again, Rapunzel appears through the editor's voice, not her own.

In "Hansel and Gretel" (#15: "Hänsel und Gretel") we see a consciously created silence descending on female characters. An analysis of the extent and content of direct discourse reveals a pattern of verbalization which undermines and contradicts Gretel's active role in implementing her own and Hansel's escape from the slavering witch. In the opening scene when Gretel tearfully says, "'Now all is over with us'" ("'Nun ist's um uns geschehen'"), Hansel adopts an appropriately consolatory attitude. His first words to Gretel, though, enjoin her silence: "'Be quiet Gretel, do not distress yourself, I will soon find a way to help us'" ("'Still, Gretel . . . gräme dich nicht, ich will uns schon helfen'"). Astonishingly, on the following two occasions on which Hansel calms Gretel, the text provides absolutely no occasion for his words; it is simply assumed that Gretel must be crying or deeply distressed. It is Hansel whom the stepmother addresses, and he who speaks in response, a situation which provides the pattern for discourse throughout the tale.

In "Cinderella" (#21: "Aschenputtel") we recognize the actual lineaments of female silence. After her piously expressed wish that her father bring her the first branch that brushes against his hat, Cinderella, aside from her formulaic incantations, says nothing further. Silent at the ball, speechless among the ashes, mute when trying on the tiny slipper, Cinderella endures the barbs and jibes of her loquacious stepsisters. Their very loquacity identifies them as wicked. In the world of Wilhelm Grimm a talkative woman meant trouble.

Trouble could come in many forms, but particularly noxious was female sloth. The woman's volubility preserved precisely this loathsome trait in "The Lazy Spinner" (#128: "Die faule Spinnerin"), where slothfulness parallels her readiness to speak. "She was always ready with her tongue" ("so war sie mit ihrem Maul doch vornen") we hear Wilhelm, the editor, add. In case the reader missed the point, the tale ends: "But you yourself must own she was an odious woman!" ("Aber das mußt du selbst sagen; es war eine garstige Frau").

These implicit and explicit assumptions diverge sharply from the French tradition and from the English and American traditions derived from Perrault, who includes no mute women. Indeed, eloquence in women is prized, as in "Riquet à la Houppe" ("Ricky with the Tuft") where the reader meets two princesses. One is beautiful but "stupide," the other ugly but eloquent. At every party the guests first gather around the beauty but quickly drift to the brilliant conversation of her ugly sister. Riquet, himself ugly but eloquent, offers eloquence to the beautiful sister in return for loving him. In his eyes her "manque de parole" (inarticulateness) is her only fault. So too in "Cendrillon" ("Cinderella") the titular heroine speaks throughout the tale, suggests remedies, and thereby meets the approval of her fairy godmother, who characteristically affirms Cendrillon's suggestions by exclaiming at one point, "You are in the right!"

Can one then generalize about speech acts in Grimms' *Fairy Tales?* At one end of the speech scale are biological mothers — good but dead — and their marriageable daughters. Both are silent. The mothers of Snow White, Cinderella, and Marienkind exemplify this group. At the other end of the speech scale appear both evil witches and witchlike figures and authority figures — the Virgin Mary, kings, princes, and men in general — all free to speak. Here the power-bearers are clearly broken down along gender lines, with the curious exception of the Virgin Mary, a case to be discussed at another point.

The foregoing discussion leads to the conclusion that muteness clearly exists on two levels in Grimms' *Fairy Tales:* first, muteness which grows out of the narrative itself, when a character is cursed with or is condemned to silence for a period of time; and second, a silence within the text which results from the author's or editor's choice in distributing direct and indirect discourse.

A further manner in which the text itself can charge a character's speech with authority (or conversely can devalue it) grows out of the lexical context, the level least noticeable at first reading. In Grimms' *Fairy Tales* this set of distinctions is made with the verbs introducing direct speech: "ask" (*fragen*), "answer" (*antworten*), "cry" (*rufen*), "say" (*sagen*), and "speak" (*sprechen*). The author or editor probably employs this set of distinctions least consistently. Despite this, a pattern emerges from Grimms' *Fairy Tales*, a message on a subliminal level.

It is tempting to develop a theory about the distribution of the two verbs "speak" and "say," which appear to offer an entry to the unconscious world in which Wilhelm ordered his folklore characters hierarchically according to gender, social class, and licit or illicit speech and power. In many of the tales, though by no means in all of them, "speak" appears far more often in conjunction with authority figures. A count of seven tales reveals the following numbers of instances of the verb "speak": [12]

Mother	(3)
Girl	(7)
Witch	(19)
Father/King	(11)
Boy/Prince	(16)

This division of "speak" and "say" among the male or authority figures and female figures extends even to animal tales. The wolf in "The Wolf and the Seven Little Kids" (#5: "Der Wolf und die sieben jungen Geißlein") uses "spoke" four times, the nanny goat's words are preceded by "said," and the kids "cry" time after time.

Furthermore the verb "speak," in two tales, "Faithful John" (#6: "Der treue Johannes") and "The Story of the Youth Who Went Forth to Learn What Fear Was" (#4: "Märchen von einem der auszog, das Fürchten zu lernen") appears at the precise point at which the character's authority and independence emerges, that is, when he leaves his father's home:

When the day dawned, therefore, the boy put his fifty talers into his pocket, and went forth on the great highway, and continually said to himself. . . .

Als nun der Tag anbrach, steckte der Junge seine fünfzig Taler in die Tasche, ging hinaus auf die große Landstraße und sprach immer vor sich hin. . . .

In the same tale the youth's eventual wife never speaks, but is only described: "And this at last angered her" ("Das verdroß sie endlich"), although her clever maid, the sexton's wife, and the innkeeper's wife are each allowed a few words, uncharacteristically introduced by the verbs so rare for women, "ask" and "speak." It is possible that this tale points toward an implicitly held belief that the lower, serving orders somehow lay outside the norms for correct bourgeois behavior, as expressed here by the incidence of the verbs "ask" and "speak." Is it significant, one wonders, that in the same tale the bold son cries out to a ghostly figure: "speak if you are an honest fellow" ("Sprich, wenn du ein ehrlicher Kerl bist")? May the reader conclude that male speech indicates a solid, honorable character (as indicated by the adjective "candid" [*redlich*]) applied in German society principally to males, whereas female speech implies the opposite? Jacob Grimm's successors addressed the question of the distinction between "speak" and "say" in the *German Dictionary* (*Deutsches Wörterbuch*) and concluded that their meanings were equivalent:

"Speak" is unusually frequent in older New High German. In contrast to that it has somewhat diminished in daily colloquial speech in favor of "say" and has taken on a somewhat ceremonial character. (2799)

With "say" the emphasis is placed on the content. For example, he spoke without saying much. (2801)

sprechen ist namentlich im älteren nhd. auszerordentlich häufig. jetzt ist es dagegen in der altäglichen umgangssprache etwas zurückgetreten zu gunsten von sagen, und hat einen etwas feierlicheren charakter angenommen. (2799)

bei sagen [steht] die rücksicht auf den inhalt im vordergrunde. beispiel: er sprach ohne viel zu sagen. (2801)

The conclusions of this investigation, however, suggest that special considerations not addressed here, gender and social class, are conspicuously decisive in evaluating the act of speaking, regardless of content, which offers a radically new understanding of the patterns of speech distribution in Grimms' *Fairy Tales*.

In the *Fairy Tales* women answer with great frequency, they almost never pose a question, and their general helplessness leads them to cry out often. This represents much more than a random assignment of verbs introducing direct speech; it expresses the weight of an entire society enjoining compliant responses in good girls and, more important, forbidding inquiry, initiative, and, most heinous of all, impertinence. The consequences of such powerful paradigms for gender-differentiated behavior recorded or introduced into Grimms' *Fairy Tales* made themselves felt at every level of German society in the nineteenth century, from the apprentice carrying his printed kerchief, through Fanny Lewald, to Cosima Wagner herself.

Any doubt at this point about the relationship between language and power can be dispelled by a close examination of the images associated with muted females. Marienkind is banished from heaven, imprisoned by an impenetrable thornhedge, nourished on roots and berries, exposed naked to snow and ice, condemned as a cannibal, and tied to a stake with flames burning around her. The sister in "The Twelve Brothers" also ends up bound to the stake:

And when she was bound fast to the stake, and the fire was licking at her clothes with its red tongue. . . .

Und als sie schon an den Pfahl festgebunden war und das Feuer an ihren Kleidern mit roten Zungen leckte. . . .

The youngest sibling, the sister, in "The Six Swans" endures the same fate, though in her story, the fire has not yet been lit as she stands on the faggots. The nine days' hunger endured by the princess in "The Iron Oven" as a punishment for speaking more than the allotted three words to her father seems mild in comparison to these ghastly concluding scenes.

Sexual vulnerability also permeates tales of muteness. Before a king out hunting discovers Marienkind, her clothes rot and fall off her body in the several years she spends in the forest. Wielding a phallic sword, he hacks his way through the thicket and carries her off naked to his castle. The central fact of the girl's sexual vulnerability, her nakedness, is raised into high relief when this motif reappears in "The Six Swans," where against all logic the girl — having taken refuge in a tree — tries to drive off the king's hunters by throwing her clothes down at them, piece by piece, until she has only her shift left:

The huntsmen, however, did not let themselves be turned aside by that, but climbed the tree and fetched the maiden and led her before the king.

Die Jäger ließen sich aber damit nicht abweisen, stiegen auf den Baum, hoben das Mädchen herab und führten es vor den König.

The evident fact that no amount of security is protection enough for a woman emerges from my reading of "The Glass Coffin," where the onset of speechlessness coincides with the revelation of the protagonist's vulnerability, that is, her powerlessness against intrusion (and, of course, this forced entry may be understood in many ways):

I wanted to summon my waiting-maid who slept in the next room, but to my astonishment I found that speech was taken away from me by an unknown force. I felt as if a nightmare were weighing down my breast, and was unable to make the very slightest sound. In the meantime I saw the stranger enter through two doors which were fast bolted.

[Ich] wollte mein im Nebenzimmer schlafendes Kammermädchen rufen, allein zu meinem Erstaunen fand ich, daß mir, als lastete ein Alp auf meiner Brust, von einer unbekannten Gewalt die Sprache benommen und ich unvermögernd war, den geringsten Laut von mir zu geben. Indem sah ich bei dem Schein der Nachtlampe den Fremden in mein durch zwei Türen fest verschlossenes Zimmer eintreten.

Speechlessness also occurs in conjunction with breaking a girl's will ("The Virgin's Child"), with reducing a girl's pride ("The Glass Coffin"), with spinning and sewing, the archetypal female occupations ("The Six Swans," "The Twelve Brothers," and "Allerleirauh"), and with practicing Christianity ("The Virgin's Child"). "The Twelve Brothers" exemplifies these tendencies: Here a Christian vocabulary (the sister wants "to redeem" [*erlösen*] her brothers) with repeated supplication to the Almighty frames the striking image of the sister sitting in a tree spinning, while the mother's silencing prefigures her daughter's later muted state: "'Dearest child,' she answered, 'I may not tell you'" ("'Liebstes Kind,' antworte sie, 'ich darf dir's nicht sagen'"). Female verbosity signals not only evil incarnate but also sloth. While the lazy spinner natters away, Wilhelm Grimm stands on the proscenium denigrating her in an editorial aside: "She was always ready with her tongue" ("so war sie mit ihrem Maul doch vornen").

Conclusion

In his own time Wilhelm Grimm codified a generally accepted behavioral code both as he found it in oral narrative and as he rewrote it in the collection. In the *Fairy Tales* he expressed the values of the German social structure out of which these tales grew, by holding up specific models of behavior as essential and necessary and exhibiting terrible punishments as the just fate of the wayward and dilatory. In this way, Grimm preserved and passed on these values in image and narrative.

One may well ponder the social function of these appalling representations of silenced girls and women. Kenneth Burke asserts that certain images may assist in tolerating the intolerable.[13] Both men and women in the nineteenth century, though not all women, certainly not Fanny Lewald, accepted the rightness of the image of the quiet woman, whether silent or silenced. However, the extensive buttressing of this image by a purported or real folk tradition as expressed in Grimms' *Fairy Tales* suggests the intolerability of the image for many girls and women of the nineteenth century. In trying to understand these images and to ponder the effect they may have had on their readers and listeners then and now, one must conclude that fairy tales offered an apparently innocent and peculiarly suitable medium for both transmitting and enforcing the norm of the silent woman. To the extent that these tales corroborated and codified the values of the society in which they appeared, they reinforced them powerfully, symbolizing and codifying the status quo and serving as paradigms for powerlessness.

Notes

1. The material in this chapter represents an extension into literary history of the lively discussion in linguistic circles about the relationship between gender, language, and social structure. For illuminating discussions and an extensive bibliography see Barrie Thorne, Cheris Kramarae, and Nancy Henley, *Language, Gender and Society* (Rowley, MA: Newbury House, 1983). An earlier study by Max Adler summarizes research in this area from 1879 to 1978. See *Sex Differences in Human Speech* (Hamburg: Helmut Buske, 1978).

2. Dagmar Grenz, *Mädchenliteratur* (Stuttgart: Metzler, 1981), p. 86 ff. Two recent and relevant studies should also be mentioned here. They are John C. Fout, ed., *German Women in the Nineteenth Century* (New York: Holmes and Meier, 1984) and Ruth-Ellen B. Joeres, and Mary Jo Maynes, eds., *German Women in the Eighteenth and Nineteenth Centuries: A Social and Literary History* (Bloomington: University of Indiana Press, 1986).

3. A valuable exposition of the real and psychological space accorded women in the home, in love, marriage, divorce, law, feminism, politics, and the academy in Germany, France, England, and Italy can be found in Priscilla Robertson, *An Experience of Women: Pattern and Change in Nineteenth-Century Europe* (Philadelphia: Temple University Press, 1982).

4. From *Deutscher Jugend Kalender*, ed. H. Bürkner (Leipzig: Wigand, 1855), p. 59.

5. Originally published in Augsburg, 1733; repr. in the series Frau in der Literatur, ed. Ursula Schröder (Frankfurt: Ullstein, 1982).

6. Musée de l'impression des étoffes 954.619.1 M.A., Mulhouse, France.

7. Letter of 10 October 1885, Bayreuth. Quoted in *Liebe Mutter, Liebe Tochter*, ed. Jutta Radel (Frankfurt: Ullstein, 1982), p. 112.

8. *Signs*, Spring 1982, p. 605.

9. Unless otherwise noted, English tale titles, names, and translations are taken with permission from *The Complete Grimm's Fairy Tales*, trans. Margaret Hunt and James Stern (New York: Pantheon, 1944, 1972). Quotations from the *Tales* in German come from the 1857 edition of *Kinder- und Hausmärchen*. A recent, and widely available, reliable German edition is that edited by Heinz Rölleke (Stuttgart: Reclam, 1980).

10. Although this tale is clearly a variant of "The Twelve Brothers," Wilhelm Grimm included both in the large edition.

11. This forms the conclusion of my article, "The Transformed Queen: A Search for the Origins of Negative Female Archetypes in Grimms' Fairy Tales," in *Amsterdamer Beiträge* 10 (1980): 1–12.

12. This graph is based on the incidence of the verb "sprechen" in seven tales: #13: "Die drei Männlein im Walde"; #12: "Rapunzel"; #15: "Hänsel und Gretel"; #21: "Aschenputtel"; #50: "Dornröschen"; #53: "Sneewittchen"; and #16: "Die drei Schlangenblätter."

13. Discussed in Marcia Landy, "The Silent Woman," in *The Authority of Experience: Essays in Feminist Criticism* (Amherst: University of Massachusetts Press, 1977), p. 24.

Bibliography

Bettelheim, Bruno. *The Uses of Enchantment: The Meaning and Importance of Fairy Tales.* New York: Random House, Vintage Books, 1977. Introduced the broader public to the notion that the fairy tale mirrors and explains a child's basic emotional response to problems of maturation; limited by lack of awareness of the editorial history of Grimms' tales.

Gilbert, Sandra M., and Susan Gubar. *The Madwoman in the Attic: The Woman Writer and the Nineteenth-Century Literary Imagination.* New Haven: Yale University Press, 1979. Sections relating to fairy tales offer a feminist reading of thoroughgoing gender differentiation.

Kramer, Cheris; Barrie Thorne; and Nancy Henley. "Perspectives on Language and Communication." *Signs* 3 (1978): 638–51. A review essay covering discussions of language and the sexes in the 1970s; clearly outlines and analyzes the question of gender vs. social status.

Stone, Kay F. "Things Walt Disney Never Told Us." *Journal of American Folklore* 88 (1975): 42–49. An early reflection on gender distinctions and their consequences in fairy tales.

Thorne, Barrie; Cheris Kramarae; and Nancy Henley: *Language, Gender and Society.* Rowley, MA: Newbury House, 1983. Excellent essays on the relationship between gender, language and social structure; annotated bibliography covers "Stereotypes and Perceptions of Language Use," "Genre and Style," "Language Varieties in American English" (with reference to age, race, ethnicity, sexuality and social class), etc.

7. Folklorists as Agents of Nationalism: Asturian Legends and the Problem of Identity

JAMES W. FERNANDEZ

Recognition: Our Culture Heroes Find Themselves a Home

Once upon a time, in those halcyon days before the greening of America and its subsequent graying, before the vultures of the Vietnam War came home to roost and peck at our vitals, before the invention of the doomsday machine and the forecast of a nuclear winter, when America was still innocent or could believe itself to be so, for it still dwelt in the afterglow of our heroic battles of the Second World War against a truly "evil empire," two young cultural anthropologists set out with their two very young children to find in the scarcely explored mountains of northern Spain — in the land of the Asturians — a village in which to undertake a year's research. But how, in the midst of that multitude of villages and tiny hamlets in those upper valleys would they recognize that village which had been destined for their work? They hit upon the stratagem of stopping in the plaza of each

This is a slightly revised version of the paper read at the conference "Fairy Tales and Society." I am grateful for comments by Alan Dundes and Ellen Feinberg. And for his careful and detailed work in La Torre (a pseudonym), we are indebted to Richard Detwiler. Ruth Bottigheimer provided perspicacious comment upon the manuscript. Support for this research was provided by the Spanish Northamerican Joint Committee.

village and releasing first — out of the tiny car in which they all were piled — their one-and-a-half-year-old: an enterprising infant who would unhesitatingly make off for whatever attracted his eye or ear. The villagers' response to this Trojan Toddler would be a sign of a predestined relationship. And in many villages indeed this one-and-a-half-year-old was smiled upon and patted. But in one village an old and gnarled man sitting upon his bench before his house was suddenly galvanized by this careening child, and rising and stepping forth quickly and with a preternatural smile, he swept the boy into his arms. All became immediately clear, and that was the village into which we settled to do our fieldwork and the village to which we have returned ever after.

That is the story we like to tell those who ask us — it is a frequent question to anthropologists — how we chose our research site. There *is* some truth to it. We did let our children wander a bit in every village we visited, and we noted the reaction to them. And there were significant differences between villages. But there was much more to our choice: village size, location, dialect, history, age composition, all went into it. Still, our final choice — and such things can rarely be finally calculated — did rest upon some surpassing sense of congeniality, some sense of where it would be best to do fieldwork and to raise our children for a time. The stories that men and women tell often say more about them and their commitments than do the strategies they must adopt in order, successfully, to do the work of this world.

The villagers we worked among told us stories — legends really — about themselves and about their villages that they thought important for us to know. They recounted these legends partly in response to the inundation of questions that we were addressing to them, and partly, I think, because they felt that there was something in them truer than the truth to be found in the statistics, maps, population graphs, genealogical tables, life histories, and health records we were accumulating. If we really wanted to know about them, we could find it in these legends.

In this paper I will discuss the legends told to us in three different villages in the mountains of south-central Asturias on the north coast of Spain. I will say something about why these legends were singled out, and I will say something about the challenge that the diversity and dialectic of local legends poses to any theory of local, regional, or national character. For several reasons I believe this to be an important question. First, in these recent democratic years Spain has moved toward federalism and toward regional autonomy. There has been a desire to assert regional identity over against the national identity celebrated (and often enough imposed) by the authoritarian centrist-nationalist regime of General Franco. And so Spain is in a period of renegotiating the identities of the whole and its parts.

The question of local, regional, and national identity that I raise here is, therefore, relevant there now as it would not have been in the Franco years. But there is a larger question for folklorists, and that is the question of the degree to which in our generalizations about the folklore of nations — French folklore, German folklore, Spanish folklore — we oversimplify the complexities of folklore dynamics, that is, the vast reservoir of motifs and tale-types which is rarely if ever neatly distributed by the national boundaries of recent centuries. The rising nationalisms of the nineteenth century made much use of folklore to typify and thus create new national identities around new national boundaries, but there is no reason for folklorists to be the acquiescent agents of such nationalisms.

"The Straw Dragon [Cuelébre] *of Escobines"*

Asturias among the Spanish provinces — this mountainous north-ernmost province overlooking the Cantabrian Sea is also its own region — was long regarded by the church as a redoubt for super-stitious beliefs. This is to be seen in the special attention paid to local superstitions in a succession of synodal documents throughout the centuries. An early fourteenth-century document issued by Alfonso XI for the conservation of the faith (1343) singled out Asturias and Andalucia as provinces where the residence of "sortilegos, maleficos, adivinos, encantadores, augures, aruspices, nigromanticos, geoman-ticos y otros magos" was to be suppressed. And indeed if we are to take Asturian folklore as evidence for this impious superstition — this alternate view of religious worlds and supernatural possibility to that presented by the church — there is indeed a resistant imagination in residence. The *cuelébre* — an Asturian and very rural and almost do-mestic version of the European dragon — is only one among many of the province's legendary creatures. There is the *nuberu*, a cloud and storm spirit, the *espumeru*, a spirit of the seaside and stormy coast, the *levandera*, a spirit of the riversides, waterfalls, and cascades, the *ven-tolín*, a spirit of the light breezes, moonbeams, and firesides, and the *xanas*, genies of the mountains and springs. And there are an abun-dance of mischievous troll-like creatures, *busqosu* and *trasqu*. Only the *quaya*, who feeds on the young, is truly malignant and vampirelike.

All these creatures correspond roughly to similar figures in European folklore, and one would have thought like so much of that lore, that such beliefs were principally the stuff of nostalgic recollection — not really believed in since the nineteenth century. But suddenly in the early 1960s the *cuelébre* made an appearance in Escobines. Early one misting evening, at the very end of the haying season, under an overcast sky brightened by a full moon Maria de la Puente ran down breathless from the upper meadows known as Fresneo. She had seen a *cuelébre* in the meadow next to her own. Like all *cuelébres*, its snake body had the head of an animal, a donkey, or was it a cow? Her story went rapidly round the village and much further as it turned out. Many credited Maria's vision to the effects of drink on an elderly widow who frequently comforted a lonely old age in this manner. But Victor the village butcher, who also had a meadow in the vicinity, allowed that he too had heard a strange hiss in the meadows that evening.

Over the years reports of *cuelébre* half serious and half jesting had been heard frequently enough in village life. But this report suddenly had a much greater echo. For one thing, a short item sent in by an upper valley correspondent of the provincial press was followed up by the visit of reporters and feature articles in the two main papers of the capital. Also, the Civil Guard made an appearance and a brief investigation. Was someone frightening people in the mountains? It was not so long before, in the early sixties, that the last of the Republican *refugiados* from the Civil War had either escaped abroad or been shot. And the Franco regime, after all, had risen to power in what it regarded as a glorious crusade against evil — an epic tale, that of the Civil War, that it never ceased recounting to Spaniards. Perhaps there was some real evil behind this credulous rural tale. Perhaps there *was* a real "snake in the mountains" — some lingering Republican refugee. The Great Story of the Civil War gave local authorities reason to give their own credence to the "incredible *cuelébre* of Escobines."

Many interpretations arose out of the event. There was the slightly tongue-in-cheek attitude of the provincial press, which was not much different from the attitudes of many villagers who were skeptical that there was anything more than drink there — and an elderly imagination. Luis de Carmina, a pragmatic soul, went up to the meadow the next day and observed that from a certain angle the remains from last year's hay stack had the look of a snake on its tail. The perennial summer visitor, Don Manuel, a man who loved the village for the "cunning innocence" and foxy credulity of the villagers and who had first called the provincial press, reflected that it was a tale told to a purpose. It was a dry summer that year and there was tension about water rights to one of the few irrigation channels in the upper meadows. The meadows owned by Maria and some of her relatives, such as the butcher, flourished because the irrigation channels ran naturally into them and water did not have to be diverted. Don Manuel offered a sophisticated explanation in which he saw society and social tensions symbolized in this supernatural creature. The *cuelébre* was a phantom projection by Maria and the butcher of the menacing resentments they felt in their fellow villagers. Was the hissing the butcher heard and attributed to the snake a surreptitious diversion of the water up channel by envious villagers?

These euhemeristic or Durkheimian attempts to account for the actual history of this apparition are clearly relevant to the political economy of village life. The apparition may well symbolize some of its deeper tensions. But the point I wish to make here is that the tale continued to be told by the villagers as a wry comment upon themselves and as a way of probing the stranger's view of them. For example, when I first heard this tale from Eladio, an old ribald bachelor, he watched me carefully, peering up under slightly hooded eyes to see what its effect would be. We tell tales to please ourselves but also to obtain some authentic reactions from others.

But he who most profited from this tale, it was increasingly elaborated over the years, was Antonio, the owner of the only village inn. Indeed, he more than others sedulously repeated and cultivated the tale. He had just finished installing new facilities, and he must have recognized that the story would be good for business, and it was. It attracted some weekend curiosity seekers, though nothing like the tourism of the seventies when the Upper Valley villages became weekend tourist meccas — escapes from the over industrialized, overcrowded, and smoggy cities of the coast. What Antonio was trying to exploit in urban and downriver Asturians was their continuing rural orientation: their readiness to celebrate and explore — even with tongue in cheek — both its virtues and its superstitions. The credulity of the people of Escobines was matched by the belief among the urban dwellers in the simplicity of country life. Indeed "The *Cuelébre* of Escobines" became more a tale told for the delectation of summer vacationers, urban dwellers, and other sophisticated strangers.

The village, in its foxy innocence, has known how to exploit such tales of its rustic credulity. Indeed, the *cuelébre* affair produced various poems in the Concejo in which an apparent gullibility is turned astutely against the outsider. Here is an example by Jose Campo of Moreda, the best-known poet of the concejo of Aller.[1]

Pachin y el Cuelébre

Toparonse nel mercau Manolin y la tia Angelines, y aquel, algo preocupau, preguntoi per un cunau que vivia en Escobines.	Finding each other in the market, Manolin and Aunt Angelines, The former, somewhat preoccupied, Inquired after a brother-in-law Who lived in Escobines.
La muyer, con cuidain de que nadie mas l'oyera, acercose a Manolin y a la oreya, muy suavin, susurroi d'esta manera:	The woman, very carefully That none should overhear her, Came close to Manolin And in his ear, very softly, Whispered in this manner:
— "Ay, como tien l'azotea Pachin el de la Caleya! Ta corrio per l'aldea de que'l to cunau chochea. Ta mas llocu au'na oveya!	— "Ay, how he suffers Pachin, he of the alleyway! It's the talk of the entire village Your brother-in-law's in his dotage. He is as foolish as a sheep!
Metiosei en la tarrena que hay un cuelébre co casa, xunto a la parva de leña; y el prubitin con el sueña les noches en vela pasa!	He's got it into his head That there's a *cuelébre* in the house, Close to the woodshed; And the poor fellow with such visions Suffers many sleepless nights!
Pa escapar del animal metese baxo la cama, y el probe, d'alli, non sal; tien que terminar muy mal si otra vida non entama."	To escape from that creature He crawls under the bed, And the wretch does not come out; It is going to end badly If he doesn't change his ways."
Marcharon home y muyer per diferent camin, al mes volvieronse a ver, y el home quiso saber algo a cerca de Pachin.	They departed man and woman By different roads, Meeting again a month later, And the man wished to know What had happened to Pachin.
Manolin oyo asutau lo que tia Rosa i conto — "Pero non tas enterau que paso co'l to cunau! Pues voy decitelo yo!	Manolin listened astonished To what Aunt Rosa told him — "But are you not informed Of what happened to your in-law! Well I'll tell it to you myself!
Con Pachin de la Caleya paso una cosa muy celebre. Non te dize yo a la oreya que 'staba com'una oveya? Pies, chachu, comiolu el cuelébre!"	With Pachin of the Caleya Something very celebrated occurred. Didn't I whisper into your ear That he'd become foolish as a sheep? Well, my dear, the *cuelébre* ate him!"

Miraculous Animal Helpers: "The Cows of the Hermitage" and "The Pig of Corralín"

The straw dragon of Escobines was an apparition which arose, at once, out of the reservoir of provincial folklore and the social and economic tensions prevalent in the village. The apparition was elaborated into several legends told in the village in several registers and from several points of view: as a rueful commentary on village identity, as a playful commentary on village credulity, as a test of strangers' attitudes and identities, and as a strategy to provide an image of the village attractive to visitors. In what way would it be relevant to our understanding to isolate a privileged telling of this story that should have precedence over all the others, and that should come to stand for the village version? The fact is there was a constant dialectic in which the elaborated versions of this apparition were in constant negotiation to various purposes.

It may be that there was a greater dialectic with respect to the *cuelébre* than with other lore for the reasons I have mentioned having to do with the transitional status of these mountain villages between a moral economy and a political one. It is true that there were two tales — legends really — told to us with greater piety and less diversity of register. We found these legends to be apt symbolizations of the central concerns of this agriculture community whose livelihood depends upon the providence of animals. But let us note here not so much the differences within villages as the differences between villages. The first of the two legends is told about the founding and construction of the village chapel called the Hermitage.

The Cows of the Hermitage

The chapel of the hermitage is very old. And the Virgin there we call her the Antigua. And it was built in this way. It happened that every morning as the herders passed on the way to the mountain meadows they saw where the chapel now stands a herd of beautiful, sleek cattle. But whose were they? They belonged to no one. Were they stray cattle from the herd of some senor? Then a herdsman had a dream, and San Anton, the patron of all herdsmen, came to him and told him to go gather in and sell the cows and found a hermitage chapel with the proceeds. And thus it was, and our chapel dedicated to the Virgin of the Antigua was founded. No one ever found out to whom those cattle belonged. It was a miracle.

The Pig of Corralín

There used to be a time, but our priest has done away with all that, when a herd of cows belonged to the church. And the church gave them out to the poor "a medias" — on half shares, letting them take half of the milk and half of the calves in return for taking care of the cows. There also was a pig that belonged to the church, and it went from house to house for its supper, and eventually it provided sausage for the poor. One night it snowed hard and an elderly couple in Corralín was expecting the pig. Theirs was an old house. Finally they went to bed. Not long after they heard a snuffling at the door. "Oh, leave the pig," said the husband, "let him wait until morning." But the wife got up and got her husband up to go out and feed the pig in the stable. And they were in the stable when the roof of the house, heavy with snow, fell in. It was a miracle that the house did not fall in upon them.

These legends deserve much commentary. They evoke a former time, during the old regime before the disentailment of church lands and properties, when the church maintained its own lands and animals and shared them out to the villagers. The piety and obeisance of these legends reflects the characteristic conservatism of cattle-keeping communities which for centuries were tied in to the hierarchical system of ecclesiastical and señorial patronage. And they also evoke the necessary dependence of husbandmen, ultimately, upon the providence of animals.

Because our studies in Asturias were comparative, we worked in several mountain villages. And because we were interested in the social and cultural consequences of the shifting from cattle-keeping to mining — a process that has been going on in these mountains over the last hundred years — these villages were chosen for different mixes of these two ways of life. In the two other villages in which we worked most intensely, La Torre and Rinconcon, villagers told us two very different legends about their villages — stories truer than true about themselves.

"The Old Stranger Denied" and "The Last Gasp of the Candle"

The two villages are differently situated on the continuum between cattle-keeping and mining. La Torre, whose legend we consider first, is deeper in a valley and closer to the mines than is Rinconcon. There is a much higher percentage of miners living there and much more pronounced social-political cleavages between Socialist and conservative factions. The Socialist movement, except for the suppression of the Franco years, has been active there since the teens. La Torre lies on the main route between the coastal cities and mountain passes. It takes great pride in its rustic beauty and in its appeal as a way station for the tourist and traveler. It prides itself, therefore, on its hospitality. The miners, because they have more leisure time than the cattle-keepers, have undertaken to beautify the town, and it has won many prizes for its attractiveness. This political and economic context explains some of the aptness of the legend in the minds of the villagers and the reason it gets frequently retold.

In the Great House (*casona*) of La Torre a verse is roughly carved in the stone lintel over one of the windows facing the street.

Dará posada a los pobres	He will give shelter to the poor
Quien habitara esta casa	Whoever lives in this house
Y no la ocupe ni herede	Neither occupying nor inheriting it
El que no quiere darle.	He who refuses to give it.

The legend concerns the origin of this inscription and the loss of the Great House's coat of arms, which belonged to a hidalgo of the town, granted to his family by the king for services rendered in the war against the Moors.

Dará Posada a los Pobres (You will give restful lodging to the poor)

The Hidalgo Don Juan was owner not only of this great house but also of much land around. One fierce winter night he heard a knock at the door. Opening the window, he looked out and shut it quickly again upon a ragged old man seeking shelter in the name of the Saviour and "por amor de Dios." Later in the winter on a hunting trip in the high mountains, this hidalgo lost sight of his companions and soon found himself wandering in high winds and driving snow. Freezing slowly, he found himself at a village but, knocking at every door, he received no response. Wandering on and close to collapse, he called upon the name of the Saviour. At once the Old Man whom he had refused appeared before him and asked what right he had to appeal to the Saviour when he himself had refused lodging to another who had so appealed. The Old Man then showed his nail-pierced palms. Fainting in the snow, the hidalgo woke to find himself in the church close to his village, lying under the statue of the Saviour. In a few days the villagers were surprised to see the Noble Coat of Arms chiseled away from over the window and that the verse "Dará posada a los pobres" had been carved there instead.

No more than in Escobines must we imagine that this legend was told in the same register by all villagers. Indeed, there was an interesting dialectic between the miners and the conservative cattle-keepers. The miners, when they did not mock the legend, told it emphasizing the tightfisted character of the gentry and the identity of the poor with the Saviour, while the cattle-keepers emphasized the noblesse oblige in the story, the religious and miraculous elements, and the general piety for the teachings of Mother Church to be learned from it. For both constituencies, proud of their village and its hospitable reputation, the legend is satisfying.

The legend we heard in Rinconcon is known to all the villagers and, more than these other legends, to other villages as well. When we had come back from our first visit to Rinconcon, we were asked by our friends in Escobines: Did they tell you the story of the "Last Gasp of the Candle"? And indeed they had. This legend has been elaborated around a historical fact — the purchase back (*redención*) of their lands in the late sixteenth century from the senorial administration of the Knights of Santiago. The legend involves some of the choicest lands of Rinconcon, an *encomienda* belonging to the knights since the late twelfth century.

The Last Gasp of the Candle

When news came to the pueblo of Escobines that the Knights of Santiago wished to alienate their *encomiendas*, the villagers rang the church bells, entered into ingenious speculation, gathered together their savings, and named a commission of three men to attend the auction. They knew that they would be faced with wealthy *Señores* who would be seeking to buy the *encomiendas* from the Knights of Santiago. The bidding would take place while a tallow candle burned. The last flicker of the candle would be the signal of the final bid. The commission bided its time, and indeed, few bids were made, so convinced was everyone that the rich landholder, Don Pedro Solís de Oviedo, would carry the day, for he could not be outbid. So there was little competitive surging in the bidding. Don Pedro made only a show of raising his original bid a fraction as the candle burned down to its final flicker. All seemed lost to a village that so desired its independence. The judge accepted the final bid of Don Pedro. But then as the three villagers, knowing the ways of candles, had anticipated, there was a vague glimmer and the candle flared up one final time. A flash of light and a moment of opportunity and one of the commission members shouted out, "10,000 *maravedís*," topping Don Pedro's bid with just the amount of the village's savings. Neither the judge-auctioneer nor Solís would accept this final bid, so it was taken to judgment in Valladolid at the king's court and there it was admitted. And thus the village freed itself from Señorial rule.

This story, like the others we have considered, is told in several versions in the village. In some Don Pedro is a pronouncedly evil character and in others a dupe. As we have come to expect when, as folklorists, we compare versions of any tale, we find genius in some tellers and not in others. Some add more convincing corroborative detail. Some create more suspense about the bidding. Some give us more apt imagery. But much more than in the legend "The Old

Stranger Denied," there is a commonly accepted version of "The Last Gasp of the Candle." It does not provoke different versions from progressive and conservative factions. It is a legend, therefore, more typical of a town. Still, we cannot easily generalize from the town's consensus about one legend to the entire municipality, or to an entire valley and, much less, to an entire province.

Tell Us a Story of Spanish Folklore: The Problem of Provincial and National Identity

This brief account of these legends of three villages provides the background for the dilemma I face when I am asked, as anthropologists often are, to say something in general about the Asturian character or the Spanish character as seen in folklore. It is tempting to respond to such a question: What kind of a story do you want me to tell or do you want to hear? For, from the perspective of participant observation in village life (and this may contrast, to be sure, with the perspective of those who are dealing with collections already made), one is most aware of abundant lively argument. There is a dialectic of legends both within villages and between villages. It is not so different really, though perhaps not as sophisticated and informed, from the abundant lively argument going on in folklore about, for example, whose voices we should be hearing in "Little Red Riding Hood" or about whose voice is really evoked in the spinning of a tale, the weaving of a legend.

In these mountain villages what choices could I make for purposes of generalization amidst that abundant argument that would not magnify some villages and villagers and slight others? Whose *cuelébre* do we choose — the butcher's *cuelébre*, or Eladio's *cuelébre*, or Antonio's *cuelébre?* Do we want Escobines' "The Pig of Corralín," or Rinconcon's "The Last Gasp of the Candle," or La Torre's "The Old Stranger Denied." Can I really talk about *the* Asturian character, as seen in folklore, when Escobines emphasizes piety and a rather playful and canny innocence in their legend, when La Torre emphasizes noblesse oblige and hospitality, when Rinconcon emphasizes their legendary cleverness, and when even these generalizations about villages are perturbed by the lively argument in each village about the import and the veracity of their characteristic legends? The argument of lore is the thing we want to grasp and illuminate if we can, not some abstraction from it that might give us some illusory assurance that, somehow, despite all the complexity and the dialectic, we have gotten at *the* character of the people.

But surely, an interlocutor might reply, one must be prepared to make some generalizations. That is what science is all about, the source of its power. "Of course," I might reply, "and perhaps usefully so. But let me tell you why I worry about doing so in this instance." It not only has to do with the difficulty of generalizing about this abundant argument of lore going on within and between villages. It also has to do with that "storytelling" that anthropologists, whose principal interest it is, call ethnocentrism. Ethnocentrism is that ancient tribal impulse much exacerbated in the modern era by nationalism that exalts the state and the nation-state. I worry that I could not make a selection that would be perfectly objective and would seek neither to exalt nor somehow to debase either Asturian identity or Spanish identity, and that would not itself somehow be ethnocentric in a laudatory or derogatory sense. One always worries in the social sciences about any generalization lest it contain an invidious seed of comparison and somehow exalt or debase those who are included and excluded. One worries even more when these generalizations concern national character, about which it has been argued that every generalization inescapably contains "the seed of detestation."[2]

We know ourselves from the Nazi era and Ernst Cassirer's richly informed discussion *The Myth of the State* how some of the elements of German folklore were taken to exalt German identity and to ultimately animate dark and barbarous deeds. And though only in passing I have mentioned another authoritarian national socialism, the Franco one, which used folklore and made legendary claims in order to exalt its crusading mission, I worry that when we generalize about folklore in relation to such geo-political categories as Asturias or Spain (or France or Germany),[3] we are required, even with the best will in the world, to make arbitrary selections that are somehow ethnocentric in either a positive or a negative sense. One of the forces in the nineteenth century that acted to promote folklore studies was the rise of nationalism. Should we not be wary lest we find ourselves inadvertently in its service? It seems likely that nationalism is only a passing though a rather dangerous phase in our evolution toward world order.

Many of the legends told in Asturias are very like those told elsewhere in Europe, if not in the Indo-European tradition, for motifs and tale types are supranational and the folklore reservoir is very large — pan-human and multivocal. In my view what folklore testifies to in all its abundant argument is a widespread human quest for identity amidst the contrarieties and the inchoate quality of our human condition. Folklore as folklorists know it and should teach it should be an antidote for the infectious enthusiasm of nationalism and not a sustenance to it. The material of folklore long antedates the creation of national frontiers and the cultural attempts to justify them.

Inevitably a part of that quest for identity that folklore embodies is the present national and ethnic quest for identity. It is a quest that is always at risk of denying as much as it affirms. Of course we must study the folklore of ethnic and national identity whether this be the *Nibelungenlied* turned to millenarian militarism or ethnic jokes.[4] These are grist for our mill. But we need not acquiesce in this geopolitical ethnocentrism, much less pretend that there are easy generalizations to be made about national lore. We may end up by telling a bad ethnic joke in the guise of scientific generalization.

What was so gratifying about the conference in which this paper first appeared was the way we allowed the folktale to work upon us, the way we worked with the folktale, as the psychiatrist participating in our debate, Dr. Simon Grolnick, urged that we do, for psychological and philosophical insight. We were not, even inadvertently, seeking geopolitical exaltation or debasement. My view as an anthropologist is that there is no folklore from anywhere in the world whose nontendentious study will not carry us far into such humanistic illumination. I regret that the farthest we could carry you in this adventure in the wisdom of other cultures — my wife and I and our two small children in our tiny car — was to those not-so-distant mountain villages of northern Spain.

Notes

1. Jose Campo, *Per les caleyes de Aller* (Moreda, 1968).

2. The Argentine-Spanish publisher and essayist Mario Muchnik argues that any generalization on national or group character contains "una semilla de odio." This appears in a column in which he seeks to point out and correct the stereotypes in a report on Israel by a Spanish correspondent of the Madrid daily, *El País* (26 July 1984).

3. I have in mind here the too acquiescent generalizations about French and German folklore by Robert Darnton ("The Meaning of Mother Goose," 1984) and Alan Dundes (*Life Is Like a Chicken Coop Ladder*, 1984): the former in an otherwise valuable article — an historian's corrective of the too easy psychoanalytic interpretation of folklore — on the peasant world expressed in folktales; and the latter in an otherwise engrossing and in the end cathartic study of the cloacal in German culture. Dundes's monograph is instructive to us all, not just to Germans, about the sleazy underside of compulsive cleanliness and the terrible social suffering it can produce. For the methodological difficulties involved in either defining a nation as a unit of study or in defining the criteria for studying its character in any objective way, see Daniel Bell, "National Character Revisited" (1980).

4. See my "Folklore as an Agent of Nationalism," *Bulletin of the African Studies Association* 5, no. 2 (May 1962): 3–7.

Bibliography

Bell, Daniel. "National Character Revisited: A Proposal for Re-negotiating the Concept." In *The Winding Passage: Essays from a Sociological Journey*, pp. 167–83. Cambridge, Mass.: ABT Books, 1980.

Campo, Jose. *Per les Caleyes de Aller*. Moreda, 1968.

Darnton, Robert. "The Meaning of Mother Goose." *The New York Review of Books* (2 February 1984), pp. 41–47.

Dundes, Alan. *Life Is Like a Chicken Coop Ladder: A Portrait of German Culture Through Folklore*. New York: Columbia University Press, 1984.

Part Three

FAIRY TALE RESEARCH TODAY

8. Gender-Related Biases in the Type and Motif Indexes of Aarne and Thompson

TORBORG LUNDELL

Folktales, a term usually embracing fairy tales such as the Grimm tales as well as traditional prose narrative handed down over the years, are largely known through popular editions with a narrow view of women aimed to fit ideals promoted by nineteenth-century patriarchal sensibilities. A reader of unabridged collections of folktales, and fairy tales, soon realizes, however, that the model for female conduct reflected in such tales over a wide geographical area is far from confined to the submissive beauty of popular selections and Walt Disney's dramatizations. Furthermore, a folktale scholar soon finds that a similar tendency to present an image of a passive and subordinate heroine exists in such scholarly research tools long considered fundamental as Antti Aarne and Stith Thompson's *The Types of the Folktale* and Thompson's *Motif Index of Folk Literature.*[1] Admittedly, the Indexes were first published in the early thirties and revised in the mid-fifties, and thus conceived and written before the rise of feminist consciousness in the sixties. However, the feminist movement of the sixties was not the first in history, and therefore one might at least have hoped that scholars of the calibre of Aarne and Thompson would have been aware of the possibility that folklore may reflect

This article is an expanded and revised version of "Folktale Heroines and the Type and Motif Indexes," *Folklore* 94(1983): 240–246.

ideals of female independence and strength. It should also be pointed out that though folklorists may know of the limitations of the Indexes, potential researchers from fields outside folklore may regard these works as definitive, not realizing their particular weakness in terms of gender attributions. This makes them less accurate as reference works and warrants an investigation of what more precisely constitutes their flaws.

Stith Thompson states in his introduction to the revised Motif Index that he has:

made the index very inclusive of various kinds of motifs. Sometimes the interest of a student of traditional narrative may be centered on a certain type of character in a tale, sometimes on action, sometimes on attendant circumstances of the action. Hence I have endeavoured to use all the elements of tales that have in the past been objects of special study and similar elements that are likely to serve as such objects in the future.[2]

Instead of being "inclusive," however, the Motif Index tends to promote a patriarchal view of the characters and their interactions, especially as they affect female characters. The Motif Index in general (1) overlooks gender identity in its labeling of motifs, thus lumping male and female actions or characters under the same, male-identified, heading or (2) disregards female activity or (3) focuses on male activity at the cost of female. This is true also of the Aarne and Thompson Type Index, although Thompson asserts that "it has thus far proven practicable as far as European peoples are concerned."[3]

Today we may find it less practicable. When Richard M. Dorson in *Folktales Told Around the World* (1975) suggests that one of the Micronesian tales "needs a special motif or perhaps even a type number," he seems to base his need on the fact that the tale features a woman in a traditionally male situation: "for over and over again a woman is exiled or cast away and through her son returns victorious."[4] Indeed the motif L111.1, "Exile returns and succeeds," with its lack of gender specification would not properly identify either the "type of character" or "circumstances of the action," to follow Thompson's guidelines. Three important items are missing from motif L111.1 in terms of its applicability to the Micronesian tale: (1) the sex of the exiled person, (2) the fact that she gets help, and (3) the identity of the helper. To fit in the context we would need a motif to read "Woman (or female) exile returns and succeeds with help of son."

Similar lack of clarity regarding the dramatis personae of tales characterizes also the motifs (and types) when they are applied to European material. It is then not necessarily the introduction of material from other cultures which might necessitate, as Thompson predicted, addition of types of tales.[5] (We recall that he considered his Motif Index to be "very inclusive of various kinds of motifs.") In addition, a change in cultural consciousness gives rise to a need for adding new types of motifs or rephrasing existing ones, especially those dealing with female activity. This does not mean replacing male-focused bias with female-focused bias, for naturally an index should be as free of bias as possible. It requires instead a thorough examination of existing type and motif identifications to question the way in which they have been selected and labeled. What is at stake is the theoretical validity of a trusted research tool.

This is not to say that Thompson consistently ignores heroines and other female characters. Numerous motifs referring to "girl," "princess," "wife," and "woman" certainly testify to his awareness of the presence and acts of female characters. It should, however, be pointed out that a large number of these motifs (and tales) are set in the passive mode with the girl being acted upon, thus promoting or supporting a socially supported tendency to regard the female as passive rather than active. More specifically, female characters are misrepresented in the following ways: (1) by being presented as passive and subordinate rather than active, and (2) by having different value systems applied to male and female activity. These categories will be discussed below. Female characters are also mistreated (3) by having to share type or motif number with a title referring to male characters, even if the action involves females. For example, there are only types 1115–1129, "Attempts to murder the hero." No number is used for attempts to murder the heroine as happens in Grimms' tale "Dearest Roland." The only motif we can use here is type 1119, "The ogre kills his own children: Places change in bed." We seem in other words to be led to believe either that heroines are not murdered or that "hero" is to be understood generically to embrace heroines as well, analogous to the language convention that dictates that "man" for "mankind" includes women. This would make the heroine linguistically invisible. Furthermore, female characters are (4) victimized by the general semantic-syntactic inconsistency throughout the index which sometimes identifies items with complete sentences in active form, sometimes with phrases in the passive, and sometimes with short emphatic phrases (this affects male characters as well).

We get, for example, the following motifs: K953, "Murder by squeezing"; K953.1, "Murder by lacing corset"; K953.2, "Murder by wrapping snake around man"; K953.4, "Murder by crushing in false embrace"; and K955, "Murder by burning"; there is no indication of the gender or social identity of the murderer and his/her victim. Such identification is not unimportant. We glean from the context that K953.1 probably involves at least one female character and K953.2

probably at least one male character, but we would gain needed clarity and sophistication of analysis if the persons involved were more clearly delineated. Also, it seems that once various ways of squeezing are introduced, it would be desirable to have a motif number to cover the circumstances in the Bulgarian tale "An Unborn Maiden" where a gypsy woman attacks the maiden and squeezes her throat until she chokes.[6]

Passive constructions abound. While they appear to project generalizations and objective statements, their effect is vitiated by their silence regarding the active person. Often circumstances surrounding the action are left out as well. For example, in type 326, "The youth who wanted to learn what fear is," the summary reads "III. *Learning. Fear.* After his wedding he learns fear when cold water is thrown on him or eels are put down his back while he is asleep." In Grimms' tale it is, for example, his wife who throws cold water on him.[7] This is not unimportant because it would be quite another tale if, for example, his father-in-law or brother had done it. The same objection applies to motif H1441, "Fearless hero frightened by being awakened with cold water." Here the wedding context is also left out, thus further obscuring the significant aspects of the motif, an important "circumstance of the action" to recall Thompson's guidelines. In K2116.1.1, "Innocent woman accused of killing her newborn children," and K2116.1.1.1, "Innocent woman accused of eating her newborn children," the accuser is not identified. It is usually the stepmother or mother-in-law or occasionally sisters, which again is very different from it being, for example, the husband. As in motif H1441, the family dynamics in these motifs are significant and should be identified because they do vary.

Just as some characters are not represented, others, especially female characters, are misrepresented to fit into a patriarchal stereotypical pattern of female behavior and qualities.

The misrepresentation of character in the two Indexes can be divided into different categories of bias, each with the same two dimensions: (1) external, that is, in reference to heroines or other female characters as they appear in specific tales, and (2) internal, that is, inconsistency in semantics of the Indexes regarding identical events, depending on whether they refer to female or male character, and incongruity between title and plot synopsis disfavoring the female. In some instances these dimensions overlap. The largest category is characterized by selective labeling in which the female activities are made to seem less active or heroic than they in fact are.

A typical example of selective labeling concerns the concept of "helper" in the folktale world. To "help" carries with it a connotation of assistance rather than leadership. Both heroines and heroes in the folktales need and receive help to complete their tasks and overcome obstacles. They meet helpers in the form of animals, old women and men, magic objects, and supernatural creatures who, for example, spin and weave, sift peas from the ashes, carry the protagonist from one place to another, or give good advice. Helpers are supportive, their power is limited, and they do not demonstrate a broader view of the situation.

According to the Aarne and Thompson Type Index, the heroine of the Norwegian tale "Mestermø,"[8] for example, would be classified as belonging to this useful but limited group of tools for the hero. In English translation she turns to "Mastermaid," a literal translation with implications of a subordinate role which does not exist in the original, whose connotation is "a girl who is the master." But the title of this type, "The girl as helper in the hero's flight" (type 313), hardly does justice to the girl in "Mastermaid."

Incidentally, we may ask what constitutes a hero (or heroine). The Type Index sees the boy of this tale as the hero and he is, in the sense that the tale initially focuses on him. However, the girl may be claimed as heroine considering the fact that she carries most of the action in the major portion of the tale. Obviously we are here dealing with a tale featuring two major protagonists, a hero and a heroine, who should be given equal billing in the Type Index. We could, for example title the tale "Hero frees heroine, enabling them to escape from troll." As we learn from the following paraphrase focusing on the girl's activities in the tale, she certainly is a far more independent character than the type title indicates.

Imprisoned by a troll, Mastermaid sits in a room which the hero has been forbidden to enter. He does, of course, open the door, but that is the end of his initiative. As soon as he has opened the door to her room, she takes over the action. She tells him how to perform his tasks and she keeps track of the time when they are together so they will not be surprised by the returning troll. She organizes their escape, collects a few valuable objects, engineers a device which will delay the troll's pursuit, and takes off with the prince. She directs the defense strategy as the troll approaches and brings them safely out of his reach. Then the prince, passive during this whole episode, insists on going home. When he gets there he eats an apple, against the heroine's advice, and forgets her. She must now make more plans to prevent him from marrying an impostor, because he cannot see the difference between a troll hag and his true bride.

It seems, then, that rather than acting as a "helper," with its connotation of subordinate assistant, Mastermaid has demonstrated independence, superior knowledge of the mechanisms of society, skills in magic, and leadership qualities. On the other hand, we learn that the prince could not have performed the tasks with his own power; nor could he have been able to escape the troll without subordinating himself to the girl's preparations, insights, and skills. He appears weak and unable to protect himself against scheming females, and Mastermaid must rescue him a second time from a troll. If there is any help involved in this tale, it is the boy helping the heroine to unleash her powers (by opening the door).

Among the motifs in type 313 we find type D672, "Obstacle flight: Fugitives throw objects behind them which magically become obstacles in the pursuer's path." Here, too, female activity is disregarded or hidden in a language which by convention perceives "male" when "female" is not specified by form or context. While the male character may do the actual throwing as he does in "Mastermaid," and the Scottish "The Prince and the Giant's Daughter,"[9] the female character provides him with the magic objects to throw. She may have to do both as in the Russian "Baba Yaga."[10] Similarly, in a tale from Peru, "The Condemned Lover"[11] the heroine both runs away and throws the magic objects (provided by the Virgin Mary). We note also in this context that motif D671, "Transformation flight: Fugitives transform themselves in order to escape detection by pursuer," implies that the fugitives are both (or all) skilled in magic, while in fact it usually is the girl who does the transformation of both herself and her lover. This happens in, for example, the Russian "The Sea King and Vasilissa"[12] and Grimms' "Dearest Roland."[13] This type often features motif H151.1, "Attention drawn by magic objects, recognition follows," which in its wording hides the fact that the girl possesses the magic objects with which she in the end attracts the attention of her forgetful lover.

Selective labeling also operates in the indexing of the widespread tales of the Amor-and-Psyche type in which the heroine also must undergo a series of ordeals and prove her intelligence and resourcefulness before she recovers her lost husband. In a Swedish example of this type, "Prince Hatt under the Earth,"[14] the heroine also becomes responsible for the welfare of the whole family as she guides her blind husband and their small children through the forest to place them with his sisters. When he disappears, she must, like all heroines of this tale type, undertake a long journey and undergo a number of trials before their reunion. The semantics of the Type Index, however, fail to recognize this adventurous aspect of the heroine's activities. This type is called "The search for the lost husband" (type 425), while the male equivalent is entitled "The man on a quest for his lost wife" (type 400). One gets the impression that a woman *searches*, as for a lost sock, while a man sets off on a *quest*. In the Motif Index practically all female pursuits are identified as "Search" and male pursuits as "Quest." Occasional crossovers in this gender-divided semantics such as motif H1385.4, "Quest for vanished husband," and H1381.5, "Hero seeks his equal," do not obliterate the impression that male and female pursuits are looked upon with different value systems. Further, "Search" is also used with children.

The naming of the type of tales to which the Norwegian "The Finn King's Daughter"[15] belongs provides another way of ignoring a heroine's more adventurous qualities. The king fears his daughter will marry the serving boy, so he puts her in an earthen cave before he goes to war. When he has not returned after several years, the princess digs herself out with her bare hands. Not knowing where she is, she spends a night with some charcoal makers, crosses a river on the back of a wolf, and, freezing and starving, roams about the forest. Finally she arrives at the castle, where no one recognizes her, and takes a job in the kitchen. She learns that the prince is about to marry a troll hag. Having displayed strength and courage in the wilderness, she must now demonstrate superior skill in domestic work and create poetry to rescue the prince from the false bride.

Furthermore, she must deal independently with the psychologically disconcerting situation of not being recognized, a form of rejection, and she must establish her superiority from an inferior position in society. Consistent with the Aarne and Thompson downplay of female activity, this folktale type, with its aggressive and capable female protagonist, has been labeled "The princess confined in the mound" (type 870), which implies a passivity hardly representative of the thrust of the tale. "The princess escaping from mound" would fit better. Thompson also neglects the heroine's methods of escape in his Motif Index which lists the motif "Captivity in mound (cave, hollow, hill)" (R45) but has no listing for her various ways of getting out of the mound under the R200 motifs covering "Escapes and pursuits." Nor does Thompson assign a motif number to the heroine's forest experiences under "Test of endurance and power of survival" (H1500–1549), though this is precisely what is tested in this episode.

The heroine's independence and capacity to make decisions about her own life is also disregarded in the motifs referring to a princess who marries a man who has been able to guess her riddles or make her speechless. In some of these tales her father declares that he who can beat the princess in her own game will get to marry her, but in other tales she herself sets the condition for marriage. For example, the Swedish tale "Lögnbrackan" (The liar guy)[16] begins: "Once upon a time there was a princess who had made up her mind to take for a husband none but a man who could lie so well that she would get angry and then say it was a lie." Grimms' "The Riddle"[17] talks about a "beautiful but arrogant princess who had let it be known that she would marry the man who gave her a riddle she couldn't solve." The Russian tale "The Princess Who Wanted to Solve Riddles" likewise features a princess determined to mind her own affairs: "She said to her father: Permit me to solve riddles, father. If I solve a man's riddle let his head be cut off; but him whose riddle I cannot solve, I will marry." But Thompson assigned no motif number for this contingency, though he did include the Russian tale in his *One Hundred Favorite Folktales*.[18] There is only the motif H551, "Princess offered to man who can out-riddle her," and none to cover the fact that in many tales the princess offers herself.

Furthermore, in the Motif Index, marriages resulting from winning games of intelligence and wit are labeled differently depending on whether a woman or a man is the subject. While motif H551 reads, "Princess offered to man who can out-riddle her," a similar situation applied to a man is called "Man marries girl who guesses his riddles" (H552). Even though motif T68, "Princess offered as prize," is semantically matched with motif T67, "Prince offered as prize," the subcategories slant each motif differently. The index sustains the notion of the princess as passive object but labels the prince less passive. In fact, even under the main motif of T67, the heroine instead of the prince is sometimes labeled as the implied passive partner, as seen in T67.1, "Marriage to prince as reward for disenchanting him," and T67.2, "Marriage to prince as reward for curing him," instead of, for example "Prince offered as reward. . . ." The motifs referring to the heroine avoid ambiguity. Motif 68.1 is called "Princess offered as prize to rescuer," and T68.2, "Earl's daughter as reward to knight who helped kill fierce buffalo," and T68.3, "Princess as prize to man who saves his country."

Different standards for evaluating behavior of women and men are also revealed in the labeling. We find, for example, a motif T55, "Girl as wooer: Forthputting [pushy] woman," but no motif number for a "forthputting" man. Judging from the Motif Index, adulterous women, especially deceptive women, outnumber men in this type of literature. The motifs K1500–1599, "Deception connected with adultery," covers only wives who are consistently called "adulteress" with an occasional motif referring to a wife's "paramour." Husbands appear to be models of fidelity. The General Index lists references to "adulterer" on little more than two lines while references to "adulteress" span twenty-three lines. A closer look at the Motif Index reveals, however, that selective semantics also in this context have been used to convey different images of men and women. Thompson simply tends to give men who commit adultery a less shameful label. We get, for example, K1271.3.1, "Wife surprises husband in adultery and shames him into giving her all she desires," instead of "Adulterer surprised by wife who shames him into giving her all she desires," which would be consistent with the language used for wives in identical situations. It is also tempting to suspect that husbands are favorably treated in the motif complex K2210, "Treacherous relatives," which covers all immediate family members: wife, brother, sister, daughter, son, and in-laws, plus uncle and nephew, but does not mention husbands. Whether this omission is due to Thompson's unconscious reluctance to acknowledge the existence of treacherous husbands or to the fact that there exist indeed no treacherous husbands in folk literature, the absence of such husbands in the Motif Index provides yet another example of the underlying patriarchal value system governing the literature and indexes.

Titling convention detrimental to the heroine appears in a comparison of type 884B, "The girl as soldier," with type 514^{++}, "The court physician." Both types refer to tales in which the heroine performs admirably in a male profession and each deserves to be identified in the title.

Misleading labeling occurs in some types where the male instead of the female receives credit in the title. In AT 312A, "The brother rescues his sister from the tiger," two of the three listed variants credit the girl herself with her rescue, either by killing the tiger or by escaping. Still, only the brother's deed is reflected in the title. In type 300^+ the incongruity between title and summary favors the male: "The boy rescues the princess through her magic power: She changes herself into a golden bird." We find a similar incongruity in type 329, "Hiding from the devil." Here, a plot summary reads: "The task. (a) A princess (devil) assigns her suitors the task of hiding themselves. (b) She has magic windows. . . ." In fact, this summary outlines a tale that should be called "Hiding from the princess."

The wording of type 881A, "The abandoned bride disguised as man," suggests that the heroine is more vulnerable than she actually is; the summary offers a contrasting view: "A prince and his bride are separated in a forest. (1) She escaped from would-be seducers by shooting an arrow. . . ." She seems quite capable of fending for herself just as the heroine of type 519, "The strong woman as bride (Brynhilde)." Strong women, however, rarely receive their full due, as we have noted previously. For this type, the plot summary tells: "(1) The Suitor. A prince with his extraordinary companions woos a bride who is beautiful, strong and warlike and who will have as husband no man who is not her equal in strength." The motif for this context listed with the type index includes H345, "Suitor test: Overcoming princess in strength."

Plot summaries may reveal other types of bias: the index often ignores or deemphasizes strong or independent qualities of female characters. Although one cannot object to the title in the Type Index for tales concerning a quick-tongued princess: "The hero catches the princess with her own words" (type 853), because this he does, one can question the image of the princess conveyed in the plot summary. It reads: "The contest: A princess is offered in marriage to the youth who outwits her in repartee." This insistence on the princess as a medium of exchange disregards her active role, paralleling a similar thrust in the Motif Index. The third item of this plot summary (confusingly also called "The contest") reads: "By producing these objects at the proper time he brings all the princess' words to scorn (often obscene)." First, the ambiguity in the reference to the obscene language does not make clear that the speaker of obscenities is the princess, which gives her an earthy quality and distances her from the idealized character usually connoted by "princess." Second, this description does not convey the fact that the heroine challenges the hero's masculinity by testing his ability to handle a sexually aggressive woman.

Although in many versions of the tale this is toned down or euphemistically obscured, a wonderful Swedish version[19] exemplifies how the hero is tested in this respect. First the hero is dumbfounded by the princess's beauty and manages only an unimaginative start of the conversation as have the other suitors; but soon he regains his composure:

"It's dreadfully warm in here," said he.

"Ha, ha," laughed the princess, "it's much warmer in my behind."

"Is that so," said the boy, "then maybe I can fry this magpie there and get something to eat before my head is cut off."

And he brought forth his dead magpie and showed it to the princess. The princess was quiet and almost at a loss for a reply, but then she pulled herself together:

"Sure you can," she said, "but I don't think you can get it in there."

"Well, well," said the boy, "I can manage if I use this wooden wedge."

And so he brought forth the old wedge he had found on the road and showed it to the princess.

Then she was embarrassed and hardly knew what to say but at last she said:

"Then my little behind will crack."

"Oh no," said the boy, "if that's the only problem I know what to do. I'll just put this thing around your behind. It'll keep it from cracking."

And he pulled out the old fence-clamp he'd found on the road. One more round and the princess has to admit that she has found her man.

Just as the summary for this plot glosses over the heroine's sexuality, so does the summary to type 875, "The clever peasant girl," ignore the fact that a husband has to yield to his wife's intelligence. The conclusion of the type description states that the king is moved "to forgive her," yet the plot clearly indicates that rather than "forgiving" her, he is accepting her.

Using a nondescript, passive structure to describe the heroine's activities provides another way to deprive her of credit for her acts. The short plot synopsis of type 327A, "Hansel and Gretel," does not mention that it is the girl who pushes the witch into the oven, but says only: "The witch thrown into the oven." Yet, many women best remember Gretel from the better-known Grimms' tale precisely because of her aggressive act.[20]

Another way in which the heroine is short-changed in the Type Index is demonstrated in choice of focus. A Danish tale, "The Green Knight,"[21] reveals this type of bias: The king puts his daughter on an island to protect her from a scheming stepmother. The unhappy princess longs for the Green Knight, her name for death. But when the king returns from a journey he gives her a book from the Green Knight, who turns out to be a handsome prince. The princess's father cannot read the book himself, but she has no difficulty in doing so and her reading brings the prince to her. He arrives in the form of a bird and then turns into a man. After her jealous stepmother discovers them, he is wounded by a pair of scissors she has strategically placed, and he becomes sick, unable to return. The princess, too, weakens, but she learns from two ravens how to cure the prince. In spite of her weakness, she rolls away a heavy stone, escapes, and walks for weeks over high mountains and dense forests until she reaches his castle, where she takes service in the kitchen and prepares a healing soup. The Type Index credits her with none of her accomplishments: her ability to read a language her father does not know, her physical prowess, or her medical knowledge. In fact, she sinks from sight in the classification of this tale "The prince as bird" (type 432). It could have been called, for example, "Princess redeems prince as bird," to better reflect the thrust of the tale.

Type 433B, "King Lindorm," adequately describes some of the tales of this type but neither the title nor the plot synopsis gives justice to the events in a Swedish version. The Type Index tells the following story: "King Lindorm. A childless queen bears a boy who stays in serpent form. When he grows up he demands a wife and his father finds a maiden who is willing. (In some versions he devours the bride and only after several have tried does the bride survive.) She (or her father) disenchants him by bathing or burning his serpent skin while he is transformed." In the Swedish tale chosen by Thompson for his *One Hundred Favorite Folktales,*[22] however, we find another story. In this tale a woodcutter's youngest daughter goes into the forest to get her father's coat. She meets a snake and accepts his offer to ride out into the world on him, and finally she disenchants him by chopping off his head. In this version the girl is the main character, but there is no way of identifying this version though it differs radically from the tale used as norm in the index. It could, for example, be labeled "Girl disenchants serpent prince."

Another way of downplaying the heroine involves naming the tale type after an object rather than after her. For instance, the plot summary of type 434, "The stolen mirror," tucks away another active heroine: "The princess as doctor cures the lovesick prince . . ." (who has stolen her mirror and picture and is pining away from love until she finds him and cures him). Type 545A is called "The cat castle," but to be applicable to a Swedish tale it should be called "Girl wins prince with help of cat," considering the fact that the castle appears only at the end of the tale, while the girl's way of winning the prince includes a number of listable features.[23]

There is also a tendency to overlook activities of cruel mother figures, not surprisingly, because active and strong women as well as cruel mothers both offer aspects of womanhood heartily disapproved of by a patriarchal consciousness. Motifs for "Cruel mother" (S12) and "Cruel stepmother" (S31) exist, but only the stepmother gets the blame in the plot summary to type 720, "My mother slew me, my father ate me: The juniper tree." Although this covers the better-known Grimm version, it does not adequately represent the Scottish tale "The Milk-White Doe."[24] The cruelty of stepmothers and other mother figures is, on the other hand, ignored or obscured in references to birth episodes. She is, for example, left out in K2116.1.1.1, "Innocent woman accused of eating her newborn children." The accuser is frequently the stepmother (who also took away the baby),[25] occasionally the mother-in-law[26] or more seldom (step)sisters.[27] Although a negative mother figure often assists at the heroine's birth, only the motif T584.03, "Childbirth assisted by angel," records this, and no motif exists for the negative mother figure's far-from-angelic assistance. Another missing event related to birth involves the husband. Although motif T583.1.0.1, "Husband goes into seclusion at wife's pregnancy," exists, none lists his going to war or out hunting when the birth approaches, a standard motif in tales.

Conclusion

As a research tool for folktales the Type and Motif Indexes must obviously be used with a great deal of caution by modern scholars exploring female roles in folktales and fairy tales. However, impressive as pioneer accomplishments, these works are clearly dated. The latest revision of the Type Index is almost twenty years old and the revised Motif Index is over twenty years old. In the meantime a radical change of consciousness has affected the way we perceive the portrayal of women in literature, folktales, and fairy tales.

There is enough evidence to show that the Indexes generally classify the female protagonist as passive and subordinate, supportive rather than full of initiative, weak rather than strong. This image misrepresents many folktale and fairy tale heroines and should be corrected.

A revision of the Indexes need not mean a radical change of the system itself, which does not appear to be alarmingly sexist. It is, however, alarmingly inconsistent in its semantic-syntactic conventions. Why is the sex of characters sometimes indicated and sometimes not? Thompson's own guidelines need to be applied in a more structured fashion. Decisions have to be made about what constitutes a hero or heroine, and whether type titles should focus on the activities of the hero and heroine, leaving the identification of specifics such as "The prince as bird" to the Motif Index. Further, there should be some indication of the criteria used for plot summaries. Tales radically different from the major trend of tale content, or best-known tale versions, should be given a separate number. (There are numerous examples of Thompson's willingness to accommodate uniquely occurring motifs in the Motif Index.)

Basically, the components within the two systems need to be modernized and made to conform better to the tale material. Some can be simply relabeled with plot summaries rewritten and alternatives added. For other tales one can create subcategories. That there is an urgent need for revision of these research tools is made particularly clear when we read the following cross-reference in the Motif Index: *"Man,* see also *Person." "Woman,* see also *Wife."*

Notes

1. Antti Aarne and Stith Thompson, *The Types of the Folktale,* Folklore Fellows Communications no. 184, 2d revision (Helsinki, 1961); Stith Thompson, *Motif-Index of Folk Literature* (Bloomington: Indiana University Press, 1955–58).

2. Thompson, *Motif-Index,* p. 11.

3. Ibid., p. 9.

4. Richard M. Dorson, *Folktales Told Around the World* (Chicago and London: University of Chicago, 1975), p. 314.

5. Thompson, *Motif-Index,* p. 9.

6. Assen Nicoleff, ed. and trans., *Bulgarian Folktales* (Cleveland, Ohio, 1979), pp. 31–42.

7. Grimm, "A Tale of a Boy Who Set Out to Learn Fear," in Stith Thompson, *One Hundred Favorite Folktales* (Bloomington: Indiana University Press, 1968), p. 48.

8. P. Chr. Asbjørnsen and Jørgen Moe, *Norske Folke-eventyr,* vol. 2, 8th ed., revised by Moltke Moe (Kristiania: H. Aschehoug & Co. [W. Nygaard], 1914), p. 188. Reidar Th. Christensen, ed., *Folktales of Norway* (Chicago: University of Chicago Press, 1964), pp. 213–28.

9. Barbara Ker Wilson, *Scottish Folk-Tales and Legends* (1954; repr. London: Oxford University Press, 1975), pp. 156–72.

10. "Baba Yaga," in Alexander Afanasev, *Russian Fairy Tales* (New York: Pantheon Books, 1973), pp. 363–66.

11. Dorson, *Folktales,* pp. 533–41.

12. "The Sea King and Vasilisa the Wise," in Afanasev, *Russian Fairy Tales,* pp. 427–37.

13. Jacob Ludwig Karl Grimm, *Grimms' Tales for Young and Old,* trans. Ralph Manheim (New York: Doubleday, 1977).

14. Benjamin Thorpe, ed., *Yule-Tide Stories: A Collection of Scandinavian and North German Popular Tales and Traditions* (1853; repr. New York: AMS Press, 1968), pp. 11–35.

15. Christensen, *Folktales of Norway,* pp. 147–53.

16. Jan-Öjvind Swahn, ed., *Svenska Folksagor* (Stockholm: Albert Bonniers Förlag, 1959), pp. 224–26. Translation by Torborg Lundell.

17. Grimm, *Tales,* pp. 90–92.

18. Thompson, *One Hundred Favorite Folktales,* pp. 345–47.

19. Swahn, *Svenska Folksagor,* pp. 224–86.

20. Kay Stone, "Things Walt Disney Never Told Us," *Journal of American Folklore* 88 (1975): 49.

21. Svend Grundtvig, *Danish Fairy Tales* (1919; repr. New York: Dover Publications, 1972), pp. 17–28.

22. Thompson, *One Hundred Favorite Folktales,* pp. 127–28.

23. Thorpe, *Yule-Tide Stories,* pp. 64–75.

24. Hannah Aitken, ed., *A Forgotten Heritage: Original Folk Tales of Lowland Scotland* (Totowa, N.J.: Rowman & Littlefield, 1973), pp. 76–79.

25. Grimm, "Little Brother and Little Sister," "The Three Little Men in the Woods," in *Tales,* pp. 41–46, 49–54; Thorpe, "The Beautiful Herd-Gird," "Little Rosa and Long Leda," pp. 35–50.

26. Grimm, "The Six Swans," in *Tales* pp. 171–75; "The Twelve Wild Ducks," in George Webbe Dasent, *East o' the Sun and West o' the Moon* (1888; repr. New York: Dover, 1970), pp. 51–59.

27. "The Wicked Sisters," in Afanasev, *Russian Fairy Tales,* pp. 356–60.

Bibliography

Georges, Robert A. "The Universality of the Tale-Type as Concept and Construct." *Western Folklore* 42, no. 1 (Jan. 1983): 21–28. Argues that "the construct identifiable as the tale-type is based upon a concept which is itself a manifestation of the human abilities to conceptualize reality phenomenologically" and "grouping phenomena together." The tale type then "would appear to be biologically based" and "seems destined to determine and to influence our conceptualizations, characterizations and analysis of narrating and narrative."

Jason, Hedda. "Structural Analysis and the Concept of the Tale Type." *ARV* 28 (1972): 36–54. Notes that the Aarne tale-type concept is based on the Grimm collection, which has had important consequences for classifications. For example, "Sleeping Beauty" in Grimms' version is type 410, while its longer Mediterranean form would place it in the tale group 880–899, *"Persecuted heroine."* Jason also points out that 30 to 40 percent of the Middle Eastern fairy tales do not fit neatly into a single Aarne and Thompson type and many may not fit in at all, indicating the questionable validity of the concept "type" and of "the theoretical significance and usefulness" of their method.

Liungman, Waldemar. *En traditionsstudie över sagan om Prinsessan i jordkulan.* Diss., Göteborg, 1925. Discusses type 870, dealing with an active and courageous heroine without giving much, if any, credit to her strong qualities. For example, the heroine's different names in various versions are discussed, but not her abilities to survive on her own or her way of getting out from the mound.

Lundell, Torborg. "Folktale Heroines and the Type and Motif Indexes." *Folklore* 94 (1983): 240–46. Discusses some of the biases in terms of "selective labelling," "misleading plot summaries," and "focus on male character instead of heroine."

9. The Structure of "Snow White"

STEVEN SWANN JONES

Two of the most important approaches to folk narrative study include the historic-geographic and structural methods of analysis.[1] Both, in their turn, have made significant contributions to our understanding of folktales. However, their coexistence as methods of folk narrative study has not always been peaceful; they have been regarded to date somewhat more as competing methodologies and not as mutually supportive systems of analysis.[2] It is my contention that these two approaches to folktale study may be usefully combined into one synthesized methodology for the study of the formal features of folk narratives. Specifically, this essay represents an attempt to identify the structure of one folktale, "Snow White," by applying certain principles of structuralist methodology (primarily those of Vladimir Propp and Alan Dundes) to a concept previously identified and extensively studied by the historic-geographic school — the tale type. This essay suggests ultimately that there is a structural basis for identifying tale types based on recognizing narrative patterns found in those tale types.

The narrative patterns underlying tale types consist of the sequence of dramatic events that are a consistent part of these tale types

Reprinted from *Fabula* 24 (1983): 56–71, by permission of Walter de Gruyter Publishers.

even when they are told in different versions with varying motifs. The structural methodology of identifying allomotifs (that is, related motifs that fulfill the same dramatic purpose in the same point in a narrative in different versions) is used here to identify the significant actions of the story of "Snow White." For example, in "Snow White" the heroine may be killed in different versions by a poisoned staylace, needle, raisin, or apple, but in every version *she is killed*, which is the significant action of that episode or event. These significant actions of tales, then, are the morphological components of the tale types; they are the definitive and descriptive elements that make up a tale's structural typology. Accordingly, these common events found in versions of the same narrative are termed *episodes* in this essay, and their identification is proposed as the basis for defining the tale type of "Snow White" and differentiating it from other tale types.

I should make it clear here that a different typological pattern underlies each different tale type, and not simply one structural pattern as Propp suggests; in other words, each tale type has its own particular code or combination of episodes, and individual tale types consistently follow these uniquely characteristic, typological patterns of action. In addition to these typological patterns, however, related folktale types may follow generalized structural patterns, such as Lord Raglan's hero pattern, Propp's fairy-tale typology, and Dundes's nuclear motifemic sequences, which I call generic patterns. The morphological components of these generic patterns are functions, as proposed and defined by Propp. Thus, folk narratives appear to be structured in two ways: the typological structure characterizes the action consistently found in the different versions of the same story, while the generic structure describes action commonly undertaken in different stories. Ultimately, then, this study is an attempt to identify the typological and generic patterns in "Snow White" and show how they underlie the construction of that folktale.

Typological Structure of "Snow White"

The method I employ to identify the typology of "Snow White" is essentially a revised application of the historic-geographic theory to versions of this folktale.[3] It is suitable for analyzing any other folktale for which numerous variants exist. By examining versions comparatively, I have discerned nine significant events in that folktale that are consistently repeated actions, or "episodes," characteristic of different versions. This proposed structure of nine episodes in "Snow

White" represents a slight revision of previous studies that have identified seven, eight, or five major actions in that story.[4] For example, Antti Aarne and Stith Thompson's typology of the folktale of "Snow White" has five major characteristics preceded by a brief description:

[709] *Snow-White.* The wicked stepmother seeks to kill the maiden [a]t the dwarfs' (robbers') house, where the prince finds the maiden and marries her.

I. Snow-White and her Stepmother. (a) Snow-White has skin like snow, and lips like blood. (b) A magic mirror tells her stepmother that Snow-White is more beautiful than she.

II. Snow-White's Rescue. (a) The stepmother orders a hunter to kill her, but he substitutes an animal's heart and saves her, or (b) she sends Snow-White to the house of the dwarfs (or robbers) expecting her to be killed. The dwarfs adopt her as a sister.

III. The Poisoning. (a) The stepmother now seeks to kill her by means of poisoned lace, (b) a poisoned comb and (c) a poisoned apple.

IV. Help of the Dwarfs. (a) The dwarfs succeed in reviving her from the first two poisonings but fail with the third. (b) They lay the maiden in a glass coffin.

V. Her Revival. A prince sees her and resuscitates her. The stepmother is made to dance herself to death in red hot shoes. (p. 245)

As a number of critics have pointed out, however, the approach employed by Aarne and Thompson and other users of the Finnish method is seriously flawed. The most important flaw is that not one of the major motifs or events associated with a given narrative is necessarily found in every version of that narrative.[5] The Finnish method leads to inaccurate results, as can be seen, for example, in the typology suggested for "Snow White" by Aarne and Thompson. Their typology implies that the narrative has five major episodes and, more important, that motifs such as red as blood/white as snow, the magic mirror, the compassionate executioner, the dwarfs, the poisoned lace, comb, and apple, the glass coffin, and the red-hot shoes are a crucial part of the narrative.[6] This is generally not true — some versions include none of these motifs.[7] Furthermore, a more logical and consistent analysis indicates nine, not just five, episodes or significant actions in the narrative of "Snow White." (We can recognize these episodes, as we will below, by the *accumulation* of motifs that are used to illustrate them in different versions, that is, by the variety of motifs employed in the various versions to describe a particular episode.) Thus, the Aarne–Thompson typology is clearly flawed in two ways — in its reliance on specific motifs to describe the tale and in its resulting taxonomy of significant events. It is certainly a weakness to describe, as Aarne and Thompson do, a folktale such as "Snow White" by a set of motifs that may not appear at all in same versions and by an incomplete sequence of major events. They list popular motifs associated with "Snow White," as it appears in the Grimms' *Kinder- und Hausmärchen*, but do not provide a true typological description of the folktale type in its essential form.

To correct the flaws in the Aarne–Thompson methodology and provide a truly typological description for the folktale type of "Snow White," we need to identify the constituent episodes that recur in numerous versions of this story. From the coinciding motifs in different accounts, we can deduce the essential paradigm of action common to these narratives. When applied to "Snow White," this method of analysis yields nine major episodes that are themselves organized into two parts.

In Part 1, the heroine is expelled from her home and adopted by someone else. Four episodes are commonly used to describe this part of the story. The first episode is termed Origin, and in it an introductory etiological motif explains the creation or conception of the heroine or describes the heroine's familial situation. For instance, a woman pricks her finger or has a nosebleed on a snowy day and wishes for a child as red as blood and white as snow. Or she may eat a pomegranate and wish for a child to call Little Pomegranate. Or she may eat a tangerine and wish for a child to call Little Tangerine. In the second episode, Jealousy, the persecutor (the mother, stepmother, sisters) becomes jealous of the heroine's beauty. Some common motifs in this episode are the magic mirror, sun, moon, or passerby that tell the persecutor that the heroine is more beautiful than she is. Alternatively, the mother may feel the father prefers the daughter, throw a temper tantrum, and ask the father to choose between herself and the daughter. In the third episode, Expulsion, the persecutor orders the heroine's death or otherwise expels her from home. Popular motifs include abandoning the heroine in the woods or ordering a servant to kill the child and bring back her heart, lung, liver, intestines, blood-soaked dress, or a bottle of her blood stoppered with her little toe or finger; the compassionate executioner instead frees her in the woods and substitutes some other token of her death. The fourth episode is Adoption, in which the heroine is rescued from her homeless plight. Frequently, the motif of the mysterious housekeeper appears in this episode, that is, the heroine finds an empty house, cleans and cooks, and then hides. Eventually, the occupants, who may be thieves, giants, dwarfs, or others, discover their visitor and let her stay.

Part 2, with five episodes, involves a repetition of the pattern of rivalry, attack, and rescue from Part 1, but with more serious consequences. In the first episode, Renewed Jealousy, the persecutor again becomes jealous of the heroine upon hearing that she has survived her ordeal of expulsion, has been adopted by someone else, and is still more beautiful. Generally, this episode is filled by the allomotifs of the magic mirror, sun, old beggar woman, or other, that reveal to the persecutor the heroine's situation. The next episode in this second part is Death, in which the persecutor apparently kills the heroine despite the interference of the heroine's companions. As in the Expulsion episode of Part 1, a series of attacks may fill the Death episode, but the end result is the heroine's death. Common means of achieving that end include giving the heroine a poisoned ring, a pair of bewitched slippers, a poisoned dress, or simply sticking a needle or similar object into her hair or head. Following the heroine's Death is the Exhibition episode, in which the heroine's companions prepare and exhibit the corpse. She is generally placed in a beautiful coffin and then either hung from a tree, cast into the sea, set loose on the back of a horse, or placed on a mountain. The fourth episode in Part 2, Resuscitation, describes the heroine's revival: in moving the coffin or examining the corpse, the magic object is fortuitously displaced and the heroine revives. For example, a prince finds the heroine's coffin and takes it back to his room; there his sisters discover the corpse and comb its hair while playing with it like a doll. In doing so, they find the magic needle stuck in her skull, remove it, and awaken the heroine. The final episode of Part 2, Resolution, details the ultimate outcome of the drama. This generally includes the heroine's marriage and the persecutor's punishment. Some of the grisly punishments include rolling the persecutor out of town in a brimstone barrel with nails pounded in it, burning her, or walling her up in a doorless and windowless room.[8]

These episodes constitute a comprehensive typology of the folktale of "Snow White"; they describe the action as it is commonly presented in more than one hundred versions of "Snow White" that I have examined.[9] By way of corroboration here, I would like to demonstrate how two particular versions conform to this typological description.[10]

In one version collected by Fortier in Louisiana, the story opens with the Origin episode — a suitor, refused by a haughty lady, prophesies that in a year she will have a daughter prettier than herself; the prediction is fulfilled. The story then moves to Jealousy — the lady realizes the child's beauty and shuts her up in a room with her nurse. There, the child sees a peacock, and declares her intention to marry King Peacock. Next is Expulsion — the mother orders the nurse to kill the child with a knife; instead, the nurse gives the child three seeds and tells her to swallow one and throw herself in the well. The child drops a seed as she falls into the well and the water dries up.

Then, in Adoption, the girl walks to the house of an ogre, whose wife warns the child that the ogre will eat her. The ogre, however, wishing to spare the beautiful child, takes her instead to an elegant room and orders his wife to fan the child with peacock feathers while she sleeps.

Part 2 usually begins with Renewed Jealousy, but it is omitted in this version. Instead, Death follows when the heroine decides to eat one of the seeds because she is convinced her mother will kill her anyway; she falls into a deep sleep. In Exhibition, the ogre, believing the girl is dead, buys a gold coffin for her, puts her in it, and places it in the river. And in Resuscitation, King Peacock sees the coffin in the river, has it retrieved, and takes it to his chamber. There he sprinkles her with eau de cologne; when he opens her mouth to see what pretty teeth she has, he sees something red, and removes it with a golden pin. The seed falls out, and the girl recovers. Finally, in Resolution, the girl marries King Peacock. As we can see, with some minor variations and with some very imaginative and suggestive motifs (for example, the magic seeds and the examining of the girl's teeth), this version follows the typological pattern previously identified.

We can further verify the existence of the typological structure underlying "Snow White" by analyzing the episodes in a version collected by Juan Rael from Spanish oral tradition in the Southwestern United States (see note 10). Entitled "Los Chapincitos de oro" (The golden slippers), this text omits the Origin episode (as many versions do) and begins directly with Jealousy — a mother has a daughter of unequalled beauty. Seeing this in her magic mirror, the mother grows envious. Expulsion — the mother orders that the daughter's eyes be put out and that the daughter be taken to the mountains and abandoned; it is done. Adoption — the blind girl follows a deer, who is the Virgin Mary, to a thieves' den. There she learns the password for the magic door and secretly cleans house. When the thieves discover their mysterious housekeeper, they adopt her as a sister and give her a pair of golden slippers.

Part 2 begins with Renewed Jealousy — the mother hears from village gossip that the daughter is still alive. The mother goes to an old witch to dispatch her rival. Death — the witch, on the mother's command, exchanges the girl's slippers for a pair of poisoned ones. The girl puts them on and dies. Exhibition — the thieves put the heroine's lifeless body in a golden chest, which they throw into the ocean. Resuscitation — a fisherman recovers the chest and brings it to a prince, who places it in his room. There a curious serving girl opens the chest and removes one of the slippers. The heroine begins to revive, and the prince takes the other slipper off; the girl awakes. Resolution — the girl marries the prince, and the mother is burned to death.

Once more, we can see how this narrative follows the typological pattern that characterizes the tale type of "Snow White." The variety of colorful motifs in this version, such as the blinding of the heroine and her abandonment on a mountain in Expulsion, the aid of the Virgin Mary in Adoption, and the bewitching of the heroine with a magic pair of slippers in Death, still conform to the essential action of the episodes of this tale type and thus maintain the typological structure.

Thus, from these examples we can see an essential model of folktale type construction: conformance to a prescribed set of episodes that are illustrated by a cross section of allomotifs. The findings here, while only slightly revising previous typologies of "Snow White," suggest more far-reaching theoretical conclusions. In the first place, the typological pattern of nine episodes identified here may explain the identifiability and stability of this narrative. Folktales are highly susceptible to alteration in oral tradition, and this typological pattern provides a skeleton that keeps the shape and form of the narrative, somewhat like a genetic code. It enables the narrator to incorporate changes in detail and motif while retaining a narrative that presents the same basic plot with its proven appeal; the typological pattern explains the narrative stability of the folktale type, and the selection of motifs accounts for the stylistic variation in the different versions. The typological pattern of episodes, then, organizes the story in a memorable and appropriate way, building the narrative's dramatic impact from episode to episode.

Additionally, this pattern of nine episodes validates the concept of tale types as proposed by Aarne and Thompson; it suggests a structural basis for these tale types by conceptualizing these episodes as structural units of narrative plot. The pattern of episodes characteristic of a particular tale type is, in essence, a structural description of that tale type because it is based on the formal narrative actions consistently present in different versions and illustrated by different motifs. Finally, this pattern of episodes identified in "Snow White" allows us to discern more general narrative patterns underlying that folktale as well as other related folktales. As we shall consider in the following section, identifying the typological structure of "Snow White" leads us to clues about possible generic structures in that narrative.

Generic Structure of "Snow White"

The generic structure of "Snow White" is a pattern of action underlying that narrative that reveals the essential connection between

"Snow White" and other related folktales of persecuted heroines as well as the fundamental relationship between these tales and the society from which they grew. Propp suggests that we can describe these generic structures by identifying the tale's functions, the pattern of basic events common to different stories.[11] Specifically, the fundamental pattern of action of "Snow White" and certain related folktales of persecuted heroines depicts a repetition of hostilities directed against the heroine. These hostilities recur with increasingly serious consequences until the drama is resolved. This succession of incremental hostilities may be considered the essential paradigm both of "Snow White" and of other folktales of persecuted heroines, and it reveals an underlying connection between this folktale and its audience.[12]

In "Snow White," the cycle of hostilities directed against the heroine involves three steps: first, a threat is directed against the heroine; second, that threat is realized in some form of hostility; and finally, a rescue or escape from the hostility is effected. This cycle is generally repeated twice in the narrative of "Snow White": first, when she is initially threatened, expelled, and then adopted; and second, when she is attacked, killed, and finally resuscitated and married. Versions of "Snow White" follow this persecution pattern faithfully, presenting us generally with two instances or separate occasions of hostility directed against the heroine.[13]

The evidence supporting the presence of a twofold repetition of a persecution cycle in "Snow White" is difficult to present in an abbreviated form, because we cannot review scores of versions in order to show the manifestation of the persecution pattern. However, we can summarize the general action of the story and show how the motifs from three sample versions illustrate the presence of the generic persecution pattern in "Snow White." Accordingly, in Table 9.1, I have outlined the generic pattern of actions (labeled "functions" after Propp's terminology) found in "Snow White." Furthermore, I have listed the corresponding episodes and motifs that illustrate the generic pattern outlined here.[14] For reasons of familiarity, I have listed the motifs from the Grimm version, but by way of corroboration, I have included motifs from one version from Italy (recorded by Thomas Crane) and one from Asia Minor (recorded by Henry Carnoy).[15]

The way the episodes identified in Part 1 are essentially duplicated in Part 2 suggests the idea that a double pattern of hostility underlies "Snow White." As we can see from Table 9.1, the events of the second half repeat more intensively the events in the first half of the story: once again the mother (persecutor) becomes jealous and tries to attack the heroine, but the heroine is ultimately rescued. In the beginning of both parts, a villainous figure contrives an intense dislike for the heroine in an initial threatening situation; then the persecutor becomes envious of the heroine and wishes to be rid of her, as we see in the motif of the magic mirror, in the motif of the breaking of plates and glasses, or in the motif of the boastful eagle. And accordingly, in both parts, a hostile action is subsequently initiated. In Part 1, as illustrated by the motifs in the table, the heroine is expelled or ordered to perform a dangerous chore or taken away to be killed, while in Part 2 the heroine is killed by the use of a poisoned staylace, comb, apple, ring, raisin, sweetmeat, or dress. Finally, in both parts, the heroine manages to escape from the hostility in a way that significantly alters her situation, status, and environment. In Part 1, she leaves home and finds a new home with her companions, while in Part 2, she leaves the companions' establishment for the home of her new husband. The crucial distinction that reveals the structural repetition of the generic pattern in "Snow White" is the heroine's change of environment. Her move from her parents' house to the companions' house provides the structural coda of the story. Like musical annotation, it signals a repetition of the primary melody or theme of the piece. Both in terms of narrative treatment of the transition between cycles (the dramatic transportation, hiatus, and subsequent renewal of action somewhere near the middle of the story) and in terms of the parallel pattern of action in both cycles (the coincidence in the action of the episodes in the first and second parts of the story), the structural repetition of the events in "Snow White" seems an explicit and significant feature of this narrative.

Some unusual treatments of "Snow White" also confirm the validity of the persecution pattern as an important part of that folktale's formal construction. For example, certain oicotypal versions of this tale include a third instance of this cycle of threat, hostility, and escape.[16] In about 20 percent of the versions that I have examined, a third repetition of hostilities follows the heroine's marriage. In these, the punishment that normally occurs at the conclusion of "Snow White" is omitted, and the heroine simply marries after her resuscitation. When the persecutor hears that the heroine has revived and married, the persecutor again tries to dispatch her rival. Thus, these longer versions, by incorporating a third cycle of persecution, further support the idea that these cycles of persecution are units of dramatic structure apparent to narrators, who may double or treble them in the story.

Furthermore, the events in Part 3 correspond to events in related folktales. For example, the motif of the "Calumniated wife" (motif K 2110.1), which is sometimes used in Part 3 of the extended oico-

Table 9.1 Pattern of Action in Three Versions of "Snow White"

GENERIC PATTERN (FUNCTIONS)	TYPOLOGICAL PATTERN (EPISODES)	VERSIONS* (MOTIFS)
Part 1		
Threat — the protagonist is threatened	Jealousy — persecutor becomes jealous of the heroine	(a) The persecutor learns from a magic mirror that the heroine is more beautiful (b) A stepmother resents her new stepdaughter (c) A stepmother feels that the father prefers the stepdaughter — breaks plates and glasses
Hostility — a hostile action is directed against the protagonist	Expulsion — the persecutor orders the heroine's death or otherwise expels her from home	(a) The queen orders a servant to kill the heroine; she is abandoned in the forest (b) Stepmother orders the heroine to water a dangerously situated basil plant (c) The father, on the request of the stepmother, abandons the heroine with a basket of food on a faraway mountain
Escape — the protagonist escapes from her predicament	Adoption — the heroine is rescued from her homeless plight and adopted by someone else	(a) The heroine is taken in by some dwarfs after they discover her in their house (b) An eagle carries the heroine to a fairy palace (c) The heroine secretly cooks and cleans at the palace of forty giants, who adopt her when they finally find her

GENERIC PATTERN (FUNCTIONS)	TYPOLOGICAL PATTERN (EPISODES)	VERSIONS* (MOTIFS)
Part 2		
Threat	Renewed Jealousy — the persecutor is informed that the heroine is still alive and still more beautiful	(a) The persecutor learns from her magic mirror of the heroine's new home (b) The eagle boasts to the stepmother of the heroine's new home (c) The stepmother asks the sun if there is any prettier woman in the world and learns about the heroine's new home
Hostility	Death — the heroine dies at the hands of the persecutor or her agent	(a) The queen tries to kill the heroine with a staylace and a comb, and then succeeds with a poisoned apple (b) The stepmother asks a witch to kill the heroine, who tries first with poisoned sweetmeats, and finally succeeds with a poisoned dress (c) The stepmother tries to kill the heroine with a gold ring and then succeeds with a poisoned raisin
Escape	Resuscitation — the heroine is resuscitated, usually after someone sees and acquires her corpse	(a) A prince obtains the heroine's body; the coffin is jostled, and the heroine revives and marries the prince (b) A prince obtains the heroine's body; his mother removes the dress to clean it, and the heroine revives and marries the prince (c) A prince finds the heroine's body; his father presses the heroine's chest and she spits up the raisin, revives, and marries the prince

*(a) Grimm; (b) Crane; (c) Carnoy. (See note 15.)

typal versions of "Snow White," surfaces in "The Three Golden Sons" (AT 707), "The Maiden Without Hands" (AT 706), and "Crescentia" (AT 712). In "Snow White" this motif illustrates the postmarriage incidence of the Threat, Hostility, and Escape pattern in which the heroine is accused of destroying her own children and is, as a consequence, ejected from her home; this correspondence suggests the possibility that the generic pattern of Threat, Hostility, and Escape underlies the action in related tales of persecuted heroines. I contend that the generic persecution pattern of Threat, Hostility, and Escape can be shown to underlie the narrative action of several related folk narratives of persecuted heroines, such as "Cinderella" (AT 510A), "Rapunzel" (AT 310), "The Maiden Without Hands" (AT 706), "The Black and White Bride" (AT 403), "Sleeping Beauty" (AT 410), "The Maiden Who Seeks Her Brothers" (AT 451), "Born from a Fish" (AT 705), "Our Lady's Child" (AT 710), "Crescentia" (AT 712), and "The Innocent Slandered Maiden" (AT 883A), thus corroborating the presence of this generic pattern in "Snow White." Limitations of space prevent a thorough exposition here of how this generic pattern underlies these related tales of persecuted heroines. However, Ilana Dan has already anticipated the presence of a persecution pattern in the "Female Fairy Tale," as she terms those related tales. In her article, "The Innocent Persecuted Heroine: An Attempt at a Model for the Surface Level of the Narrative Structure of the Female Fairy Tale,"[17] she points out in seventeen texts of AT types 403 ("The Black and White Bride"), 706 ("The Maiden Without Hands"), 712 ("Crescentia"), and 883A ("The Innocent Slandered Maiden") the common characteristic of "double persecution of the heroine, both in her parental home and in her husband's house." Although Dan excludes analyses of "Snow White" and other relevant folktales, she has recognized the same crucial feature of these tales — repeated persecution of the heroine in at least two environments. Since it is a crucial feature of a number of different folktales in addition to "Snow White," the pattern of persecution is apparently functioning as a generic structure for those narratives.[18]

The generic persecution pattern in "Snow White" serves a number of important purposes. First, it enhances the dramatic tension of the narrative. The events of the second part of the tale metaphorically duplicate the first part in a new, expanded, and intensified context. By establishing a parallel structure of events, the narrator increases audience participation and concern by encouraging them to anticipate the perils of the heroine. The structural equivalence or correspondence of the events of the second part of "Snow White" to the events of the first generates echoes and reverberations of association and meaning, serving as a warning and a stimulation to the audience.

Second, the dramatic repetition serves a stylistic purpose; it divides the story roughly in half, provides a sense of balance and symmetry, and operates as an effective fundamental plot outline giving coherence and order to the story and organizing the details simply and sharply. The symmetry of the formal arrangement of the action, in which the persecutor in two separate situations or places threatens the heroine, confirms the folktale community's preference (as pointed out by Max Lüthi) for order, balance, and consistency.[19]

Finally, not only is the structural repetition in "Snow White" stylistically and dramatically a crucial element of the narrative but it also underscores that tale's thematic message. In essence, the structural pattern of episodes in "Snow White" recapitulates the personal development of the heroine; in other words, the sequence of episodes is structured to correspond to the basic trials and transitions of the maturing young woman in order to illustrate for the audience the process of maturation. This connection between theme and structure is evidenced by the way that the successive acts of the persecution pattern coincide with what may be considered three of the most crucial transitions in the heroine's life — puberty, marriage, and childbirth.

The first incidence of the persecution pattern appears, for a number of reasons, to correspond to the heroine's approaching sexual puberty. Generally, the heroine is at the appropriate age; even though some texts, like the Grimms', indicate the heroine is around seven, most portray her as being in her early teens and approaching young womanhood. Furthermore, the physiologically appropriate act of menstruation is suggested indirectly by the flow of blood that accompanies, in many versions, the first act of persecution.[20] Finally, the puberty period is suggested also by the heightened rivalries and tensions with the mother. This aspect of the physiological and sexual development of the heroine is illustrated by the motifs in which the suitors prefer the daughter to the mother or the magic mirror says that the heroine is more beautiful than the mother. These pubescent tensions are further illustrated by the motifs where the mother or stepmother tries to lock the heroine up in a room or cave or attempts to cut off her hair or otherwise disfigure her. Thus, the first act of the folktale appears to be set in a crucial period in the heroine's life when she is initially maturing into a young woman, and it metaphorically mirrors the anxieties and concerns typical of this adolescent stage of development.

The next act of the persecution pattern culminates in the heroine's marriage, illustrating the transition from adolescence to adulthood. This instance of the persecution pattern dramatizes the heroine's acceptance of the responsibilities and prerogatives of adulthood, especially sexuality, as illustrated in the motifs of the poisoned apple, dress, or slipper. The clothes and shoes are means of enhancing her physical beauty and confirm her status as a mature woman. With these clothes, the heroine is assuming the suits and trappings of womanhood. The other common motifs of the heroine eating various kinds of poisoned fruit (apples, grapes, raisins, and so on) represent the heroine metaphorically experiencing a socially euphemized sexual initiation. Thus, the second act dramatizes the heroine's transformation into a mature, married woman.

The final presentation of the persecution pattern (found only in the oicotypal extended versions of "Snow White," but commonly a part of many other tale types of the "Persecuted heroine" cycle) coincides with the heroine's becoming a mother. The anxiety of motherhood and childbirth are depicted in the descriptions of the wife being accused of eating her newborn children or of giving birth to monsters or animals. Thus, the folktale appears to dramatize in these three acts of the persecution pattern, three significant stages in the growth of the child into a woman.

Presumably the purpose of this patterning of the folktale to correspond to a woman's typical life crises is that it attempts to assist the heroine in her passage through these major life changes by providing her with psychological, sociological, and philosophical instruction along the way. By tracing and anticipating her journey, the folktale serves as a guide and model for the young woman. Specifically, the key accomplishment of each of the acts is the relocation of the heroine in a new situation. Thus, the pattern of the tale is designed to encourage change and growth. Furthermore, there is an underlying developmental logic to the relocations. The heroine moves from the childish environment of the parents' home, to the adolescent environment of her friends' home, to the young woman's environment of her husband's home, and finally to the mature woman's environment of her own home. Thus, there is a progression in the ensuing acts of the persecution pattern toward self-independence and self-assertion, an underlying goal of achieving autonomy.

It must be noted that few of the tale types in the "Persecuted heroine" cycle, including "Snow White," present the full incidence of the pattern; they usually present only a portion of the overall moves and thus do not afford us the opportunity to see in one tale the entire life cycle. However, we do not expect every novel or play to present the entire life story; similarly, different tale types in the "Persecuted heroine" cycle may alternately focus on different stages in the heroine's development. The important point is that, generically, they may all be viewed as part of a larger narrative outline that does sketch the main changes in the typical overall experience of women. Thus, viewing the tales of the "Persecuted heroine" cycle as a group, we see that one very important function of this generic pattern is to illustrate the psycho-social development of the heroine, an outline of the normal process of maturation, as she passes through different stages in her life.

Another way that the generic structure of the folktale of "Snow White" mirrors the development of a young woman may be seen in its emulation of the pattern of certain socially enacted rituals as identified by Arnold van Gennep.[21] Van Gennep studied a wide variety of rituals associated with changes in an individual's status (such as puberty rituals, marriage rituals, and so on), and he found that these rituals follow a definite pattern in their depiction of the crossing of these thresholds. They dramatize the participants as going through the steps of separation, liminality, and reincorporation as a means of facilitating their transition from one social status to another. This pattern appears to underlie the various acts of the "Persecuted heroine" cycle as well. The acts effect the heroine's separation from one setting, depict her liminal condition in the wilderness, and then reincorporate her into a new social situation. In the first act, the heroine is expelled, wanders through the forest, and then is adopted by the companions. In the second act, the heroine is killed, her body is then placed in a liminal situation (for example, tossed into the ocean or hung from a tree), and finally, she is married and moves into a new house. Thus, the order of the specific steps within each act of the "Persecuted heroine" cycle essentially duplicates the pattern of social rituals.[22]

Presumably, the goal of the acts also duplicates the goal of the ritual to facilitate the heroine's transition from one social position to another. The acts correspond to certain important transitions in a young woman's life that would themselves logically be the subject of such rituals. As noted previously, the first act contains certain associations with puberty (bleeding, physiological maturation, sexual competition with a mother figure, or attraction to a father figure), the second act with marriage, and the third act with childbirth. All of these transitions are crucial changes for the young woman — changing first from an asexual to a sexual individual, from an unattached and unmarried woman to a married one, and finally from a childless woman to a child-rearing mother. These acts apparently serve the function of assisting the heroine in coping with these changes by echoing the traditional formulas used by rituals to guide initiates through those transitions.

One of the ways that the narratives appear to differ from the rituals, however, which may interfere with seeing this connection clearly, is that in the ritual the motivation for the transition is inherently accepted and understood by the actors of the ritual; thus, there is no need to explain it. In contrast, the narrative finds it necessary to dramatize the motivation for the heroine's separation from her old environment, by depicting the threat and hostility offered by past relationships that are preventing her from maturing further. Thus, we have the explanation for the persecution by the stepmother; it serves as an illustration of the obstacles to the child's development and as a motivation for the child to transcend that oppression. Apart from this additional elaboration by the fairy tale, however, both the ritual and tale dramatize the same basic process of personal and social change, prompting and assisting the heroine in her maturation.

Van Gennep's ritual pattern not only underlies the specific acts of the "Persecuted heroine" cycle but also underlies the typological pattern of "Snow White." A number of previous studies have pointed out how the folktale of "Snow White" follows the pattern commonly found in rituals — Snow White's expulsion from her parents' house is seen as the ritualistic separation, her adoption by the companions is seen as the liminal stage, and her rescue by the prince is the reincorporation. This reading is a slightly different application of the ritual paradigm to the folktale, in that only one instance of the separation, liminality, and reincorporation pattern is seen in the tale rather than two. N. J. Girardot, for example, sees "Snow White" as corresponding to puberty rituals in which the young women are isolated in huts in the forest during their first menstruation and then are reincorporated back into the village afterward. During their stay in the hut, the women are taught various domestic skills, much as Snow White learns to care for her companions. Thus, Girardot sees the dwarfs' house as representing a liminal domain where Snow White is initiated into the domestic arts, before she is reincorporated in the prince's house.

While I accept the merit of this reading I would argue that van Gennep's pattern also underlies the composite persecution cycle that is repeated one, two, or three times. Thus, the tale apparently conforms in two ways to the ritual paradigm; both its microcosmic acts and its overall plot depict a pattern of separation, liminality, and reincorporation. This elaborate patterning confirms the noted proclivity in folklore for order and repetition. It also illustrates the purpose of the folktale to assist the child in understanding and coping with her personal development by presenting in dramatic form the ritualized methods for coping with social and personal changes. For example, the heroine's death in the companions' house might be regarded as corresponding to van Gennep's observation that frequently young initiates in the coming-of-age rituals are regarded as being dead for a period and then reborn. Thus, Snow White's death may be seen as an illustration of the transformation of social position (dying in an old form in order to be reborn in a new one), rather than as simply acquiescence to sexist, passive role models. Furthermore, the quasi-human nature of many of the heroine's companions in this liminal situation is appropriately explained, in this light, as evidence of their role as liminal mediaries, fictional shamans as it were. Thus, we can see how the structure of "Snow White" is designed from the ritualistic model to dramatize the problems and the process of a young woman's maturation. As part of the "Persecuted heroine" cycle, this particular folktale depicts two of the important stages in the growth of the child into a woman in order to serve the function of assisting the heroine in coping with these changes, becoming, in effect, a literary dramatization of the rites of passage.

In sum, we find that the narrative structures in "Snow White" serve useful functions for the audience of that folktale and are accordingly important elements of that story. Studying these structures helps us to realize the deceptive complexity of folktales. Like crystals that have been formed by years of pressure, folktales have an intricate beauty that is simultaneously the product of their exceptional longevity as well as an explanation for it. Given their history of being continually recreated by individual narrators in different social settings, under changing political conditions, with varying psychological concerns, it is no wonder that, under these pressures, they have become like diamonds, precisely structured and elegantly arranged gems of human expression.

Notes

1. I wish to thank Alan Dundes, Jan Brunvand, Richard Bjornson, and Mark Workman for their assistance in formulating and revising the argument proposed in this essay. For the exposition of the historic-geographic method, see Antti Aarne, *Leitfaden der vergleichenden Märchenforschung*, FFC 13 (Haminia, 1913), and Kaarle Krohn, *Die folkloristische Arbeitsmethode* (Oslo, 1926). For the exposition of the structural approach, see Vladimir Propp, *Morphology of the Folktale* (Austin: University of Texas Press, 1968); Claude Lévi-Strauss, "The Structural Study of Myth," *Journal of American Folklore* 68 (1955): 428–44; and Alan Dundes, *The Morphology of North American Indian Folktales* (Helsinki: Suomalainen Tiedeakatemia, 1964).

2. Two of the most significant and explicitly critical studies are Hans Honti's Märchenmorphologie und Märchentypologie," *Folk-Liv* 3 (1939): 307–18 and Alan Dundes's "From Etic to Emic Units in the Structural Study of Folktales," *Journal of American Folklore* 75 (1962): 95–105. Additionally, many structural studies implicitly, and sometimes explicitly, criticize the Finnish approach. See, for example, Vladimir Propp, *Morphology of the Folktale* (Austin: University of Texas Press, 1968); C. Bremond, "Le message narratif," *Communications* 4 (1964): 4–32; A. J. Greimas, "Le conte populaire russe (analyse funtionelle)," *International Journal of Slavic Linguistics and Poetics*, 9 (1965): 152–75; Heda

Jason, "The Russian Criticism of the 'Finnish School' in Folktale Scholarship," *Norveg*, n.s. 14 (1970): 285–94; and C. Lévi-Strauss, "L'analyse morphologique des contes russes," *International Journal of Slavic Linguistics and Poetics* 3 (1960): 122–49.

3. To a great extent, my method of typological analysis is as much a logical product of the Finnish comparative approach as it is an extension of the structural approach. Following the procedures proposed by Kaarle Krohn in *Die folkloristiche Arbeitsmethode* (Oslo, 1926; available in English translation in Roger L. Welsch, *Folklore Methodology* [Austin, Texas: AFS Bibliographical and Special Series, no. 21, 1971]), studies such as Walter Anderson's *Kaiser und Abt* (Helsinki: Suomalainen Tiedeakatemia, 1923), Warren E. Roberts's *The Tale of the Kind and Unkind Girls* (Berlin: W. de Gruyter, 1958), and Stith Thompson's "The Star Husband Tale" (in Alan Dundes, ed., *The Study of Folklore* [Englewood Cliffs, N.J.: Prentice-Hall, 1965], pp. 414–74), have demonstrated the value of comparing different versions of a particular tale type and of thereby defining the type through the multiplicity of versions. However, while I accept the basic logic of their approach, I do have my differences with the Finnish school. In the first place, some of the underlying assumptions and goals of their approach—such as their search for the ur-form of a folktale—are unnecessarily devolutionary and restrictive. We must remember that a folktale is the sum of its versions; the versions are not partial reflections or evolved examples of an original, ideal text. Also, in their zealous attempt to trace minute connections between geographically or historically related tales, they overanalyze individual versions at the expense of the larger pattern that manifests itself in the tale. As a result, the historic-geographic approach overlooks the structural pattern that underlies the tale; their studies are not examinations of how individual folktales are constructed but instead are detailed lists of the traits found in various versions. Rather than minutely tracing the supposed evolution of the subsequent retellings of a tale in order to follow the trail back to some apocryphal "original versions," this study of "Snow White" comparatively studies different versions of the tale in order to deduce the common pattern of events or actions that occur.

4. Currently, the main typology of "Snow White" is found in Antti Aarne and Stith Thompson, *The Types of the Folktale*, Folklore Fellows Communications no. 184 (Helsinki, 1961), p. 245. Two other preceding typologies of "Snow White" were proposed by Ernst Böklen and Bolte-Polivka. Böklen's typology is presented in his study of this folktale, entitled *Sneewittchenstudien* (Leipzig: J. C. Hinrichs, 1910), p. 74, and Bolte-Polivka's description is found in *Anmerkungen zu den Kinder -und Hausmärchen der Brüder Grimm* (Leipzig: Dieterich'sche verlagsbuch handlung, 1913–23), p. 453. Böklen suggests a typology that includes seven elements: (1) hatred of female relatives, (2) abandonment in forest, (3) compassionate executioner, (4) rescue by dwarfs, (5) poisoning of Snow White, (6) resuscitation, sometimes followed by persecution after the wedding directed at Snow White's children, and (7) punishment. Bolte-Polivka modify this typology slightly but still identify seven common traits: (a) the beauty of the heroine, (b) the jealousy of the stepmother, (c) the compassionate executioner, (d) the stepmother's attempts to kill Snow White with poisoned lace, comb, and apple, (e) the attempts of the dwarfs to save Snow White, (f) the resuscitation of Snow White by the Prince, and (g) the punishment of the stepmother. N. J. Girardot also has studied the typological structure of "Snow White" in "Initiation and Meaning in the Tale of Snow White and the Seven Dwarfs," *Journal of American Folklore* 90 (1977): 274–300. He divides the story into "twenty-five key statements or narremes"; however, I do not believe that these narremes represent an accurate morphological description of versions of "Snow White" because they cannot be applied to versions other than the Grimms'; we cannot consistently find these same narremes in all versions of "Snow White." Rather, the narremes represent as a rule the specific motifs employed in the Grimm version to fulfill the action (the typological structure) of "Snow White"; see S. Jones, "The Pitfalls of Snow White Scholarship," *Journal of American Folklore* 92 (1979): 69–73, for a further critique of Girardot's methodology and for a discussion of other examinations of "Snow White."

5. Alan Dundes, "From Etic to Emic Units in the Structural Study of Folktales," *Journal of American Folklore* 75 (1962): 103.

6. See Aarne and Thompson, "Type-Index," in *Types of the Folktale*, p. 245–46, for the motif numbers of these motifs.

7. See for example "La mère jalouse et la jeune persecutée" in M. Cerquand, *Legends et recits populaires de pays basque*, 4 vols. (Paul: L. Ribaut, 1875–82), vol. 4, no. 106; or "La locandiere di Parigi" in Giuseppe Pitre, *Novelle Popolari Toscane* (Palermo: P. Montaina, 1878), no. 9. Another example of such a version is the Fortier text summarized later in this study. As a matter of fact, a great majority of the versions of "Snow White" that I have examined (more than 100) eschew most of the "traditional" motifs taken from the Grimms.

8. Some 20 percent of the versions I have examined continue the story after the heroine's marriage and hence include more than nine episodes. In these, the punishment part of the Resolution episode is omitted and the heroine simply gets married after her resuscitation. When the persecutor hears that the heroine has revived and is now married, the persecutor tries once more to dispatch her rival. This three-part presentation of the narrative is not as well known as the two-attack model; consequently, I consider it to be an oicotypal variation of the typical typological pattern (a specialized rendition common to certain specific areas). I discuss its relationship to the standard typological pattern of "Snow White" in more detail in the following section.

9. I have previously shown how the typological pattern suggested here operates in twenty-four versions of "Snow White." See S. Jones, "The Construction of the Folktale: 'Snow White,'" Ph.D. diss., University of California, Davis, 1979.

10. These versions are found in Alcée Fortier, *Louisiana Folktales* (New York: Houghton Mifflin, 1895), pp. 56–61; and Juan B. Rael, *Cuentos Españoles de Colorado y de Neuvo Mejico* (Stanford: Stanford University Press, 1957), pp. 254–56.

11. These functions form the basis for the structural patterns identified by Propp and Dundes, i.e., Propp's thirty-one–function sequence and Dundes's two-, four-, and six-motifeme sequences. However, just as the functions that Dundes found characteristic of North American Indian folktales were different from those identified by Propp, so I have found a distinctive set of functions characteristic of "Snow White" and other folktales of persecuted heroines. While I have borrowed Propp's methodology, I have deduced different results. The exposition of these results is the focus of this final section of this essay.

12. I noted this pattern of hostilities in "Snow White" in the *Journal of American Folklore* 92 (1979): 69–73, where I referred to this pattern of repeated hostilities but did not explore the concept in depth. This essay is an attempt to document and analyze that pattern more thoroughly.

13. Except those oicotypal versions that present a third instance of hostility.

14. Propp actually anticipates the relationship of motifs, episodes, and functions as I outline them here in Table 9.1, when he lists his functions as occurring in variants, which are realized by motifs; thus his variants are more specific manifestations of the general action described by a particular function, much as the episodes that I identify are. However, he makes no attempt to correlate these variants to individual tale types or to describe the typological sequences of variants that might define tale types, whereas I use the concept of the episode as a morphological unit to identify typological structures in folk narratives. As a rule, structural studies have not attempted to identify the typological units or pattern of events common to and characteristic of a particular narrative (such as comparative versions of a particular tale type), and hence, their structural categories (the functions) have remained very general. Some studies approach structural analysis of individual tale types, for example, Dov Noy, "The Jewish Versions of the 'Animal Languages' Folktale (AT 760): A Typological-Structural Study," *Studies in Aggadah and Folk-Literature* (Jerusalem: Akdamon, 1971): 171–208; Heda Jason, "Structural Analysis and the Concept of the 'Tale-type,'" *Arv*, 28 (1972): 36–54; Lubomir Dolezel, "From Motifemes to Motifs," *Poetics* 4 (1972): 55–90; and E. M. Meletinskij, "Typological Analysis of the Paleo-Asiatic Raven Myths," *Acta Ethnographica* 22 (1973): 107–55. However, for the most part, they do not advance structural typologies for those individual tale types; instead, they fit their tale to the Procrustean bed of Propp's generic typology of thirty-one functions. Unlike the other structural studies, however, Noy's article attempts to combine generic and typological analyses (much as I do). He shows how the versions of AT 670 found in the Israel Folklore Archives are actually oicotypal variants of the tale type identified by Aarne-Thompson, thus verifying the traditional concept of a type as employed by Aarne-Thompson. Moreover, he shows how these oicotypal variations do not interfere with the sequence of events, but instead are

added on to them at the start and end of the tale, hence suggesting to me that a significant typological pattern (which Noy fails to identify) is at work in versions of "The Animal Languages," much as one functions in "Snow White." Finally, Noy shows how motifs are changed in the oicotypes of this folktale as the result of ethnic preferences, but their structural slot is maintained in the tale type, which supports my argument. For example, Noy points out that the snake, which figures prominently in European versions of "The Animal Languages" as the donor of the gift of understanding animal speech, is not a popular figure in Hebraic lore, and hence it is usually replaced by Leviathan or sometimes a raven in the Israeli versions of this folktale. In sum, Noy's structural study comes the closest to duplicating my approach, and his article provides additional proof for some of my findings, but he stops short of identifying the structural typology (or pattern) of the tale; instead, he applies Propp's structural model to it.

15. These outlines are derived from: *The Complete Grimm's Fairy Tales* (New York: Pantheon Books, 1972); E. Henry Carnoy et Jean Nicolaides, *Traditions populaires de l'Asie mineure* (Maisonneuve & C. Leclerc, 1889), no. 5; Thomas Frederick Crane, *Italian Popular Tales* (Boston: Houghton Mifflin, 1889), no. 21.

16. See, for example, James Bruyn Andrews, *Contes ligures, traditions de la Rivière recueillies entre Menton et Genes* (Paris: E. Leroux, 1892), no. 58; M. Cerquand, *Legends et recits populaires du pays basque*, 4 vols. (Pau L. Ribaut, 1875–82), vol. 4, no. 106; Jon Arnason, *Islandic Legends*, translated by Powell and Magnusson (London: D. Nutt, 1883), pp. 108–14; W. Henry Jones and Lewis L. Kropf, *The Folktales of the Magyars*, collected by Kriza, Erdelyi, Pap, and others (London: E. Stock, 1889), no. 35; and Henri Alexandre Junod, *The Life of a South African Tribe* (London: D. Nutt, 1935), p. 266 ff. Some unusual versions of "Snow White" from the Caribbean conversely present only one cycle of persecution — the heroine is rivaled, killed, and then rescued. In these accounts, for example, the heroine will be living elsewhere at the start of the narrative, the persecutor becomes jealous, the heroine is killed, and finally, the heroine is rescued. The fact that some narrators consider one instance of the persecution cycle as dramatically significant, suggests the narrative integrity of these cycles is reasonably strong. Thus, these single-cycle versions are additional support for the dramatic and narrative validity of this cycle as a generic structure.

17. Ilana Dan, "The Innocent Persecuted Heroine: An Attempt at a Model for the Surface Level of the Narrative Structure of the Female Fairy Tale," in Heda Jason, ed., *Patterns in Oral Literature* (Paris: Mouton Publishers, 1977), pp. 13–30.

18. In another essay in progress, I have undertaken to document in more detail the way this pattern of repeated persecution underlies the related folktales of persecuted heroines noted in the text. Unfortunately, such an argument is too lengthy for presentation here; for the purposes of this essay, we must content ourselves with the documentation supplied by Dan. Additionally, a similar instance of such a repeated pattern of action underlying a folk narrative is presented by Dell Hymes in "Folklore's Nature and the Sun's Myth," *Journal of American Folklore* 88 (1975): 345–69. Hymes's article points out a doubled pattern of action (the hero desires, travels, discovers, and stays twice in the narrative) in a Kathlamet Chinook myth.

19. Max Lüthi, *Once Upon a Time: On the Nature of Fairy Tales* (Bloomington: Indiana University Press, 1976).

20. See Bruno Bettelheim, *The Uses of Enchantment: The Meaning and Importance of Fairy Tales* (New York: Random House, Vintage Books, 1977) and A. S. Macquisten and R. W. Pickford, "Psychological Aspects of the Fantasy of Snow White and the Seven Dwarfs," *Psychoanalytic Review* 29 (1942): 233–52, for interpretation of the bleeding as a sign of menstruation. See these and the other studies referenced in "The Pitfalls of Snow White Scholarship" for further discussion and corroboration of the interpretations suggested here.

21. Arnold van Gennep, *The Rites of Passage* (Chicago: University of Chicago Press, 1960).

22. In addition to the interpretation suggested above, the structural patterning in "Snow White" may also be correlated to Joseph Campbell's monomyth and to Jung's process of individuation (the heroine achieves a reconciliation of conscious and unconscious anxieties through a journey into her unconscious), and to Lévi-Strauss's orchestrated score

(the heroine achieves a reconciliation of the dialectical extremes of life and death, sexuality and asexuality, through mediation between opposites). These correlations suggest that several general patternings are at work in the narrative simultaneously. The structures that I identify in "Snow White" do not preclude the possibility that other structures underlie that folktale; they simply appear to be the most apparent formal organizations of that narrative.

Bibliography

Aarne, Antti, and Stith Thompson. *The Types of the Folktale: A Classification and Bibliography.* Helsinki: FFC 184, 1961. Provides the long-standard typological descriptions of the major folktales in the Indo-European tradition, based on the morphological unit of the motif. Presents nearly 2,000 analyses of tale types identifying predominant events and motifs.

Bremond, Claude. "Le message narratif." *Communications* 4 (1964): 4–32. Proposes some revisions for Propp's structural theory, which include his differentiation between deterministic and probabilistic motifemes; "multidimensional" syntax is proposed, which includes a number of sequences that are superimposed within a given folktale.

Campbell, Joseph. *The Hero with a Thousand Faces.* Princeton: Princeton University Press, 1968. Identifies the separation, initiation, and return pattern described by van Gennep as a generic model underlying many fairy and folktales.

Dan, Ilana. "The Innocent Persecuted Heroine: An Attempt at a Model for the Surface Level of the Narrative Structure of the Female Fairy Tale." In Heda Jason, *Patterns in Oral Literature,* pp. 13–30. Paris: 1977. Follows Proppian theory and identifies a common pattern of the double persecution of heroine in two environments underlying five fairy tales.

Doležel, Lubomír. "From Motifemes to Motifs." *Poetics* 4 (1972): 55–79. Presents a theoretical discussion of the method of structural analysis in order to propose a tripartite scheme of the strata of the story structure: motifeme, motif structure, and motif texture, which reflect increasing degrees of specificity.

Dundes, Alan. "From Etic to Emic Units in the Structural Study of Folktales." *Journal of American Folklore* 75 (1962): 95–105. Argues for abstracted structural analysis of folk narratives in place of item-oriented descriptive analysis of previous folklore research. Adapts linguistic theory to folktale analysis in order to identify the (phon)emic level of narratives as distinct from their (phon)etic level.

Greimas, A. J. *Sémantique structural.* Paris: Larousse, 1966. Revises Propp's set of seven actants in fairy tales and suggests describing actants in terms of the syntactic relationship of the binary pairs of subjects and objects of essential verbs.

Meletinski, Eleasar M. "Typological Analysis of the Paleo-Asiatic Raven Myths." *Acta Ethnographica* 22 (1973): 107–55. Applies Propp's model to a group of Eskimo folktales and shows their conformance to the prescribed typological pattern.

Nathhorst, Bertel. *Formal or Structural Studies of Traditional Tales: The Usefulness of*

Some Methodological Proposals Advanced by Vladimir Propp, Alan Dundes, Claude Levi-Strauss and Edward Leach. Stockholm, 1969. Presents an informative comparative discussion of some major structural methodologies. Mostly useful as a survey of these approaches.

Noy, Dov. "The Jewish Versions of the 'Animal Languages' Folktale (AT 670): A Typological-Structural Study." In J. Heinemann and D. Noy, *Studies in Aggadah and Folk-Literature.* Jerusalem: 1971. Shows how versions of AT 670 are oicotypal variants of the tale type identified in Aarne and Thompson, thus verifying their conception of the tale type.

10. The Encyclopedia of the Folktale

HANS-JÖRG UTHER

Since 1975 a reference work in German has been appearing fascicle by fascicle which aims at presenting the results of over 150 years of international research in the field of past and present folk narratives.[1] The title, *Enzyklopädie des Märchens* (Encyclopedia of the folktale) is not intended to suggest a genre restriction of the type found in modern definitions. The work is concerned with all those categories which the Grimm brothers included in their *Household Tales*, animal stories, fables, religious legends, etiologies, legends, novellas, jocular tales, fairy tales, and so on.

"One of the goals of the Encyclopedia," according to the editors and staff in the foreword to volume 1,[2] is to compare "the rich traditions of oral and written folk narrative material from many different ethnic groups [and establishing] the relevant social, historical, psychological and religious backgrounds." In addition, the Encyclopedia clearly exemplifies the interrelationship between the folk narrative tradition and literature. The processes by which themes and motifs are passed on are illustrated by reference to literary sources such as exempla and legend collections, sermon books, chronicles, and chapbooks. The mutual influence of literature and the oral tradition which

I would like to thank Ruth B. Bottigheimer for translating my contribution.

has always existed is thus made clear. The functions and regularities of the genres, their contentual and formal qualities, and their social background are addressed as part of the theoretical inquiry. This collective program is expressed in the subtitle, *Reference Book for Historical and Comparative Folk Narrative Research*. Approximately 3,600 articles, with about 1,000 cross references, are anticipated. These are listed alphabetically and are available to scholars and interested parties as a list of entries.[3] There are five kinds of articles:

1. Theories and methods, genre questions, problems of style and structure
2. Monographs on important tale types and motifs
3. Biology of folk narratives
4. Biographies of scholars, collectors, and authors of literary works relevant to folk narrative research and
5. National and regional surveys providing information about folk narrative tradition and folk narrative research.

Twelve volumes are planned, each consisting of five fascicles. They, as well as a supplementary volume, will appear approximately once every two to three years.

Four volumes with approximately 1,200 research articles, which is one-third of the number planned, are now available. They comprise articles from "Aarne" to "Formelhaftigkeit, Formeltheorie" (The formulaic, theory of the formulaic).

Some examples of published entries from different kinds of articles indicate the variety of the entries:

1. Well-known and internationally occurring stories: "Aladdin," "Ali Baba and the Forty Thieves," "Cinderella," "Doctor Know-All," "The Three Brothers," "The Dwarf and the Giant," "The Dragon Slayer," "The Monster as Bridegroom," "The Predestined Wife," "The Crop Division"
2. Recurring narrative figures: the doctor, deceiver, fairy, blind man, braggart, beggar, Billy the Kid, Brer Rabbit, Eulenspiegel, Davy Crockett, Faust, Dracula
3. Founders of religions, saints, religious aspects and legendary material, Jesus and Christian traits in folk narrative tradition, demons, demonology, possession, and exorcism
4. Mythological figures: Achilles, the Argonauts, Danae and Danaids, Circe
5. Animals and fabled creatures: eagle, ape, basilisk, elephant, unicorn, fish, bear
6. Thematic groupings and motifs: old people, bribery, theft, adul-

tery, amity and enmity, character attributes and tests, the external soul

7. Problems of structure and style: abstractness, absurdity, adaptation, association, exoticism, factuality, fictionality, authenticity, reworking, esthetics, ambivalence and the extreme situation
8. Theories and methods: experimental folk narrative research, computer technology and analysis, archaic traits, fakelore, fieldwork, theory of fragments, anthropological theory
9. Genres: ballads, bestiaries, anecdotes, the epic, comics, exempla, chapbooks, Aesopic fable and tradition, coyote tales, endless tales, fables and fable books, film, broadsides, women's tales
10. Context of narrative material: acculturation, biology of folk narratives, narration, narrators
11. Important sources and biographies of authors: Giambattista Basile, Giovanni Boccaccio, Erasmus of Rotterdam (sources); Martha Beckwith, Franz Boas, Linda Dégh, Richard M. Dorson, Alan Dundes, Sigmund Freud (biographies of scholars)
12. Countries and regions: Albania, Algeria, Argentina, Basque country, Afro-American narrative, Anglo-American narrative material, Brazil, Bulgaria, Denmark, Ecuador, Chile, China, France, etc.

An early evaluation of the articles already published makes clear that the contributions about tale types, motifs, and works of world literature relevant by virtue of their content predominate in number and extent (approximately 50 percent). It is further evident that the strict division between oral and literary tradition maintained in folk narrative research for decades is a fiction; at best one can posit an interdependence between the two forms of transmission. The articles point at shifts in function and content of tales, genre shift, and sociohistorical backgrounds. Most entries had to be freshly conceptualized and are not to be found in any other reference work. The editors and editorial staff are primarily concerned with aspects relevant to folk narrative research.[4] This primary concern is justified if they are to maintain the encyclopedic claim of the title, that is, to represent the entire scholarship of a particular area of specialization. Only selected information, however, can be published. This is a problem that all specialized reference works must confront. The material presented centers on aspects relevant to folk narrative research, for example, in connection with information about the use of computers ("Computertechnik und -analyse") or in connection with biographical data (such as "Walt Disney"). Each article, however, provides bibliographical references facilitating access too further information.

As experience has shown, most differences between contributors on the one hand and the editors and editorial staff on the other hand grow out of the fact that the contributor conceives of the entry from his or her own perspective and thus does not meet the needs of folk narrative research in general, so that reworking or including additional material is necessary. The editorial staff's guidelines, provided to the contributors at the time of assigning entries, emphasize the relationship to historical and comparative narrative research and offer the first point of departure for avoiding problems in defining the particular function of the entries. This problematic point is being closely pursued by the editors who hope to find a middle ground between the requirements for specialized information and the justifiable desire of the contributor for his or her own presentation of the material. A further problem, which became apparent directly after the completion of the first few articles, is the documentation of the narrative material, which reflects to a certain extent inadequate research conditions in some countries. Despite encyclopedic requirements, certain limitations regarding regions and ethnic groups had to be accepted. The following statement appears in the foreword to volume 1 of the Encyclopedia:

On the one hand, the areas to be compared should not be limited prematurely, if the virtually unbounded supranational interconnections of the narrative material was to be respected. On the other hand, an equal representation of all parts of the world would have required completely different means of gaining contributors, and one would have had to await the research results of further generations. To achieve a defensible comprehensiveness it has been agreed that, above all, the oral and written narrative forms for Europe and of cultures affected by European influence, as well as of Mediterranean and Asian cultures, be embraced and treated. On the other hand, the narrative material of peoples who have been without written records until relatively recently are taken into consideration in the reports summarizing regional research. A certain weighting corresponding to the current state of research was accepted as unavoidable. The possibility cannot be excluded that Central European and particularly German examples dominate in the articles: this, too, is rather an expression of the state of research in this country [Germany] than of ideological ethnocentrism.[5]

Since its appearance much notice has been taken of the Encyclopedia among experts in the field. The variety and thematic breadth of the contributions have met unbounded praise. It has been widely and favorably reviewed (to date 115 reviews from 55 journals) with only peripheral criticism about the presentation of individual facts or the geographical orientation of some of the articles. Thus G.-L. Fink objected, with some justification, "que le monde occidental paraît presque fatalement favorisé,"[6] a problem of which the editors are fully aware, as mentioned above. The ethnologist R. Schott aptly ascertained that unfortunately the entire African continent was taken note of with only very few entries, which here means survey articles.[7] Further research in the African nations themselves is awaited, so that the African continent can be considered more extensively in the supplementary volumes when they appear.

Such an undertaking as the Encyclopedia naturally has a history, which in conclusion should be briefly touched upon.[8] Since the 1920s the still relatively new discipline of folklore has been aware of the need for comprehensive reference books for instructors, students, and the general public, which could describe specific areas of the field. Two reference works developed with this in mind were the well-known *Handwörterbuch des deutschen Aberglaubens* and the *Handwörterbuch des Märchens*, the latter of which was discontinued after volume 2 in the confusion of World War II.[9] The *Handwörterbuch der Volkssage*,[10] planned in the 1950s, also remained truncated, with only three fascicles appearing[11] — and further projects, such as a reference work of the *Schwank* (jocular tale) or of the *Sage* (legend) have still not been realized.[12] A continuation of the *Handwörterbuch des deutschen Märchens*, which remained thematically limited to German-speaking areas, was conceptually outdated by broader approaches and could no longer be justified on a scholarly basis. When the publishing house of Walter de Gruyter (which published the *Handwörterbuch des deutschen Märchens* and the *Handwörterbuch des deutschen Aberglaubens*) approached the folklorist Kurt Ranke, then teaching at Kiel University, with the request to complete this reference work, Ranke rejected their proposal but suggested at the same time an encyclopedia that would encompass the entire field of folk narrative research with special emphasis on the Eurasian and Mediterranean cultural zone as a center of influence.[13]

In 1956 Ranke founded a research group: Enzyklopädie des Märchens. For the encyclopedia he planned, a comprehensive archive was to be gathered and sources and collections from the whole world were to be worked up. From these modest beginnings in Kiel, the research group developed with the financial support first of the Deutsche Forschungsgemeinschaft and later (1967–72) of the Stiftung Volkswagenwerk. In Göttingen since 1960, the research group has developed an archive with approximately five hundred thousand texts, specialized literature in the less accessible languages, and a large specialized library.[14] Since 1980 the encyclopedia has been a project of the Akademie der Wissenschaften in Göttingen, where the editorial staff is also located.

After twenty years of preparation, the editing phase began in 1973.

To guarantee organizational continuity for the project, the editor-in-chief, Kurt Ranke, created an editorial staff. Hermann Bausinger (Tübingen), Wolfgang Brückner (Würzburg), Max Lüthi (Zürich), Lutz Röhrich (Freiburg), and Rudolf Schenda (Göttingen, now Zürich) joined him as co-editors. Since 1981 Rolf Wilhelm Brednich, now the head of the Göttingen research group, has also been a co-editor. Present editorial staff members are Ines Köhler, Elfriede Moser-Rath, Christine Schmidt, and Hans-Jörg Uther.

Besides undertaking this enormous project, Kurt Ranke also founded the international journal *Fabula,* which has appeared since 1958. He organized the international Folktale Studies Congress in Kiel and Copenhagen in 1959, which was followed by the founding of the International Society for Folk Narrative Research (ISFNR), thus bringing about scholarly contacts among researchers on every continent. Many contributors to the Encyclopedia are also contributors to *Fabula* or members of the ISFNR. The Encyclopedia is precisely the sort of project which relies on the cooperation of internationally proven specialists. More than 330 researchers from the most diverse disciplines have worked together on the articles already published: folklorists, classicists, theologians, ethnologists, educators, art historians, media experts, and philologists of English, German, Slavic, and Romance languages. Half of the contributors come from German-speaking areas, the others from more than forty countries. Particularly well represented are the United States and the countries of eastern Europe. The Encyclopedia is meant to serve a broad spectrum of scholars besides folklorists as a reference work: ethnologists, anthropologists, theologians, social scientists, psychologists, educators, art historians, media experts, and philologists and literary scholars. The editors and the editorial staff hope to maintain the continuous appearance of the work, so that the project can be completed in the year 2000 or very soon thereafter. At that point, the way would be clear for a translation into other languages, an undertaking which many reviewers have already called for.

Notes

1. K. Ranke et al., eds., *Enzyklopädie des Märchens: Handwörterbuch zur historischen und vergleichenden Erzählforschung,* 4 vols. to date. (Berlin and New York, 1975–84), vol. 1: 1975–77; vol. 2: 1977–79; vol. 3: 1979–81; vol. 4: 1982–84.

2. Ibid., 1:vi.

3. The 3rd edition of the "Stichwortliste" was published in 1976; a new edition will appear in 1985.

4. See also the foreword to the *Enzyklopädie,* 1:vii.

5. Ibid., p. vi.

6. Review in *Études germaniques* (1977), p. 58.

7. Review in *Zeitschrift für Ethnologie* 103 (1978): 127–30.

8. H.-J. Uther, "Bericht über die *Enzyklopädie des Märchens und den gegenwärtigen Stand der Forschung,*" *Fabula* 15 (1974): 250–55.

9. E. Hoffmann-Krayer and H. Bächtold-Stäubli, eds., *Handwörterbuch des deutschen Aberglaubens* (Berlin, 1927–42); L. Mackensen, ed., *Handwörterbuch des deutschen Märchens,* 2 pts. (Berlin, 1930–40), pt. 1: 1930–34; pt. 2: 1934–40.

10. See W. E. Peuckert in *Fabula* 1 (1958): 164 ff.

11. W.-E. Peuckert, ed., *Handwörterbuch der Sage* (Göttingen, 1961–63).

12. K. Ranke, "Deutsche Beiträge zur internationalen Erzählforschung: Nach einem Arbeitsbericht vorgetragen auf dem Volkskunde-Kongreß vom 20–25. Oktober 1958 in Nürnberg," *Zeitschrift für Volkskunde* 55 (1959): 280–84.

13. For Ranke's biography and bibliography see *Fabula* 24 (1983): 1–10.

14. On the development and history of The Archive, see Uther, "Bericht über die *Enzyklopädie*" and R. Wehse, "Die Enzyklopädie des Märchens," *Artes Populares* 4–5 (1978–79); 1979: 272–83. A detailed study of the constitution of the *Arbeitsstelle* and of the editorial work recently became available: M. Grätz, "Die Enzyklopädie des Märchens: Untersuchungen zu Konzeption, Erstellung und Nutzungsmöglichkeiten," dissertation prepared for admission to Advanced Library Service, Köln, 1984.

11. Fairy Tales from a Semiotic Perspective

ANNA TAVIS

With the publication of Vladimir Propp's classical work *Morphology of the Folktale*,[1] the genre of the folktale became a popular object for structuralist research. Formalist studies of folklore material concentrated primarily on similarities and archetypal features shared by folktales of various cultures and different historical periods. The search for repetitive patterns and their generalized meanings overshadowed concern with the creativity and uniqueness of individual tales. As a result, the relevance of the creative element in folklore became questionable.

Students of folklore recognize, however, that such conclusions come as a result of analytical speculations, yet scholars should go beyond pure theory to folklore's individual and creative nature. The traditional definition of creativity as something nonrepetitive and unique is inappropriate in folktale research and can lead to a perceived discrepancy between analytical and empirical results. If we were to reconcile these differences, we should first redefine creativity itself. The conceptual framework for the new approach to the creative process is suggested by the Soviet semiotician Juri Lotman and the Tartu school of semiotics.[2] Tartu scholars approach the concept by redefining the creative process as it occurs in different types of texts in different cultures.

In terms of Tartu semiotics, culture is understood as a hierarchical system of an almost infinite number of texts or secondary modeling systems.[3] By a "secondary modeling system" Lotman and his colleagues understand literature, art, religion, folklore, and myth as systems within a culture which are secondary to "natural" languages.[4] Different cultures rearrange these hierarchies of secondary systems in an individual way.[5] Lotman divides all existing texts into two basic categories according to the orientation of their communication:

Texts in the first category, which includes folk tales, follow a single system of rules or a canon.[6] When considered on the level of a natural language, these texts retain their individuality. On the level of culture, as secondary modeling systems, the texts in the first category do not contain any information unfamiliar to the members of that culture. Texts of this type represent a syntagmatic[7] rearrangement of what is already known.

The second category includes texts oriented toward two or more systems of norms. When a text meets one of these norms it cannot fulfill the requirements of the others. These texts often deviate from their "logical intention" and "defeat" readers' anticipations.[8] Texts of the second category "deconstruct" what is perceived by the readers as their origins.[9]

The structure of texts in the first category parallels the structure of natural languages. Both structures operate with signs and a limited number of combination rules of these signs. Semioticians have noticed this similarity and have tried to create a grammar of plots and their functions for folktales, detective stories, myths using the principles of the grammar of natural languages. Vladimir Propp's *Morphology of the Folktale* is the classic work of this kind of scholarship.

After outlining a general conceptual framework, Lotman examines specific features of different "secondary systems." A closer look at the structure and functions of natural languages and folktales uncovers their essential differences.[10] In a natural language the form of expression is highly predictable, but the message or content is open and unpredictable. In a tale not only the form but also the content is governed by a limited number of rules and stipulations which the audience knows. According to communication theory, this should mean that a folktale is devoid of creativity.[11] If this conclusion is true it becomes necessary to consider how a folktale retains its value and originality in society.

A possible explanation of the source of creativity in a folktale lies in the semiotic nature of culture and the types of communication present within that culture. The conclusion that a folktale cannot be creative is derived from the assumption that the process of communication works according to the following three-stage model:[12]

Addresser — Context/Message/Contact/Code — Addressee.

An addresser delivers his message to an addressee. This is an "I to you" type of communication.

In contrast to Roman Jakobson, Lotman and his group see a possible alternative type of communication which they call "auto-communication." This communication works on the following pattern:

Addresser — Message/Content — Shift of Content — Addresser.

The addresser himself transforms the message. This is an "I to me" type of communication. Both the addresser and the addressee are represented by the same subject. The majority of folktales belong to the "I to me" type of autocommunication.

It could be argued that "I to me" communication is only the modi-fication of a relationship where a distance in space is substituted by a distance in time. A closer look at the autocommunication confirms that there are qualitative differences between the two types: "I to you" and "I to me." [13]

Since the majority of folktales tend to manifest an "I to me" type of communication, it is worth considering the existing subdivisions within autocommunication. Lotman points out two distinct types: (1) a mnemonic type, and (2) a "discovery" type.

A mnemonic type of autocommunication is a reminder to oneself about something already known. [14] An abbreviation in a notebook can be reconstructed into the exact information that has been recorded. This mnemonic type of communication would also be the "reading" of familiar sacred texts by someone who does not know how to read. Specialists have pointed to the historical instance of this phenomenon in the early written tradition of the Koran. [15] In the "Scriptio defectiv" the absence of both short and long vowels and diacritical marks made it impossible to decipher except by those who already knew the text from having heard it read.

Autocommunication of the discovery type includes not only actu-alization of the originally recorded information but also a significant addition of information. The discovery type of autocommunication rearranges structural elements of a text. The text's function changes. In mnemonic communication the text carries complete information, whereas in the discovery communication the text serves as a stimulus for the increase of information.

Both dichotomies, an "I to you" and an "I to me" communica-tion, as well as the mnemonic and discovery types within auto-communication, are common for other semiotic systems and texts. An obvious example comes from the visual arts. Compare, for instance, the different effects produced by an elaborate pattern on the wall of a mosque and a nineteenth-century European painting. The function of the pattern is to trigger the imagination, an example of "I to me" communication. The painting, on the other hand, is a means of communicating a new message or an "I to you" type of communication. Another example of the discovery communication type is the Japanese Buddhist ritual: a Buddhist monk contemplating a stone garden, stones carefully arranged within a small square. What makes it "a garden" is the presence of an informed observer.[16]

Lotman's theory of two possible communication patterns assigns the folktale a new place in the overall culture. The folktale is a "discovery" text in the autocommunication channel. It can be analyzed strictly in terms of language, motifs, and "functions," but its inspirational effect on an individual must also be explored.

The following analysis of the brothers Grimm tale "Marienkind" illustrates different aspects of autocommunication.

Narrative prose does not normally have a regular pattern of rhythms and rhymes. These specifically "poetic" features are compensated for by other means in the works of prose and especially in the folktale. Repetition of syntactic, phonetic, and semantic elements of the text becomes equivalent to the rhythm of a poem. Grimms' tale "Marienkind" in two versions, 1807 and 1857, provides an example of how the interaction of codes takes place in a folktale.[17]

Scholars have often commented on the changes in the text that were codified in the last, the so-called "Large" 1857 edition of the tales. For our purposes it is more important to look at what Wilhelm Grimm did not and could not change in this tale, and to find elements that constitute "the memory of the genre."[18] Changing the vocabulary and imagery in the 1857 version, Grimm does not violate the basic syntactic structure of the tale. He strictly follows the syntactical pattern of inversion as it is introduced in the first line:

Vor einem grossen Walde lebte ein Holzhacker mit seiner Frau. (1808)

Es war einmal ein grosser Wald, davor wohnte ein Holzhacker. (1857)

The first line sets a narrative rhythmic pattern occasioned by the retention of specific elements in the tale. This pattern is repeated throughout the entire text.

Da nun der Holzhauer eines Tages sehr traurig darüber in dem Wald war. (1808)

Eines Morgens ging der Holzhacker voller Sorgen hinaus in den Wald an seine Arbeit. (1857)

Wie nun die Jungfrau Maria von ihrer Reise zurückkehrte. . . . (1808)

Gar nicht lange, so kam die Jungfrau Maria von ihrer Reise zurück . . . (1857)

Most sentences maintain inversion with the help of semantically re-
dundant words, such as "so," "nun," "da," which serve the narrative
pattern.

Da legte sie ihre Hand auf sein Herz.

Da sprach sie noch einmal.

Da versank das Mädchen in einen tiefen Schlaf. (1857)

Da nun der Herbst kam. . . . (1808)

Syntactic inversion is reinforced by semantic repetition. The concrete, analytical information of subject-predicate is retarded to emphasize the semantic openness of modifiers. The model is set in the
first sentence.

Vor einem grossen Walde — lebte — ein Holzhacker. (1808)

Es war einmal ein grosser Wald. (1857)

The proportion of changeable elements in the tale is small compared to the number of the repeated patterns. The syntactic, semantic, and lexical rhythms maintain conformity with the canon of the
genre. Thus, despite many "ideological" changes, such as a more pru-
dent religious context, Grimm does not violate the basic rhythmic
pattern of the tale. A tale is only a tale when it contains a number of
repetitions common to the folktale as a secondary modeling system.

The notion of autocommunication is a valuable tool for folklore
research. The majority of folklore texts are oriented toward "I to
me" communication of the discovery type. It is possible to find examples of mnemonic folklore texts, but they are outside of the focus
of this essay.

In conclusion, I want to return to Vladimir Propp's *Morphology of
the Folktale*. In Russia and after its translation into English in 1958, it
was at first enthusiastically received but later criticized for its for-
malism.[19] I would defend Propp against his critics by arguing that the
formal structural approach, if defined in terms of communication theory, aims at describing possible stimuli for the imagination rather
than at creating an exhaustive, self-explanatory scheme. Lotman provides a cultural context for Propp's theories by applying hs concept of
universal communication channels and their role in society to the

study of secondary modeling systems. This approach allows for an individual creative contribution to be seen in relation to the cultural background of the contributor. Lotman's theory opens new perspectives for an understanding of the folktale as a creative genre.

Notes

1. V. Propp, *Morphology of the Folktale* (Moscow, 1928). The first English translation was published in 1958.

2. It is important to note that the semiotic theory of the Tartu school is not based exclusively on the concepts of the American semiotician Charles S. Pierce. Tartu semiotics is an independent development which stems from many sources: Russian as well as East and West European, and American.

3. See a series of articles in *Trudy po znakovym systemam* (Tartu, 1968–82) and especially "O Dvux Modeliax Kommunikazii v systeme kul'tury ("On two models of communication in a cultural system")," in *Materialy vsesojuznogo simposiuma po vtorichnym modelirujushim systemam* (Tartu: Tartu University Press, 1975), pp. 227–43.

4. English, Russian, French, for example, would be natural languages or "primary" systems. Lotman's secondary modeling system recalls Roland Barthes' study of the nature of a myth with the difference that Lotman uses the concept in a general cultural context. Barthes, *Mythologies* (Paris: Aux Editions de Seuil, 1957), p. 222.

5. Different rearrangements of these hierarchies constitute the subject matter for Lotman's typology of culture. I. Chernov offers a comparison of three models of culture (Ju. Lotman, C. Lévi-Strauss, S. Lemm) in an article, "Tri Modeli Kultury" ("Three models of culture") *Quinquagenaria: Collection of Works by Young Philologists to Celebrate Professor Ju. Lotman's 50th Birthday* (Tartu: Tartu University Press, 1972), pp. 5–18.

6. Medieval literature and works of the eighteenth-century European classicism are among other texts in this category.

7. Lotman uses "syntagmatic" and "paradigmatic" in the Saussurian sense. Texts are members of a syntagm, a successive structure, or a paradigm, a hierarchical structure.

8. Roman Jakobson in the essay "Linguistics and Poetics" uses a similar term "frustrated expectation" in a different context. *Collected Writings* (The Hague, Paris and New York: Mouton Publishers, 1981), 3:33.

9. The novel as it developed in Europe in the nineteenth century is an example of such self-deconstructive genre. It deviates from its original intention and thus is constantly in the making.

10. By a function Lotman means the social and cultural role of a secondary modeling system. Propp's definition of function is more specific: "Function is understood as an act of a character, defined from the point of view of its significance for the course of the action." *Morphology of a Folktale*, 5th ed. (Austin and London: University of Texas Press, 1968), p. 21.

11. As anthropologists notice, the semantics of a fairy tale was originally created in its relation to ritual. With time, however, this connection lost its immediacy and folktales became asemantic in their cultural function. Lévi-Strauss noted similar tendencies in myth, which eventually loses its semantics and becomes a reorganization of a known pattern on the level of culture. Psychoanalytical, Christian, feminist, and Marxist critics may disagree with the term "asemantic." In fact, the existence of a variety of different interpretations may be explained only as a result of loosening links between the original intention and independent existence of individual tales.

12. Jakobson, "Linguistics and Poetics," p. 22.

13. Already in the 1930s the Russian psychologist Lev Vygotsky studied the phenomenon of "inner speech," which constitutes the psychological foundation for Lotman's "two channels of communication."

Inner speech is not the interior aspect of external speech — it is a functon in itself. It still remains speech, i.e. thought connected with words. But while in external speech thought is embodied in words, in inner speech words die as they bring forth thought. Inner speech is to a large extent thinking in pure meanings. It is a dynamic, shifting, unstable thing, fluttering between word and thought, the two more or less stable, more or less firmly delineated components of verbal thought. Its true nature and place can be understood only after examining the next plane of verbal thought, the one still more inward than inner speech.

That plane is thought itself. . . . every thought creates a connection, fulfills a function, solves a problem. (Lev Vygotsky, *Thought and Language* [Cambridge, Mass.: MIT Press, 1981], p. 149)

14. The traditional beginning of "Once upon a time" may be considered an example of a "mnemonic element" in a fairy tale on the level of the language. The level of the plot contains a mnemonic element of, say, traditional three sons, one of whom is thought to be a "fool." A "discovery" element consists of the individual variations on all the levels: plot, language, character development.

15. *Koran*, translated into Russian and commentary by I. Ju. Krachkovsky (Moscow, 1963), p. 674.

16. Katsuo Saito and Sadaji Wada, *Magic Trees and Stones: Secrets of Japanese Gardening* (New York, Rutland, and Tokyo, 1970), pp. 101–4.

17. The tale tells how the Virgin Mary adopted a little girl from a poor family. The girl became known as the Marienkind. Once she disobeyed Mary's orders but refused to confess her transgression. In retaliation Mary deprived the child of speech and banished her from heaven. For years afterward the girl refused to admit her guilt even after Mary took away her three children. In the end, under threat of death, Marienkind confessed and Mary gave back her speech and returned the children to their mother.

18. The term is used by Mikhail Bakhtin in his study of the novel: *Problems of Dostoyevsky's Poetics*, trans. R. W. Rotsel (Ann Arbor: University of Michigan Press, 1973).

19. Claude Lévi-Strauss, "L'analyse morphologique des contes russes," *International Journal of Slavic Linguistics and Poetics* 3 (1960): 122–49; Archer Taylor, "The Biographical Pattern in Traditional Narrative," *Journal of the Folklore Institute* 1 (1964): 114–29.

Bibliography

Archer, Taylor. "The Biographical Pattern in Traditional Narrative." *Journal of the Folklore Institute* 1 (1964): 114–29. Explores repetitive patterns in traditional narrative in a rather unconventional manner and critically evaluates Propp's method.

Barthes, Roland. *Mythologies*. Paris: Edition du Seuil, 1957. "Le Mythe, aujourd'hui" is particularly insightful from the semiotic point of view.

Lévi-Strauss, Claude. "L'analyse morphologique des contes russes." *International Journal of Slavic Linguistics and Poetics* 3 (1960): 122–49. Lévi-Strauss's speculative and deductive method is in many ways a critical response to Propp's empirical and inductive study.

Lotman, Juri. *The Structure of Artistic Text*. Translated by Ronald Vroon and Gail Vroon. Ann Arbor: University of Michigan Press, 1977. An overall picture of Lotman's application of semiotic concepts in literature. The first half is a theoretical introduction to semiotics of human sciences; the second an analysis of literary texts that illustrates Lotman's theories.

Matejka, L., ed. *Readings in Soviet Semiotics*. Michigan Slavic Materials no. 15. Ann Arbor: University of Michigan Press, 1977. Comprehensive collection of translations encompassing a wide variety of subjects, ranging from machine translations to history, art, and music. Each article is supplied with an editorial commentary that offers explanations for the basic theoretical concepts.

Meletinsky, E. M. *Poetika Myfa.* Moscow: Vysshaja shkola, 1976. (Not yet translated into English.) Meletinsky is one of the leading contributors to the folklore research among Soviet semioticians. The monograph summarizes Western and East European theories of the genesis of the myth and investigates the roles that myth has in different societies.

Propp, Vladimir. *Morphology of the Folktale.* Austin: University of Texas Press, 1968. The work that pioneered structuralist inquiry in folklore scholarship and that triggered intensive research and controversy.

12. Fairy Tales
and Psychotherapy

SIMON A. GROLNICK

Fairy tales and psychotherapy have been related to each other throughout this past century of psychological, or, as some would have it, Freudian, man. I would like to provide a brief historical perspective and then discuss how some of the recent shifts in the theories of psychotherapy (more specifically, Freudian psychoanalytic psychotherapy and psychoanalysis), have affected the way the psychoanalyst sees and uses fairy tales, and how these shifts point to potential areas of research into the psychology of the fairy tale. The current sense of research in applied psychoanalysis is actually a re-searching of the theories of psychoanalysis, with an emphasis on early infant and child development, the psychologies of the first few (pre-oedipal) years of life, as well as the application of hermeneutic and general system theory to the analyst-analysand and child-parent dyads.[1] It is hoped that this time of shifting, change, and controversy among psychoanalysts will lead to more specific reassessments of the nature of and the therapeutic workings of the fairy tale as one of its byproducts.

Psychoanalysis has antagonized, and continues to antagonize, many scholars involved in the historical, structural, anthropological, and even psychological study of the fairy tale.[2] The following quotation from one of the earliest psychoanalytic attempts to study the fairy tale systematically may illuminate the all too slow growth of the cooperative spirit between psychoanalysis and its sister disciplines. Franz Ricklin, an analyst from Zurich, began his 1915 monograph, *Wish Fulfillment and Symbolism in Fairy Tales*, with the comment, "In psychiatry and the related sciences there has lately broken out a struggle for and against the Freudian theories. I count myself fortunate to be able, by means of such beautiful, inviting material as fairy tales, to bear a weapon in this conflict."[3]

The paradox of a fairy tale club or spear defending psychoanalysis from its enemies is a telling metaphor.

Since psychoanalysis straddles the arts and the sciences, attacks have always been expected from both quarters. The artists felt psychoanalysis reduced art to its primitive motives. The scientists claimed analysis could show no experimental evidence that the theories were speculative. The analysts attempted to find proof in so-called objective reality, within the dualistic reality-versus-fantasy thinking that characterized early psychoanalysis. The dream was Freud's "royal road to the unconscious" — but ultimately other roads were sought out; since then the manifestations of magical thinking, metamorphosis, and poetic mechanisms such as metonomy and synechdoche have been found in folklore, fairy tales, mythology, poetry, and imaginative literature.[4]

Circular reasoning prevailed during the inevitable but unfortunate early period of "applied psychoanalysis" (that is, the application of analysis to areas beyond the clinical treatment of a patient on the couch). Freud's original observations on mythology, Greek drama, and literature, as well as his clinical observations led him to spell out the various magical "primary process" mechanisms (quick transfers of labile psychic energy) of the unconscious (displacement, condensation, and symbolization), the libidinal stages (oral, anal, and so on), and the psychological complexes, especially those derived from the Oedipus, Electra, and Narcissus stories. When called upon to defend the findings of psychoanalysis, aside from the publications of case histories, early psychoanalysts used cultural manifestations such as folklore, fairy tales, and imaginative literature to re-find the stages, mechanisms, and complexes.[5] The system became so closed that Ricklin was able to write in his monograph: "I arrived at the pleasing and important conclusion that for my work, it was not necessary for the investigation of fairy tales, in a psychological sense, to know their historical pedigree first."[6] The concept of a universal unconscious began to develop and reached its most intense and reductionistic form. The historical, cultural, and political contexts of a fairy tale tended to be not so much ignored as taken for granted, a situation that unfortunately still occurs. Much of this appears to be an unconscious survival from a time when psychoanalysis struggled against both its real and its projective enemies, reminding us how much the early adventurers into the dark caves of the unconscious felt they were close to the treasure of the "truth."

The tendency to deal with the fairy tale reductionistically persisted. In a 1953 article entitled "Fairy Tale and Dream," which appeared in the respected series the Psychoanalytic Study of the Child, the first psychoanalytically trained anthropologist, Géza Róheim, wrote:

> It seems that dreams and myths are not merely similar, but that a large part of mythology is actually derived from dreams. In other words, we can not only apply the standard technique of dream interpretation in analyzing a fairy tale but actually can think of tales and myths as having arisen from a dream, which a person dreamed and then told to others, who retold it again, perhaps elaborated in accord with their own dreams.[7]

In truth, the early analysts tended to *equate* the dream with fairy tales, folklore, and romantic literature. Added to the list were children's dreams, which Freud thought of as relatively simple wish-fulfillments. During a time when Lévy-Bruhl's concept of remainders of savage practices was influential in anthropology, psychoanalysis, caught in the same intellectual currents, thought of the fairy tale as a rather pure culture of unconscious, "primary process" mechanisms, and treated the fairy tale, along with folklore and myth, as if it were a cultural dream. This period in psychoanalysis, now called "id analysis," contrasts with the more recent phase of "ego analysis,"[8] wherein the workings of the ego (more abstract, more logical, more in keeping with cultural reality, and more adaptive) were taken into account when attempts were made to understand any psychic event, personal or cultural.

It is interesting to review Freud's handling of fairy tales before the earliest advent of ego psychology. As is well known, Freud did indulge in universal symbolism. In a 1911 paper written with classical scholar Ernst Oppenheim, Freud said, for example: "In dreams in folklore, gold is seen in the most unambiguous way to be a symbol of faeces,"[9] a point that seemed hardly debatable. Yet only two years later, in "The Occurrence in Dreams of Material from Fairy Tales," Freud noted:

> If we carefully observe from clear instances the way in which dreamers *use* fairy tales *and the point at which they bring them in,* we may perhaps also succeed in picking up some hints which will help in interpreting remaining obscurities in fairy tales themselves.[10] [My italics.]

Here Freud emphasizes the manner in which the fairy tale is handled, how it finds an equivalency in the psychological thematics of the patient. Freud seemed to carry his reductionistic weapons along with more sophisticated, broader concepts which foreshadowed the capacity for modern ego psychoanalysis to be a "general psychology," in which the findings of other fields, from biology and genetics to the philosophy of science, anthropology, literature, and history, must be taken into account when assessing any psychological entity. In the 1950s, Erik Erikson also stressed the point at which personal psychology and culture touch and resonate.[11]

With the advent of ego psychology, psychoanalysis began to emphasize the way individuals use their cultural lore, and some of the possible ways and under what circumstances fairy tales and folktales are created.[12] Rather than treating these tales as virtual equivalents of dreams or samplings of the unconscious or symptons such as phobias, analysts are beginning to think of the interplay between personal and cultural psychology. Individuals are shaped by their culture, and at the same time, their own psychology, resonating with the culture, helps to create the culture. When both child psychoanalysis and psychoanalytic anthropologists became more interested in child-rearing methods and their ultimate outcome, the early interplay between the mother and the child and its later elaboration in the interplay between the individual and the culture became increasingly important areas of research. But it was no longer a one-way street — the postulation of feedback mechanisms led to a more serious use of general system theory, with less tendency to regard outer reality and inner psychic life as dualistic entities.

One important influence in guiding psychoanalysis toward this less reductionistic direction was the paper "Ego Psychology and Mythology" by psychoanalyst Jacob Arlow.[13] He stressed the need for inner, personal fantasy to find validation in the communal fantasies that appear within fairy tales, folklore, and mythology. Significantly, his bibliography included not only psychoanalytic references but also the writings of Joseph Campbell, Richard Chase, Richard M. Dorson, Robert Graves, Claude Lévi-Strauss, Bronislaw Malinowski, and Henry Murray. After Arlow's frequently cited paper, analysts would at least hesitate to analyze cultural products before doing their extra-disciplinary homework.

It would be hoped that with an increasingly sophisticated, psychoanalytic view of the fairy tale, criticisms of Freud's writings on fairy tales, such as Harold Bloom's,[14] would no longer apply. Bloom, in a review of Bettelheim's both praised and maligned book, *The Uses of Enchantment*, reminded us that Freud did not believe fairy tales elicited feelings of the uncanny.[15] For Freud, the uncanny inevitably arose from something that had been familiar but had been repressed.[16] Since fairy tales did not conform, and probably because he felt they were too close to children's dreams and consequently did not use repression as a mechanism in their formation (Freud felt that children's dreams were simple wish-fulfillments), fairy tales did not evoke the sense of the uncanny for him. However, if we now believe fairy tales are complex narratives, partaking of all psychological structures — id, ego, and superego — as well as manifesting the use of repression, for Bloom, they can qualify.

Let us now discuss some trends that have occurred in parallel fashion, both in folklore research and methodology and in psychoanalytic theory. From the beginning, there were always folklorists who felt that the tale could not be taken from the context of the teller, the audience, and the culture. This is exemplified by Edwin Hartland in his 1895 *The Science of Fairy Tales:* "The student must know something of the habits, the natural and social surroundings and the modes of thought of the people whose stories he examines."[17] Hartland stressed the importance of the storyteller: "It is difficult to sever the occasion and the mode of the tale telling from the character of the teller; nor would it be wise to do so." He quotes from Giuseppe Pitré's description of a master tale-teller in Sicily. She could not be separated from Pitré's childhood experience, as, according to Pitré:

Messia witnessed my birth and held me in her arms: Hence I have been able to collect from her mouth the many and beautiful traditions to which her name is appended. She has repeated to the grown man the tales she had told to the child thirty years before; nor has her narration lost a shade of the old sincerity, vivacity and grace. The reader will not find the cold and naked words.

This appears in Hartland's first chapter, significantly entitled, "The Art of Story Telling."[18]

The Russian folklorists traditionally were concerned about the storyteller, especially in descriptions of the epics called the *Byliny.* This tradition was carried out tellingly by Linda Dégh in her studies of Hungarian peasant society and its folktales.[19] Dégh pointed out the differences in both the tellers and the students of the folktale — those who were most interested in edification, in the content and structure of the folktale, in contrast to those more attuned to the emotion, a processual view of the tale-telling experience. Dégh writes:

We have become convinced that it is inflexible devotion to one version which spoils a tale. The creative and talented storyteller has no way of proving his talent other than through smaller or more considerable modifications. . . . Most of the excellent storytellers like to talk, and the attention which the audience offers them contributes to the utmost to the drawing out of the story.[20]

These more functionalist trends in folklore studies correspond to the current interest in the dyadic interplay between the mother and child during early development. One could easily include here the current interest in development phases, for example, in Mircea Eliade's view of the fairy tale as exemplifying a rite of passage, the pursuing and mastery of an ordeal, and issues of separation and individuation which appear in early toddler stages (Mahler et al.) and during the adolescent recapitulation of these phases.[21] Pertinent too are Victor Turner's views of ritual taking place within a realm that is neither reality nor fantasy but "liminal."[22] Turner and others (Erving Goffman, Antonin Artaud, Jerzi Grotowski, Richard Schechner) emphasize performance theory, which would include the telling of a story as a performance, an actor-audience experience.[23] More and more, those studying literary and drama theory are using the latest psychoanalytic studies of the interactive process as it proceeds throughout development, from the earliest mother/child interaction, through the toddler stages of separation and the formation of the self, adolescence, pregnancy, adulthood, mid-life, and old age.

The work of the current British psychoanalytic "object relations school" offers a chance to conceptualize the way fairy tales are involved in the developmental process, and therefore to better understand their nature and their capacity to promote growth and development, and hence to have potential therapeutic value.[24] This is especially significant now that fairy tales seem to be so much involved in bedtime rituals in an age of separate beds and bedrooms.[25] Unless for social or economic reasons there are bed partners, infants and children tend to develop security objects. The security, or transitional object, as D. W. Winnicott called it, is our first illusion, a kind of half-conscious "let's pretend."[26] It is both me and "not me," both reality and fantasy. It could be a blanket, but also a crib space, a mobile hanging over a crib, or a tune. As the developmental line progresses, an imaginary companion can appear. So does the whole process of externalizing dream symbols into ludic (play) symbols,[27] and, ultimately, when maturation allows abstract thinking, an imaginary, metaphorical or potential space, as Winnicott termed it, can develop.

The fairy tale is made of the stuff of the enchanted and the prosaic, the real and the unreal. It is read by an empathic caretaker who provides a steady base and a constant presence that assuages the fear of loss of self and body image that occurs before sleep, when the child is ill, or when he or she is able to conceptualize and fear death.[28]

Winnicott once said there is no such thing as a baby. He could not picture an infant without its dyadic caretaker. Here we could say, there is no such thing as a fairy tale, or a folktale in isolation — no fairy tale without a narrator and a listener. So there is a correspondence between many trends in modern psychoanalysis and those in folklore and anthropology — we are all becoming more interested in the process of the creation of, the telling of, and the listening to the fairy tale, and the interaction of all of these. In both fields, however, there is continued realization that a tale, or a fantasy, has its own structure, and that a purely functional or processual approach would be a narrow one. But the influences of hermeneutic thinking on the literary aspects of folklore and its equivalent influence on psychoanalysis have led to more and more acceptance of a *hermeneutic* circle, and further away from the dangers of circular reasoning and reductionistic thinking.

Let me be more specific about the implications of Winnicott's concept of the transitional, or security, object for psychoanalytic therapeutics.[29] The security object, in its concrete form, is a treasured, vitally important aspect of the child's life. Optimally its comfort-producing properties gradually become internalized into the autonomous capacity for self-comfort. Traces of the need for security objects persist normally and can be seen in some of our habits (the ritualistic aspect of smoking, drinking, our interests in texture, even influences on the specific aspects of our collecting art objects).

How does this apply to the fairy tale? There have always been reports in the psychoanalytic literature of fairy tales that become organizing schema for an individual's life course. If the specific fairy tale becomes a transitional object (or transitional "phenomena" as Winnicott would have termed it), then there is a greater tendency to retain it inside and feel comforted when it is being reenacted in life — where it becomes a kind of script creating a drama that is unconsciously being played out by the individual. On another level, the general function of the telling of fairy tales can be internalized. Perhaps this can help us to explain some aspects of certain artists, especially those whose life corresponds, often unfortunately, with the content of their productions. The very young Antoine de Saint Exupéry, for example, was immersed in his mother's storytelling.[30] Is it only coincidental that in *The Little Prince* his little pilot disappears in the vastness of the desert, and that an accident-prone and counterphobic Saint Exupéry disappeared in 1944 during a reconnaisance flight that led him over the area of his birth in southern France?

The Uses of Enchantment, Bettelheim's contribution to the psychoanalytic study of fairy tales, has been important and most provocative. He can be faulted for his continued application of reductionistic universal symbols to understand fairy tales. But interspersed in his loosely organized book are ideas that are not incompatible with more comprehensive views of the fairy tales. Bettelheim especially stressed the need for the child to *externalize* his or her inner fantasy life in the fairy tale and its equivalents. Healthy development involves the alternating and simultaneous processes of internalization and externalization. If as infants we only internalized the functions of our caretakers, we would become totally self-sufficient creatures, self-involved, and hardly able to adapt to the reality of the world around us. Piaget implied this with his complementary concepts of assimilation and accommodation.[31]

When told by a loving caretaker, the fairy tale triggers a response in the young child's imaginative life consistent with its developmental level at the moment. This is particularly true at the stage when the blanket or doll is experienced as part-me, and part-not-me, when it is not a true symbol (where the symbol and the referent are for the most part distinguished from each other) but a pre- or protosymbol.[32] Here the fairy tale is received more for its form, body, texture, and content. Split worlds of good and bad cannot be integrated yet by the immature mind; the tale is experienced as comforting because of the steadying, stabilizing effects of having it read at a potentially threatening time (bedtime) by a constant, comforting parent. Just as the blanket gradually becomes a symbol for the mother (or caretaker), the fairy tale becomes accepted at a symbolic level — that is, the same fairy tale and the same blanket are utilized at a different, more advanced cognitive and affective developmental level. Meaning, interpretation, and narrative gradually enter. Bettelheim and Winnicott imply that if the parental "owner" of the blanket, or the fairy tale, is able to provide the illusion that they belong to the child, and if the interaction has been empathic and developmentally tuned, then blankets, dolls, and fairy tales, and the imaginative mental play involved can serve, along with other aspects of the growing child's experience, as parental helpers in negotiating the many developmental tasks that beset each parent-child unit. It is when empathy is missing and parental inconstancy and trauma are too prevalent that the fairy tale can become an instrument of fear, even the core of a future maladaptive pattern.

Bettelheim wondered whether a study could be done to show the effects of fairy-tale deprivation on children, to see whether or not there is a syndrome analagous to the negative effect of dream deprivation on personality development.[33] Another area deserving more methodical study is the bibliotherapeutic[34] use of fairy tales in the treatment of so-called "borderline" children, that is, children who have had difficulty with internalization of psychological functions, who tend to lack a sense of self-object constancy, and who cannot integrate polar splits, especially the "goods and bads."[35] In the context of a good therapeutic relationship, just as in the healthy developing child, the fairy tale provides an evocative, concrete Zoroastrian view of the world that might be relevant to the borderline child, and might provide a step on the way toward the realization of more progressive levels of psychological structure. Another potentially fruitful area to study might be the result of introducing student psychotherapists to the world of the fairy tale to sensitize them to the child's and the adult's imaginative world. Psychotherapy seminars using more sophisticated literature have been conducted for this purpose. Then, one could challenge Bettelheim's call for a return to the literary fairy tale by comparing the effect of traditional fairy tales to that of our modern folklore as portrayed in movies, on television, and in children's stories and comic books. I would expect that, at a certain point in the child's development, the anachronistic fairy tale would begin to lose out to the more culture-appropriate story or movie.

Another interesting area is the direct observation and the electroencephalographic study of early infantile "protodreams" (not yet symbolic) and the protosymbolic nature of transitional objects. These protodreams appear around six months of age. The capacity to have a transitional object and a protodream seem to be part of the same process of affective and cognitive development. If this is one of the roots of the creative, imaginative process, then it might provide a way of understanding the relationship of the dream to creativity, the fairy tale, and folklore in a scientific sense.

Psychoanalysis is becoming increasingly aware of its intrinsic involvement in narrative — the patient's story, with all its manifest and latent drama, tragedy, majesty, mystery, and "magic." Freud was a master storyteller and writer.[36] His earliest case histories have been peopled by protagonists now known as, for example, "Little Hans," "The Wolf Man," and "The Rat Man." This is how Freud closes the story of Little Hans, the first description of a child analysis:

In conclusion, let me add these words. With Hans' last phantasy, the anxiety which arose from his castration complex was also overcome, and his painful expectations were given a happier turn. Yes, the Doctor (the plumber) *did* come, he *did* take away his penis — but only to give him a bigger one in exchange for it. For the rest, our young investigator has merely come somewhat early upon the discovery that all knowledge is patchwork, and that each step forward leaves an unsolved residue behind.[37]

Fairy story, cautionary tale, fable — what is the model? Freud's narrative form speaks of his ability as a universal storyteller. There have been virtually countless retellings of his original case studies — each psychoanalytic writer retells the story, adding his or her own interpretation, depending on the prevailing theoretical psychoanalytic culture of the day. The Wolf Man, for example, was treated after Freud by two important analysts, each of whom wrote extensively on their experiences and revisions of his story.

In other words, psychoanalysis itself stands within the folkloristic tradition. The patient and the analyst tell and retell, interpret and re-interpret the story of the patient. Oral tradition prevails until, in the fashion of Perrault or Grimm, the decision is made to write up and publish a case report. Although psychoanalysis is more than folklore, and its scientific status is crucial to it, perhaps there is now less necessity for it to over-scientize itself by retaining mechanistic metaphors in its theory. The object-relations school described above tends to see the self and the other as the basic motivational units — in other words, to concretize into theory Freud's statement that psychoanalysis could never reach beyond anthropomorphization.[38] This, combined with hermeneutic and interactive influences, might help to bring it closer to its basic folkloristic nature. As a byproduct, it is hoped that we may learn more about the spirit and the process that helps to create fairy tales and folklore in the first place.

Notes

1. The importance of interactionism in social and psychoanalytic theory can be gleaned from Von Bertalanffy's writings on general system theory. See *General System Theory: Foundations, Development, Applications* (New York: George Braziller, 1968), as well as *Perspectives on General System Theory: Scientific-Philosophical Studies* (New York: George Braziller, 1975).

2. A recent example can be found in Robert Darnton's essay, "Peasants Tell Tales: The Meaning of Mother Goose," *The Great Cat Massacre and Other Episodes in French Cultural History* (New York: Basic Books, 1984).

3. Ricklin, *Wish Fulfillment and Symbolism in Fairy Tales* (New York: The Nervous and Mental Disease Publishing Company, 1915; repr. New York: Johnson Reprint Corporation, n.d.), p. 1.

4. The kind of thinking involved in this searching can be found in some of the writings of Ella Freeman Sharpe, especially her essay "Mechanisms of Dream Formation," in *Dream Analysis: A Practical Handbook for Psycho-analysts* (London: The Hogarth Press, 1959).

5. See an interesting article touching on this subject: W. Grossman and B. Simon, "Anthropomorphism: Motive, Meaning, and Causality in Psychoanalytic Theory," in *The Psychoanalytic Study of the Child*, vol. 25 (New York: International Universities Press, 1969).

6. Ricklin, *Wish Fulfillment*, p. 2.

7. Róheim, "Fairy Tale and Dream," Psychoanalytic Study of the Child, vol. 8 (New York: International Universities Press, 1953), p. 394.

8. For one of the early, basic texts on ego psychology, refer to Heinz Hartmann, *Ego Psychology and the Problem of Adaptation* (1939; repr., New York: International Universities Press, 1958).

9. Freud and Oppenheim, "Dreams in Folklore" (1911), *Standard Edition*, vol. 12, pp. 177–211.

10. Freud, *Standard Edition*, vol. 12 (London: Hogarth Press, 1953–74), p. 283.

11. Good examples are Erikson's early books, *Childhood and Society* (New York: W. W. Norton, 1950), and *Toys and Reasons* (New York: W. W. Norton, 1977).

12. See Hartmann's text, footnote 8.

13. Arlow, "Ego Psychology and Mythology," *Journal of the American Psychoanalytic Association* 9 (1969): 371–93.

14. Bloom, "Driving Out Demons," *The New York Review of Books*, 15 July 1976 (review of Bettelheim).

15. Bettelheim, *Uses of Enchantment: The Meaning and Importance of Fairy Tales* (New York: Random House Vintage Books, 1977).

16. Freud, "The Uncanny" (1919), *Standard Edition*, vol. 17, pp. 218–56.

17. This interesting but quite dated book by Edwin S. Hartland is entitled, in full, *The Science of Fairy Tales: An Inquiry into Fairy Mythology* (London: Salter Scott, 1895; repr. Detroit: The Singing Tree Press, 1968).

18. Ibid., p. 11.

19. Dégh, *Folktales and Society: Story-Telling in a Hungarian Peasant Community* (Bloomington: Indiana University Press, 1969).

20. Ibid., p. 224.

21. Eliade, *Rites and Symbols of Initiation: The Mysteries of Birth and Rebirth* (1958; repr. Harper Colophon Books: New York, 1975); M. Mahler, F. Pine, and A. Bergman, *The Psychological Birth of the Human Infant: Symbiosis and Individuation* (New York: Basic Books, 1975).

22. Turner, *From Ritual to Theatre: The Human Seriousness of Play*, Performing Arts Journal Publications, 1982.

23. Goffman's performance theories mesh well with the work of Artaud, *The Theatre and Its Double* (1938; repr. New York: Grove Press, 1958); and Richard Schechner (the environmentalist, theater director, and theoretician), *Essays on Performance Theory, 1970–1976* (New York: Drama Book Specialists, 1977).

24. A balanced and reasonable summary of the principles of object relations theory can be found in John Sutherland's article, "British Object Relations Theorists: Balint, Winnicott, Fairbairn, Guntrip," *Journal of the American Psychoanalytic Association* 28: 829–60.

25. P. Ariès, *Centuries of Childhood: A Social History of Family Life* (1960; repr. New York: Vintage Books, 1962).

26. Winnicott, "Transitional Objects and Transitional Phenomena" (1951), in *Collected Papers: Through Pediatrics to Psychoanalysis* (New York: Basic Books, 1958), pp. 229–42.

27. J. Piaget, *Play, Dreams and Imitation in Childhood* (1951; repr. New York: W. W. Norton, 1962).

28. See S. Grolnick and A. Lengyel, "Etruscan Burial Symbols and the Transitional Process," in *Between Reality and Fantasy: Transitional Objects and Phenomena*, ed. S. Grolnick and L. Barkin, in collaboration with W. Muensterberger (New York: Jason Aronson, 1978).

29. See Winnicott, "Transitional Objects."

30. See Curtis Cate, *Antoine de Saint-Exupéry: His Life and Times* (New York: G. P. Putnam's Sons, 1970), pp. 14–18.

31. For an exposition of these concepts, see Piaget, *Play, Dreams and Imitation*.

32. See a fine description of a developmental, object relations, and affect-oriented approach to the creation of symbols that meshes well with the work of Winnicott: H. Werner and E. Kaplan, *Symbol Formation* (New York: Wiley, 1963).

33. Bruno Bettelheim, *The Uses of Enchantment: The Meaning and Importance of Fairy Tales* (New York: Random House, Vintage Books, 1977).

34. See C. Shrodes, "Bibliotherapy: An Application of Psychoanalytic Theory," *American Imágo* 17 (1960): 311–19.

35. A number of examples of the use of fairy tales in the psychoanalytically oriented therapy of borderline children can be found in R. Ekstein, *Children of Time and Space, of Action and Impulse: Clinical Studies on the Psychoanalytic Treatment of Severely Disturbed Children* (New York: Appleton-Century-Crofts, 1966).

36. The classic here is Stanley Hyman, *The Tangled Bank: Darwin, Marx, Frazer and Freud as Imaginative Writers* (1959; repr. New York: Grosset & Dunlap, 1966).

37. Freud, "Analysis of a Phobia in a Five-Year-Old-Boy" (1909), *Standard Edition*, 10:100.

38. See H. Nunberg and E. Federn, eds., *Minutes of the Vienna Psychoanalytic Society, 1906–1908* (New York: International Universities Press, 1962).

Bibliography

Bettelheim, Bruno. *The Uses of Enchantment: The Meaning and Importance of Fairy Tales*. New York: Random House, Vintage Books, 1977. Now the most comprehensive and ambitious work on the current psychoanalytic view of fairy tales. Suffers from some reductionism, a lack of good organization, and a lack of sophistication in other disciplines; yet it is interesting and a good book for the reader to grapple with.

Cath, C., and S. Cath. "On the Other Side of Oz: Psychoanalytic Aspects of Fairy Tales," in *The Psychoanalytic Study of the Child* 33 (1978): 621–39. Using the *Wizard of Oz* as a take-off point, the authors demonstrate a number of psychological factors that describe the creation of and the use of the fairy tale. Short and well-written.

Freud, Sigmund. *The Occurrence in Dreams of Material from Fairy Tales*. London: Hogarth Press, 1913. By definition, dated, but a good example of how Freud observed that a fairy tale could become psychological, a theme, appear as associations to dreams, or as "screen" (or disguised) memory.

Greenacre, P. "Hans Christian Andersen and Children." *The Psychoanalytic Study of the Child* 38 (1983): 617–35. Discusses the interplay between Andersen's life and his work; an excerpt from a forthcoming book.

Grolnick, S. and M. Grolnick. "The Little Lame Prince: Transitional Phenomena in a Nineteenth-Century Children's Story." *The Psychoanalytic Study of Society* 9 (1981): 160–79. Using the children's story by Dinah Craik, an attempt is made to understand the dynamic of both the story and the author's life, utilizing principally the ideas of Winnicott on transitional objects and phenomena.

Hagglund, T. and V. Hagglund. "Mourning and Death in Fairy Tales and Folklore." *Psychiatria Fennica* (1976), pp. 25–33. Analyzes the theme of death and mourning in fairy tales, a subject more available in the Jungian literature. The authors try to show that the fairy tale helps the child to deal with the meaning of death.

Ricklin, F. *Wish Fulfillment and Symbolism in Fairy Tales*. New York: The Nervous and Mental Disease Publishing Company, 1915. Reprint. New York: Johnson Reprint Corporation, n.d. An early, very dated but ambitious study analyzing the fairy tale, using it to prove and justify contemporary psychoanalytic theory. Discusses wish fulfillment, symbolism, and defense mechanisms (as understood in 1915) as they appear in fairy tales.

Rinsley, R. and E. Bergmann. "Enchantment and Alchemy: The Story of Rumpelstiltskin." *Bulletin of the Menninger Clinic* 47 (1983): 1–13. An example of a recent "object-relations theory" view of a specific fairy tale. The psychoanalytic theory here is somewhat closer to the reader's experience than the earlier, mechanistically tinged studies.

Schwartz, E. "A Psychoanalytic Study of the Fairy Tale." *American Journal of Psychotherapy* 10 (1956): 740–62. Even though this paper is almost twenty years old, it is one of the best short expositions of the psychoanalytic point of view on fairy tales. Balanced and shows only a minimum of the heavy-handed reductionism that is all too characteristic of such studies.

13. The Criminological Significance of the Grimms' Fairy Tales

GERHARD O. W. MUELLER

In September 1983, leading newspapers[1] reported the surfacing of another fairy tale from the Grimm brothers' collection — either fairy tale number 201, or, more likely, legend number 11. It was front-page news for the *New York Times*.[2] People young and old, and scholars in particular, were delighted. Apparently of relatively recent origin, the tale refers to a war that lasted thirty years, probably the Thirty Years War of 1618 to 1648. That war raged particularly in the central German area in which the Grimm brothers collected most of their tales. In this latest story mother takes her "dear child" into the forest to protect her from the ravages of the impending war. Of course there is a happy ending. No punishment for child abandonment befalls the mother. After all, had she not acted with good motives and for justifiable ends? How juridical a moral! Juridical indeed, and that is the crux of the matter! Virtually every tale in the Grimm collection contains a message of law — not necessarily criminal law[3] — of justice, of punishment, or of pardon.

This discussion encompasses only the Grimms' fairy tales, in which legal historians perceive a legacy of legal lore. Of less relevance for law are fairy tales collected or composed by others, ingenious literary products, many of which are in the realm of fiction and often exude little more than the originator's imagination, while yet others are the repository of history, geopolitics, religion, geography, or travel lore. The legal lore in the Grimms' fairy tales has its counterpart in the law lore revealed by anthropologist E. Adamson Hoebel and jurisprude Karl N. Llewellyn — revealed for the Cheyennes, in the epic *Cheyenne Way*.[4] Precedent provides the element common to both collections.

Jacob Grimm had studied law with one of the greatest legal philosophers of all times, Friedrich Karl von Savigny, the founder of the "historical school" of jurisprudence. For a time von Savigny had served as Prussian minister of law codification. Yet he steadfastly refused to codify anything. To him true law lived in the spirit of the people, the *Volksgeist*, and that spirit changed gradually over time in accordance with the *Zeitgeist*. Jacob Grimm incorporated this basic tenet into his own literary, linguistic, and folkloric studies.

In preliterate societies the legal tradition of a given age, of a given people, reveals and transmits itself through rituals or tales. It is contained in what old-timers and youngsters are told, around the hearth, the campfire, or wherever generations meet. Jacob Grimm and his brother Wilhelm, both practiced in philology, went to work. And they reaped a rich harvest of *Märchen* ("tales"). The word *Märchen* is derived from the medieval High German word *Maere*, denoting messages that are important and that are to be remembered. Lawyers may feel inclined to translate *Maere* as "precedent," because the *Märchen*, taken together, provide a consistent guide of conduct, as do the precedents of law as a body. For the *Märchen* to be considered precedents of legal lore, the external and internal consistencies of their morals must be established.

German legal historians had worked on that problem for a century and a half. Jacob Grimm himself had initiated that research in his *German Legal Antiquities* (1828),[5] and in his seven-volume *Wisdoms* (commenced 1840),[6] a collection and interpretation of folk wisdom, and contained in maxims, slogans, parables, and stories, as sources of law. But the foundations for this research had been laid by the two-volume collection of fairy tales ("Children-and-House [or Family]") stories, published in 1812 and 1815.[7]

The fairy tales caught the immediate attention of German scholars of law, and the legal historians in particular, who found therein the mirror reflection of positive law. The law itself was that which was contained in the (Latin language) codes, the *Leges Barbarorum*, of the early Middle Ages, that is, of the time before lawyers emerged as a class or profession in northern Europe. During the late Middle Ages, after lawyers had established themselves as a dominant caste, positive law could be found in imperial decrees, city codes, and the judgments of city courts and high tribunals. But living law, especially as applied at the local level, was not the (Latin) lawyers' law; it was, instead, the law as transmitted from generation to generation among nonlawyers (law receivers, rather than law-givers), in the German tongue. In this sense, the fairy tales were not just a reflection of positive law, they were indeed positive law.

One cannot view the fairy tales collected by the brothers Grimm as a homogeneous mass, or as a set of rigid legal propositions. The fairy tales vary in age, and they metamorphosed with changing social and political conditions. In other words, just as precedents of law do change and must change over time to properly serve the ends of temporal justice as understood at a given time, the fairy tales had to change. Thus, they were indeed precedents.

Jens Christian Jessen, in a decades-long research undertaking, demonstrated this point clearly. He found many bridges between the law in the Grimms' fairy tales and the law of official documentation.[8] Legal references to the fairy tales can indeed be dated to anywhere from the seventeenth century back to the seventh century, with fragments of fairy tales from even earlier dates.

The *external* consistency of the Grimms' fairy tales with officially documented law is, thus, fairly well established. Their *internal* consistency has been established more recently. By internal consistency I mean that the messages of the fairy tales as a body of largely self-sufficient propositions do not grossly conflict with one another but instead form a harmonious whole. Applying "balance theory," Carol Auster demonstrated that 94 percent of fairy tales ended with completely balanced, positive relations,[9] leaving the reader or listener with an overall harmonious body of precepts and propositions.

It is astounding that so few criminologists have seen the value of Grimms' fairy tales as a source of criminological information. One of these few was Hans von Hentig, surely the greatest of German-American criminological scholars.[10] His observations on the revelations of the fairy tales, about the nature, form, and severity of punishments, are a major contribution to the history and psychology of crime and punishment.

Half a century earlier, in 1910, a Dresden prosecuting attorney, Eric Wulffen, had published his epoch-making research entitled "The Criminal Element in German Folk Tales," in the *Records of Criminal Anthropology and Criminalistics*, the journal edited by the Austrian Criminologist Hans Gross.[11] Wulffen analyzed the German fairy tales of the Grimms — as well as those of Ludwig Bechstein, J. K. A. Musäus, and others — from the perspective of criminological psychology. In the tales, he uncovered every conceivable criminal motivation,

Table 13.1 Fairy Tale Crimes and Their Punishments

CRIMES	HISTORIC PUNISHMENTS	TALE NUMBER (GRIMM)	FAIRY TALE	MÄRCHEN	COMMENTS
Witchcraft and attempted cannibalism	Death by fire	15	"Hansel and Gretel"	"Hänsel und Gretel"	Incineration
(Alleged) witchcraft and cannibalism	Death by fire	3	"Our Lady's Child"	"Marienkind"	At the stake (unrelated penitence)
Witchcraft and murder	Death by fire	46	"Fitcher's Bird"	"Fitchers Vogel"	Incineration — criminalistics
Witchcraft	Death by fire	49	"The Six Swans"	"Die sechs Schwäne"	At the stake
Witchcraft and solicited homicide	Death by fire	53	"Little Snow-White"	"Sneewittchen"	Red-hot shoes
Perversion of justice causing false execution (attempted)	Death by fire	9	"The Twelve Brothers"	"Die zwölf Brüder"	
Witchcraft and murder	Death by fire, outlawry, and death in forest	11	"Brother and Sister"	"Brüderchen und Schwesterchen"	
Murder and cannibalism	Drowning	26	"Little Red-Cap"	"Rotkäppchen"	Wolf = outlaw
Murder and cannibalism	Drowning	5	"The Wolf and the Seven Little Kids"	"Der Wolf und die sieben jungen Geißlein"	Wolf = outlaw

Crime	Punishment	Page	English title	German title	Notes
Witchcraft	Drowning	51	"Fundevogel"	"Fundevogel"	
Murder and causing cannibalism	Stoning to death	47	"The Juniper Tree"	"Machandelboom"	Conscience-death Frisian law? Ignorance of fact = impunity! Criminalistics
Attempted murder, fraud, and deceit	Capital: iron maiden	13	"The Three Little Men in the Forest"	"Die drei Männlein im Walde"	Barrel with nails — rolled into water
Impersonating royalty and deceit	Capital: iron maiden	89	"The Goose-Girl"	"Die Gänsemagd"	Barrel with nails — dragged by horses
Impersonating royalty	Capital: iron maiden	135	"The White Bride and the Black Bride"	"Die weisse und die schwarze Braut"	Barrel with nails — drawn through town
Impersonation and involuntary servitude	Blinding	21	"Cinderella"	"Aschenputtel"	
Impersonation and attempt to obtain property by false pretences	Tarring	24	"Mother Holle"	"Frau Holle"	
Grand theft	Hanging	192	"The Master-Thief"	"Der Meisterdieb"	Pardon — exile (for cunning)
Larceny	Corporal punishment	36	"The Wishing-Table, the Gold-Ass and the Cudgel in the Sack"	"Tischchendeckdich, Goldesel und Knüppel aus dem Sack"	

from base greed to the grossest form of psychopathology. Yet Wulffen was very apologetic. In an age that regarded fairy tales as sacrosanct, he had lifted the veil. Had he broken the magic? He apologized for having revealed the basic — the criminal — instincts which had always rested in the fairy tales.

In these tales of precedent, which the Grimms preserved for us, every category of crime appears along with the punishments to be imposed upon those found guilty (Table 13.1). The exact definition and scope of these crimes need not concern us here. But one crime, cannibalism, requires special mention. It is the only crime to appear in the fairy tales — and frequently at that — which does not have a counterpart in the positive law of the Middle Ages. It seems that the problem of cannibalism had been solved by society. Legal prohibitions were no longer needed, yet, in the minds of the people, cannibalism lived on, if only as a nightmare. Two of the fairy tales refer to cannibalism as having occurred long ago: "perhaps two thousand years ago,"[12] which means as much as a very long time. The thought of, and reference to, cannibalism, may have survived in the form of puberty rites in preliterate German society.[13] Certainly, some of the sting had been taken out of cannibalism by turning devoured children into kids of the animal variety, their mother an old goat, and the cannibal a wolf, as in "The Wolf and the Seven Little Kids" (#5: "Der Wolf und die sieben jungen Geisslein").

Tales appertaining to witchcraft represent one of the most heinous crimes. This crime frequently, though not necessarily, includes cannibalism or attempted cannibalism, as in "Hansel and Gretel" (#15).[14] In that tale the witch dies by fire, incinerated in her own stove. In "Mary's Child" (#3: "Marienkind") the witch likewise dies in the fire, at the stake (at least her penitence saves her from ultimate hell-fire). Incineration is also the punishment for the sorcerer (and murderer) in "Fitcher's Bird" (#46: "Fitchers Vogel") — a story rich in criminalistic lore and wisdom. Again, in "The Six Swans" (#49: "Die sechs Schwäne"), the witch dies at the stake, and fire death (having to dance in red-hot iron shoes) is the fate of the witch in "Little Snow White" (#53: "Sneewitchen"). (The witch in *Snow White* had also been guilty of solicitation to murder and attempted murder.) In "Brother and Sister" (#11: "Brüderchen und Schwesterchen") witchcraft and murder likewise lead to death by fire. The conclusion is inescapable: The principal punishment for witchcraft is burning. Indeed, Merowingian law (A.D. 481–751) provides for precisely that punishment and as late as 1310 Prussian law proclaimed that punishment for witchcraft.

But one other punishment may befall the witch or the murderer:

death by drowning. Such was the punishment in "Fundevogel" (#51: "Fundevogel"). Murder and cannibalism likewise are punished by drowning in "Little Red-Cap" (#26: "Rotkäppchen") and in "The Wolf and the Seven Little Kids" (#5: "Der Wolf und die sieben jungen Geißlein"). Legal history tells us that drowning was the preferred punishment for murder among some German tribes, for example the Saxons, certainly since the end of the Middle Ages, that is, the probable time of origin of these fairy tales in the form in which they have come down to us.[15] In "Juniper Tree" (#47: "Machandelboom") the witch, who had also induced cannibalism, dies under the weight of a falling stone. Stoning to death disappeared as a punishment in German tribal laws in the early Middle Ages, but it lived on in fairy tales.[16] Thus, "Juniper Tree" is another tale transmitting not just criminal law (including the rule that ignorance of fact, with resulting lack of criminal knowledge or intent, leads to impunity), but criminalistic widsom as well.

In three of my selected fairy tales we find one of the most interesting forms of punishment: being placed in a nail-studded barrel and being dragged through town by a team of horses ("Goose Girl" [#89: "Die Gänsemagd"] and "The White Bride and the Black Bride" [#135: "Die weisse und die schwarze Braut"]), or ultimately being dumped into the water ("Three Little Men in the Forest" [#13: "Die drei Männlein im Walde"]). The punishment in these three tales is imposed for forms of treason, deceit, or impersonating royalty, coupled with false imprisonment in one. The nail-studded barrel appears later in history in a much perfected form as the "iron maiden," an iron, spike-studded cage, in which the convict was literally punctured to death. Impersonation and involuntary servitude in "Cinderella" (#21: "Aschenputtel") are punished by blinding, which German tribes regarded a one of the most severe punishments, imposable only for treasonous acts and serious frauds, exactly as in "Cinderella."[17] But such serious crimes can also be punished by tarring, as in "Mother Holle" (#24: "Frau Holle"). Tarring and feathering can be found as punishment in north German and Scandinavian law, where the convict is turned into a bird as a preparation for the death penalty—the traditional sacrifice to appease the gods for having been outraged by the crime.[18]

Grand theft is punishable by hanging, as threatened in "The Master-Thief" (#192: "Der Meisterdieb") who, however, so impressed the monarch with his skill and cunning that he was pardoned and exiled. Petty larceny was punished corporally, as "The Wishing-Table, the Gold-Ass, and the Cudgel in the Sack" (#36: "Tischchendeckdich, Goldesel und Knüppel aus dem Sack") amply demonstrates.

Indeed, German tribes in the Middle Ages routinely hanged for grand theft and punished corporally for petty theft.[19]

Imprisonment as a punishment for crime does not exist in any of the fairy tales; imprisonment became a punishment in German territories only in the fourteenth century. By that time the central motifs of most of the fairy tales had been well formulated.

Being boiled in oil into which vipers were thrown is the most unusual punishment found in Grimms' fairy tales. It was decreed in "The Twelve Brothers" (#9: "Die zwölf Brüder") for perverting justice and causing (or attempting to cause) an innocent person to be executed. This punishment first appears in early Roman law, where the severest form of capital punishment consisted of being sewn into a sack, together with a viper, a rooster, and a monkey, and then being thrown into the water. A remnant of animal symbolism and sacrifice combined with the execution of the convict, it also points to the interrelatedness of the crimes and punishments among Indo-Germanic peoples, of whom the Romans and the Germans were equally a part. Both peoples worshipped gods with similar functions, though with different names. Among the most important religious rituals were sacrifices to these gods to appease them for offenses to deity.

One remaining criminological mystery in the Grimms' fairy tales is the frequent appearance of the wolf as aggressor, whether in "Little Red-Cap" or in the "Wolf and the Seven Little Kids." Psychoanalysts have made much of the symbolism which inheres in wolfdom.[20] But as far as the wolf's appearance as an aggressor in the fairy tales is concerned, the answer can be found more easily in law than in psychoanalysis. The barbarian codes refer to a convicted felon, punished by outlawing from the community, as wargus, or vargus. In his work on German legal antiquities (1828), Jacob Grimm wrote: "Wargus, however, signifies wolf and robber because the banished criminal becomes a resident of the forest, just like a predatory animal, and he may be hunted, just like a wolf."[21]

Professor Wilhelm Eduard Wilda devoted considerable attention to this issue in his work *The Criminal Law of the* [ancient] *Germans,* dedicated to, among others, Jacob Grimm, "as a token of intimate esteem and loyal and devoted friendship."[22] He recognized expulsion from the community as the principal and most severe form of punishment, and as the very crux for the understanding of Germanic criminal law. To him the same idea inhered in all German tribal laws (the *Leges Barbarorum*), whether the Salic, the Frankish, the Norwegian, or the Icelandic. For the most severe crimes, the culprit was sentenced to banishment from the community to the dreaded forest, there to be devoured by wild beasts, to perish, to become one of the wild beasts (werewolf), or to be hunted and killed.[23] The convict is a *vargus*, writes Wilda: "But vargus is also the name of the wolf, so that both concepts truly merged; that of the unprotected animal, pursued by all, and that of the human who finds himself in the same position."[24] Wilda points to the oldest source he could find for his proposition, Ulfilas' Gothic Bible translation in which the phrase "sentencing to death" is translated as *gavorgian ðanpan*.[25] The term *gavorgian*, the Gothic equivalent of the latin *vargus*, had at one point perhaps denoted little more than stranger, or, at worst, robber. The Gothic adaptation of the word as [*ga*]*vargian*, or [*ga*]*vergian*, clearly has the meaning (in modern German) of *würgen*, that is, somebody (man or beast) who jumps at the throat, who throttles and kills: the wolf, or the wolf-man — banished to the forest. Similarly, the German legal historian Heinrich Brunner could proclaim that "the common Germanic designation of the banished criminal was 'warc, wary', which literally means as much as Würger [throttler] or wolf"; and he cites precedent from several points in the Germanic law area equating the banished human convict with the wolf. The laws of the Norman kings (as early as 1130) refer to the outlaw as *lupus* (Latin for "the wolf").[26] Later German legal historians (no longer under the direct spell of the historical school of jurisprudence of Friedrich Karl von Savigny or Jacob Grimm) reiterated this interpretation, although none referred to the wolf of the fairy tales. In a contribution to Paul's work on German philology, at the turn of the century, the legal historian Karl von Amira wrote of the felon convicted to banishment as one who is "hunted like the wolf and is called such: vargr, . . . warg . . . vearh. . . . He bears the 'wolfes heafed' . . . and leads the life of a wolf (wargida)." He is also referred to as a forest walker, a term equally applied to the wolf.[27]

Some contemporary legal historians have rejected this interpretation, attributing the identification of the outlaw as the wolf only to high medieval Scandinavian sources. However, when Professor Karl Kroeschel (Freiburg) explains that "in the time of Germanic law, the term [*vargus*] means nothing more than robber,"[28] it accords poorly with the alternate Latin term *lupus*, in lieu of *vargus*, used in English law as early as 1130. Thus, explanations of the banished felon as a wolf (*lupus*/*vargus*/*Würger*) seem irrefutable. Bishop Ulfilas' (A.D. 311–81) *gaworgjan ðanpan* ("wolf declaration") meant exactly that. Outlawing the human convict gave him the status of wolf.[29] Banned from the campfire, he had to live like the four-legged wolf in the dreaded forest, there to die or to be killed.[30] It is this two-legged wolf that we see tromping around the fairy tales. Banished to the forests along the Fulda, the Werra, and the Weser rivers during the Middle

Ages, he survived until the brothers Grimm recorded the remnants of a long-dead law transformed into lore.

Notes

1. Anon., "Wo Dornröschen wachgeküsst wurde — Die Saba — Burg wird 650 Jahre alt," *Frankfurter Rundschau* 7 April 1984, p. M3.

2. Edwin McDowell, "A Fairy Tale by Grimm Comes to Light," *New York Times,* 28 September 1983, p. 1.

3. Jens Christian Jessen, *Das Recht in den Kinder — und Hausmärchen der Gebrüder Grimm* (Diss., Kiel, 1979). See also Gabrielle A. Brenner, "Why Did Inheritance Laws Change?" in Reuven Brenner, *Betting on Ideas: Wars, Invention, Inflation* (Chicago: University of Chicago Press, 1985), pp. 116–30.

4. Karl N. Llewellyn and E. Adamson Hoebel, *The Cheyenne Way* (Norman: University of Oklahoma Press, 1941).

5. Jacob Grimm, *Deutsche Rechtsalterthümer* (1828), 4th ed. (A. Heusler und R. Hubner, 1899).

6. Jacob Grimm, *Weistümer,* 7 vols. (begun 1840).

7. Jacob Grimm and Wilhelm Grimm, *Kinder- und Hausmärchen,* 2 vols. (1812, 1815).

8. Jessen, *Das Recht in den Kinder- und Hausmärchen,* esp. p. 234. Jessen humbly admits that "an attempt to date the age of individual fairy tales or motifs, is doomed to failure" (ibid). With all due respect, he has done remarkably well in dating individual episodes or practices in the fairy tales in accordance with the "official" law of given periods. Obviously, this raises an interesting question: When were the fairy tales "frozen" as legal precedent and when did they cease reflecting "official law?" Obviously, it was some time before the Grimms collected them.

9. Carol J. Auster, "Balance Theory and Other Extra-Balance Properties: An Application to Fairy Tales," *Psychological Reports* 47 (1980): 183–88. Balance theory is employed to determine the consistency of relations within a given group structure, overall, as well as through various time sequences. Auster applied this process to sixteen selected fairy tales. The originator of balance theory is F. Heider. See his *Psychology of Interpersonal Relations* (New York: Wiley, 1958).

10. Hans von Hentig, *Die Strafe,* 2 vols. (Berlin: Springer Verlag, 1954–55).

11. Erich Wulffen, "Das Criminelle in deutschen Volksmärchen," in *Archiv für Kriminal-Anthropologie und Kriminalistik,* vol. 38 (Leipzig, 1910), pp. 341–70.

12. Jessen, *Das Recht in den Kinder,* pp. 19, 173–75.

13. Hans Ritz, *Die Geschichte vom Rotkäppchen,* 8th ed., (Göttingen: Muriverlag, 1984), pp. 11–13.

14. William Arens, in his provocative and controversial study, *The Man-Eating Myth: Anthropology and Anthropophagy* (New York: Oxford University Press, 1979), redefines cannibalism as a designation by individuals or society of the most basic form of malevolence, rather than as an actual social act or institution.

15. Rudolf His, *Deutsches Strafrecht bis zur Karolina* (Munich and Berlin: R. Oldenbourg, 1928), p. 82.

16. Ibid., p. 82.

17. Ibid., p. 87.

18. Ibid., p. 56. This could also be related to the ancient Germanic legal practice of declaring a malefactor "vogelfrei," without further protection under the law — ED.

19. Ibid., p. 85.

20. Ritz, *Die Geschichte vom Rotkäppchen;* Gerhard O. W. Mueller, "Wolf und Vulva," in *Kriminologische Wegzeichen,* ed. Mergen and Schäfer (1967), p. 53; id., "Tort, Crime and the Primitive," *Journal of Criminal Law and Criminology* 46 (1955): 303, 309.

21. Jacob Grimm, *Deutsche Rechtsalterthümer,* 11 : 334, et seq.

22. Wilhelm Eduard Wilda, *Das Strafrecht der Germanen* (Halle: C. A. Schwetschke und Sohn, 1842).

23. Ibid., p. 279.

24. Ibid., p. 280.

25. Richard Schröder, *Lehrbuch der Deutschen Rechtsgeschichte* (Leipzig, 1894); and see Mueller, "Tort," p. 309.

26. Brunner, *Deutsche Rechtsgeschichte*, 3d ed. (Berlin: Duncker and Humblot, 1961; unchanged reprint of 1906), 1:235. "Leges Edw. 6, 2a. Lupinum enim gerit caput . . . quod ab Anglis wulfesheved nominatur. Vgl. Bracton, fol. 125 b, Fleta 1, c 27, § 13 (p. 41)."

27. Karl von Amira, *Die Germanischen Todesstrafen*, Abhandlungen der Königlichen Akademie, vol. 31 (Munich, 1922), p. 35.

28. Karl Kroeschell, "Germanisches Recht — ein Forschungsproblem," manuscript on file with the author, and authorities cited there, esp. p. 14.

29. See above, n. 25.

30. My reading of the Grimms' fairy tales has been based on *The Complete Grimms' Fairy Tales*, with an introduction by Padraic Colum, and folkloristic commentary by Joseph Campbell (New York: Pantheon Books, 1984); and *Kinder- und Hausmärchen der Brüder Grimm* (Leipzig: Verlag von Hegel und Schade, n.d.). And if I needed any boost for enthusiasm, I obtained it from Lawrence G. Wrenn, "Law and the Brothers Grimm," *Studia Canonica* 13:429–54.

Bibliography

Havelock, Eric. *The Greek Concept of Justice*. Cambridge: Harvard University Press, 1978. A detailed and controversial discussion of the concept of justice found in the oral education among the pre-Platonic poets; particular emphasis on the *Iliad* and the *Odyssey*.

Jessen, Jens Christian. *Das Recht in den Kinder- und Hausmärchen der Brüder Grimm*. Diss., Kiel, 1979. Discusses law and justice as they emerge in the Grimms' *Fairy Tales*.

14. Feminist Approaches to the Interpretation of Fairy Tales

KAY F. STONE

The *Märchen* has lent itself to a variety of literary, psychological, and sociological interpretations based primarily on the examination of printed texts. Feminist writers have been attracted to the *Märchen* by its popularity as a genre of children's literature. Initially it was viewed, in its form as the well-known fairy tale (primarily from selected tales from the Grimms, Charles Perrault, Hans Christian Andersen, and Andrew Lang[1]), as an unfortunate source of negative female stereotypes. The passive and pretty heroines who dominate popular fairy tales offer narrow and damaging role-models for young readers, feminists argue. Thus much writing has been a sharp critique of the genre.

In early feminist writing (1950s and 1960s) the *Märchen* was uncritically considered as one of the many socializing forces that discouraged females from realizing their full human potential. Few writers from this period focused exclusively on the *Märchen* since it was only one of many sources of stereotyping. Thus critical descriptions tended to be vague and generalized. Both Betty Friedan and Simone de Beauvoir, for example, refer to generalized "Cinderellas"

Since recent feminist writings consider both *Märchen* and feminism together, it is inappropriate to entitle this "Approaches to *Märchen*," as it was called when it was presented at the 1984 Princeton conference "Fairy Tales and Society." Carol Mitchell and Marta Weigle have contributed considerably to my survey of feminist scholarship here.

and "Sleeping Beauties" who were urged to wake up and take charge of their own lives rather than wait for "Prince Charming" to act for them.[2] A more recent book boldly titled *Fairy Tales and Female Consciousness* takes the generalized approach to its logical extremes in its overly vague images of "the fairy tale princess."[3] The author, Barbara Waelti-Walters, insists that future generations must be protected from the negative effects of fairy tale stereotyping but seems unaware that feminist scholarship has been examining the problem for three decades now.

Later feminist work has examined *Märchen* in more detail. An article written in 1972, for example, reaches its conclusions on the damaging passivity of heroines only after an examination of all the heroines in Andrew Lang's multivolume fairy books. Marcia Lieberman insists here, with ample literary evidence, that the fairy tale romance, the "happily ever after" endings, have "been made the repositories of the dreams, hopes, and fantasies of generations of girls."[4] Similarly, Karen Rowe refers to specific tales (though not such a wide sampling) in attempting to demonstrate connections between fairy tales and popular romantic stories in books and magazines.[5] Once again "Prince Charming" appears as the villain for whom girls foolishly await in both fairy tales and romantic stories. Rowe views such tales as problem-creating rather than problem-solving. She thus challenges writers like Bruno Bettelheim who see fairy tales as gender-free stories that help children of both sexes to solve their problems and define themselves as human beings.[6]

In addition to challenging gender-stereotyping through critiques, feminist writers have also responded by offering more aggressive heroines. In "The Practical Princess" and "Petronella," original stories by Jay Williams, we meet princesses who slay their own dragons and rescue spoiled princes from magicians.[7] Other writers offer traditional tales culled from lesser-known international collections in which heroines assume more active roles. Among these are Rosemary Minard's *Womenfolk and Fairy Tales* and Ethel Phelps' *The Maid of the North: Feminist Folktales from Around the World*.[8] Such writers felt that the availability of strong and enterprising women would counterbalance stereotypic passive princesses and offer a new paradigm for female consciousness.

Feminist writings discussed thus far have been concerned with the effects of gender-stereotyping and have justifiably aimed their criticisms at popularly known tales. In so doing they tend to attack the same heroines—notably Cinderella, Snow White, and Sleeping Beauty—again and again, until the feminist view of such heroines has itself become a stereotype. Even Rosemary Minard and Ethel

Phelps, despite their attempts to introduce more challenging figures, fail to discover active heroines much closer to home. Several twentieth-century gatherings of Anglo-American tales feature heroines who take responsibility for their own destiny.[9] While these collections are not obscure and inaccessible, they are little known outside of folkloric circles. And because feminist folklorists have concentrated on other forms of verbal expression,[10] the potential connections between these little-known tales and their popular counterparts have not developed in feminist scholarship.

When I began examining *Märchen* heroines in the early 1970s, I attempted to expand the sample of tales to include lesser-known Anglo-American collections and to contrast their heroines with those of popular collections. I accepted the feminist stereotype of popular princesses and challenged it with more aggressive heroines, further supporting my views with interviews in which contemporary readers discussed the degree to which they felt themselves negatively affected by narrow female images.[11]

My approach along with that of other feminists came under attack by critics who pointed out that only the surface story was being considered and deeper levels of meaning ignored.[12] Even as these critiques were being formulated a new feminist view of *Märchen* heroines was beginning to emerge. Feminists agreed that earlier studies ignored the subtle inner strength of heroines. Cinderella, for example, emerged as resourceful rather than remorseful, but not aggressively opportunistic like her sisters. Leah Kavablum insisted that Cinderella really gains freedom from kitchen and fireside, and that her "prince" is symbolic for inner strength. She reminds readers that Cinderella's slipper in Freudian symbolism is her own vagina, and thus her regaining of it establishes her as an independent woman.[13]

Other feminist writers have reworked old stories in new ways, to emphasize unrecognized aspects of feminine strength. Angela Carter's *The Bloody Chamber,* for example, reinterprets ten versions of beauty/beast tales beginning with "Bluebeard."[14] Similarly, the poems of Anne Sexton and the stories of Tanith Lee attempt to re-view *Märchen* women both negatively and positively.[15]

In the critiques and the rewritten stories, *Märchen* women, both as heroines and as secondary characters, were set in irreconcilable opposition to male characters. Thus the *Märchen* was regarded as no longer a romantic tale about living happily ever after but instead as about the inner development of the unique female persona. Men could only be a hindrance in this development — or at best (as in Kavablum's Cinderella) symbolic of its attainment.

A third view of women and of heroines has emerged in feminist writings of the late 1970s. Here women are seen as necessarily separate from but not inherently antagonistic to men. Feminist critiques have expanded to include *Märchen* heroines and mythic figures together, since the separation of myth and tale was now regarded as artificial and misleading; both myth and tale interweave the separate realities of the liminal and numinous worlds. Many such works attempt to offer the missing voices of female deities and challenging witch/wisewoman figures in *Märchen*. In *The Book of Goddesses and Heroines,* for example, Patricia Monaghan lists and describes hundreds of major and minor female deities and folktale personages from around the world. She notes in her introduction that some of these had previously been described only as "votive figures."[16] In another A-to-Z collection, *The Woman's Encyclopedia of Myths and Secrets,* Barbara Walker agrees that female figures have often been presented too negatively. In describing Pandora and her box, for example, she notes that it "was not a box but a honey-vase, *pithos,* from which she poured out blessings."[17] Ignoring the limited erotic imagery of the honey-box, Walker shows Pandora, like Eve, as a bringer of knowledge to the world rather than a trouble-maker.[18]

Similarly, Sylvia Brinton Perera in *Descent of the Goddess* interprets the renewed interest in goddesses and heroines as essential for redeeming "our own full feminine instinct and energy patterns," which have been regarded by patriarchal religions "as a dangerous threat and called terrible mother, dragon or witch."[19] Her study includes *Märchen* protagonists like Cinderella and secondary figures like Baba Yaga as descendants of supernatural figures.

An even more detailed examination of myth and *Märchen* as paradigms for inner growth is found in Marie-Louise von Franz's *Problems of the Feminine in Fairytales,*[20] published a decade earlier than the Monaghan and Perera works. As a Jungian analyst, von Franz is able to present concrete connections between the feminine in traditional literature and in the real world of women. Using Jung's concepts of anima and animus she insists that women come to terms with their masculine force as well as with the dark side of their feminine force. It is precisely this dark side that women have been taught to ignore and repress, according to many feminist writers. Von Franz also suggests that men develop familiarity with their feminine forces, but she does not comment on the fact that the dark sides of their masculine forces already have full expression. In the opinion of von Franz and other Jungians, full individuation for both females and males is encouraged by understanding myth and *Märchen* and other forms of archetypal expression such as dreams. As a Jungian rather than a feminist, von Franz is too moderate. She does not fully acknowledge the additional difficulty women face in attaining individuation in a male world.[21]

In a more radically challenging examination of femininity and fairy tales, *Kiss Sleeping Beauty Good-Bye,* Madonna Kolbenschlag demonstrates clearly and concisely how the feminine mystique exists negatively and positively.[22] She too sees the need for both women and men to understand their conflicting feminine and masculine forces and to open themselves to transformation and transcendence. Kolbenschlag agrees with other feminist mythologists that a new language must be learned fully by women and men if human culture is to continue growing. In her concluding chapter, "Exit the Frog Prince," she warns that if the feminine voice continues to be silent, or unheard when spoken, then women will have to separate themselves from men in order to develop fully. In her imaginary letter to the frog prince she writes:

> My own anger and depression finally forced me to transform my life. What will it take to transform yours? Is rejection the only way to open your eyes? Do I have to leave you, abandon you to your self-serving universe? If we go our separate ways, there will be pain and loss. The tapestry of relationships that we have woven with our lives will be rent.[23]

Feminists have favored the weaving and spinning image for its connection with traditional female occupations and its optimistic images of connecting and creating positive patterns. A recent book by folklorist/anthropologist Marta Weigle, *Spiders and Spinsters,* interweaves an impressive amount of material on women and folklore.[24] Weigle's underlying assumption is that women are naturally separate because they perceive and react to the world differently from men, and consequently express their perceptions and reactions differently. Her book is an attempt to do the same. As she says, simply, "for the most part, the voices assembled here spin and weave their own story."[25] She arranges these voices with connecting comments that interweave but do not bind material to restrictive strands of narrow interpretation or theory.

Weigle and others express the challenging realization that the feminine voice is indeed different from the masculine but suggest that this voice is not absolutely limited to women. We make a serious error in equating "female" with "feminine" and "male" with "masculine." The most recent feminist writers insist that new perceptions of female and male are needed by all human beings if we are to break the magic spell of gender stereotyping.[26]

Three differing assumptions have underlain the development of feminist writing in general, and in their approaches to *Märchen* and myth. The earliest feminists saw women as artificially separated from and wrongly considered unequal to men; the next generation of writers insisted that women were naturally separate from men and rightly superior; and many recent writers consider both women and men as naturally separate but potentially equal — if men shape up. The *Märchen* has been examined from all three approaches, and feminist reactions have ranged from sharp criticism to firm support of the images of women presented in them. Early writers, unhappy with the images they perceived as reflected in the *Märchen* insisted that the mirror was at fault, while later writers pointed out that other images could be perceived in the same mirror. If we care to look again at both *Märchen* and myth we might see that they offer flexible paradigms for positive transformations — female *and* male. Eve was the first consumer of the fruit of knowledge, and she shared this dangerous delight with Adam.

Notes

1. These are the collections most often cited by both casual readers and scholarly researchers. The Grimm tales are more often read in books selecting 30–60 tales rather than all 210, and in these selections heroines in general, and passive heroines in particular, account for a much higher ratio than in the collection as a whole. The courtly French tales of Charles Perrault, also featuring passive heroines ("Cendrillon" being the most famous), have remained popular since they were published in 1697. Hans Christian Andersen's literary tales create even more downtrodden heroines, including "good" girls like "The Little Mermaid" and "The Little Matchgirl" who are destroyed. Andrew Lang's several volumes of tales mostly gleaned from other collections also favor helpless heroines, particularly in his earliest volumes in which tales from Grimms, Andersen, and Perrault and his imitators (Madame D'Aulnoy and Madame de Beaumont) are featured.

2. Betty Friedan, *The Feminine Mystique* (New York: Dell Publishing Co., 1963), particularly pp. 118 and 292; and Simone De Beauvoir, *The Second Sex* (New York: Alfred A. Knopf, 1953), particularly pp. 126, 128, 158 for "The Cinderella Myth," pp. 163, 178 for "Snow White," and p. 171 for "Sleeping Beauty." She does not list "Prince Charming" in her index, but references to this imaginary character are found on pp. 126, 171, and 178.

3. Barbara Waelti-Walters, *Fairy Tales and Female Consciousness* (Montreal and Quebec: Eden Press, 1982). Despite the broad title this is a narrow literary study of a handful of French and French-Canadian women writers. It has little beyond vague observations that relate to the topics promised by the title.

4. Marcia Lieberman, "Some Day My Prince Will Come," *College English*, December 1972, particularly pp. 383–95; quotation from p. 385.

5. Karen E. Rowe, "Feminism and Fairy Tales," *Women's Studies* 6 (1979), particularly pp. 237–57.

6. Bruno Bettelheim, *The Uses of Enchantment: The Meaning and Importance of Fairy Tales* (New York: Alfred A. Knopf, 1977).

7. Jay Williams, "The Practical Princess," *Ms.*, August 1972, pp. 61–64; *Petronella* (New York: Parents, 1973).

8. Rosemary Minard, *Womenfolk and Fairy Tales* (Boston: Houghton Mifflin, 1975); Ethel Phelps, *The Maid of the North: Feminist Folktales from Around the World* (New York: Holt, Rinehart and Winston, 1981).

9. See references to Campbell, Fauset, Gardner, Randolph, Roberts, and Spray in bibliography.

10. See, for example, Claire Farrer, ed., *Women and Folklore* (Austin: University of Texas Press, 1975); and Rosan Jordan and Susan Kalcik, eds., *Women's Folklore, Women's Culture* (Philadelphia: University of Pennsylvania Press, 1985).

11. Kay Stone, "Things Walt Disney Never Told Us," *Women and Folklore*, ed. Claire R. Farrer (Austin: University of Texas Press, 1975), pp. 42–50; "Romantic Heroines in Anglo-American Folk and Popular Literature" (Ph.D. diss., Indiana University, 1975); "Fairy Tales for Adults: Disney's Americanization of the *Märchen*," *Folklore on Two Continents*, ed. Burlakoff and Lindahl (Bloomington, IN: Trickster Press, 1980), pp. 40–48; and "Aschenputtel als Weiblichkeitsideal in Nordamerika," in *Über Märchen für Kinder von Heute*, ed. Klaus Doderer (Weinheim and Basel, 1983): 78–93.

12. See N. J. Girardot, "Initiation and Meaning in 'Snow White and the Seven Dwarfs,'" *Journal of American Folklore* 90 (1977): 274–300; Polly Stewart Deemer, "A Response to the Symposium," *Journal of American Folklore* 88 (1975): 101–14.

13. Leah Kavablum, *Cinderella; Radical Feminist, Alchemist* (Guttenberg, NJ, 1973).

14. Angela Carter, *The Bloody Chamber* (New York: Harper and Row, 1979).

15. Anne Sexton, *Transformations* (Boston: Houghton Mifflin, 1971); Tanith Lee, *Red as Blood* (New York: Daw Books, 1983).

16. Patricia Monaghan, *The Book of Goddesses and Heroines* (New York: E. P. Dutton, 1981), p. xiii.

17. Barbara Walker, *The Woman's Encyclopedia of Myths and Secrets* (San Francisco, 1983), p. 12. This is an uneven work with some entries ("Cinderella," for example) that are extreme.

18. For other examinations of Pandora, see Dora Panofsky and Erwin Panofsky, *Pandora's Box: The Changing Aspects of a Mythical Symbol* (Princeton, NJ: Princeton University Press, 1962); and Sarah Pomeroy, *Goddesses, Whores, Wives, and Slaves* (New York: Schocken Books, 1975). For further examinations of Eve, see Mary Daly, *Beyond God the Father: Toward a Philosophy of Women's Liberation* (Boston: Beacon Press, 1973); Raphael Patai, *The Hebrew Goddess* (New York: Avon Books, 1978); J. A. Phillips, *Eve: The History of an Idea* (New York: Harper and Row, 1984); and Phyllis Trible, "Depatriarchalizing in Biblical Interpretations," in *The Jewish Woman: New Perspectives*, ed. Elizabeth Koltun (New York: Schocken Books, 1976).

19. Sylvia Brinton Perera, *Descent of the Goddess* (Toronto: Inner City Books, 1981), p. 7.

20. Marie-Louise von Franz, *Problems of the Feminine in Fairytales* (New York: Spring Publications, 1972).

21. For further comments, see Naomi Goldenberg, "A Feminist Critique of Jung," *Signs* 2 (1976): 443–49.

22. Madonna Kolbenschlag, *Kiss Sleeping Beauty Good-Bye* (Garden City, NY: Doubleday, 1981).

23. Ibid., pp. 199–200.

24. Marta Weigle, *Spiders and Spinsters: Women and Mythology* (Albuquerque: University of New Mexico Press, 1982).

25. Ibid., p. ix.

26. Of interest are recent and as yet unpublished papers presented at annual meetings of the American Folklore Society. For example: Marta Weigle, "A Mythology of One's Own: Mundus vs. Mythos" (1981); Carol Mitchell, "The Garden of Eden Revisited" (1982); and Carol Edwards, "Feminism and Fairytales Revisited" (1983).

Bibliography

Farrer, Claire, ed. *Women and Folklore*. Austin: University of Texas Press, 1975. A collection of articles by folklorists on women's expressive culture.

Jordan, Rosan, and Susan Kalcik, eds. *Women's Folklore, Women's Culture.* Philadelphia: University of Pennsylvania Press, 1985. An anthology of women's folklore concentrating on contemporary North America.

Lieberman, Marcia. "Some Day My Prince Will Come." *College English* 34 (1972–73): 383–95. Examines heroines in Andrew Lang's multivolume "fairy books."

Rowe, Karen E. "Feminism and Fairy Tales." *Women's Studies: An Interdisciplinary Journal* 6 (1979): 237–57. Examines selected popular folktales from the perspective of modern feminism.

Stone, Kay. "Fairy Tales for Adults: Walt Disney's Americanization of the Märchen." In *Folklore on Two Continents.* Edited by Burlakoff and Lindahl. Bloomington: University of Indiana Press, 1980.

———. "The Misuses of Enchantment." In *Women's Folklore, Women's Culture.* Edited by Rosan Jordan and Susan Kalcik. Philadelphia: University of Pennsylvania Press, 1985.

———. "Things Walt Disney Never Told Us." In *Women and Folklore.* Edited by Claire Farrer. Austin: University of Texas Press, 1975.

Von Franz, Marie-Luise. *Problems of the Feminine in Fairy Tales.* New York: Spring Publications, 1972. A Jungian interpretation of fairy tale heroines from such tales as "Sleeping Beauty," "Snow White and Rose Red," "The Handless Maiden," "The Six Swans," and the Russian "The Beautiful Wassilissa."

Weigle, Marta. *Spiders and Spinsters.* Albuquerque: University of New Mexico Press, 1982. An extensive gathering of comments on women in mythology, including *Märchen* heroines. Excellent bibliography.

15. Marxists and the Illumination of Folk and Fairy Tales

JACK ZIPES

Before I discuss the relationship of Marxists to folk and fairy tales, I want to quote three German Marxists whose ideas were heavily influenced by the social and political changes of the Weimar period, and who became interested in and concerned with the meaning and power of fairy tales.

The proletariat will create the new fairy tales in which workers' struggles, their lives, and their ideas are reflected and correspond to the degree which they demonstrate how they can continually become human, and how they can build up new educational societies in place of the old decrepit ones. [Edwin Hoernle, *Die Arbeit in den kommunistischen Kindergruppen* (1923)][1]

Of course, the fairy-tale world, especially as a magical one, no longer belongs to the present. How can it mirror our wish-projections against a background that has long since disappeared? Or, to put it a better way: How can the fairy tale mirror our wish-projections other than in a totally atavistic obsolete way? Real kings no longer even exist. The atavistic and simultaneously feudal-transcendental world from which the fairy tale stems and to which it seems tied has most certainly vanished. However, the mirror of the fairy tale has not become opaque, and the manner of wish-fulfillment which peers forth from it is not entirely without a home. It all adds up to this: the fairy tale narrates a wish-fulfillment which is not bound by its own time and the apparel of its contents. [Ernst Bloch, *Das Märchen geht selber in Zeit* (1930)][2]

"And they lived happily ever after," says the fairy tale. The fairy tale which to this day is the first tutor of children because it was once the first tutor of mankind, secretly lives on in the story. The first true storyteller is, and will continue to be, the teller of fairy tales. Whenever good counsel was at a premium, the fairy tale had it, and where the need was greatest, its aid was nearest. The need was the need created by the myth. The fairy tale tells us of the earliest arrangements that mankind made to shake off the nightmare which the myth had placed upon its chest. [Walter Benjamin, *Der Erzähler* (1936)][3]

Hoernle, Bloch, Benjamin. Three different Marxists who shared different fates at the hands of fascism. Hoernle, a member of the Communist party, fled to the Soviet Union and returned to East Germany after World War II to become a minister of forestry. He did not continue his work with youth groups, and his ideas for a new proletarian fairy tale were never realized. He died in 1952. Bloch spent the major portion of the fascist period in America (1938–48) working on his most significant book, *Das Prinzip Hoffnung*. In 1949 he returned to East Germany, where he became a professor of philosophy in Leipzig until 1961. At that time, because of his disagreement with the cultural policies of the East German bureaucracy, he moved to Tübingen, where he spent the rest of his life, espousing utopian notions of philosophy and society while criticizing the depraved social and political conditions in both Germanys. He died in 1977. Benjamin sought exile in Paris during the 1930s and worked in association with the famous Institute of Social Research, otherwise known as the Frankfurt School. Like many of its members, he wrote scintillating essays against fascism during this time while endeavoring to make new contributions to Marxist thought and methodology. Forced to flee Paris in 1940 because of the Nazi invasion, he was overtaken by fear and committed suicide on the Spanish border.

Hoernle, the dedicated party member; Bloch, the eclectic Marxist philosopher of hope; Benjamin, the eccentric *flaneur* of the Frankfurt School: their lives were anything but fairy tales. Yet, their concern for the meaning and power of fairy tales had great ramifications in West Germany during the late 1960s. It was then that the leftist student movement rediscovered, so to speak, the formidable Marxist tradition of the Weimar period, a tradition that had been obfuscated at school and in the university. Among the "treasures" rediscovered were the writings of Hoernle, Bloch, and Benjamin on folk and fairy tales.

This rediscovery is important for the Marxist approach to folk and fairy tales because German critics and scholars have been at the forefront of critical endeavors to reexamine folk and fairy tales from a Marxist point of view.[4] In fact, to discuss the development of Marxist criticism and its relationship to folklore and fairy tale research, it is necessary to focus primarily on West Germany, at least when one addresses post–World War II developments in this field. With few exceptions, Western Marxists outside Germany have not delved into the meaning of folk and fairy tales.[5]

Beginning with Bernd Wollenweber's essay, "Märchen und Sprichwort" (1974),[6] and Dieter Richter and Johannes Merkel's book, *Märchen, Phantasie und soziales Lernen* (1974),[7] there has been a virtual flood in West Germany of Marxist studies dealing with folk and fairy tales. Since it would be too difficult to discuss all the works that have been produced during the last ten years, I will concentrate on three areas of folk and fairy tale research opened up by Hoernle, Bloch, and Benjamin to demonstrate where and why contemporary German Marxists have sought to go beyond them. Despite their differences, Hoernle, Bloch, and Benjamin shared much common ground on socialization, utopianism, and ideology. From their work in these three areas, contemporary Marxists have drawn the stimulus to develop their own ideas. In examining these three areas I shall synthesize the notions of the three authors into three general theses and discuss their elaboration by contemporary Marxists.

1. Fairy tales are closely tied to the real situation of children and have both a positive and a negative impact in the socialization process. Here the work of Manfred Klein and Werner Psaar, Ulrike Bastian, Bernd Dolle, and Christa Bürger[8] has complemented the studies of Wollenweber, Richter, and Merkel. In general, they have examined the changing role of the fairy tale in history and the uses to which the fairy tale has been put in order to influence the behavior and thinking of children and adults alike. In contrast to Hoernle, Bloch, and Benjamin, they are historically more specific and thorough in their analyses and demonstrate how the transformation of the tales and their employment have been ideologically determined to legitimate the interests of capitalist societies.

2. The original fairy tales, that is, the oral folk tales in their *Urform*, contain elements of political protest and wish-fulfillment that demonstrate the ways through which oppressed peoples can withstand and overcome the power of rich and exploitative rulers. It is almost as if they had a messianic mission and illuminated the way to a golden age. Here Wollenweber, Richter, Merkel, and Heide Göttner-Abendroth have qualified those elements of wish-fulfillment and

protest by analyzing their anachronistic and feudal features.[9] In particular, Göttner-Abendroth focuses on the patriarchalization of the tales from a historical feminist viewpoint. Despite sexist and feudal components, most contemporary Marxist critics believe that both the oral and the literary fairy tale can be modernized and reshaped to incorporate a critique of present-day society along utopian lines.

3. The utopian "aura" of the authentic folk tradition must be preserved and developed in modern society. Hoernle, Bloch, and Benjamin are insistent about this notion of preservation but vague in their analyses of folk and fairy tales. Contemporary Marxists are more careful in the distinctions that have to be made about the folk and fairy tale. For instance, Jens Tismar has written two books that examine the literary fairy tale as a type of commodity which results from the "bourgeoisification" of the oral folk tale.[10] Friedmar Apel traces the evolution of the literary fairy tale (*Kunstmärchen*) to the French court of Louis XIV and discusses the aesthetics of the tale in relation to bourgeois standards that were emerging at this time.[11] Other critics, such as Otto Gmelin and Bernd Dolle, analyze the diminution of the utopian element in folk and fairy tales as they are passed down through history while emphasizing the utopian efforts of particular groups to reformulate the concerns and needs of oppressed groups.[12]

Perhaps the most important conclusion to be drawn from the ideas of Hoernle, Bloch, Benjamin, and their followers is that the fairy tale, whether it be oral or literary, is a social product stamped by its times, and its power resides in its utopian potential to illuminate ways by which we can come to terms with injustice and pursue our dreams of a golden age. Implicit in their ideas is the notion that the most *authentic* folk and fairy tales speak in the name of the common people and justice. Here the idealistic side of the German Marxists reveals itself and is in need of a corrective, for it is extremely difficult to discern what is or what is not an authentic tale. For instance, many of the so-called folk tales that bespeak the interests of peasants are sexist and racist. In other words, it is important not to set oral or literary tales on a pedestal just because they originate from the common people or because the author purports to speak in the name of the people. More Marxist research must be conducted in the area of socio-historical origins of the tales and the transformations that they undergo as a result of changes in general taste, cultural standards, and their social function.

This need for more Marxist research is emphasized by Vladimir Propp, not the structuralist Propp of the *Morphology of the Folktale*, but the Marxist Propp, whose later writings have just become available in

English.[13] He justifies his earlier work by maintaining that one cannot grasp historical transformations within a genre without knowing its poetics and mode of composition: "The comparative study of plots opens up wide historical perspectives. What needs historical explanation is not individual plots but the compositional system to which they belong. This approach will bring out the historical connections among them and pave the way for the study of individual plots."[14] Since Propp always focuses on the oral tradition of folk tales, he outlines a Marxist approach to tales produced in what he calls precapitalist societies. Even if the mode of production played a very limited role in those societies, he argues, we must then look at social institutions such as marriage, death, initiation into a tribe or community, and the succession of power. In particular, he remarks that "the wondertale preserves traces of vanished forms of social life,"[15] and we must return to rituals and customs to understand motifs in the tale. Although he tends to idealize the folk and to examine precapitalist ritual uncritically, Propp's Marxist writings are significant because they link ethnography and folklore ideologically. He establishes this link by stressing that the people have cultivated folk art in resistance to the oppression of the ruling classes. Since ethnography focuses on the study of material culture and social organizations, historical folklore research must rest upon ethnography.[16] As a historical discipline, folklore research tries to demonstrate what happens to old folklore under new historical conditions and to trace the appearance of new formations. Propp argues that folklore must be studied by stages that can be characterized by the economic development of the society. Research must deal with hybrid formations and contradictions by using the comparative method. By studying various peoples at various stages of their development, one can comprehend the specific significance of an individual tale.

In some respects, the German Marxists anticipated Propp's theses without knowing them and have actually gone beyond him. In other respects, particularly with regard to the ideological tradition within Western folklore research, Propp's position needs further evaluation and elaboration. Here Claude Lévi-Strauss's debate with Propp[17] is helpful as is the remarkable book, *Traumzeit*, by Hans Peter Duerr,[18] who questions the colonialist attitude of ethnologists and provides a new perspective on the links between ritual, art, and ideology. Certainly, the recent appearance of Propp's Marxist writings will prompt more discussion about the relationship of Marxism to the study of folk and fairy tales.

If Marxists have been fascinated by the illumination of folk and fairy tales, it is because they are interested in real social contradictions that they hope to resolve. By critically historicizing the study of folk and fairy tales, they have challenged other approaches and have shed light on areas that need further exploration.

Notes

1. In *Das politische Kinderbuch,* ed. Dieter Richter (Darmstadt: Luchterhand, 1973), p. 220.
2. In Jack Zipes, *Breaking the Magic Spell* (Austin: University of Texas Press, 1979), p. 133.
3. In *Illuminations,* trans. Harry Zohn (New York: Harcourt, Brace & World, 1968), p. 102.
4. Ironically, East German Marxists have not continued the tradition of Hoernle, Bloch, and Benjamin because of the orthodox limits set by the state's cultural policies. Nevertheless, there have been some interesting studies such as Waltraut Woeller's *Der soziale Gehalt und die soziale Funktion der deutschen Volksmärchen* (Habilitations-Schrift der Humboldt-Universität zu Berlin, 1955).
5. See José Limon, "Western Marxism and Folklore," *Journal of American Folklore* 96 (1983): 34–53; then my reply entitled "Folklore Research and Western Marxism: A Critical Replay," *Journal of American Folklore* 97 (1984): 330–37; then Limon's reply to my reply, "Western Marxism and Folklore: A Critical Reintroduction," *Journal of American Folklore* 97 (1984): 337–45.
6. In *Projektunterricht,* vol. 6, ed. Heinz Ide (Stuttgart: Metzler, 1974), pp. 12–92.
7. Berlin: Basis, 1974.
8. Klein and Psaar, *Wer hat Angst vor der bösen Geiß? Zur Märchendidaktik und Märchenrezeption* (Braunschweig: Westermann, 1976); Bastian, *Die Kinder und Hausmärchen der Brüder Grimm in der literatur-pädagogischen Diskussion des 19. und 20. Jahrhunderts* (Giessen: Haag und Herchen, 1981); Dolle, "Märchen und Erziehung: Versuch einer historischen Skizze zur didaktischen Verwendung Grimmscher Märchen," in *Und wenn sie nicht gestorben sind . . . Perspektiven auf das Märchen,* ed. Helmut Brackert (Frankfurt: Suhrkamp, 1980), pp. 165–92; Bürger, "Die soziale Funktion volkstümlicher Erzählformen: Sage und Märchen," in *Projekt Deutschunterricht 1,* ed. Heinz Ide (Stuttgart: Metzler, 1971), pp. 26–56.
9. Göttner-Abendroth, *Die Göttin und ihr Heros* (Munich: Frauenoffensive, 1980).
10. Tismar, *Kunstmärchen* (Stuttgart: Metzler, 1977) and *Das deutsche Kunstmärchen des 20. Jahrhunderts* (Stuttgart: Metzler, 1981).
11. Apel, *Die Zaubergärten der Phantasie. Zur Theorie und Geschichte des Kunstmärchens* (Heidelberg: Winter, 1978).
12. Gmelin, *Märchen für tapfere Mädchen* (Giessen: Schlot, 1978); Dolle, "Märchen und Erziehung," pp. 165–92. See also the afterword essays by Dolle and Zipes in *Es wird einmal . . . Soziale Märchen der Zwanziger Jahre,* ed. Dolle, Richter, and Zipes (Munich: Weismann, 1983); Zipes, "Der Märchen im Prozeß der Erziehung," pp. 153–60; Zipes and Dolle, "Aus alten Mären da klingt es: . . . Die etablierte Märchenszene der Weimarer Republik," pp. 161–64; and Dolle, "Märchen der Wirklichkeit," pp. 165–75.
13. Propp, *Theory and History of folklore,* ed. Anatoly Liberman, trans. Ariadna Martin and Richard Martin (Minneapolis: University of Minnesota Press, 1984).
14. Ibid., p. 72.
15. Ibid., p. 105.
16. Ibid., pp. 3–15.
17. Cf. Lévi-Strauss's essay "Structure and Form: Reflections on a Work by Vladimir Propp," in Propp, *Theory and History of Folklore,* pp. 167–88, and Propp's "The Structural and Historical Study of the Wondertale" (1976), in *Theory and History of Folklore,* pp. 67–81.
18. The subtitle of Duerr's book is *Über die Grenze zwischen Wildnis und Zivilisation* (Frankfurt: Syndikat, 1978).

Bibliography

Barchilon, Jacques. *Le conte merveilleux français de 1690–1790*. Paris: Champion, 1975. A socio-psychological examination which explores different aspects of the literary fairy tale during its most fruitful period in France.

Bastian, Ulrike. *Die Kinder- und Hausmärchen der Brüder Grimm in der literatur-pädagogischen Diskussion des 19. und 20. Jahrhunderts*. Giessen: Haag und Herchen, 1981. A socio-historical study of the pedagogical use of the Grimms' fairy tales and the different approaches taken by educators over the course of 150 years.

Bloch, Ernst. *Ästhetik des Vor-Scheins*. Edited by Gert Ueding. 2 vols. Frankfurt: Suhrkamp, 1974. A selection of Ernst Bloch's essays on culture, literature, art, and music. The collection contains important essays on the fairy tale and its connection to popular culture.

Darnton, Robert. *The Great Cat Massacre and Other Episodes in French Cultural History*. New York: Basic Books, 1984. A collection of essays essentially on the social background of French cultural history. Also contains a comparative essay on French and German folktales that focuses on the development of "Little Red Riding Hood."

Ellis, John. *One Fairy Story Too Many*. Chicago: University of Chicago Press, 1984. A critical examination of how the brothers Grimm allegedly duped the German public by falsifying the sources of their fairy tales.

Rölleke, Heinz, ed. *Die älteste Märchensammlung der Brüder Grimm*. Cologne and Geneva: Fondation Martin Bodmer, 1975. A significant edition of the Grimms' handwritten manuscript containing the first versions of the tales (1810) along with the first printed edition of the tales (1812) and important historical notes about sources and development of editions.

Storrer, Mary Elizabeth. *La Mode des contes de fées (1685–1700)*. Paris: Champion, 1928. A study of the rise of the literary fairy tale during the reign of Louis XIV.

16. Past and Present Folkloristic Narrator Research

RAINER WEHSE

Like Aristides, Philostratus, and others, Plato speaks pejoratively of the tales current in the nursery as *titthōn mythoi* ("old wetnurses' tales").[1] The Romans used the expression *aniles fabulae* ("crones' tales"). These expressions have a twofold implication: first, that folk narrative material is regarded as unimportant, childish, and beneath notice; and second, that this disdain also carries over to the tale-tellers. Neither tales nor tale-tellers seemed worth studying at that time, at least not by scholars or philosophers. A great distance separates present scholarly interest in the genre, *Märchen* and folktales, and in their narrators. A perceptual shift is prerequisite to recognizing that behind the form, the tale, there is someone who *forms* the tale and that the tale is inconceivable without the one who forms it. To arrive at this realization, one must first see traditional material, not as a constant rigid entity but as entities — contents and forms — newly created and altered by a series of oral transmissions. The text of a tale type, despite its characteristic unmistakability, is something more than a self-enclosed entity; in addition, it directly reflects the character of the bearer of the tradition and of his or her specific human

Translated by Ruth B. Bottigheimer.

situation. And a "product" can only be completely understood by an acquaintance with the "producer."

These producers, the narrators, generally belong to peripheral or lower social groups: wetnurses, servants, agricultural workers, peddlers, vagabonds, minstrels, bards, and so on. Only now, when attention has turned away from an exclusive preoccupation with epoch-making individuals, have these people become objects of scholarly inquiry. Scholarly consideration today includes the "unimportant" accomplishments of "unimportant people," a change comparable to developments within literature, where, for example, interest in courtly drama was followed by interest in bourgeois drama, then — with Henrik Ibsen and the naturalism of Gerhart Hauptmann — the analysis of "lesser" people was taken up, a process that has developed into a genuine mania for the lower classes. It took this broadening of the circle of "people worth noticing" in art and many areas of scholarship to perceive the narrator behind the tale.

Regard for the value of folktale and *Märchen* materials was not, however, completely absent in former times. Poets used tales and tale elements. Homer used them in the *Iliad* and the *Odyssey;* Strabo reported an Egyptian version of a Cinderella motif; and Apuleius, born in A.D. 124, inserted the tale of Amor and Psyche into *The Golden Ass.* The first accounts of tale-tellers are similarly embedded in a literary matrix. Vishnusharman the Wise appears as the tutor of princes and tells them eighty-six stories in the *Panchatantra,* the ancient Indian collection of fables, stories, proverbs, and animal tales, which served to instruct princes and later became a general child-rearing book. The book was translated into sixty languages.

Alf laila waleila is better known. Translated as *The Arabian Nights* or the *Thousand and One Nights,* this frame tale of Indian origin is composed of more than three hundred tales. The king of Samarkand, deceived by his wife with a Moorish slave, loses his faith in women's fidelity. Therefore, every evening he marries a new woman and has her murdered the next morning. Scheherazade, the clever daughter of the royal vizier, ensnares the king with the tales she carries over from night to night until, after 1001 nights, the king reprieves her. Here the narrator — in a highly precarious situation — is assigned great significance, notwithstanding the fact that the point in question is amusement, fictional characters, and imaginary situations. Wanderers who plied their hosts with stories night after night so that they could continue to enjoy hospitality for as long as possible made use of a related ploy.[2]

A device similar to that used in the *Thousand and One Nights* appears in Boccaccio's *Decameron* (1348–53). With modest European reserve, there are only ten days in which one hundred stories are told by seven ladies and three gentlemen staying on an estate near Florence at the time of the Great Plague of 1348. This work has often been imitated. In Margaret of Navarre's *Heptamerone,* for example, a group of ladies and gentlemen pass the time telling stories while they wait in a monastery garden for the roads to become passable again after a heavy storm. One may also mention famous examples such as Geoffrey Chaucer's *Canterbury Tales* or the tales of the *Seven Wise Masters,* in which a young man is saved from the gallows by telling stories. In addition to these fictive narrators who, we may assume, reflect narrative practices and situations to a certain extent, there is much evidence about actual narrators, especially those professional storytellers of the eastern Mediterranean. In Europe the number of professions associated with narrative grows during and after the medieval period. Folktales and other oral material were used in *exempla* and above all in sermons in both Protestant and Catholic churches, particularly in the Baroque period.[3]

As in many areas of folklore, archival material — especially prohibitions and legal decisions — provide a further important source for the study of narrators. For centuries, stories were censured as "lies" by religious and secular authorities. Symbolic language was often suspected of being an expression of dissatisfaction with social conditions and was thus perceived as a possible threat to the social order. Because of this, gatherings in the spinning room (*Spinnstubenabende*) and other high-spirited entertainments were prohibited from time to time in various European countries and the storytellers excommunicated, flogged, or imprisoned. In Russia the czars even banished peasant storytellers of traditional tales to Siberia.[4] In contrast hardly any importance is assigned to storytellers today, who are mostly regarded as harmless, at least in a political sense.

Despite whatever occasional bright views of the subject of storytellers exist before the nineteenth century, the entire field was generally regarded negatively. The Enlightenment, above all, makes use of the expression "wetnurses' tales" (*Ammenmärchen*). In the foreword to *Dschinnistan* (1786), Christoph Martin Wieland writes: "Nurses' tales, told in their style, may be transmitted orally, but they mustn't be printed." But the way was being prepared for a new era, and soon thereafter such tales were found worthy of publication. In 1791–92, two volumes of *Märchen*-like stories attributed to Christian August Vulpius appeared in Weimar with the title *Ammenmärchen.* Ludwig Tieck also termed his *Ritter Blaubart* (Berlin, 1797) a nurses' tale (*Ammenmärchen*). Heinrich Heine wrote in *Deutschland, ein Wintermärchen* (1844): "They sound so dear, they sound so sweet, the fairy

tales of the old nurse" (chap. 14). In the period of Romantic sensibilities and literature a great change sets in, after even the educated
classes came to appreciate folk tradition. From now on, no matter
how hesitatingly, one approached storytellers themselves. The text
alone still occupied the center of attention, but it was by no means the
text as it was actually recounted. For the most varied reasons the text
was corrected and improved. One need only compare the Grimms'
sources according to the Ölenberg manuscript[5] with the versions in
later editions. Yet meager notes about the storytellers themselves can
occasionally be found as fieldwork byproducts, for example, the
Grimms' storytellers like "die Viehmännin," to whom the brothers devote a famous description in Volume 2 of the *Kinder- und Hausmärchen*
edition of 1819, Dortchen Wild, Marie Hassenpflug, the Haxthau-
sens, and "Old Marie," as she was portrayed by generations of Grimm
scholars.

How peripheral narrators themselves were regarded at that time
and how unimportant they seemed to be is indicated by the fact that
because of inadequate information about informants, almost 200
years passed before Heinz Rölleke was able to show that one of the
Grimms' informants, the "Old Marie" who everyone assumed was the
Wilds' housekeeper, was actually Marie Hassenpflug and thus a
young, not an aged, storyteller.[6]

Those were all preludes; genuine research concerning folk narrators begins later. John Francis Campbell of Islay with his *Popular
Tales of the West Highlands 1–4* (Edinburgh, 1860–62) and the Sicilian
Giuseppe Pitrè, with his *Fiabe, novelle e racconti popolari siciliani 1–4*
(Palermo, 1874–75) take the lead. The latter writes about his best
storyteller: "Anything but pretty, she nonetheless possesses a verbal
facility, an effective choice of words and a captivating storytelling
manner, which reveal an extraordinary natural gift" (p. xvii).

In Russia in the first three decades of this century, N. E. On-
čukov, the brothers Boris M. and Jurii M. Sokolov, and Mark
Azadowskii, to name a few, follow the example of those researchers
who studied the rich tradition of epics sung in Scandinavia.[7] These
scholars describe the independently creative accomplishments of narrators and detail how their experiences influence their own telling of
the stories. The Russian School's research emphasis rejected earlier
theories which laid claim to anonymity and a mystically perceived
collective origin for the development of folk narrative. The Russian
researchers' aim was to recognize the folk poet as the equal of the
author of written literature. Azadowskii's *A Siberian Tale Teller* emphasizes the principle of individuality with the characteristic attention
which is accorded the person of the narrator. These principles are

exemplified in the figure of the fifty-year-old Natalia Ossipowna Winokurowa, whom Azadowskii met in 1915. Winokurowa was illiterate and spent her entire life in the place of her birth. The attention fixed characteristically on informants from the agricultural lower classes as objects of inquiry remained valid internationally until recently. We will meet the exact opposite of Winokurowa later in connection with a most up-to-date study, Juha Pentikäinen's *Life History and World View.*

How does narrator research develop after these first beginnings, a detailed view of which appears very modern? Finnish and Scandinavian researchers next come into view. The Swede, Carl Wilhelm von Sydow, undertook a first division of narrators into active and passive bearers of tradition, that is, into those who pass *Märchen* and folktales on and those who only listen to them. He thereby modified the theory of purely mechanistically linear diffusion of folk narrative material assumed by the Historico-Geographic School, also called the Finnish School, which is particularly well represented by the work of Antti Aarne and of Kaarle and Julius Krohn.

Untested and unverified in the field, some of the earlier theories had been developed at the desk and in the minds of scholars. That situation changed with increasing collecting activity. Although leafing through dust-covered folios in search of folktales of earlier centuries remains necessary in order to arrive at a historical perspective, collecting in the field draws collectors out of their offices and turns their attention to storytellers themselves. It is true that attention to texts still takes precedence, as one can easily see by looking at the holdings of the Archives of German Folk Narrative in the Folklore Seminar of the University of Marburg or (for the folksong) at the collections in the German Folksong Archive in Freiburg. But researchers nowadays get their material from people themselves and become correspondingly curious about these people in order to develop insights and theories based on this knowledge. Perhaps one could term this attitude the Epoch of Realism in research. At the same time folklore begins to view itself no longer just as philology but also as a social science or as anthropology in the broadest sense, knowledge of human beings.

This development characterizes, for example, the founding of the Irish Folklore Commission in Dublin in 1930, organized according to the guiding principles of von Sydow and the Norwegian Reidar T. Christiansen, and systematically documenting the repertoires of specific storytellers as well as also studying them individually.

The school of the Germanist Julius Schwietering looks at yet another aspect, the narrative situation. Not the folk narrator as a creative artist, but the social function of the narrative act now takes center stage:

Folkloristic formulation of the interpretation and meaning of specific folk material sees folk material as an instrument or tool, which can be comprehended not from its form, but from its cultural context, from the totality of events in life with which it is inextricably bound up, not as an independent detachable pattern, product or structure. The object of such research is . . . not the story, but the telling of a story or how a story is told . . . not only its outward appearance, but also everything that is at the same time an inner act of experience of the soul and mental acquisition, not by the individual but by the community.[8]

One sees the emphasis move away from the individual to a consideration of the narrator as part of a community and to the act and the situation of narrating rather than to form and content, a widening of the research horizon. For the earliest researchers, the center of interest was *content*, then came the *teller*, and currently the *telling* in terms of performance, situation, and relationship to vital processes. The three most important viewpoints in oral folk tradition have thus been made explicit. On this level of abstraction, nothing basically new can be added. All further research will differ only according to whichever formulation dominates the thinking of the scholar in question: according to method and technique, as well as according to the kind of narrators being investigated, whether defined by gender, ethnic group, age, or job.

The best example for a synthesis of all practices and formulations previously tested is the work of the late Hungarian folklorist and minister of culture, Gyula Ortutay. In his "epochmaking" (as Linda Dégh termed it) essay on the storyteller, Miháli Fedics, he writes in 1972:

In folk culture the essence and process of the "public poetry" are provided by the tension that naturally arises from the relations between individual talent and the tradition of the community. It also follows from the nature of oral tradition itself and from the social relations existing between the creative talent of folk culture and their material, the tradition preserved by the community and the judgment of their audience.[9]

Ethnological oral narrative researchers were stimulated above all by the German-American Franz Boas, who integrated the study of storytellers into his principle of holistic observation of culture. For him the storyteller was only one component of his or her contemporaneous socio-cultural system.

Juha Pentikäinen's *Oral Repertoire and World View* is based on the same premises.[10] The "object" of his investigation was Marina Takalo (1890–1970), a Lake Ladoga Karelian expelled from Russia to Finland under political pressure in 1922. A member of the lower class, illiterate, conservatively orthodox, from a small village community, she fits all the traditional criteria. However, if one pictures the development of such studies of individual bearers of tradition, then it becomes clear that a new folklore practice is emerging. To repeat: In the beginning there were repertoire studies without reference to informants; then a selection of good mediators of tradition followed along with an evaluation of them as esthetes and individuals. Both approaches seem to have finally been replaced today by a method which Pentikäinen also follows, that is, the bearer of tradition is investigated as an individual and as a representative of his or her culture taking into account the personal role which he or she plays in the community, his or her repertoire seen in relationship to its use, and his or her attitude to the repertoire. The object of research is thus no longer the human "product" isolated from its context, the person and his or her utterances. The study itself is based on one hundred hours of tape recordings with 1,592 individual pieces recorded between 1959 and 1969, not all of which are folkloristic. In this undertaking Marina Takalo proves herself to be an outstanding preserver of every important genre in the Karelian and Finnish tradition. However, her repertoire was not static in function and constitution. In 1944 she had made the transition from passive to active tradition-bearing; she adapted material to her changing world view as well as to her altered circumstances and absorbed new material in her new homeland. That, together with modifications to her repertoire, brought about by different contexts (including emotional ones) is all taken into account by her biographer. Takalo's collection can be summed up roughly under the following headings: folk belief, daily and annual custom, magic practices, folk medicine, story, and song.

A final developmental stage in narrator studies has been attained by that group of American folklorists which — with attacks on text-, tradition-, and narrator-research — aims at making the situational context of a storytelling event the only legitimate object of study. Representatives of this approach — Dan Ben-Amos, Richard Bauman, and Robert Georges, for example — take their inspiration from ethnology, linguistics, behavioral psychology, literary criticism, and field studies of preliterate cultures. What they want is a new fundamental concept for the study of human communication, which is defined by Robert Georges as "a process, which is integrally interrelated to, and which is an expressive manifestation of, fundamental physiological and cognitive processes."[11]

But this obsession with context which is especially evident in ethnology has already attracted criticism for its loss of perspective, for it overlooks the fact that the storyteller faces an audience, to which he or she is joined by a *story*.

In the following section one problem area among many in narrator research will be scrutinized more closely. What happens with a fairy tale or a folk narrative when it is transmitted orally? At first the answer seems quite simple. The story is changed, just as the message is transformed in the parlor game "Telephone," in which a certain message is whispered from person to person around a circle. The humor consists in comparing the original message with what the last person thinks he or she has heard, a message which often bears no resemblance to the original. On the other hand, certain fairy tale and folktale content can exist almost unchanged for centuries, sometimes for millenia and over several continents. Take the example of "Cinderella." Geographically it is known in nearly 1,000 variants from Hawaii to Japan, South Africa, and Arabia, known practically throughout the entire world, and historically with evidence for two thousand years. How can that be explained?

It is difficult, if not impossible, to observe on the spot the process of dissemination in its spatial range as well as its geographical depth, particularly since contemporary chains of tradition provided by mass communication and travel have been made even more incalculable. A fortuitous insight into one particular case made it glaringly clear to me how communication and travel affect ideas concerning the provenance of a particular tale. In a Swedish archive there is an urban legend about the baby in a microwave oven. How did it get there? It was sent in by a Canadian woman in 1974. I, a German, had previously told her the story in Finland. I no longer remember who it was who told me the story, but it was somewhere in the American Midwest in the year 1969!

Studying the oral transmission of stories as it naturally occurs is, as already stated, nearly impossible. One must set up a controlled experiment to come to any conclusions. Walter Anderson undertook just such an experiment in 1947. He says:

The unusual stability of folktales can be explained as follows: 1) Each narrator has, as a rule, heard the tale (or jest, legend, and so on) from his predecessors not once but many times. 2) He or she has heard it, as a rule, not from a single person, but from a series of people (and in different versions). The former condition eliminates errors and omissions potentially arising from the listener's poor memory, as well as alterations which the narrator might have allowed him- or herself on a single occasion; the latter eliminates the errors and omissions which are peculiar to one or the other narrator from his or her sources. . . . I by no means deny that one often hears a tale, particularly a long one, only once in one's lifetime; but it occurs very rarely that someone dares to recount a tale he or she has heard only once.[12]

To prove his hypotheses, especially those which from then on were called the Law of Self-Correction, Anderson undertook the following: First he determined what was produced when a tale or legend actually was repeated twelve times according to the Principle of the Single Source.[13] Together with students of German literature at the University of Kiel he formed three chains of tradition, each with twelve members. He read a Pomeranian legend about the devil to three participants who had never heard it before and had them write it down from memory the next day. Each of these three students then read this tale separately to one of their colleagues, who in turn wrote it down the following day, and so on. The entire procedure was repeated twelve times.

The conditions of the experiment were more clearly defined and more favorable for the stability of the legend's text than those which obtain for the actual propagation of folk narratives in oral tradition, according to adherents of the Principle of the Single Source:

1) A short, simple, and thus very striking text was chosen.
2) The participants listened to the text with close attention, in order to be able to reproduce it as faithfully as possible on the following day.
3) They were told to avoid all voluntary alterations and embellishments.
4) Each time only 24 hours passed between hearing the legend and writing it down.[14]

One would actually have anticipated that memory lapses on the part of the participants would have caused the legend to become shorter and less detailed as it was repeated. This was true only in a general sense, since individual narrators, despite all warnings, let their fantasy or their rich vocabulary range free and as a result the word count rose steeply. But let us let the original text and the variant of the twelfth recipient of one of the chains of tradition speak for themselves:

Original Version: Once there lived on the island of Usedom a nobleman, who led a sinful and dissolute life, and who pursued young girls, so that very few escaped his clutches.

Final Version: Once there was a baron. He possessed great wealth and had many jewels in his castle; he also liked to play the flute.

Original Version: He once drove to the edge of the sea and saw a coach approaching from afar, in which a beautiful girl sat. . . .

Final Version: One day he rode out with one of his ministers. On the way they were met by a coach, in which a beautiful lady sat. . . .

Original Version: . . . immediately he sprang from his coach and wanted to approach her, when his coachman called after him: "My lord, look at her feet!" Then he looked and noticed that the girl had a horse's hoof. . . .

Final Version: The baron desired to talk with this lady. Since the coach was in his realm, he stopped it. He got into conversation with the lady, which lasted for a long while, for she pleased him greatly. The minister, however, noticed that she had a horse's hoof. Since his lord did not seem to have noticed this, he brought all his arts to bear to move his lord to a speedy departure, in order to protect him from the influence of the devil, whom he suspected of having taken the form of the beautiful lady. He was successful only after a prolonged effort. The next day the baron rode out again with his minister and hoped to meet the beautiful lady again, and he was not disappointed. The same thing happened again, for the baron did not seem to have noticed the horse's hoof this time either, while the minister was again successful in his efforts and saved his lord from the devil. On the third day, the minister was again successful in protecting his lord.

Original Version: . . . he immediately leapt back, but in the same instant the girl jumped out of the coach and ran after him. He threw himself into his coach and raced home wildly, but the girl followed hard on his heels with her hair flying loose.

Final Version: On the fourth day (the baron had ridden out again to meet the beautiful lady), he looked everywhere in vain for the coach, but it didn't appear. The minister heaved a sigh of relief, for he had succeeded in saving his lord from the devil, who wanted to catch his unsuspecting lord in his trap.

Original Version: Finally he arrived at his residence, rushed inside, bolted the door behind him and hurried right up to the attic window, to see if his horrifying pursuer was still there. Then he sees how she's rising toward him up the wall like a cat, higher and higher, and now she is there: in desperation he grabs his flute from the wall and plays:

> Lord, I have sinned;
> Yea, the weight of my sins is great;
> I haven't trodden the path
> That you pointed out to me.

And with the last note the girl disappeared; the nobleman did penance and began a new life.

Final Version: Not extant.

If one compares the final versions of all three chains of tradition, one sees that only a fragmentary substrate of the original version remains in the following content:

A nobleman sees a coach passing by, in which a beautiful lady sits. He greets the lady, but is held back by his servants, because the lady turns out to have at least one hoof. The nobleman is saved.

Anderson comes to the following conclusion: "The more often the components of a chain of tradition pass from mouth to mouth, the more they depart from the original in terms of content and the more the component bearing the same number in the different chain of tradition diverges from the other. That has to do with the fact that the Urtext — reconstructible on the principle of 'two witnesses against one' based on the similarly numbered members of each chain of tradition — becomes more and more uncertain and strays further and further from the actual original text." [15] At the end of his description the author suggests that his readers continue the experiment, but he predicts that they will make the same observations and arrive at the same conclusions.

Ortutay responded to the challenge in 1953 and, using the same legend, did, in fact, achieve the same results. One of Ortutay's final versions can no longer be recognized:

> Wherever it was — or wasn't — there was once an old man. This old man was on his way to the vineyard one day to hoe. Halfway there he got tired, found a stream and bathed. While he was in the water, he saw that little elves had found his clothes on the shore, were picking them up laughing and carrying them off. The poor old man couldn't go any further. [16]

In 1955 Kurt Schier set up the same experiment in Munich, on the Starnberger See to be exact, using children, but with more refined methods (for instance, specified chains of tradition from children who conformed to tradition and others who were not particularly gifted in telling stories). The work [17] is simultaneously a critique of Anderson and an adverse criticism of the following points of his experiment:

1. The choice of subjects is questionable: One would have to take into account (a) the attitude of the subjects to the experiment, (b) their capacity to remember, (c) particular stresses, which the subjects might be exposed to at that time, for example exam preparations.
2. The actual narrative situation in storytelling communities was not sufficiently taken into account.
3. The legend used experimentally was not suitable, because it came from another area (an objection which is not completely defensible, since a *Wandersage* is in question).
4. A psychological instead of a folkloristic method was applied.
5. Oral transmission had been replaced by a written mode.

These points, valid to a certain extent, provoked Anderson to a vehement reply and countercriticism in the form of a twenty-four-page pamphlet.[18]

Both of these works considerably extend the formulation of the experiment, which was originally very simply conceived, and together they lead directly to the Conduit Theory of Linda Dégh and A. Vázsonyi (1971). According to the Conduit Theory, folklore messages do not ramble erratically from one person to another but follow definite routes consisting of communicative sequences of individuals with similar personality characteristics, who share similar attitudes toward similar messages. When a message travels through an adequate conduit it remains virtually unaltered. When, however, a message arrives at an uncomprehending or unsympathetic receiver, it either stops or is modified to a greater or lesser extent.

Conduits are not monolithic; instead, each conduit is suitable for carrying a major complex of essentially similar messages, such as a *Märchen*, and it often brachiates into subconduits which dismantle the larger complex and convey diverse subtypes, clusters, episodes, motifs or even disintegrated particles to appropriately receptive individuals.

The Conduit Theory stresses the recognition that folklore communication, like other forms of communication, is based on a series of complex choices by the participants on both ends of each section of the conduit. In a natural context they are essentially free. Restrictions on freedom of choice impair the natural functioning of the conduits, which accounts for the results of reproductive experiments (W. Anderson and others), in which many of the participants reacted with psychological defenses, recalling inaccurately or totally forgetting. On the other hand, experiments connected with the Conduit theory attempt to analyze the errors committed during reproductive processes, comparing them with the findings of objective psychological tests, in order to utilize psychological defenses as a probe to test the hypothesis that individuals with similar personality traits react similarly to similar types of folklore material.[19]

This is one of the most recent results in a small but refreshingly relevant and lively sector of contemporary research in oral narratives and narrators.[20] The relevance of the Conduit Theory gains in relationship to the empirical theory of literature, whose basic theoretical cognitive premise is the radical constructionist approach of biological (Humberto R. Maturana) and psychological (Ernst von Glaserfeld) definition. According to this, human beings are "self-creating homeopoietic systems, which are autonomous, determined by their structure, and which are operationally closed, and which function self-referentially and homeostatically."[21] Accordingly, cognition is strictly dependent on the subject. A communication between individuals requires a more or less parallel and comparable construct of (for example, cognitive) orientation processes, for which among others cultural unity and socialization as well as biological disposition set the parameters.[22] According to Siegfried J. Schmidt's theory of communicative behavior, a communication cannot be understood in the sense of immediate transmission of information between subjects.[23] This statement is consistent with the empirical observations of Anderson and Schier, in whose experiments textual alterations occurred without the experimental subject's appearing to have either a willful or a conscious intention to make the alteration. A genuine understanding between two individuals can result only from a comparison of their "communicates" (in this instance, the story that has been passed on) and a greater or lesser approximation of consensus about that "communicate." The concept of "text" in its former sense would thus have to eliminated; in any case it can only be interpreted and analyzed in relationship to the biologically, culturally, and psychologically formed structure of the narrator's and listener's personalities. Herein lies the essential task of contemporary narrator and reception research.

Notes

1. Cf. Elfriede Moser-Rath, "Ammenmärchen," in *Enzyklopädie des Märchens*, ed. Kurt Ranke et al. (Berlin and New York, 1977).

2. Linda Dégh, *Folktales and Society* (Bloomington: Indiana University Press, 1969, 1972).

3. Cf. Elfriede Moser-Rath, *Predigtmärlein der Barockzeit* (Berlin: de Gruyter, 1964); also Ernst-Heinrich Rehermann, *Das Predigtexempel bei protestantischen Theologen des 16. und 17. Jahrhunderts*. (Göttingen: O. Schwartz, 1977).

4. Dégh, *Folktales and Society*.

5. The text of this collection has been published most recently in Heinz Rölleke's *Die älteste Märchensammlung der Brüder Grimm* (Cologny-Genève: Fondation Martin Bodmer, 1975).

6. Ibid., pp. 391, 395.

7. The following discussion borrows heavily from Linda Dégh's article on narrator research, "Erzählen, Erzähler" in the *Enzyklopädie des Märchens*, vol. 4 (1984), 315–42.

8. Julius Schwietering, "Volksmärchen und Volksglaube," *Euphorion*, N. S. 36 (1935): 74.

9. Gyula Ortutay, "Mihály Fedics Relates Tales," in *Hungarian Folklore: Essays* (Budapest, 1972), p. 268.

10. Juha Pentikäinen, *Oral Repertoire and World View*, FF Communications 219 (Helsinki, 1978).

11. Robert A. Georges, "From Folktale Research to the Study of Narrating," *Studia Fennica* 20 (Helsinki, 1976): 166.

12. Walter Anderson, *Ein volkskundliches Experiment*, FF Communications, 141 (Helsinki, 1951), p. 3.

13. Ibid., pp. 4ff.

14. Ibid., pp. 6ff.

15. Ibid., pp. 44–45.

16. Walter Anderson: *Eine neue Arbeit zur experimentellen Volkskunde,* FF Communications, 168 (Helsinki, 1956), p. 6.

17. Kurt Schier, "Praktische Untersuchungen zur mündlichen Weitergabe von Volkserzählungen." (Inaug. diss., Munich, 1955).

18. Anderson: *Eine Neue Arbeit.*

19. Linda Dégh, "Conduit-Theorie," in *Enzyklopädie des Märchens* (1981), 3:124–26. See also Elliott Oring, *Experimentelle Erzählforschung,* in ibid. (1984), 4:684–94.

20. Parts of this essay appeared as "Volkskundliche Erzählforschung" in Rainer Wehse, ed., *Märchenerzähler-Erzählgemeinschaft* (Kassel 1983), pp. 7–20, 175.

21. Natascha Würzbach, "Die Empirische Literaturwissenschaft ELW: Ein Neues Paradigma," *Siegener Periodicum zur Internationalen Empirischen Literaturwissenschaft* 1, no. 1 (1982): 7.

22. According to Natascha Würzbach's review of Siegfried J. Schmidt, *Grundriß der Empirischen Literaturwissenschaft,* vols. 1–2 (Braunschweig, 1980–82), in *Poetica: Zeitschrift für Sprach- und Literaturwissenschaft* 15, nos. 3–4 (1983): 342–54.

23. Schmidt, *Grundriß.*

Bibliography

Azadowskii, Mark. Trans. James R. Dow, Monograph series no. 2, Austin: University of Texas Center for Intercultural Studies in Folklore and Ethnomusicology, 1974. (Originally *Eine sibirische Märchenerzählerin.* Helsinki: Suomalainen Tiedeakatemia, 1926 (FFC 68).) Early classical and influential study of a Siberian female narrator on *Märchen* emphasizing the principle of individuality in regard to the narrator's repertoire as opposed to the theory of communal origin.

Cahiers de littérature orale, vol. 11 (1982). Volume 11 of this periodical is dedicated to the telling and tellers of folktales.

Dégh, Linda. *Folktales and Society.* Bloomington: Indiana University Press, 1969, 1972. First published as *Märchen, Erzähler und Erzählgemeinschaft.* Berlin: Akademie Verlag, 1962. Treats the narrating of Hungarian *Märchen*-tellers originally from the Bukowina who were dislodged during World War II. Deals with general aspects of the narrative context and also surveys former research on narrators.

Dorson, Richard M. *American Negro Folktales.* New York: Fawcett Publications, 1968. Principally a collection of folktales but also a lively description of their narrators and how their stories were collected in the field.

Enzyklopädie des Märchens: Handwörterbuch zur historischen und vergleichenden Erzählforschung. Edited by Kurt Ranke et al. Berlin and New York: de Gruyter, 1975–. Among the approximately 3,600 entries in the twelve volumes planned, many deal or will deal with aspects of narrators and narrating.

Pentikäinen, Juha. *Oral Repertoire and World View.* Helsinki: Suomalainen Tiedeakatemia, 1978 (FFC 219). Detailed anthropological study of the Karelian narrator Marino Takalo, her life history, and her repertoire.

Studia Fennica, vol. 20. Helsinki, 1976. Several essays on different aspects of folk narrators (in English).

Wehse, Rainer, ed. *Märchenerzähler — Erzählgemeinschaft.* Kassel: Erich Röth, 1983. Essays on traditional and modern *Märchen*-telling by international authors.

17. Fairy Tales from a Folkloristic Perspective

ALAN DUNDES

The first thing to say about fairy tales is that they are an oral form. ✦ Fairy tales, however one may choose ultimately to define them, are a subgenre of the more inclusive category of "folktale," which exists primarily as a spoken traditional narrative. Once a fairy tale or any other type of folktale, for that matter, is reduced to written language, one does not have a true fairy tale but instead only a pale and inadequate reflection of what was originally an oral performance complete with raconteur and audience. From this folkloristic perspective, one cannot possibly read fairy tales; one can only properly hear them told.

When one enters into the realm of written-down or transcribed fairy tales, one is involved with a separate order of reality. A vast chasm separates an oral tale with its subtle nuances entailing significant body movements, eye expression, pregnant pauses, and the like from the inevitably flat and fixed written record of what was once a live and often compelling storytelling event. To be sure, there are degrees of authenticity and accuracy with respect to the transcription of fairy tales. In modern times, armed with tape recorders or videotape equipment, a folklorist may be able to capture a live performance in the act, thereby preserving it for enjoyment and study by future audiences. But in the nineteenth century when the formal study of folklore began in Europe, collectors had to do the best they could to take down oral tales verbatim without such advances in technology. Many of them succeeded admirably, such as E. Tang Kristensen (1843–1929), a Danish folklorist who was one of the greatest collectors of fairy tales of all time.[1] Others, including even the celebrated Grimm brothers, failed to live up to the ideal of recording oral tales as they were told. Instead, they altered the oral tales in a misguided effort to "improve" them.[2] The Grimms, for instance, began to conflate different versions of the same tale and they ended up producing what folklorists now call "composite" texts. A composite text, containing one motif from one version, another motif from another, and so on, exemplifies what folklorists term "fakelore."[3] Fakelore refers to an item which the collector claims is genuine oral tradition but which has been doctored or in some cases entirely fabricated by the purported collector.

The point is that a composite fairy tale has never actually been told in precisely that form by a storyteller operating in the context of oral tradition. It typically appears for the very first time in print. And it is not just a matter of twentieth-century scholars trying to impose twentieth-century standards upon struggling nineteenth-century pioneering collectors. For the Grimms certainly knew better, and they are on record as adamantly opposing the literary reworking of folklore (as had been done in the famous folksong anthology of *Des Knaben Wunderhorn* [1805] which they severely criticized). They specifically called for the collection of fairy tales as they were told — in dialect. In the preface to the first volume of the *Kinder- und Hausmärchen* of 1812, the Grimms bothered to say that they had "endeavored to present these fairy tales as pure as possible. . . . No circumstance has been added, embellished or changed." Unfortunately, they were later unable or unwilling to adhere to these exemplary criteria. So the Grimms knew what they were doing when they combined different versions of a single folktale and presented it as one of the tales in their *Kinder- und Hausmärchen*.

What this means is that anyone truly interested in the unadulterated fairy tale must study oral texts or as accurate a transcription of oral texts as is humanly possible. The reality of far too much of what passes for fairy tale scholarship — including the majority of essays in this very volume — is that such fairy tale texts are not considered. Instead, a strong, elitist literary bias prevails and it is the recast and reconstituted fairy tales which serve as the corpus for study. When one analyzes fairy tales as rewritten by Charles Perrault or by the Grimm brothers, one is *not* analyzing fairy tales as they were told by traditional storytellers. One is instead analyzing fairy tale plots as altered by men of letters, often with a nationalistic and romantic axe to grind. The aim was usually to present evidence of an ancient nationalistic patrimony in which the French or German literati could take pride. With such a laudable goal, it was deemed excusable to eliminate any crude or vulgar elements — How many bawdy folktales does one find in the Grimm canon? — and to polish and refine the oral discourse of "rough" peasant dialects.

This does not mean that versions, composite or not, of tales published by Perrault and the Grimms cannot be studied. They have had an undeniably enormous impact upon popular culture and literature, but they should not be confused with the genuine article — the oral fairy tale.

There is another difficulty with the research carried out by deluded individuals who erroneously believe they are studying fairy tales when they limit themselves to the Grimm or Perrault versions of tales. Any true fairy tale, like all folklore, is characterized by the criteria of "multiple existence" and "variation." An item must exist in at least two versions in order to qualify as authentic folklore. Most items exist in hundreds of versions. Usually, no two versions of an oral fairy tale will be exactly word-for-word the same. That is what is meant by the criteria of multiple existence and variation. When one studies the Perrault or the Grimm text of a fairy tale, one is studying a single text. This may be appropriate for literary scholars who are wont to think in terms of unique, distinctive, individual texts written by a known author or poet. But it is totally inappropriate for the study of folklore wherein there is no such thing as *the* text. There are only texts.

Folklorists have been collecting fairy tales and other forms of folklore for the past several centuries. Not all these versions have been published. In fact, the majority of these tales remain in unpublished form scattered in folklore archives throughout the world. However, one can obtain these versions simply by applying to these archives. Folklorists have carried out extensive comparative studies of various fairy tales in which they have assiduously located and assembled as many as five hundred versions of a single tale type.[4] Ever since the Finnish folklorist Antti Aarne published his *Verzeichnis der Märchentypen* as Folklore Fellows Communication no. 3 in 1910, folklorists have had an index of folktales (including fairy tales). Twice revised by American folklorist Stith Thompson, in 1928 and again in 1961, *The Types of the Folktale: A Classification and Bibliography*, is the standard reference for any serious student of Indo-European folktales. Thompson's revisions took account of the various local, regional, and national tale type indexes which appeared after Aarne's 1910 work. There are more than fifty or sixty national tale-type indexes in print, including several which are not referenced in the Aarne-Thompson

1961 index inasmuch as they were published after that date, for example for Latvia, China, Korea, Madagascar, Friesland, and Norway.[5]

The Aarne-Thompson tale-type index gives not only a general synopsis of each of some two thousand Indo-European tales, but also some sense of how many versions are to be found in the various folklore archives. In addition, if there is a published article or monograph which contains numerous versions of a tale type, it is listed followed by an asterisk. If there has been a substantial, full-fledged comparative study of a particular tale, that bibliographical citation is marked by two asterisks. Thus if one looked in the Aarne-Thompson tale-type index under tale type 425A, "The Monster (Animal) as Bridegroom (Cupid and Psyche)," one would in a matter of seconds discover no less than five double-asterisked monographs or articles devoted to this tale type.[6] One would also learn that there are eighty-seven Danish versions, twenty-eight Hungarian versions, twenty-nine Rumanian versions, and others located in archives.

The gist of this is that if one is really interested in a particular fairy tale, one has the possibility of considering dozens upon dozens of versions of that tale. Whatever one's particular theoretical interest, the comparative data is essential. If one is concerned with identifying possible national traits in a particular version of a tale, one cannot do so without first ascertaining whether the traits in question are found in versions of the same tale told in other countries. If the same traits are to be found in twenty countries, it would be folly to assume that those traits were somehow typical of German or French culture exclusively.[7]

The sad truth is that most studies of fairy tales are carried out in total ignorance of tale-type indexes (or the related tool, the six volume *Motif-Index of Folk Literature* which first appeared in 1932–36, and was revised in 1955–58). One can say categorically that it is always risky, methodologically speaking, *to limit one's analysis to one single version of a tale.* There is absolutely no need to restrict one's attention to a single version of a tale type when there are literally hundreds of versions of that same tale easily available. The fallacy of using but a single version of a fairy tale is compounded when that one version is a doctored, rewritten composite text, as occurs when one uses the Grimm version alone.

The abysmal lack of knowledge of folktale scholarship among academics in classics, comparative literature, and literature departments generally causes genuine concern among folklorists. Let one example stand for hundreds. Rhys Carpenter publishes a book, *Folk Tale, Fiction and Saga in the Homeric Epics* (Berkeley and Los Angeles: University of California Press, 1958), in which he discusses the story of the

Cyclops with absolutely no mention of the fact that it is Aarne-Thompson tale type 1137, "The Ogre Blinded (Polyphemus)." It was in fact collected by the Grimms and the Homeric version provides a useful *terminus ante quem* for that tale. How can a scholar write a whole book about folktales without any apparent knowledge of the tale-type index? (And what about the scholars who reviewed the manuscript for the university press involved?) Despite the existence of a tale-type index since 1910, most of the discussion of fairy tales occurs without the benefit of folkloristic tale typology.

It is hard to document the extent of the parochialism of the bulk of fairy-tale research. There are too few folklorists and too many amateurs. For example, one continues to find essays and books naively claiming to extrapolate German national or cultural traits from the Grimm tales. It is not that there could not be any useful data contained in the Grimm versions, it is rather that there are plenty of authentic versions of German fairy tales available which a would-be student of German culture could consult as a check. Psychiatrists writing about fairy tales commit the same error. They typically use only one version of a fairy tale, in most instances the Grimm version, and then they go on to generalize not just about German culture, but all European culture or even all humankind — on the basis of one single (rewritten) version of a fairy tale! [8] This displays a certain arrogance, ethnocentrism, and ignorance.

There is another important question with respect to fairy tales. If one were to read through symposia and books devoted to the fairy tale — such as this — one could easily come to the (false) conclusion that the fairy tale, strictly speaking, was a European form. Certainly, if one speaks only of Perrault and the Grimms, one is severely restricted — just to France and Germany, not even considering the fairy tale traditions of Eastern Europe. But is the fairy tale a subgenre of folktale limited in distribution to Europe or to the Indo-European (and Semitic) world? Are there fairy tales in Africa? in Polynesia? among North and South American Indians? If one defines fairy tales as consisting of Aarne-Thompson tale types 300 to 749, the so-called tales of magic — as opposed let us say to animal tales (Aarne-Thompson tale types 1–299) or numskull stories (AT 1200–1349) or cumulative (formula) tales (AT 2000–2199), then one would have a relatively closed corpus. Vladimir Propp, for example, in his pioneering *Morphology of the Folktale*, first published in 1928, tried to define the structure of the "fairy tale," that is, Aarne-Thompson tale types 300–749. [9] The Swedish folklore theorist C. W. von Sydow proposed the term *chimerate*, which included AT 300–749 *and* AT 850–879, which is perhaps a better sampling of the so-called European fairy tale. [10]

The point is that these Aarne-Thompson tale types are *not* universal. They are basically Indo-European (plus Semitic, Chinese, and so on) tale types. "Cinderella," for example, AT 510A, although extremely widespread in the Indo-European world is not found as an indigenous tale in North and South America, in Africa, or aboriginal Australia. In other words, more than half the peoples of the world do not have a version of "Cinderella" except as borrowed from Indo-European cultures. But they have their own tales. The question is: Are some of their tales fairy tales? Is the tale of Star-Husband which is found throughout native North America a "fairy tale"? An abundant scholarship has been devoted to this American Indian tale type, but the issue of whether or not it is a fairy tale has not been discussed.[11]

⊁ ──⟶ The term *fairy tale* is actually a poor one anyway, for fairies rarely appear in fairy tales. The vast majority of stories with fairies in them are classified by folklorists as belonging to the legend genre, not folktale.[12] So since the term *fairy tale* is so inadequate, it is not clear that there is any advantage in forcing the folktales of other peoples and cultures into such a Procrustean misnomer. Regardless of whether or not one wants to extend the notion of fairy tale to African and American Indian folktales, the fact remains that *folktale* as a folklore genre is a universal one — even if specific tale types do not demonstrate universal distribution. This emphasizes the unduly restrictive nature of treatments of folktale which in effect ignore the rich folktale traditions of so much of the world.

Folklorists who choose to study the folktales of non-Western cultures enjoy a distinct advantage. In Europe, the study of a particular tale is complicated by the fact that oral and written versions of that tale have existed side-by-side for more than a century. Sometimes the oral tradition influences the written/literary tradition; sometimes (less often) the written tradition influences the oral tradition. (Informants who mean to be helpful will often suppress their own traditional version of a tale, preferring instead to check with the standard literary version, for example, in the Grimm canon, and dutifully parrot the latter to the collector. Much evidence indicates that a number of the Grimms' "German" folktales actually came from French literary sources — including Perrault.) In non-Western cultures, where literacy may still be relatively rare, storytellers may give oral versions untainted by literary rewritten texts. If one, therefore, is truly interested in studying folktales, one would do well to consider investigating non-European tales. The study of the interrelationship of oral and printed texts is a legitimate and important one, but it is not the same as the study of a purely oral tradition.

Nowhere is the excessive bias of literary elitism more evident than in the consideration of so-called *Kunstmärchen* and children's book illustrations. The distinction between *Volksmärchen* and *Kunstmärchen* is intended to distinguish true folktales from artistic or literary tales.[13] The latter are not and were never oral tales but instead are totally artistic imitations of the oral folktale genre. The "fairy tales" of Hans Christian Andersen, for example, are *Kunstmärchen*. He wrote them himself—he did not collect them from oral performances from informants. The very distinction between *Volksmärchen* and *Kunstmärchen* becomes virtually meaningless in an oral culture. In a culture which has no written language, there can be no *Kunstmärchen*. So the distinction is once again an example of a strictly Europe-centric view of the folktale. The same holds for children's book illustrations. While the content analysis of the various children's book illustrations of a tale like "Little Red Riding Hood" (AT 333) may be fascinating, it has little to do with the oral tale. There are no picture-book illustrations in an oral tale. Personally, I find children's book illustrations of fairy tales depressingly limiting and stultifying. Why should the audience see the dragon as one particular professional illustrator depicts it? Is not the human imagination far more powerful than anything a single book illustrator could possibly draw? In the oral-tale setting, each member of the audience is free to let his or her imagination create images without limit. So once again, children's book illustrations over and above the fact that versions of fairy tales rewritten for children are often heavily bowdlerized and simplified (in contrast to most societies where children are permitted to hear the same versions of the tales as told to adults) are a peculiar feature of European culture. One should be able to investigate the nature of fairy tale book illustrations, but one should realize that one is dealing with a derivative, printed art-form, part of a literary and commercial tradition which is at least one full step removed from the original oral tale.

If one were to remove from this volume all the essays which treated literary fairy tales, for example, by Ruskin, or which treated literary rewritten fairy tales such as by Perrault, the Grimms, or the ones in the *Thousand and One Nights*, or which were concerned with fairy tale children's book illustrations, one would have very little remaining. This is a pity insofar as the true fairy tale—even if one wished to restrict the subgenre to Europe or the Indo-European world—would essentially not be considered at all. The reader should be cautioned about this bias, especially since no doubt the majority of readers will, like the authors of the other essays, come from the ranks of students of literature, not folklore. The study of *Kunstmärchen* and literary versions of fairy tales is a legitimate academic enterprise, but it is no substitute for and it ought not to be confused with the study of the oral fairy tale.[14]

Finally, what is even more of an indictment of an overly literary

bias in the studies of fairy tale contained in this volume is the nar-
rowness of theoretical approach. A host of alternative theories and
methods exist with respect to the analysis of fairy tales, but very few
of them are represented in this set of essays. Several essays are totally
literal and historical, for example, looking for traces of old German
law in the Grimm tales. Fairy tales, oral and literary, are essentially
creatures of fantasy. They do not necessarily represent historical reality. The literal approach in folklore includes mythologists who lead
expeditions to Mount Ararat searching for remains of Noah's ark or
folktale scholars who go so far as to suggest that the dragons in fairy
tales are primitive man's recollection of prehistoric pterodactyls! The
attempt to extrapolate historical features of a culture from fairy tales
is admittedly one approach, but it hardly exhausts the content analysis possibilities. Structural, ritual, Jungian, and Freudian interpretations of fairy tales are discussed in this volume, but none of these
approaches is applied to any one tale.

The folkloristic approach to fairy tales begins with the oral tale —
with literary versions being considered derivative and secondary. It
includes a comparative treatment of any particular tale, using the resources of numerous publications and the holdings of folklore archives, as indicated in the standard tale-type indexes. Ideally, the
folkloristic approach should incorporate a healthy eclectic variety of
theoretical orientations which would be more likely to reveal the
richness of the fairy-tale genre, its symbolic nature, and its enduring
fascination.

Notes

1. Kristensen published more than eighty books on folklore, many at his own expense.
He collected many different genres including approximately 25,000 legends and stories.
With respect to folktales, the figure is 2,700. See Joan Rockwell, *Evald Tang Kristensen: A
Lifelong Adventure in Folklore* (Aalborg and Copenhagen: Aalborg University Press, 1982),
p. xii. For another portrait of this remarkable collector, see Bengt Holbek and Thorkild
Knudsen, "Evald Tang Kristensen," in Dag Strömbäck et al., eds., *Biographica: Nordic
Folklorists of the Past: Studies in Honour of Jouko Hautala* (Copenhagen: Nordisk Institut for
folkedigtning, 1971), pp. 239–57.

2. Although not the first to call attention to the discrepancy between what the Grimms
claimed they did and what they in fact did, John M. Ellis in his *One Fairy Story Too Many:
The Brothers Grimm and Their Tales* (Chicago: University of Chicago Press, 1983) documents
the poetic license taken by the famous brothers, especially Wilhelm, who was responsible
for most of the rewriting of the fairy tales. For gratifying detail on the history of folktale
collecting in various countries, see Richard M. Dorson's excellent forewords to the individual volumes published in the University of Chicago Press's *Folktales of the World* series, e.g.,
Katharine M. Briggs and Ruth L. Tongue, *Folktales of England* (1965); Sean O'Sullivan,
Folktales of Ireland (1966); Kurt Ranke, *Folktales of Germany* (1966). These tales, inciden-

tally, collected by folklorists from informants and transcribed and translated as faithfully as possible provide a useful alternative or antidote to the "literary" and rewritten tales — so often found in children's books.

3. For a discussion of fakelore, see Richard M. Dorson, "Fakelore," in his collection of essays entitled *American Folklore and the Historian* (Chicago: University of Chicago Press, 1971), pp. 3–14. The essay appeared originally in the *Zeitschrift für Volkskunde* 65 (1969): 56–64, although the term was coined by Dorson earlier in "Folklore and Fake Lore," *American Mercury* 70 (1950): 335–43.

4. See, for example, Kurt Ranke's study of 368 versions of AT 300, "The Dragon Slayer" ("Die zwei Brüder"), FFC 114 (Helsinki: Academia Scientiarum Fennica, 1934); or Anna Birgitta Rooth's analysis of "Cinderella," AT 510A, *The Cinderella Cycle* (Lund: C.S.K. Gleerup, 1951) based upon some 700 versions of the tale; or Warren Roberts's historic-geographic examination of roughly 1,000 versions of "The Spinning-Women by the Spring" [Frau Holle], AT 480, *The Tale of the Kind and the Unkind Girls* (Berlin: Walter de Gruyter, 1958).

5. Most of the older tale-type indexes are listed in Antti Aarne and Stith Thompson, *The Types of the Folktale*, FFC no. 184 (Helsinki: Academia Scientiarum Fennica, 1961), pp. 10–12. For a more complete listing of such indexes, see the seventh edition of Max Lüthi's *Märchen* (Stuttgart: Metzler, 1979), where the indexes are enumerated on pp. 20–22. Among the principal indexes that have appeared since 1961 are K. Arājs and A. Medne, *Latviešu Pasaku Tipu Rādītājs* ("The types of the Latvian folktales") (Riga: Izdevniecība 'Zinātne', 1977); Nai-Tung Ting, *A Type Index of Chinese Folktales*, FFC 223 (Helsinki, 1978); In-Hak Choi, *A Type Index of Korean Folktales* (Seoul: Myong Ji University Publishing, 1979); Lee Haring, *Malagasy Tale Index*, FFC 231 (Helsinki, 1982); Jurjen van der Kooi, *Volksverhalen in Friesland: Lectuur en Mondelinge Overlevering Een Typencatalogus* (Groningen: Stifting Ffyrug/Stichting Sasland, 1984); Ørnulf Hodne *The Types of the Norwegian Folktale* (Oslo: Universitetsforlaget, 1984).

For more about type indexing, see Stith Thompson, "Fifty Years of Folktale Indexing," in Wayland D. Hand and Gustave O. Aarlt, eds., *Humaniora: Essays in Literature, Folklore, Bibliography Honoring Archer Taylor on His Seventieth Birthday* (Locust Valley, NY: J. J. Augustin, 1960), pp. 49–57; Fritz Harkort, "Zur Geschichte der Typenindices," *Fabula* 5 (1962): 94–98; and Hiroko Ikeda, "Type Indexing the Folk Narrative," in Adrienne L. Kaeppler and H. Arlo Nimmo, eds., *Directions in Pacific Traditional Literature: Essays in Honor of Katharine Luomala*, Bernice P. Bishop Museum Special Publication 62 (Honolulu: Bishop Museum Press, 1976), pp. 333–50.

For an idea of the location and number of folklore archives, see Peter Aceves and Magnus Einarsson-Mullarky, comps., *Folklore Archives of the World: A Preliminary Guide*, Folklore Forum, Bibliographic and Special Series no. 1 (Bloomington, 1968); or Gun Herranen and Lassi Saressalo, eds., *A Guide to Nordic Tradition Archives* (Turku: Nordic Institute of Folklore, 1978). It is hard to convey the enormity of the holdings of some of these archives. For example, the Finnish Literary Society, founded in 1831, has one of the largest archives. Its holdings include some 20,000 folktales, 70,000 riddles, and 500,000 proverb texts. See Jorako Hautala, "The Folklore Archives of the Finnish Literature Society," *Studia Fennica* 7, no. 2 (1957): 3–36; and Urpo Vento, ed., *The Folklore Archives of the Finnish Literature Society* (Helsinki: Suomalaisen Kirjallisuuden Seura, 1965), pp. 18–20.

6. For even more citations to scholarly sources devoted to this tale type, one could turn to Walter Scherf, *Lexikon der Zaubermärchen* (Stuttgart: Alfred Kröner Verlag, 1982), pp. 363–64. Of course, no bibliographical listing includes everything. Scherf's two dozen references omit Erich Neumann, *Amor and Psyche* (Princeton: Princeton University Press, 1956); and Detlev Fehling, *Amor und Psyche: Die Schöpfung des Apuleius und ihre Einwirkung auf das Märchen, eine Kritik der romantischen Märchentheorie*, Akademie der Wissenschaften und der Literatur, Mainz (Wiesbaden: Franz Steiner Verlag, 1977). For a convenient anthology of some of the major critical essays, see Gerhard Binder and Reinhold Merkelbach, eds., *Amor und Psyche*, Wege der Forschung 126 (Darmstadt: Wissenschaftliche Buchgesellschaft, 1968).

7. For an attempt to identify traits of national character from folkloristic data, see Alan Dundes, *Life Is Like a Chicken Coop Ladder: A Portrait of German Culture Through Folklore* (New York: Columbia University Press, 1984).

8. Those interested in locating Freudian or Jungian interpretations of fairy tales should consult Alexander Grinstein's multi-volume *Index of Psychoanalytic Writings* (New York: International Universities Press, 1950–.) Representative would be Bruno Bettelheim, *The Uses of Enchantment: The Meaning and Importance of Fairy Tales* (New York: Alfred Knopf, 1976) and Marie-Louise von Franz, *An Introduction to the Psychology of Fairy Tales* (New York: Spring, 1970), but there are dozens upon dozens of Freudian and Jungian readings of tales. Most are limited to exegeses of the Grimm tales and most confine themselves to a single version of a tale type. For further references, see H. E. Giehrl, *Volksmärchen und Tiefenpsychologie* (München: Ehrenwirth Verlag, 1970), or Max Lüthi, *Märchen*, 7th ed. (Stuttgart: Metzler, 1979), pp. 113–16.

9. Propp is very specific on this point. "By 'fairy tales,'" he says, "are meant at present those tales classified by Aarne under numbers 300 to 749." See Vladimir Propp, *The Morphology of the Folktale* (Austin: University of Texas Press, 1968), p. 19. For more of Propp's consideration of fairy tales, see his *Theory and History of Folklore*, ed. Anatoly Liberman (Minneapolis: University of Minnesota Press, 1984), which includes the fascinating debate between Propp and Lévi-Strauss on the structure of such tales.

10. See C. W. von Sydow, *Selected Papers on Folklore* (Copenhagen: Rosenkilde and Bagger, 1948), pp. 68–70, or the entry on "Chimerate" in Laurits Bødker's valuable international dictionary of generic terms used by folklorists in the formal study of folk narrative, *Folk Literature (Germanic)* (Copenhagen: Rosenkilde and Bagger, 1965), pp. 59–60. See also Marie-Louise Tenèze, "Du conte merveilleux comme genre," *Arts et Traditions Populaires* 18 (1970): 11–65.

11. Most of those who write about European fairy tales know little if anything about the folktales of non-European peoples. Star Husband is just one of several hundred American Indian tale types. The scholarhsip devoted to this tale type includes Stith Thompson, "The Star Husband Tale," *Studia Septentrionalia* 4 (1953): 93–163 (reprinted in Dundes, ed., *The Study of Folklore* [Englewood Cliffs, N.J.: Prentice-Hall, 1965], pp. 414–74); Frank W. Young, "A Fifth Analysis of the Star Husband Tale," *Ethnology* 9 (1970): 389–413; George W. Rich, "Rethinking the 'Star Husbands,'" *Journal of American Folklore* 84 (1971): 436–41; and Frank W. Young, "Folktales and Social Structure: A Comparison of Three Analyses of the Star-Husband Tale," *Journal of American Folklore* 91 (1978): 691–99. To get some idea of just how extensive the folktale scholarship can be in an area outside of Europe, see Susan A. Niles, *South American Indian Narrative: Theoretical and Analytical Approaches, An Annotated Bibliography* (New York: Garland, 1981).

12. Most non-folklorists are annoyingly sloppy about narrative genres, often confusing legends with folktales and both these genres in turn with myth. A myth in folkloristic parlance is a sacred narrative explaining how the world and man came to be in their present form. Literary scholars tend to view myth either as a synonym for erroneous belief or else as a vague euphemism for pattern or archetype. The majority of books and articles containing the word "myth" in their titles have little or nothing to do with the *oral* narrative genre of myth as defined by folklorists. For a helpful delineation of the analytic categories of myth, folktale, and legend, see William Bascom, "The Forms of Folklore: Prose Narratives," *Journal of American Folklore* 78 (1965); 3–20 (reprinted in Dundes, ed., *Sacred Narrative: Readings in the Theory of Myth* (Berkeley and Los Angeles: University of California Press, 1984).

13. For an entree into the extensive world of artificial, "literary" fairy tales, see such works as Marianne Thalmann, *The Romantic Fairy Tale: Seeds of Surrealism* (Ann Arbor: University of Michigan Press, 1964); Jack Zipes, *Breaking the Magic Spell: Radical Theories of Folk & Fairy Tales* (Austin: University of Texas Press, 1979); and Jens Tismar, *Kunstmärchen*, 2d ed. (Stuttgart: Metzler, 1983).

14. Folkloristics is an independent academic discipline. In the United States, doctoral degrees in folklore are offered at Indiana University, the University of Pennsylvania, the University of Texas (Austin), and UCLA. Serious students of the fairy tale should in theory be familiar with the *Internationale Volkskundliche Bibliographie* (1917–) and the journal *Fabula*, organ of the International Society for Folk Narrative Research which has held congresses at five year intervals beginning in 1959. There is also an ambitious *Enzyklopädie des Märchens: Handwörterbuch zur historischen und vergleichenden Erzahlforschung* (Berlin: Walter de

Gruyter, 1975–) with entries on every aspect of the folktale. This work, if completed, may run to twelve volumes. Professional folklorists are familair with these critical tools of the trade, but as a rule amateurs from anthropology or literature departments who venture only occasionally into fairy-tale research projects tend to operate in an intellectual vacuum as far as folkloristics is concerned. This should not be the case as there are a considerable number of introductory essays or books available which could guide even a total novice into the rich and exciting world of bonafide fairy tale scholarship. A representative sample of such souces might include: J. L. Fischer, "The Sociopsychological Analysis of Folktales," *Current Anthropology* 4 (1963): 235–95; Felix Karlinger, ed., *Wege der Märchenforschung* (Darmstadt: Wissenschaftliche Buchgesellschaft, 1973); Lauri Honko, "Methods in Folk Narrative Research," *Ethnologia Europaea* 11 (1979–80): 6–27, and Max Lüthi, *The European Folktale: Form and Nature* (Philadelphia: Institute for the Study of Human Issues, 1982).

There are, of course, numerous specialized studies of particular aspects of folktale research. For example, with respect to the antiquity of the genre, see Heda Jason and Aharon Kempinski, "How Old Are Folktales?" *Fabula* 22 (1981): 1–27. If one were interested in the dynamics of the tale-teller and his or her audience (as opposed to merely the text alone), he might profit from Brunhilde Biebuyck's useful bibliography, "A la recherche du conteur," *Cahiers de Litterature Orale* 11 (1982): 195–214, etc.

Those curious about the range of interpretations which have been proposed to illuminate the nature and content of fairy tales may enjoy casebooks designed to demonstrate the application of various theoretical approaches to a given tale, e.g., historical, comparative, ritual, Jungian, Freudian, structural, etc. See Dundes, ed., *Cinderella: A Folklore Casebook* (New York: Garland, 1982); and Lowell Edmunds and Dundes, eds. *Oedipus: A Folklore Casebook* (New York: Garland, 1983), for treatments of Aarne-Thompson tale types 510A and 931, respectively.

18. The Grimms and the German Obsession with Fairy Tales

JACK ZIPES

It is *not* by chance that the cover of the 11 August 1984 issue of *The Economist* portrayed a large, green-shaded picture of Hansel and Gretel with a beckoning witch under the caption "West Germany's Greens meet the wicked world."[1] Inside the magazine a special correspondent began his report as follows:

> Once upon a time (in the late 1960s), a hostile stepmother (West Germany's Christian Democrats) and a kindly but weak father (the Social Democrats) decided that they had no room for children who thought for themselves. So they abandoned Hansel and Gretel (rebellious young West Germans) in a dense wood. Far from perishing, as their parents had expected, Hansel and Gretel became Greens. They quaked at the forest's nuclear terrors and cherished its trees. Soon they spied a glittering gingerbread house (the Bundestag) in a clearing. Being hungry, they ran inside. This was their first big test. For the house belonged to the wicked witch of the establishment.[2]

The metaphorical use of a Grimm fairy tale to explain German politics and the association of Germany with a fairy tale realm are not new. Ever since the Grimm brothers' collection became a household item in the nineteenth century, the Germans themselves have repeatedly used fairy tales to explain the world to themselves. Aside from cultivating traditional folk tales, they have also developed the most remarkable literary fairy tale tradition in the West. In fact, folk and fairy tales have been preserved and investigated by Germans with an intense seriousness often bordering on the religious, and nationalist overtones have often smothered the philosophical and humanitarian essence of the tales. Yet, despite the national solemnity, German authors have not lacked humor. Take, for example, Rudolf Otto Wiemer's poem "The Old Wolf":

> The wolf, now piously old and good,
> When again he met Red Riding Hood
> Spoke: "Incredible, my child,
> What kinds of stories are spread. They're wild.
>
> As though there were, so the lie is told,
> A dark murder affair of old.
> The Brothers Grimm are the ones to blame.
> Confess! It wasn't half as bad as they claim."
>
> Little Red Riding Hood saw the wolf's bite
> And stammered: "You're right, quite right."
> Whereupon the wolf, heaving many a sigh,
> Gave kind regards to Granny and waved good-bye.[3]

While such parody of the Grimms has become common in the creative works of numerous contemporary German writers, and while German critics have made important, innovative contributions to Grimm and fairy tale scholarship, certain American academicians appear to have lost their sense of humor and perspective. They have taken Wiemer's leitmotif "the Brothers Grimm are the ones to blame" much too seriously, and, though they have not accused them of a "dark murder affair of old," they have linked the Grimms and German folk tales to a national tradition that may explain why the Germans were so receptive to fascism. In particular, both Robert Darnton and John Ellis see dark shadows and nefarious designs behind German folk tales and the nationalist leanings of the Grimms.

In "Peasants Tell Tales: The Meaning of Mother Goose," Darnton compares various French folk tales with German ones, largely taken from the Grimms' collection, and concludes that "allowing for exceptions and complications, the differences between the two traditions fall into consistent patterns. The peasant raconteurs took the same themes and gave them characteristic twists, the French in one way, the German in another. Where the French tales tend to be realistic, earthy, bawdy, and comical, the German veer off toward the supernatural, the poetic, the exotic, and the violent."[4] Taking a different approach, but also denouncing German nationalism, John Ellis has written an entire book that criticizes the Grimms for purposely fabricating a false notion about the origins of the tales in their collection which they alleged were genuinely Germanic: "The Grimms appealed strongly to German nationalism because their *own* motives were nationalistic; and so this factor is dominant both in the brothers' fabrications and deceit, and in the strong reluctance of later scholars to acknowledge what they had done when the evidence emerged. The Grimms wanted to create a German national monument while pretending that they had merely discovered it; and later on, no one wanted to seem to tear it down."[5]

Darnton's conclusions about the *German* characteristics in folk tales are of limited value because his scholarship lacks depth. He provides scant evidence that German raconteurs favored "cruel" tales in the late Middle Ages and fails to make regional distinctions at a time when Germany did not exist as a nation-state. Moreover, he bases many of his assumptions about German folk tales on French tales, which had made their way into the Grimms' collection through mediators of Huguenot descent. Finally, his depictions of the historical origins of such French tales as "Little Red Riding Hood"[6] are often misleading. There is no doubt that important discoveries about national character and nationalism can be made through ethnological and historical studies of folk tales, but not when Germans are stereotypically linked with violence and cruelty.

Ellis, too, works with stereotypes, but his general thesis is perhaps even more far-fetched than Darnton's. Undoubtedly, the Grimms knew that most of their sources for the material they used were not "older, untainted, and untutored German peasant transmitters of an indigenous oral tradition but, instead, literate, middle-class, and predominantly young people, probably influenced more by books than by oral tradition — and including a very significant presence of people who were either of French origins or actually French-speaking."[7] And Ellis is certainly correct to demonstrate that the Grimms made numerous textual changes to improve them stylistically and make them more suitable for German audiences. However, there is no evidence to indicate that the Grimms consciously sought to dupe German readers and feed them lies about the German past, nor did later scholars conspire to cover up the "nationalist" designs of the Grimms. If anyone is playing with a public, it is Ellis, who relies heavily on the original research of Heinz Rölleke[8] and other German scholars, to conjure a myth of the Grimms' duplicity.

The Grimms were indeed nationalistic but not in the negative sense in which we tend to use the term today. When the brothers began their folklore research as young men in their twenties, Germany, as we now know it, did not exist. Their "country," essentially Hesse and the Rhineland, was invaded by the French, and they were disturbed by French colonialist aspirations. Thus, their desire to publish a work which expressed a German cultural spirit was part of an effort to contribute to a united German front against the French. They also felt that they were part of the nascent national bourgeoisie seeking to establish its own German identity in a manner more democratic than that allowed by the aristocratic rulers who governed the three hundred or so German principalities. In short, the issue of nationalism, the Brothers Grimm, and the *Kinder- und Hausmärchen* is a complex one.[9] The so-called lies and fabrications which Ellis discusses emanated ironically from an honest belief held by the Grimms that they were being faithful to a German cultural tradition that they wanted to nurture. And, they came to view themselves as mid-wives, who, perhaps because of a strong affection for their material and the German people, became zealous advocates not only of German nationalism but of democratic reform.

If the issue of nationalism is at the crux of the Grimms' reformations of the tales — and I believe that it is — then Ellis does not pursue many exciting avenues he could have followed. For instance, he never discusses the significance of the subjective selection of the tales and the changes made in terms of the "republican" ideology of the Grimms. (There is also the psychological factor of the Grimms' patriarchal attitudes.) Nor does he consider the major reason for the revisions made largely by Wilhelm, who felt that all the editions after 1819 should be addressed mainly toward children. As Wilhelm Schoof in his book about the origins of the Grimms' collection has maintained, Wilhelm

was guided by the desire to endow the tales with a tone and style primarily for children. He created a literary art form for them through the use of rhetorical and artistic means. This form is a synthesis based on faithful and scientific reproduction and the popular (*volkstümlich*) narrative style. Given his own ability to capture the appropriate childlike tone, he created a uniform fairy-tale style which has prevailed in the course of time and has become known as the classical or Grimm fairy-tale style.[10]

Or, in other words, the Grimms were totally conscious and open about their endeavors to make their material more suitable for children and to incorporate their notion of family, their sense of a folk aesthetic, and their political ideals in the tales because they wanted to share cultural goods with like-minded people.[11] The brothers Germanicized their material to stay in touch with the concerns and sensibility of the German people, and this is their accomplishment not their "crime." In response, the German people have made the Grimms' collection the second most popular book in Germany and during the last 150 years only the Bible has exceeded it in sales.

The love affair of the German people with the Grimms and with fairy tales in general reveals a great deal about the German national character that cannot be understood by linking the Grimms and their tales to rabid nationalism. Although vestiges of archaic societies, feudalism, and patriarchy remain in the Grimms' tales, the brothers also imbued them with certain qualities that corresponded to the progressive aspirations of the German middle class and peasantry. Or, to use Ernst Bloch's term, there is a *Vor-Schein*,[12] an anticipatory illumination of the formation of utopia, in the tales which underlies their socially symbolic discourse. To a certain extent, the Grimms made an institution out of the fairy tale genre: they established the framework of the genre that has become a type of realm in which various writers convene to voice their personal needs and a social need for pleasure and power under just conditions. The most resilient genre in German literary history since the eighteenth century has been the literary fairy tale because it has been the most democratic institution. The aesthetic nature of the symbolic discourse as consolidated by the Grimms has enabled writers of all classes to use it, to voice their views without fear of reprisal, to seek to alter the dominant discourse, and to gain understanding from the discourse itself.

When folklorists and other critics discuss the *Kinder- und Hausmärchen,* it has been customary to type them according to the Aarne-Thompson motif index.[13] That is, they are generally classified according to such motifs as animal helpers, the beast bridegroom, the enchanted mountain, the test by fire, or the seven-league boots, so that parallels with other folktales and their origins can be traced. Such typification — and there are other formalist and structuralist approaches such as those developed by Max Lüthi and Vladimir Propp — may assist in the kind of classification work done by folklorists, ethnologists, and structural-minded literary critics, but in the Grimms' collection, it has detracted from the social and historical meaning of their work. Here I want to propose another way to type the Grimms' collection which will shed light on their major contribution to the genre as institution and which might enable us to gain a deeper grasp of the German obsession with the fairy tale in general.

With the publication of the final edition of the *Kinder- und Hausmärchen* in 1857, there were 211 tales. Strictly speaking, they are not all folk and fairy tales. There are legends, fables, anecdotes, didactic

narratives, and journeyman tales in the collection, and their mediation by educated people and then by the Grimms marks them as literary products. Their variety and mediation constitute their broad
democratic appeal: there are numerous voices to be heard in the collection, and they are not only of German descent. Their democratic
and international flavor, however, was influenced by German conditions. The tales were collected and transmitted at a time when the
German principalities were at war with France. Moreover, the Grimms
continued to collect tales after the initial publication of the first volume in 1812. They added to the collection and altered the tales up to
1857 during a time when there was a growing conscious movement to
unite the German principalities and form a constitutional state. Not
only did the Napoleonic Wars influence the social attitudes of the
Grimms and their mediators, but the revolts of the 1830s and the 1848
revolution were also significant. We must not forget that the Grimms
themselves had to leave Göttingen overnight in 1837 because they
were opposed to the tyrannical rule of King Ernst August of Hannover. They continued to support democratic causes after this incident,
and in 1848 Jacob was chosen to represent Berlin in the constitutional assembly that met in Frankfurt. A clear relationship exists between the Grimm brothers, their socio-political notions, and their
audience in Germany at that time: their household tales were items
largely in middle-class homes and among literate groups of people.
That Wilhelm kept editing the tales to guarantee that the collection
would remain a household item and that he even developed a special
smaller edition, which became a bestseller, suggest that he and his
brother, even though Jacob did not entirely approve of the restyliza-
tion, had a distinct concept of home and socialization in collecting and
rewriting the tales. The rise in popularity of the tales occurred when
the middle classes in Germany also sought to constitute a new home in
opposition to feudalism, when they struggled for a nation-state that
might guarantee their rights and those of oppressed peasants.

If we look at some of the themes and narrative components of the
211 tales collected and altered by the Grimms on the basis of the relationship between the democratic ideals of the brothers and the attitudes of the German middle classes and peasantry closely tied to
standards of the Protestant ethos which had crept into the tales, then
we can make some interesting observations that will reveal why Germans were initially attracted to the tales and why they have institutionalized the genre.

Perhaps the most striking feature of many of the tales is that the
majority of the protagonists, whether male or female, are either poor,
deprived, or wronged in some way. They stem largely from the peas-

ant, artisan, or mercantile class and, whether male or female, they experience a rise in fortunes which enables them to win a wife or husband, amass a fortune and power, and constitute a new realm. This last point is important because the constitution of a new realm is also the realization of a new home away from home. Very few protagonists return to their old home after their adventure. Also, very few heroes have the physical power or military support at their disposal to take charge of the new kingdom. Instead, they must rely on their wits: the Grimms' protagonists are clever, reasonable, resolute, and upwardly mobile. They appear to know their destiny and strive diligently to realize it. It is in the name of this destiny which celebrates upward mobility and transformation that the narrative voices of the tales collect themselves and were collected to speak in one voice. The archaic structure of the oral folk tale is modernized, endowed with the raison d'etre of transaction and commerce, polished and pruned of moral turpitude. The succession to power of lower-class figures is legitimized by their essential qualities of industriousness, cleverness, opportunism, and frankness. The private adventure becomes a social venture for power that evades middle-class and peasant readers in the German reality of the nineteenth century.

If a Grimm protagonist (even as animal or object) does not communicate with helpers, whether they be beasts, fairies, devils, giants, or hags, he or she is lost. The tales describe the need for communicative action that enables the protagonist to seize the possibility to right a wrong and move up in society, to overcome feudal restrictions, to conceive a more just realm. It is interesting that the Grimm protagonist is nothing alone, by him or herself, but becomes omnipotent when assisted by small creatures or outsiders, those figures, who are marginal and live on the border between wilderness and civilization, between village and woods, between this earthly world and the other sacred world.

The new realm to which the Grimm protagonist succeeds is that made possible through his or her own ingenuity and the help of other small creatures or outcasts. Fundamentally, the creation of the smart individual in harmony with others, its institution, is founded on a collective enterprise just as the literary institution of the Grimm fairy tales depended on centuries of oral transmission by gifted storytellers and on the mediation of middle-class informants.

It may seem strange to view the Grimms' fairy tales and literary fairy tales in general as an institution. Yet, it seems to me that the distinct German character of the tales collected by the Grimms — and perhaps their overall universal appeal — might become more clear if we take this view. In his essay *Institution Kunst als literatursoziologische*

Kategorie, Peter Bürger defines the concept *Institution* as "the factors which determine the function of art in a particular historical period and in its social context."[14] If literature is regarded this way, Bürger maintains that the

> factors which determine the function be linked to the material and intellectual needs of the conveyors (*Träger*) and placed in a specific relationship to the *material conditions of the production and reception of art.* The differentiation of the factors that determine the function results from this, and it is mediated via aesthetic norms: in the case of the producer by the *artistic material,* in the case of the recipient by the establishment of *attitudes of reception.*[15]

Within literature itself, genres become institutionalized in such interaction: they have their own history that depends on their formal attributes, production, reception, and social function in a historical development.

For the literary fairy tale as genre in Germany, one would have to trace its institutionalization first to the French court of Louis XIV, where it fulfilled the function of representing and legitimizing the norms of absolutism while providing *divertissement.* The artistic output and ingenuity of Charles Perrault, Madame D'Aulnoy, and a host of other writers testify to the establishment of an actual mode of fairy tale discourse.[16] It was this mode along with the peasant oral tradition that gave rise to the German literary fairy tale as institution. Or, in other words, the German literary fairy tale begins to break with aesthetic and social prescriptions carried by the French courtly tale and the German peasant oral tradition toward the end of the eighteenth century, and it is in the manner in which it breaks and defines itself while functioning for a different audience that we can locate the significance of the German literary fairy tale as a national institution. The fairy tales of Musäus, Wieland, Goethe, and the romantics give rise to a bourgeois literary institution which has a distinctly new and more autonomous function than the courtly fairy tales and peasant folk tales. Instead of writing their literary fairy tales for courtly audiences or telling them orally, German writers directed their tales to a middle-class reading public in the process of forming itself and the free market. They incorporated notions of bourgeois individualism and the autonomy of art in their works and endowed the genre with a unique secular religious quality based on the cult of genius. As Bürger remarks, "the institution is just as much in the individual as the individual work functions within the institution."[17] Thus, a dialectical relationship between German fairy tale writers and production conditions in regard to middle-class readers was established to form the basis of the German literary fairy tale as institution.

To view the German literary fairy tale as a literary institution does not mean to regard it statically or hypostatize form and content. Rather, this method enables us to grasp literature as it transforms itself historically in unique ways and to view the extra-literary forces which influence the immanent development of literature. Nor does this method mean that the individual work itself becomes negligible: to study a genre of literature as institution allows us to uncover the uniqueness of a work when measured against the norms set down by the institution, and it allows us to understand its historical function and appreciate its present impact in a more comprehensive manner.

Bürger maintains that

after religion had lost its universal validity in the course of the European Enlightenment and had forfeited its paradigm of reconciliation which, for centuries, had carried out the task of expressing criticism about society while at the same time making it practically ineffectual, art now assumed this role — at least for the privileged social classes with property and education. Art was supposed to restore the harmony of the human personality that had been destroyed by a strict, utilitarian regimented daily life. This can only happen when it is radically separated from the practical affairs of daily life and set in opposition to it as an independent realm.[18]

Such a separation can already be seen in the fairy tales of Musäus and Wieland written in Weimar during the 1780s. They reflect the French courtly influence and also German folk traditions and were the first major endeavors to create a bourgeois autonomous art form. The production of their tales and their reception in Germany constitute a shift in the nature of the literary fairy tale as institution. However it is first with the production of Goethe's *Das Märchen*, Wackenroder's *Ein wunderbares morgenländisches Märchen von einem nackten Heiligen*, Novalis' *Sais-Märchen* and fairy tales from *Heinrich von Ofterdingen*, and Tieck's *Der blonde Eckbert, Der Fremde*, and *Der Runenberg* all written between 1790 and 1810 along with the tales of Brentano, Eichendorff, Kerner, Fouqué, Chamisso, and Hoffmann that we see the literary fairy tale institutionalizing itself as an independent genre and functioning to provide confirmation of a new bourgeois aesthetic and attitude toward art and society.

As a literary institution, the fairy tale assumes a secular religious purpose: it incorporates moral and political critiques of society while undermining the critiques by reconciling the distraught protagonist with society. Obviously such projections of harmony are not to be found in all the literary fairy tales. Tieck and Hoffmann, for example, often leave their heroes insane or broken. Yet, the norm in the literary fairy tale is based on compensatory images of reconciliation. The overall social function of the literary fairy tale as institution at the beginning of the nineteenth century is to provide aesthetic formations of social redemption. Given the Napoleonic Wars, the censorship, the lack of unification of the German people, the ineffectual peasant revolts, and the gradual rise of bureaucracy, the literary fairy tale became a means for German writers and a middle-class reading public to pose and explore more harmonious options for the creative individual experiencing the development of a free market system, while also questioning such a system and the utilitarian purposes which the incipient bourgeois social institutions began to serve. Unlike in France, where the literary fairy tale was first and foremost courtly and declined by the time of the French Revolution, and unlike in England, where the literary fairy tale was more or less banned by the bourgeois revolution of 1688 and did not revive until the Victorian period, the literary fairy tale in Germany became a major mode of expression for German middle-class writers, a means of socio-religious compensation and legitimation.

More than Goethe, Novalis, Wackenroder, Tieck, and Hoffmann, whose complex, symbolical tales were not easily accessible for a large public — nor were they widely distributed — the Grimms were able to collect and compose tales that spoke to readers of all classes and age groups. They themselves had already been influenced by Goethe and the early romantics along with Brentano and Arnim, and their work is the culmination of a folk tradition and bourgeois appropriation of the folk tale. The Grimms were able to institutionalize the literary fairy tale as genre because they articulated the interests and needs of the German middle class and peasantry. Generally speaking, the Grimm fairy tales assumed a function in the nineteenth century which illuminates what is quintessentially German in this institutionalization: as a socially symbolic act of compensation they enabled readers to gain pleasure from different depictions of power transformation; the collection of tales celebrated the rise of seemingly ineffectual, disadvantaged individuals who were associated with such bourgeois and religious virtues as industry, diligence, cleverness, loyalty, and honesty. Moreover, the critique of unjust social and political conditions in most of the Grimm fairy tales was realized metaphorically in radical ways which reconciled the readers of the tales to their helplessness and impotence in society.

Stylistically, the Grimms combined the elegance of the simplistic, paratactical oral narrative with the logical succinct businesslike prose of the middle classes to establish a conventional form for fairy tale narration, one that became a model for most fairy tale writers and collectors in the nineteenth century and not only in Germany. What is special about Germany is that the fairy tale as institution became a sacred meeting place of readers from agrarian and middle-class sectors of the population, a place to which they could withdraw, a source from which they could draw succor and through which their aspirations and wishes could be fulfilled. Within the institution of the fairy tale they could become legitimate human beings again.

Historically, the Grimms' collection exercised this function in Germany and continues to do so more or less in present-day East and West Germany. Like the Bible, however, it has also transcended its specific social function to appeal to readers throughout the world. And, as we know, the tales — that is, a select group of tales such as "Cinderella," "Little Red Riding Hood," "Sleeping Beauty," "Snow White" — have been specifically cultivated to socialize children. In each country the tales function differently, and the way they are used and received in each country indicates something about the national character of that country. In Germany, the obsession with the Grimms is actually an obsession with the fairy tale as a vital and dynamic literary institution, a national institution. Germans depend on this institution more than people in other Western countries because its development occurred exactly at a time when the nation was forming itself and when the bourgeoisie was achieving self-consciousness. In stark contrast to the utopian and science fiction literature that emerged as more characteristic forms in France, England, and the United States, the literary fairy tale in Germany became dominant before industry was fully developed and when the people, largely influenced by agrarian life-styles and patriarchal authoritarianism, were striving for a type of familial unification. The fairy tale as institution freed writers and readers to withdraw from the conflicts of daily life, to contemplate harmonious resolutions without actually expending energy in reality, to guard their own private realms. The obsession with fairy tales in the nineteenth century — and perhaps today as well — expressed a German proclivity to seek resolutions of social conflicts within art, within subjectively constructed realms rather than to oppose authorities in public.

Much has been made out of German *Innerlichkeit*, the predilection of Germans to repress their feelings, to seek inner peace, to dwell in spiritual and ethereal realms, to avoid social conflict. While there is some truth to such generalizations, and while individual fairy tales, for example, those by Hermann Hesse, may celebrate such *Innerlichkeit*, the actual social function of the fairy tale in Germany is different: it is the compensatory aesthetic means of communication through which Germans share, discuss, and debate social norms and individual aspirations.

Once the Grimms' fairy tales had become established as the conventional model of the fairy tale in the nineteenth century, hardly a single German has escaped influence by a Grimm fairy tale, a literary fairy tale by another author, or an oral folk tale. Used first as a household item, the Grimms' tales and other tales became pedagogical tools by the early twentieth century.[19] Use at home and in schools engendered numerous literary experiments so that almost all the significant German writers from the mid-nineteenth century to the present have either written or endeavored to write a fairy tale: Gottfried Keller, Theodor Storm, Wilhelm Raabe, Theodor Fontane, Hugo von Hofmannsthal, Hermann Hesse, Rainer Maria Rilke, Franz Kafka, Thomas Mann, Bertolt Brecht, Ödön von Horváth, Carl Zuckmayer, Gerhart Hauptmann, Alfred Döblin, Georg Kaiser, Joachim Ringelnatz, Kurt Schwitters, Kurt Tucholsky, Walter Hasenclever, Hans Fallada, Oskar Maria, Erich Kästner, Siegfried Lenz, Helmut Heißenbüttel, Ingeborg Bachmann, Peter Hacks, Günther Kunert, Peter Härtling, Nicolas Born, and Günter Grass. They worked within the institution of the literary fairy tale and have viewed it as a viable means for reaching audiences and for expressing their opinions about the form itself and society.

It is not only the German creative writers who have responded to the fairy tale as institution but also the critics and philosophers. The field of folklore research and fairy tale criticism began developing in the late nineteenth century and remains prominent in both Germanys today. More interesting than the traditional field is the manner in which various astute philosophers and cultural critics of the twentieth century, such as Walter Benjamin, Ernst Bloch, Theodor Adorno, Elias Canetti, Oskar Negt, and Alexander Kluge, have employed the fairy tale to register their insights about society and the potential of the tale itself. Thus, Benjamin writes: "Whenever good counsel was at a premium, the fairy tale had it, and where the need was the greatest, its aid was nearest. . . . The wisest thing — so the fairy tale taught mankind in olden times, and teaches children to this day — is to meet the forces of the mythical world with cunning and high spirits."[20] And Bloch comments: "The cunning of intelligence is the humane side of the weak. Despite the fantastic side of the fairy tale, it is always cunning in the way it overcomes difficulties. Moreover, courage and cunning in fairy tales succeed in an entirely different way than in life. . . . While the peasantry was still bound by serfdom, the poor young protagonist of the fairy tale won the daughter of the king. While educated Christians trembled in fear of witches and devils, the soldier of the fairy tale deceived witches and devils from beginning to end — it is only the fairy tale which highlights the 'dumb devil.' The golden age is sought and mirrored, and from there one can see far into paradise."[21] Finally, Elias Cannetti remarks: "A more detailed study of fairy tales would teach us what awaits us still in the world."[22]

These statements are not so much significant for their unique perspectives — although they are well worth studying — as they are for the manner in which they similarly focus on the social function of the fairy tale as prophetic and messianic. Indeed, these critics assume that the fairy tale is an institution capable of revealing the true nature of social conditions. However, the power and communicative value which these German critics attribute to the fairy tale is not typical of the way the majority of writers and thinkers outside Germany regard the fairy tale. Undoubtedly the fairy tale as institution has its own special tradition in other countries, but it has not become such a sacred convention and used as such a metaphorical medium to attain truth as is true in Germany.

The continuities within the institution are astounding. If we consider just the productive side of fairy tales in West Germany during the last fifteen years, we can grasp the significance the fairy tale as institution has retained for Germans. In the realm of children's literature a number of anthologies have aimed at revising the Grimms' tales, while new types of provocative tales have sought to upset the normative, traditional expectations of readers weened on the Grimms' and Andersen's fairy tales. Among the more interesting books here are Paul Maar's *Der tätowierte Hund* (1968); Christine Nöstlinger's *Wir pfeifen auf den Gurkenkönig* (1972); Friedrich Karl Waechter's *Tischlein deck dich und Knüppel aus dem Sack* (1972) and *Die Bauern im Brunnen* (1979); Janosch's *Janosch erzählt Grimm's Märchen* (1972); Michael Ende's *Momo* (1973) and *Unendliche Geschichte* (1979); Hans Joachim Gelberg's anthology *Neues vom Rumpelstilzchen* (1976) with contributions from forty-three authors; Otto F. Gmelin and Doris Lerche's *Märchen für tapfere Mädchen* (1978); Wolf Biermann's *Das Märchen von dem Mädchen mit dem Holzbein* (1979); and Volker Kriegel's *Der Rock'n Roll König* (1982). The fairy tales written and collected for adults follows more or less the same pattern. Here the following works are significant: Iring Fetscher's *Wer hat Dornröschen wachgeküßt* (1972) and *Der Nulltarif der Wichtelmänner. Märchen und andere Verwirrspiele* (1982); Jochen Jung's anthology *Bilderbogengeschichten* (1974) with contributions by fifteen well-known authors; Helmut Brackert's mammoth collection *Das große deutsche Märchenbuch* (1979) with hundreds of tales from the eighteenth century to the present; Margaret Kassajep's *"Deutsche Hausmärchen" frisch getrimmt* (1980); Günter Kämp and Vilma Link's anthology of political fairy tales *Deutsche Märchen* (1981) with contributions by twenty authors; Heinrich E. Kühleborn's

Rotkäppchen und die Wölfe (1982); and Peter Rühmkorf's *Der Hüter des Misthaufens. Aufgeklärte Märchen* (1983).

Finally, there has been a plethora of literary criticism dealing with folk and fairy tales which has matched the literary production itself. The major accomplishment of these critical works has been the elaboration of socio-historical methods with which one can analyze the contents and form of the tales in light of their ideological meanings and functions within the German and the Western socialization process as well. The focus is naturally more on Germany than on the West at large. Among the best works here are: Dieter Richter and Johannes Merkel's *Märchen, Phantasie und soziales Lernen* (1974); August Nitschke's *Soziale Ordnungen im Spiegel der Märchen* (1976–77); Werner Psaar and Manfred Klein's *Wer hat Angst vor der bösen Geiß?* (1976); Friedmar Apel's *Die Zaubergärten der Phantasie* (1978); Helmut Brackert's anthology *Und wenn sie nicht gestorben sind* (1980) with contributions by several different critics; Heide Göttner-Abendroth's *Die Göttin und ihr Heros* (1980); Jens Tismar's *Das deutsche Kunstmärchen des 20. Jahrhunderts* (1981); Ulrike Bastian's *Die "Kinder und Hausmärchen" der Brüder Grimm in der literatur-pädagogischen Diskussion des 19. und 20. Jahrhunderts* (1981); Walter Scherf's *Lexikon der Zaubermärchen* (1982); and Klaus Doderer's anthology *Über Märchen für Kinder von heute* (1983) with essays by various authors.

A close examination of these creative works and criticism would reveal to what extent the literary fairy tale as institution has undergone major transformations. Several significant tendencies emerge in these transformations. First, since the 1920s, when avant-garde and political writers made the fairy tale visible as institution by attacking the institution of art, German writers have moved in the direction of making the fairy tale more usable in the socialization process.[23] Certainly such explicit use occurred during fascism, and after 1945 the fairy tale continued to be employed by schools, literary organizations, psychologists, publishers, and, of course, by writers to influence social attitudes. Second, it appears that there is a major shift in the production of the more progressive writers who generally formulate their socially symbolic discourse against the grain of the Grimms while using the conventions of the Grimms. The conservative bourgeois value system in the Grimms' tales that also incorporated feudal patriarchal notions is viewed as anachronistic, banal, and escapist. Ironically, the fairy tale as institution itself is not considered escapist as long as one renovates, revises, and reutilizes the Grimms' tales and others in the German cultural heritage. Writers such as Janosch, Waechter, Kassajep, Karin Struck, Ende, Fetscher, and Rühmkorf design their tales for a new German audience and with the hope that what they are criticizing and developing in the institution of the fairy tale will have some social impact. Whether this can be achieved by these authors, their critics, educators, and publishers is an open question, but the very fact that the fairy tale is used in this way and is regarded as having a certain communicative potential, reveals a great deal about the institution in West Germany today. Or, to put it another way, there is something very German in this attitude and hope.

Notes

1. *The Economist* 292 (11 August 1984): 37–43.
2. Ibid., p. 37.
3. In Jack Zipes, *The Trials and Tribulations of Little Red Riding Hood* (South Hadley, Mass.: Bergin & Garvey, 1983), p. 256.
4. *The Great Cat Massacre and Other Episodes in French Cultural History* (New York: Basic Books, 1984), p. 50.
5. *One Fairy Story Too Many* (Chicago: University of Chicago Press, 1983), p. 100.
6. Cf. Zipes, *The Trials and Tribulations of Little Red Riding Hood.*
7. Ellis, *One Fairy Story Too Many,* p. 35.
8. In particular, see Heinz Rölleke, ed., *Die älteste Märchensammlung der Brüder Grimm* (Cologne and Geneva: Fondation Martin Bodmer, 1975).
9. Cf. Ingeborg Weber-Kellermann's introduction to *Kinder- und Hausmärchen gesammelt durch die Brüder Grimm,* vol. 1 (Frankfurt: Insel, 1976), pp. 9–18, and Heinz Rölleke's afterword to Brüder Grimm, *Kinder- und Hausmärchen* (Stuttgart: Reclam, 1980), pp. 590–617.
10. *Zur Entstehungsgeschichte der Grimmschen Märchen* (Hamburg: Hauswedell, 1959), p. 147.
11. In his afterword to the *Kinder- und Hausmärchen,* Rölleke makes the point that the Grimms were very conscious of their audience and sought to mold the tales to suit its needs.
12. Cf. *Ästhetik des Vor-Scheins,* ed. Gert Ueding, 2 vols. (Frankfurt: Suhrkamp, 1974).
13. See Antti Aarne, *The Types of the Folk-tale: A Classification and Bibliography,* translated and enlarged by Stith Thompson, Folklore Communications no. 74 (Helsinki: Suomalainen tiedeakatemia, 1928).
14. In *Seminar: Literatur- und Kunstsoziologie,* ed. Peter Bürger (Frankfurt: Suhrkamp, 1978), p. 261.
15. Ibid., p. 262.
16. Cf. Mary Elizabeth Storer, *La Mode des contes des fées (1685–1700)* (Paris: Champion, 1928), and Jacques Barchilon, *Le Conte merveilleux francais de 1690 à 1790* (Paris: Champion, 1975).
17. *Institution Kunst als literatursoziologische Kategorie,* p. 269.
18. Ibid., p. 264.
19. See Ulrike Bastian, *Die Kinder und Hausmärchen der Brüder Grimm in der literatur pädagogischen Diskussion des 19. und 20. Jahrhunderts* (Giessen: Haag & Herchen, 1981).
20. "The Storyteller," in *Illuminations,* trans. Harry Zohn (New York: Harcourt, Brace & World, 1968), p. 102.
21. "Bessere Luftschlösser in Jahrmarkt und Zirkus, in Märchen und Kolportage" in *Ästhetik des Vor-Scheins,* ed. Gert Ueding, vol. 1 (Frankfurt: Suhrkamp, 1974), pp. 73–74.
22. *Die Provinz des Menschen: Aufzeichnungen 1942–1972* (Munich: Hanser, 1972), p. 48.
23. For a discussion of the development of the fairy tale in the 1920s and 1930s, see the chapter "The Fight Over Fairy-Tale Discourse: Family, Friction, and Socialization in the Weimar Republic and Nazi Germany" in my book *Fairy Tales and the Art of Subversion* (New York: Wildman Press, 1983), pp. 134–69.

19. The "Utterly Hessian" Fairy Tales by "Old Marie": The End of a Myth

HEINZ RÖLLEKE

Socio-literarily and folkloristically important questions about the informants for the *Kinder- und Hausmärchen gesammelt durch die Brüder Grimm* (KHM) which appeared for the first time in 1812 (vol. 1) and 1815 (vol. 2), have been posed only piecemeal, with reference to one tale or to one informant at a time.[1] Everything not considered relevant to the particular tale or informant has been generally referred to in passing as something that was generally understood and unproblematic, so that decade by decade the impression has grown that there were at most only trifling details still to be added, Grimm research and fairy tale research having long before accomplished the basic work.[2]

That is clearly not true. Chronological contradictions exist within a series of traditional data, which have never been properly discussed[3]; beyond that a quite consequential fiction seems to have developed by one of the chief Grimm scholars, a theme that is also of interest from the point of view of the history of scholarship.

Translated by Ruth B. Bottigheimer.

This essay appeared originally in *Germanisch-Romanische Monatshefte*, n.s. 25 (1975): 74–86. It appears with permission of the Bouvier Verlag Herbert Grundmann Gmbh, which included it in *Wo das Wünschen noch geholfen hat* (Bonn, 1985).

One looks in vain in the earliest manuscript material of the KHM[4] for an indication of where and when material was noted down, not to mention the informant's name. In the notes of volume 1 of the first edition (1812) only references to literary sources are to be found. Only in volume 2 (1815) and in the volume of notes which appeared separately in 1822[5] do references such as "from Zwehrn," "from Cassel," "from Hanau," "from Hesse," and "from the general Main area" appear. Even here statements about names are absent. Nonetheless Wilhelm Grimm concretized the frequent designation, "from Zwehrn," in the foreword of 1815:

One of those fortunate accidents however was the acquaintance with a peasant woman from the village of Zwehrn, near Cassel, from whom we obtained a large number of tales recounted here, as well as many additions to the first volume, whose provenance thus makes them genuinely Hessian. The name of this woman, who is still fit and not much over fifty years of age, is Viehmännin.[6]

And there the Grimm brothers left it; the scholarly and bellelettristic reading public seemingly was not to be more closely informed about the individual informants, first because the Grimms insisted on the anonymous "folk" as the bearer and shaper of this narrative material, following in the tradition of the editors of the *Wunderhorn* with its mostly indefinite statements like "oral" or "sent in"; and second, because the impression was given that the collective origin of the fairy tales (according, above all, to Jacob Grimm's theory) presupposes a collective tradition and should only be so understood. The Grimms clearly wanted this characterization of an individual informant — consciously located as it was outside the individual notes and not very revealing — to be understood as *pars pro toto;* they were not prepared to reveal more about their sources publicly.

As a consequence of their lives having been spent almost continuously together, there was hardly any need for the brothers to correspond about their informants. Nowhere in their correspondence does the occasional reference permit a direct assignment of a fairy tale to a specific informant.

Wilhelm Grimm's marginal notes in his personal copy of the KHM[7] meant exclusively for his own use thus appear all the more important and valuable for the history of these events, for numerous handwritten entries concerning names and dates are to be found there, above all in volume 1 of 1812. Nonetheless it was only a generation after the death of the Grimms that Wilhelm's son, Herman Grimm, then already 67 years old, pointed out this important document,[8] which he later left to the Grimm Collection of the Cassel Library, which initially passed it on long loan to Johannes Bolte in Berlin.[9] According to his father's marginalia, Herman Grimm had assigned around thirty fairy tales to different informants. Johannes Bolte adopted these attributions; and beyond that, he further evaluated the personal copy and tried by analogy to delineate more precisely several of the published notations of provenance which were not clearly defined. And essentially that is where the entire matter rested.

If one looks closely at Wilhelm Grimm's attributions in his personal copy in this connection, one notices that dating only becomes more detailed for the period after the beginning of 1811: the "10. March 1811" is the earliest date (noted for KHM 11, 31, and 55). Only a total of nine texts are designated with earlier dates: "1807," "1808," and "1810." This remarkable fact is explained by the date of their delivery of the first manuscript collection of fairy tales to Clemens Brentano. Until the end of 1810[10] the Brothers Grimm had collected their fairy tale notations with no specific plans for later publication and had relinquished them willingly to Brentano. Only when Brentano did not actually incorporate them into his collection did Jacob and Wilhelm keep for themselves the contributions which arrived from early 1811 onward. With these they expanded the first collection which they had kept as copies and from this point on they clearly noted the names of the informants and exact dates of recording — facts that with reference to the fairy tales recorded earlier could only be added from memory and which therefore remain less precise. Wilhelm Grimm may well have transferred this information to his personal copy before these manuscript materials were destroyed after the KHM was typeset.

In the personal copy of 1812 one encounters the names of fifteen different informants. At first no problems in identification appear in connection with the contributions, which are assigned to the Engelhard, Hassenpflug, and Haxthausen families as well as to Brentano's sister, Ludovica Jordis; the pensioned guard, Friedrich Krause; the minister's daughter, Friederike Mannel; the probationer, Ferdinand Siebert; and the wife of the apothecary, Catharina Wild. The other attributions can only be based on the Christian names noted by Wilhelm Grimm: Dortchen, Gretchen, Jeanette, Lisette, Male, Marie, and Mie.

Herman Grimm knew from personal memory about contributions from his mother, Dorothea Grimm, née Wild (born 1793) and could assign the name "Dortchen" to her with complete justification. The references to "Gretchen" and "Lisette" clearly indicate her older sisters, Margareta (born 1787) and Elisabeth (born 1782). That "Jeanette" and "Male" stand for the sisters Johanna (born 1791) and

Amalie Hassenpflug (born 1800) is proven: Herman Grimm's explanation is confirmed by evidence in the correspondence, even though
he accidentally referred to Jeanette as "the younger sister" and dated
the contributions falsely.[11]

Herman Grimm avoided clarifying the name "Mie"[12] which only
occurs once. Bolte concluded that it was Wilhelmine von Schwertzell
(born 1790).[13] Wilhelm Schoof took over this hypothesis and supported it with his erroneous reading "From *Min*. 20. Okt. 1811."[14]
The version of the name and the date, however, clearly point toward
one of Dortchen Wild's five sisters. Schoof himself mentioned this
Mie Wild in 1959,[15] but had not drawn any corresponding conclusions. Since Wilhelm Grimm had noted down fairy tales (KHM 24
and 34) at the Wilds' house in Cassel on 29 September and 13 October 1811, both Sundays, there is no reason not to conclude that he
also continued his efforts there on the following Sunday and became
acquainted with the subsequent tale, KHM 44 through Mie Wild.

In connection with the notation, "Marie," which occurs eleven
times in volume 1 and once in volume 2 of the KHM, Herman Grimm
came to the following conclusion:

Dortchen also got her trove from another source. Above the Wilds' nursery in
the apothecary building, with its many hallways, stairwells, floors, and rear additions, through all of which I myself poked as a child, was the realm of "Old
Marie," whose husband had died in the war and who read her evening prayers
every evening from her Hawermann prayerbook. The first volume of the fairy
tales got its most beautiful fairy tales from her. "Little Brother and Little Sister"
("from Marie, 10 March 1811"); "Little Red Riding Hood" ("Fall 1812"); "The
Girl Without Hands" ("10 March 1811"); "The Robber Bridegroom"; "Godfather Death" ("20 October 1811"); "Thumbling's Travels"; "Sleeping Beauty"
and others without date all derive from her. I am citing the tales in the order of
their publication. One feels immediately that Dortchen and Gretchen probably
only recounted what had been impressed upon them by Old Marie.[16]

Herman Grimm's listing proves to be a confused chaos on closer
inspection. "Red Riding Hood" was labeled by Wilhelm Grimm with
the provenance "Jeanette Fall 1812," while only the unimportant
variant has the notation "Marie Fall 1812." "Godfather Death" (KHM
44), as noted above, alludes to Mie (Wild). On the other hand, actual
references to "Marie," dated and undated were simply omitted: "The
Phoenix" (volume 1, 75, later in the Note to KHM 29, is labelled
"Marie 10 February 1812"); "The Water Nixie" (KHM 79) is signed
"Marie"; "The Smith and the Devil" (volume 1, 81, later in the Note
to KHM 82) has the entry, "Marie 1 December 1812"). For the tale
which always concluded the KHM editions, "The Golden Key" (vol-

ume 2, 70, later KHM 200), Wilhelm Grimm noted "Marie May 1813"; in addition, there are the notations in the Notes to "The Frog-King" (KHM 1) "from Marie 8 March 1813" and for "Snow-White" (KHM 53) "Marie 13 October 1812."

In his notes to the individual tales, Johannes Bolte, who in his standard reference work on fairy tale research [17] names "Old Marie in the Wilds' house in Cassel" as the first informant, largely corrected the errors and omissions in Herman Grimm's listing. His attributions, summarized in the supplement of 1930, remained nonetheless incomplete.[18] In a far-ranging article about the first fairy tale contributors which appeared in the same year, Schoof did not devote a separate section to "Marie," but he confused Bolte's attributions in another connection [19] and again summed up the results (with fewer omissions but with the same errors) in 1959.[20] Table 19.1 with the KHM numbering of the first edition, shows the state of the matter.

It is characteristic of the discontinuity of folkloristic and literary-historical research in Grimms' fairy tales that neither Herman Grimm's errors and omissions nor Bolte's and Schoof's inadequate classifica-

Table 19.1

	ATTRIBUTIONS IN THE BROTHERS GRIMMS' PERSONAL COPY	H. GRIMM 1895	J. BOLTE 1930	W. SCHOOF 1930	W. SCHOOF 1959
I	1		1		1
				5	5
	11	11	11		11
				25[21]	25[21]
	26/2	26	26/2		26
	31	31	31		31
	40	40	40	40	40
		44			44(?)
	45	45	45	45	45
	50	50	50	50	50
	53		53		
	75		75		75
	79		79	79	79
	81				
II	70				70

tions have ever been expressly pointed out or even corrected. Thus it is less astonishing that people also accepted Herman Grimm's identification of the contributor, "Marie," not only without reservation, but also with apparent satisfaction, and passed it on, and augmenting it with many a new insight. The stature of the Grimm's son (and nephew), who stood at the zenith of his fame as a professor and journalist at the turn of the century in the capital city, Berlin, impeded anyone's registering doubt or criticism, despite his evident negligence in dealing with the facts. His purely apodictic attribution of the most important contributions to the first volume of the KHM to the housekeeper of the Wild apothecary in Cassel seems on first notice strangely like a personal memory with the force of genuine evidence. In his report on his visits to the Wild home, "I myself" * suggests an impossible continuum: "Old Marie" had moved away from Cassel in 1812, she died in Ziegenhain in 1826,[22] and Herman Grimm was not born until 1828.

Be that as it may, the outlines of the figure of "Old Marie" obviously got sharper and filled the role of the earliest and most important informant. Her family tree was constructed;[23] Joseph Lefftz even published a drawing by Ludwig Emil Grimm, in which one felt able to recognize "Old Marie" despite factual and chronological contradictions,[24] an apparent effort to raise her to the status of the Zwehrn Fairy Tale Woman, whose portrait opened the second edition (1819). In brief, one did everything possible to make her a second Viehmännin. These efforts peaked in Schoof's 1959 description, in which "Old Marie" stood at the head of the line of Hessian informants:

A 62 year old housekeeper lived at that time in the Wild Household, who was known as "Old Marie" and who was naturally sounded (about fairy tales). The first volume took its most beautiful tales from her . . . The best informants for the Grimms were old country women who had a good memory . . . If we reckon among these the fairy tales from the years 1807 and 1808, which up to now have been attributed to Gretchen and Dortchen Wild, then we come to the result — little known before now — that more than a quarter of the 86 tales of Volume I derive from "Old Marie." She is the Grimms' oldest fairy tale teller and deserves a place of honor next to the Zwehrn Fairy Tale Woman. What she is to Volume II "Old Marie" is to Volume I.[25]

Thus at the end of this exposition Schoof elevated Herman Grimm's feeling that the fairy tale repertoire of the Wild siblings was, in the end, traceable to "Old Marie" to the status of fact. How "more than a quarter" is calculated remains mysterious. One would have to add to

---

* The German, *ich selbst noch* conveys a strong sense of simultaneity — TRANS.

Marie's 11 contributions 21 further tales which have been attributed to Dortchen (13), Gretchen (6), Lisette (1), and Mie Wild (1); that would, however, yield more than a third of the 86 tales in question.[26]

Schoof's conclusion, with some loss of refinement, has become *opinio communis* of the most recent fairy tale research, as far as I can tell. Ingeborg Weber-Kellermann's methodologically and intellectually fine essay, "Interethnische Gedanken beim Lesen der Grimmschen Märchen" (1970) may be taken as a characteristic example:

"Old Marie" became renowned. . . . She recounted some of the best known Grimm's Tales, and even those versions contributed by Dortchen and Gretchen Wild might well have been drawn from Old Marie as a source. Collecting her repertoire and that of the Wild sisters took place in the years 1810 and 1811, whereby probably a fourth of the fairy tales of Volume I are to be attributed to their nursemaid. She . . . grew up in a smithy in Rauschenberg . . . and was thus . . . a "Hessian source," if one will.[27]

It is questionable enough that elaborate hypotheses have been and continue to be constructed on the bare foundation supplied by Herman Grimm's statement and nothing else. But it remains totally incomprehensible how research into individual tales attributed to "Marie," which are otherwise excellent in terms of their critiques of source and style, can be so led astray by Herman Grimm's statements that the authors either question or withdraw pertinent observations and try by all means to skirt the enormous discrepancies by moving like knights on a chessboard:

When Wilhelm Grimm names "Old Marie" from the Wild household in Cassel as the source in his personal copy of 1812, that refers in the strictest sense only to the version in the first edition. . . . Clearly only an oral source is meant. The fact that "The Sleeping Beauty" is noted as having come "from Hesse" in the volume of notes both in 1822 and 1856 contradicts to a certain extent the attribution to Old Marie, of course, while otherwise the pieces attributed to Marie nearly always bear the notation, "from the Main area" . . . Perhaps . . . Wilhelm Grimm had Marie tell her tales aloud to fill out the brothers' notes for the edition of 1812. . . . In any case the ultimate oral source is Marie, a woman of the people, who has preserved fairy tales from oral tradition and told them in the nursery. The notation in Jacob's hand, "This seems drawn from Perrault's 'Belle au bois dormant'" does not fit well with the notation "oral." . . . That there were connecting links leading from Marie to French oral tradition is certainly possible. . . . The Notes of the Grimms indicate the "Main area," . . . which like Cassel where the fairy tale came to light, was strongly permeated by Huguenot immigration. . . . It can be assumed that people in the Wild family were acquainted with Perault's (*sic*) work. . . . The resonances with Perrault's text alter nothing of the popular form. . . . That Marie in the Wild household in Cassel had a strong part in the popular shaping of the fairy tale can be regarded as very probable.[28]

After everything is considered, it remains unclear where "Old Marie" in the Wild household is supposed to have gotten the first part of "The Sleeping Beauty" and the second part of "Little Red Riding Hood." It must be doubted that the simple old woman told KHM 50 in the form that it has come down to us, and it seems strange on the other hand, that the Hassenpflugs, who preserved the other Perrault fairy tales so completely, should have known only the second part of "The Sleeping Beauty." In consequence the strong suspicion arises that Bolte's allegation that KHM 50 was imparted "by Old Marie in the Wild household" is based on an error.[29]

"Old Marie," to whom we owe "The Sleeping Beauty," is there in the beginning . . . if I understand rightly, it may not be unimportant that her maiden name was Clar. Thus probably from a Huguenot family? One may immediately add that the Wilds came from Bern, that the "Viehmännin" was a daughter of the Huguenot innkeeper, Pierson, and that the mother of the Hassenpflug siblings was of Huguenot extraction.[30]

The various pieces of information introduced here all end in the paradox that certain fairy tales cannot possibly derive from "Old Marie," if one wishes to accept the purely German (and thus non-French) extraction of the Wilds' housekeeper, for which no proof can be found. The resistance to going one step further and asking about the reasons why Bolte or Herman Grimm attributed the essential contributions to the first volume of the KHM to this particular housekeeper makes one think of the German proverb that what is not supposed to exist cannot exist. "Old Marie" was really a fairy tale teller after the heart of many a fairy tale scholar oriented in a definitely Hessian or nationally German direction. Since the Grimm idealization of Viehmännin in the second KHM foreword had been shown to be a fiction — Frau Viehmännin was not a peasant, but the wife of a tailor, whose fairy tale repertoire was *not* genuinely Hessian (see above, p. 288) but in part clearly of French origin — one could always refer to "Old Marie" as a clearly Hessian informant.[31]

The grave question presents itself here, why the Brothers Grimm should have so distinguished Viehmännin in word and portrait as the ideal Hessian fairy tale agent but have remained so completely silent on the role of "Old Marie" even in their correspondence, although she would appear to correspond so completely to their preconception of an old Hessian folk fairy tale teller.[32] The answer is easy to find. That didn't happen, because "Marie" was clearly an informant like the bourgeois young women, about whom they expatiated equally little and who were noted in the personal copy as "Dortchen," "Gretchen," or "Jeanette." The identification of "Marie" as the Wilds' housekeeper, Maria Müller, née Clar from Rauschenberg near Cassel (1747–1826) rests on a capital error.

In addition to this deduction, weighty reasons may be adduced:

1. Wilhelm Grimm names with their Christian names solely those informants whom he knew well and who were the same age or younger than he was. All other informants are noted with their surnames (for example, Frau Wild, the old guard Krause, and so on).

2. The Grimms' oldest fairy tale records, as they are preserved in the so-called Ölenberg manuscript together with the notations in the personal copy, reveal that Wilhelm and Jacob Grimm attended to separate contributors in the earliest stage of the collection. While all the tales that came from the Hassenpflug family up to 1810 were written in Jacob's hand, it was Wilhelm who took down all the contributions from the Wild family. The ones which were later published as KHM 40, 45, 50 and 70 and were attributed to "Marie" were all recorded by Jacob.[33] It would be hard to see why Wilhelm Grimm would have so notably missed "Old Marie" as a fairy tale teller with his frequent visits to the Wilds, reserving this richly productive source for his brother's researches. This abstruse assumption proves to be even more nebulous, when one takes into account the exact dates of the later recordings. On 18 April 1811 and on 10 February 1812 three and two, respectively contributions were added. Each time one from "Marie" and the others from the Hassenpflugs. The idea that the Grimms had called at the Wilds as well as at the Hassenpflugs on these days to collect fairy tales is just as insupportable as the assumption that the Wilds' housekeeper should have taken part in one of the literary teas in the circle of the Hassenpflug and Ramus siblings.[34]

3. The regional attributions, in all cases that can be checked, correspond to the attributions by name on the personal copies of 1812 and 1815 in the volume of notes (1822). Both contributions from Frau Wild are, for example, described with the notation "from Cassel"; those tales contributed by the Wild siblings are always characterized as "Hessian" or "from Hesse"; the tale which came from Ludovica Jordis-Brentano who came from Frankfurt am Main bears the notation, "from the Main area." Four tales attributed to "Marie" also have this designation; another one bears the notation "from the Hanau area"; six are marked "from Hesse." That strikes one as odd only at first glance. The Hassenpflug family's contributions are characterized variably throughout — probably rightly, when one considers that the family moved from Hanau (the Main area) to Cassel (Hesse) in 1798. Apparently the fairy tales which the Hassenpflug siblings remembered from their childhood in Hanau were later marked "from the Main area," while those which they only came to know in Cassel were introduced as "Hessian." In any case there would not have been the slightest cause for the Grimms to characterize fairy tale contributions of "Old Marie," who came from the Hessian village Rauschenberg

and lived in the Hessian city of Cassel, in so varied a manner or — as in one instance — to connect it directly with Hanau. This observation removes the last shred of credibility from the fiction of "Old Marie" as an important folk fairy tale teller.

Who is meant by the characterization "Marie" in Wilhelm's personal copy can be quickly decided.

Dating makes it possible to determine that the Hassenpflugs' and "Marie's" contributions came in on the same day; the same observation can be made for 29 September 1812, when two contributions "from the Hassenpflugs" and one from "Jeanette" (Hassenpflug) were collected. That is similarly an indication that "Marie" must be looked for in the Hassenpflug household,[35] as is the strikingly exact agreement of the designations of origin in the volume of notes of 1822 of the texts which came from her and the Hassenpflugs and the fact that Jacob Grimm's earliest attributable notations are traceable exclusively back to the Hassenpflugs and "Marie." That the Grimms made as little fuss about "Marie" as a fairy tale contributor as they did about the Hassenpflug and Wild brothers and sisters has already been pointed out and places this informant likewise in the vicinity of the young women of the upper levels of Cassel's bourgeoisie.

Ludwig Hassenpflug (1794–1862) writes in his autobiography:

It was probably in the year 1808 that I experienced a great upheaval in the opinions formerly customary in our home because of the connection of my elder sister Marie . . . with the Engelhard daughters. Marie's intellectual interests had outstripped the traditional family circle, and at the Engelhards she was introduced to Jacob Grimm and his brother Wilhelm. . . . Through this connection my sister entered a completely different intellectual atmosphere. Literature and poetry, interest in Goethe and every intellectual movement, namely also in fairy tales and old German poetry arose as objects of domestic discussion and touched my second sister, who has only recently died, as well as me, then a 15 year old youth. . . . In the meantime, my sister's loose connection turned into a regular gathering; to it belonged, in addition to the Engelhard sisters, my sister Marie and Johanna and also the Grimms' sister, Lotte, and because of the Grimms' separate situation it came about, that we always met there in their apartment in the Marktstraße next to the Wild apothecary and spent very cheerful evenings there.[36]

On 3 September 1809 Jacob Grimm writes to Wilhelm:

I spoke recently with [Miss] Engelhard, who doesn't know much, but through her the Hassenpflugs, whom I also like in other respects, have told me some completely new fairy tales.[37]

The reference at that time to "Hassenpflugs" could hardly mean Amalie, then only nine years old, or her sister Jeanette, who once told a nephew of the Brothers Grimm that "the Danish Hero-Songs had already appeared (1811) when I met your dear departed mother and her brothers."[38] According to that, Jacob Grimm's letter can only refer to the sisters Susanna (born 1790) and Marie Hassenpflug.

Marie Hassenpflug, born 27 December 1788 in Altenhasslau am Main, married Captain Phillipp Ludwig von Dalwigk zu Schauenburg in Hoof near Cassel 21 August 1814 and after 1820 was a lady-in-waiting for the divorced Duchess Friederike of Anhalt-Bernburg in Wabern. She died 10 November 1856. In her childhood she was sickly, suffering from "sudden loss of consciousness with accompanying loss of use of her limbs"[39] and she may have been particularly receptive to the telling of fairy tales as a result. This is confirmed in a letter of February 1810 to Friederike Theobald, née Mannel from Wilhelm Grimm, who also indicates that he, instead of his brother, had assumed responsibility for the Hassenpflugs' fairy tale contributions:

The bearer of this letter, if it is Mlle. Hassenpflug, intends to stay the summer there, in order to recover her health. You will certainly like her, she has something quite charming and intelligent about her and is, I believe and as she also says, related to Theobald. I have also asked her for fairy tales and if you both collect diligently, you will find a lot.[40]

Not only does Marie Hassenpflug deserve the place of honor among the fairy tale contributors which has heretofore been reserved for "Old Marie," but beyond that she must be honored for having initiated the Grimms' acquaintance with the Hassenpflug family which was to a large extent decisive for the quality and quantity of the Grimm collection. Her mother, Maria Magdalena Hassenpflug, née Dresen (1767–1840), was descended from a Huguenot family named Droume from the Dauphine and was "reared completely in the French spirit": "In 1880 conversation at table at the Hassenpflugs was still carried on in French."[41] The contradictions, in which different fairy tale scholars were caught up in connection with "Marie's" clear familiarity with Perrault's and d'Aulnoy's fairy tale, are thus resolved.

In addition to the twelve fairy tales attributed to Marie in Wilhelm's personal copy of the KHM one must take note of the ones characterized as "from the Hassenpflugs," which several siblings performed at the regular gatherings mentioned by Ludwig Hassenpflug. Whether one can—following Bolte's model—attribute those tales which bear the notation "from the Main area" in the 1822 volume of notes to Marie or her siblings (KHM 5, 25, 26 in part) remains to be seen and would require a stylecritical analysis. Moreover the manuscript materials allow one to conjecture that KHM 53 and 64—collected before 1810—as well as the variants for 15, 61, and 63[42] might also derive from Marie, the eldest of the Hassenpflug contributors.

The Brothers Grimm had all the more good luck with the Cassel fairy tale woman, "Old Marie," . . . from whom the first volume got its most beautiful fairy tales. . . . Therefore . . . we are certainly justified in regarding Grimm's Fairy Tales as an indigenous Hessian book with national value.[43]

What the Grimms offered at Christmas 1812 was an utterly Hessian fairy tale harvest.[44]

As far as the actual derivation of the text is concerned — naturally not only the more or less accidental location in which they were re-corded — it is necessary to take leave of images such as those above as well as to dethrone "Old Marie." Ingeborg Weber-Kellermann was fully justified in writing that "the characterization of the KHM as 'mythic material which was German to the core' begins to totter noticeably with insight into the origins of Frau Viehmännin and the Hassenpflugs."[45] The only thing that preserved this myth from actual collapse was the fiction of "Old Marie" as an outstanding Hessian in-formant.[46] This line of argument has now been turned on its head, since it is precisely the contributions of Marie Hassenpflug which show familiarity with the fairy tale stories of Perrault and d'Aulnoy. Fairy tale research is thereby forcibly directed toward the Euro-pean context even in connection with the Grimm collection.[47] The awareness that without comparative research important aspects and relationships are overlooked and false literary, cultural, and socio-historical conclusions can hardly be avoided must also be recognized as valid for folkloristic and philological work with Grimms' fairy tales. All that can be lost is an unseemly national arrogance, but much can be gained, precisely in the spirit of Wilhelm Grimm who asserted in 1811:

. . . and thus it seems to become more evident how peoples have had an effect on one another, what they have shared with each other . . . When we have recog-nized this completely, then we may dare to follow the threads spun by old fables and borne throughout the world in marvelous shapes and circuits. But how would it be possible to comprehend the life of poetry, its development and its growth, without this research into migrations among various peoples?[48]

Notes

1. Compare *Anmerkungen zu den Brüder Grimm*, ed. Johannes Bolte and Georg Polivka, vols. 1–3 (Leipzig, 1913–18), Wilhelm Schoof, *Zur Entstehungsgeschichte der Grimmschen Märchen, Hessische Blätter für Volkskunde XXIX* (1930), pp. 1–118, and *Zur Entstehungs-geschichte der Grimmschen Märchen* (Hamburg, 1959).

2. There was a similar misunderstanding about the question of the contributors to *Des*

Knaben Wunderhorn, which was incorrectly believed to have been adequately dealt with by Karl Bode, "Die Bearbeitung der Vorlagen in Des Knaben Wunderhorn," *Palaestra 76* (Berlin, 1909).

3. Thus KHM 4 in the version of 1812 was ascribed to Ferdinand Siebert from Treysa, although he did not write until 20 January 1813: "Auch habe ich das Märchen Gut Kegel- und Kartenspiel von einem Schwälmer aufgeschrieben, im Ganzen völlig mit dem Abdruck übereinstimmend, und nur nicht so vollständig" (Wilhelm Schoof, *Zur Entstehungsgeschichte* [Hamburg, 1959], pp. 81–87).

4. *Märchen der Brüder Grimm: Urfassung nach der Originalhs, der Abtei Ölenberg im Elsaß,* ed. Joseph Lefftz (Heidelberg, 1927). A critical edition of these manuscripts now in the Bodmer Collection, vol. 1, in Geneva appeared in 1975 in the series, *Bibliotheca Bodmeriana.*

5. *Kinder- und Haus-Märchen: Gesammelt durch die Brüder Grimm,* vol. 3 (Berlin, 1822).

6. *Kinder- und Hausmärchen der Brüder Grimm,* ed. Friedrich Panzer (Wiesbaden, o.J. [1953]), p. 341 ff.

7. 8°Grimm79 1.2 in the Murhard Library of the City of Cassel. I would like to thank the director of the library, Dr. Dieter Hennig for his friendly permission to use this volume.

8. "Die Brüder Grimm: Erinnerungen von Herman Grimm," in *Deutsche Rundschau 82* (March, 1895): 85–100, repeated as the foreword to the twenty-ninth printing of the *Kinder- und Hausmärchen* (Berlin, 1897), as well as in Herman Grimm, *Beiträge zur Deutschen Culturgeschichte* (Berlin, 1897), pp. 214–47, and *Aufsätze zur Literatur,* ed. Reinhold Steig (Gütersloh, 1915), pp. 161–83.

9. Bolte and Polivka, *Anmerkungen,* 4:431.

10. The manuscript collection of fairy tales was sent to Brentano in Berlin on 25 October 1810 (Reinhold Steig, *Clemens Brentano und die Brüder Grimm* [Stuttgart and Berlin, 1914], pp. 118, 152). Since Brentano never returned the papers, they were preserved in his literary remains.

11. "Die Hassenpflugschen Märchen beginnen 1811" (*Deutsche Rundschau* [1895], p. 98); Jacob Grimm himself reports on the Hassenpflugs' contributions in 1809 (see n. 19); the tale, "Herr Korbes (KHM 41) was in the Grimms' possession in Jeanette Hassenpflug's own hand in December 1810.

12. With reference to KHM 44: "vom Mie 20 oct. 1811."

13. Bolte and Polivka, *Anmerkungen,* 4:434.

14. *Hessische Blätter für Volkskunde XXIX* (1930), p. 66: "womit zweifellos Wilhelmine von Schwertzell gemeint ist."

15. *Zur Entstehungsgeschichte* (Hamburg, 1959), p. 61.

16. *Deutsche Rundschau* (1895), p. 97.

17. Bolte and Polivka, *Anmerkungen,* 1:1.

18. Ibid., 4:432.

19. *Hessische Blätter für Volkskunde XXIX* (1930), pp. 15ff., where beyond this the following tales are given false attributions: "Rumpenstünzchen" to the Wild sisters instead of to the Hassenpflugs (as indicated in the personal copy) or "Die zwei Schornsteinfegers Jungen" to Gretchen instead of Dortchen Wild, and "Die wunderliche Gasterei" without discernible reason to "Malchen Hassenpflug."

20. Compare n. 1, pp. 59–61.

21. Schoof's unsubstantiated attribution of KHM 5 and 25 derives from Bolte's notation (Bolte and Polivka, *Anmerkungen,* 1:227): "'Die drei Raben' aus den Maingegenden (also wohl von der zu Nr. 11 erwähnten Marie)". In the analogous conclusion Schoof then attributed KHM 5 ("aus der Maingegend") to "old Marie." But the Grimms also supplied KHM 26/1, 38/II, 41, 42, 43, 52, and 66 with this derivation, without Schoof's having come to a similar conclusion about them.

22. *Zur Entstehungsgeschichte* (Hamburg, 1959), p. 61.

23. Eduard Grimmell, "Die Ahnen der 'alten Marie,' einer zweiten Märchenfrau der Brüder Grimm," *Hessische Familienkunde 4* (1957), col. 237–40.

24. Compare n. 4, p. 130; Bolte and Polivka, *Anmerkungen,* 4:433. Corrected in Schoof, *Zur Entstehungsgeschichte* (Hamburg, 1959), pp. 227–30.

25. Schoof, *Zur Entstehungsgeschichte* (Hamburg, 1959), pp. 59–61.

26. One must actually reckon with one hundred individual pieces in the first volume of the KHM, because of the division of individual titles into two to four pieces.

27. *Acta Ethnographica Academiae Scientiarum Hungaricae,* vol. 19 (Budapest, 1970), pp. 425–34 (427). The datings are incorrect: the first contributions from Gretchen Wild come from the year 1807; a few pieces came in from "Marie" as early as 1808. That a quarter of all the fairy tales are attributed to "old Marie" completely without reservation is only noted here by the by.

28. Alfred Romain, "Zur Gestalt des Grimmschen Dornröschenmärchens," *Zeitschrift für Volkskunde* 42 (1933): 84–116, esp. 88ff and 97–99.

29. Rolf Hagen, "Perraults Märchen und die Brüder Grimm," *Zeitschrift für deutsche Philologie* 74 (1955): 392–410 (409ff).

30. Friedrich Neumann, "Aus der Welt der Brüder Grimm," *Zeitschrift des Vereins für hessische Geschichte und Landeskunde* 71 (1960): 171–79.

31. Ingeborg Weber-Kellermann, see n. 27, p. 427.

32. Ludwig Denecke, *Jacob Grimm und sein Bruder Wilhelm,* Sammlung Metzler, vol. 100, (Stuttgart, 1971), p. 67ff.

33. Compare Lefftz, 119, 77, 81, and 126; compare n. 4 above.

34. See below, n. 36.

35. Rolf Hagen clearly suspected that (see n. 29), but did not dare to express a corresponding conclusion.

36. Ludwig Hassenpflug, *Mein Leben bis zum Regierungsantritt des Kurfürsten Wilhelm II* (notebook 1), in the copy made by Nora Hassenpflug, pp. 178, 179, and 186. The original manuscript was lost in World War II; the copy is in the private possession of Else Hassenpflug, Rinteln, to whom I am grateful for permission to publish excerpts. I am indebted to Dr. Friderici of Cassel for referring me to this document.

37. *Briefwechsel zwischen Jacob und Wilhelm Grimm aus der Jugendzeit,* 2d ed., ed. Wilhelm Schoof (Weimer, 1963), p. 152.

38. Letter of 18 June 1845 to Friedrich Hassenpflug. Sign. Gr. Slg. Autogr. 374, Brüder Grimm-Museum, Cassel. I am also indebted to Dr. Friderici for referring me to this letter.

39. Ludwig Hassenpflug; see n. 36, p. 180.

40. *Hessische Blätter für Volkskunde XXIX* (1930), p. 56 (see n. 1). In Wilhelm's letter to Jacob of 18 November 1814 it says: "Die Marie soll noch getraut werden, eh ihr Offizier ins Feld zieht, sie dauert mich und erschreckt mich, sooft ich sie sehe." *Briefwechsel,* see n. 37, p. 240.

41. Hagen, see n. 29, p. 409. With reference to the Perrault version of "Blaubart" procured from the Hassenpflug family, the brothers wrote as early as 1822 in their volume of notes (see n. 5) that "das Französische auch an dem Ort, wo wir sie hörten, bekannt seyn konnte" (76).

42. Nr. 85/d and a variant of Nr. 11 should be noted in this regard; they are only represented in the KHM edition of 1812.

43. Wilhelm Schoof, "Die Brüder Grimm und die hessische Märchenforschung," *Volk und Scholle* 7, (1929): 383–387 (386).

44. Bolte and Polivka, *Anmerkungen,* 4:437.

45. *Acta Ethnographica,* p. 432.

46. Ibid., p. 427.

47. One may perhaps regard it as meaningful and characteristic, that the Grimms avoided calling their collection of fairy tales "German" — in contrast to Arnim and Brentano's *Wunderhorn,* which has the subtitle, *Old German Songs* and in contrast to their own *Deutsche Sagen* (German legends [1816–18]).

48. *Altdänische Heldenlieder, Balladen und Märchen,* trans. Wilhelm Carl Grimm (Heidelberg, 1811), foreword, p. v.

Contributors

Ruth B. Bottigheimer received her doctorate in German from the State University of New York at Stony Brook. She lectures widely and has published several articles on Grimms' Fairy Tales. Her contribution forms part of a content analysis of a study entitled *Bad Girls and Bold Boys: The Moral and Social Vision of Grimms' Tales*. She is Adjunct Assistant Professor in the Department of Comparative Literature at the State University of New York at Stony Brook. The conference on which this volume of essays is based was organized while she was on the faculty of Princeton University.

Jerome W. Clinton studied English and American literature before two years in Iran with the Peace Corps redirected his interests to the Middle East. He received his doctorate in Persian and Arabic Literature from the University of Michigan and is Professor of Near Eastern Studies at Princeton University. Among his publications are *Spoken and Written Persian* (with Donald L. Stilo) and a study of medieval Persian court poetry, *The Divan of Manuchihri Damghani*. He is now writing a book on the Iranian national epic, the *Shahname*.

Alan Dundes, born in New York City in 1934, was educated at Yale (B.A., English, 1955; M.A.T., English, 1958) and at Indiana University (Ph.D., Folklore, 1962). He has written or edited more than a dozen books on folklore. His major scholarly interest lies in the application of psychoanalytic theory to the materials of folklore. He is Professor of Anthropology and Folklore at the University of California, Berkeley.

James W. Fernandez is Professor of Anthropology at the University of Chicago. His main interest has been cultural change and social and religious movements. He has conducted field research over three decades in several parts of Africa and in the mountains of northern Spain. He reports upon the latter research in his article in this collection.

Simon A. Grolnick, Associate Professor of Clinical Psychiatry at the Cornell University College of Medicine, serves as the Director of Education and Training of the North Shore University Hospital Department of Psychiatry Residency Program and is also a faculty member of the Columbia and N.Y.U. Institutes of Psychoanalysis. He co-edits the annual, *The Psychoanalytic Study of Society,* and has written articles on the applications of psychoanalysis to children's stories, funereal art, dreaming, play and transitional (security) objects.

Steven Swann Jones, currently an Associate Professor at CSULA, received his Ph.D. in English and Folklore from the University of California. He co-edited *Directions in Folklore Research,* a survey of folkloristic methodologies; his publications include *Folklore and Literature in the United States* and articles on folklore and literature including a study of the legend of Santa Claus and the relationship between popular fairy tales and contemporary jokes. His contribution forms part of a book-length study of the structure and themes of "Snow White."

Torborg Lundell received her Ph.D. in Comparative Literature from the University of California at Berkeley and is currently Associate Professor in the Department of Germanic, Oriental and Slavic Languages at the University of California at Santa Barbara. Her research on the development of the mother image during the nineteenth and twentieth centuries forms part of a book-length study of the mother figure in folk and fairy tales, which uses a structural and psychological approach.

Gerhard O. W. Mueller, J.D., LL.M., Dr. Jur. (hon.), is Distinguished Professor of Criminal Justice, Rutgers — The State University of New Jersey and Chief (ret.), United Nations Crime Prevention and Criminal Justice Branch. Among his publications are some two hundred scholarly articles and thirty books, including *Crime, Law and the Scholars* (1969); *International Criminal Law* (1965); *Sentencing: Process and Purpose* (1977); and *Outlaws of the Ocean* (1985).

Lutz Röhrich is Professor of Germanic Philology and Folklore and Director of the Folklore Institute at the University of Freiburg and a co-editor of the *Enzyklopädie des Märchens*. He has written *Märchen und Wirklichkeit, Sage und Märchen, Sage,* and *Erzählungen des späten Mittelalters und ihr Wieterleben in Literatur und Volksdichtung bis zur Gegenwart.* He received the Chicago Folklore Prize in 1974 and the Grimm Prize in 1985.

Heinz Rölleke studied history, philosophy, and German literature at the Universities of Cologne and Zurich. He completed his doctoral dissertation at Cologne and habilitated in German philology with a six-volume critical edition of Arnim and Brentano's *Des Knaben Wunderhorn.* Currently at the Bergische University in Wuppertal, he has also taught at Düsseldorf and the University of Cincinnati. He won the Hessian Cultural Award in 1985.

Karen E. Rowe, Associate Professor of English at UCLA, has published articles on Edward Taylor, the colonial American poet, as well as *Saint and Singer: Edward Taylor's Typology and the Poetics of Meditation.* She has also published essays on fairy tales and women's literature in *Women's Studies* and *The Voyage In.* She was a fellow in residence at the Radcliffe Institute (1977–78) and is presently Director for UCLA's Center for the Study of Women.

Rudolf Schenda studied Romance and English literature at Amherst, Paris, and Munich, where he received his doctorate. He has taught at the Universities of Palermo, Tübingen, and Göttingen, and is now Professor of European Folk Literature at the University of Zurich. He has published *Eine sizilianische Straße, Volk ohne Buch, Das Elend der alten Leute, Lebzeiten,* and *Folklore e letteratura popolare.*

Kay F. Stone, Associate Professor of Folklore in the English Department at the University of Winnipeg, received her Ph.D. in Folklore from Indiana University with a dissertation on *Romantic Heroines in Anglo-American Folk and Popular Literature.* She has subsequently written extensively on storytelling and on women in folktales, with special reference to Walt Disney.

Maria M. Tatar received a Ph.D. in German Literature from Princeton University and is currently Professor of German at Harvard University. She is the author of *Spellbound: Studies on Mesmerism and Literature* and has published articles on the German Romantics, modern German literature, and the Grimms' collection of fairy tales. Her contribution to this volume figures as part of a larger study on sex, violence, and social climbing in the Grimms' *Nursery and Household Tales* entitled *The Hard Facts of Fairy Tales*.

Anna Tavis received her B.A. and M.A. at the Leningrad Herzen Institute and is now a doctoral candidate in Comparative Literature at Princeton University. Her principal interests lie in the area of German-Slavic literary connections and she is working on the problems of text and semiotic interpretation.

Hans-Jörg Uther studied folklore, German literature, and history in Munich and Göttingen. He did his doctoral work with Kurt Ranke in Göttingen with a dissertation on *The Disabled in Popular Narratives*. He is a member of the editorial staff of the *Enzyklopädie des Märchens* and is particularly concerned with content, type, and motif research. He has published numerous articles in the field of folk narrative research.

Rainer Wehse studied English and German literature at the Universities of Würzburg, Vienna, Munich, Newcastle-upon-Tyne, and Freiburg. He received an M.A. in Folklore from the University of Indiana and a Ph.D. in Folklore from Freiburg working with Lutz Röhrich. He has edited books and published articles in English and German on folk narratives, folksongs, children's lore, street literature, and graffiti. His *Flugblatt und Schwanklied in Großbritannien/ Broadsides and Humorous Songs in Great Britain* won the Chicago Folklore Prize in 1980.

Jack Zipes is Professor of German and Comparative Literature at the University of Florida–Gainesville. His major publications include *Breaking the Magic Spell; The Trials and Tribulations of Little Red Riding Hood; Fairy Tales and the Art of Subversion;* and *Don't Bet on the Prince: Feminist Fairy Tales and the Feminist Critique in America and England*. He co-edits *New German Critique* and has written numerous articles on classic and modern fairy tales.

Index

The spellings of many tales and characters which are indexed here vary by language and through time: for example, the "Scheherezade" familiar to the Western reader is transliterated as "Shahrazade" by the Persian scholar. I have tried to minimize these difficulties by cross-referencing variant spellings. Similarly the same tale frequently has different titles: "Sleeping Beauty" appears as "Briar (or Brier) Rose." What might occasionally look like a misspelling or lost accent in the listings represents an accurate rendering of historical orthography. Secondary works and fairy tale scholars discussed in the essays are included in the index; those cited in footnotes and bibliographies generally are not.

ST. LOUIS
AT FL